Pennsylvania

Gardener's Guide

Pennsylvania
Gardener's Guide

Liz Ball

COOL
SPRINGS
PRESS

Nashville, Tennessee
A Division of Thomas Nelson, Inc.
www.ThomasNelson.com

Published by Cool Springs Press, a Division of Thomas Nelson, Inc., P. O. Box 141000, Nashville, Tennessee, 37214.

Ball, Liz
    Pennsylvania gardener's guide / by Liz Ball.
        p. cm.
    Includes bibliographical references (p.   ).
    ISBN: 1-930604-79-3 (pbk. : alk. paper)
    1. Landscape plants--Pennsylvania. 2. Landscape gardening--Pennsylvania.
    I. Title.
  SB407 .B287 2002
  635.9'09748--dc21
                                    2001007135

First printing 2002
Printed in the United States of America
10 9 8 7 6 5 4 3 2

Managing Editor: Billie Brownell
Horticulture Editor: Charles Cresson
Horticultural Copyeditor: Diana Maranhao
Copyeditor: Dimples Kellogg
Designer: Sheri Ferguson
Production Artist: S.E. Anderson

On the cover: Flowering Dogwood (*Cornus florida*), photographed by Alan Detrick

Visit the Thomas Nelson website at www.ThomasNelson.com

Dedication

To Rick:

for all that he knows and cares about, and for all that he shares with me.

Acknowledgments

One of the great good fortunes of my life is to have discovered gardening in Southeastern Pennsylvania, a place that abounds with friendly, enthusiastic gardeners and horticulturists. I am indebted to these wonderful people for the uncounted hours I have enjoyed in their company and in their gardens learning through their informal sharing of their wisdom and expertise. I am also grateful for the many stimulating formal conferences and lectures available to me and to other homeowners and gardeners in Pennsylvania by institutions such as the Tyler, Morris, and Scott Arboretums, Longwood Gardens, and the Pennsylvania Horticultural Society (PHS).

There are also the very special people who have helped me with this book. Special thanks to Dottie Andrassy for her research and computer skills, and to Nancy Beaubaire for advice and information about resources for native plants in Pennsylvania. I am grateful to Chris Firestone for helping me find information on invasive plant species. Further, I am indebted to D. B. Kellogg for her skillful copy edits and to Charles Cresson for his valuable horticultural editing.

Another great good fortune that I have enjoyed is having Cool Springs Press, one of the Thomas Nelson companies, as a publisher. Thanks to Hank McBride for his confidence in me and his patience. A special appreciation goes to managing editor extraordinaire Billie Brownell for being at the end of the telephone at every twist and turn of this project and cheering me on. Thanks always to Cindy Games for her terrific energy and skill in promoting all my books.

Finally, I also have the great good fortune to have in my private life understanding family and friends who put up with me during the time I worked on this book. Thank you Rick, Ronnie, Vinnie, Jimmy, Bob, and Keith for taking on the lion's share of the landscape work at Creek House and helping to make up for the time I had to miss in the garden.

Featured Plants *for Pennsylvania*

(See individual entries for the corresponding botanical name of the above listed common plant names.)

Table of Contents

Welcome to Gardening
in Pennsylvania

Pennsylvanians are familiar with the fact that in its earliest days our state played a pivotal role in the formation of our new nation. Everyone knows that our first city, Philadelphia, is the "Cradle of Liberty." The fact that it is also the "Cradle of American Horticulture" is not so widely recognized and appreciated. Yet anyone who lives here very long comes to gradually understand that our Commonwealth is as special horticulturally as it is historically.

The seeds of both traditions were sown by a community of thoughtful, passionate settlers, many of them Quakers, who shared Enlightenment values, curiosity about the natural world, and a commitment to knowledge, especially about plants of all kinds. They began a gardening tradition that waves of subsequent settlers carried with them as they moved beyond the colonial confines of Philadelphia into the far reaches of what would become the Commonwealth of Pennsylvania. Wherever they settled they enjoyed Pennsylvania's wonderful natural environment—relatively mild climate, generous rainfall distributed throughout the year, and good soil—that fostered their success as farmers and gardeners. Wherever they settled, there were wonderful trees. In a very fundamental way Pennsylvania has always been about trees. And in their shade our rich and diverse gardening tradition, known and appreciated worldwide, continues.

A Sense of Place

The trees of the Eastern Seaboard's hardwood forest have always strongly defined the sense of place here in Pennsylvania. They have covered most of Pennsylvania from the rolling Piedmont Plateau of the Philadelphia area to the Allegheny Mountains, which parade diagonally across the vast central portion of the state, then to the Allegheny Plateau near Pittsburgh, and finally to Lake Erie Lowland. The accumulated humus from eons of fallen leaves from a rich assortment of stately deciduous and evergreen trees has created and protected fertile, well-drained, slightly acidic spongy loam over this state that literally and figuratively nourished the seeds of its horticultural tradition. Except for a few areas where shale is very close to the surface, or where the sandy soil of the coastal plain extends across the Delaware River from New Jersey, this good soil in Pennsylvania supports a wide range of agricultural and ornamental plants.

Through the ages, trees have flourished here and moderated a climate that has provided ample rainfall, hot, sunny summers, and relatively mild, but real, winters. Depending on whether the prevailing winds bring Gulf Stream or Arctic temperatures, winters may be intermittently somewhat harsh, but these vagaries (including the occasional ice storm) notwithstanding, conditions in this region have always favored the cultivation of lots of kinds of plants. Situated nicely between North and South, Pennsylvania is cold enough to provide the necessary chill for Northern plants, yet is mild enough to accommodate many Southern ones. The earliest Pennsylvania gardeners—the Lenni Lenape community of Delaware Indians, Shawnee and Iroquoian Susquehannocks, Erie, and Seneca—cultivated pumpkins, corn, and many other edible native plants that flourished here. Today almost 17 million acres of Pennsylvania are still covered with forest.

The Quaker Influence

The towering trees that sheltered the Lenni Lenape for thousands of years greeted William Penn when he arrived to survey the 45,000 square miles of forested land granted to him by King Charles II as payment for a debt he owed Penn's father. His delight in the great forest prompted William Penn to call his colony Pennsylvania, or Penn's Woods, to honor both his father and this inspiring natural phenomenon. Under the huge Oaks and Maples of this woods, he negotiated treaties with the Lenni Lenape so that he could create parcels of land to grant to the Quakers whom he encouraged to emigrate from England and participate in his "Holy Experiment."

As fundamental to his vision of this colony as a place of religious freedom was Penn's desire to have its first city be a "greene countrie towne" where trees continued to dominate the landscape. Reflecting his devotion to trees, Penn's detailed plan for the layout of Philadelphia specified that several main streets be named for them. To this day Walnut, Chestnut, Pine, Spruce, and Cherry Streets are at the hub of life in this city. Today it bustles beneath the benign eye of William Penn himself, memorialized as a sculpture atop Philadelphia City Hall.

Although the Swedes, the Dutch, and some English had already settled and farmed parts of eastern Pennsylvania for three generations prior to Penn's grant in 1681, the later Quaker arrivals were the ones who responded to its natural wonders most enthusiastically and laid the foundation for its horticultural prominence and tradition. The conviction of members of the Society of Friends that one way to know and understand God was to know and understand His natural creations had stimulated the interest of Quakers in gardening back in England. Many arrivals to the New World also devoted themselves to gardening. Some intensely studied and collected the fascinating flora they found here, their Enlightenment-era confidence in reason and order fueling their careful exploration and documentation of these interesting plants. As they prospered in Pennsylvania, Quaker businessmen built estates in the (then) outlying parts of Philadelphia, as Penn did at Pennsbury Manor, where they indulged their interest in growing plants and displaying them in gardens.

The grounds of the Friends' meeting houses that dot the environs of Philadelphia are still shaded by great trees, and the great homes of affluent Quaker businessmen, preserved and restored, still testify to the intense interest in gardening of these "founding fathers" of Pennsylvania horticulture.

The Amish Way

Another group of settlers from Europe has also enormously influenced and advanced horticulture in Pennsylvania. These are the Amish. In the 1600s a Mennonite minister named Jacob Amman promulgated a strict code of behavior for his adherents in this small, persecuted religious group. With about six hundred followers he established an Amish community devoted to a simple life, rejecting the distractions and luxuries of the larger society. They relied on the soil to achieve self-sufficiency. Forced to be tenant farmers in Europe, the Amish welcomed the opportunity to have religious freedom and to own land in Penn's new colony. They arrived in Pennsylvania Colony in the early 1700s, settling on Lancaster County's undulating farmland.

These Amish farmers developed numerous environmentally sound practices that not only maintained their rich soil, but also improved it. Among their innovations were rotating crops, using manure to restore fertility, and growing nitrogen-fixing cover crops on poor soil to enrich and preserve it. The gentle stewardship of Pennsylvania soil by succeeding generations of Amish farmers is legendary. Lancaster-area farmland is better after two centuries of farming than it was when the Amish arrived. This is a model and inspiration for gardeners everywhere.

Our Gardening Legacy

The history of horticulture in general and gardening in particular in Pennsylvania is one of many firsts. Numerous individuals and institutions have contributed to our rich gardening tradition both here and nationwide.

It is a tree, the Franklinia, that shall be forever associated with the Delaware County Quaker farmer John Bartram. He best typifies the confluence of Quaker and Enlightenment sensibilities that launched horticulture in our state and the nation as well. It was a Daisy in the path of his plow, however, that initially arrested his attention and awakened his interest in botany. Before long, the modestly educated farmer gave himself over to the task of systematically collecting, studying, and cultivating native plants all over the East. So extensive were his activities and travels that King George III recognized Bartram as Royal Botanist for the mainland North American colonies. He and his son William, a trained naturalist who shared his passion, identified and introduced more than two hundred of our native plants into cultivation in Europe. John Bartram was saluted by Linnaeus, who was busy developing the modern system for categorizing and naming plants, as "the greatest natural Botanist in the world."

On a new farm fronting the Schuykill River, Bartram and his son raised as many plants as they could, including the aforementioned Franklinia tree (named for friend Benjamin Franklin) which they discovered in Georgia. After his father's death, William continued to travel and collect plants, and he sold plants and seeds from his garden to contemporary horticultural enthusiasts such as Thomas Jefferson. He issued the first mail-order catalog, a single sheet of paper, or "broadside," which evolved by 1807 into a small bound booklet for the public. Among Bartram's customers were the Painter brothers, Jacob and Minshall, Quakers who farmed seven hundred acres near Media in Delaware County. Before they were finished indulging their love of trees, they had planted more than one thousand of them on the property. Their property is now part of Tyler Arboretum, the oldest and largest arboretum on the East Coast.

Bernard M'Mahon, an Irish immigrant who settled in Pennsylvania at the beginning of the nineteenth century, published the first gardening book in America for the general public, *The American Gardener's Calendar*. Through eleven editions this book was the best available compendium of the most advanced horticultural knowledge of the day. M'Mahon presented information in a calendar format. His innovation was adapting the latest English gardening practices to conditions in this country.

The Bartrams' idea of sending seeds through the mail was adopted by eighteen-year-old W. Atlee Burpee, who parlayed a $1,000 loan from his mother in 1886 into the first mail-order seed company. He was concerned that plant varieties that immigrants from Europe and elsewhere were accustomed to growing were not suited to the soil and climate in this country. He set about identifying and developing strains that were. He established Ford Hook Farm in Bucks County, Pennsylvania, a site recommended by Luther Burbank, as a testing ground for new varieties that he found in his travels and developed through hybridization. Eventually, his Burpee Seed Company would become a household name throughout the country, greatly influencing both food and ornamental gardening.

Pennsylvania took the lead in academic horticultural education as well. About the same time that W. Atlee was mailing seeds around the country, Rabbi Dr. Joseph Krauskopf was worried about the success of Jewish and other immigrants raised in urban areas who would have to depend on farming in this country. He established a special school for them in Doylestown, Bucks County. In 1896 he purchased a one-hundred-acre farm there, built a building, and hired two teachers for his National Farm School, the first school of its kind in America. Over one hundred years it has evolved into a full four-year college that features programs in food industry, biology, chemistry, and liberal arts. In its present incarnation

as Delaware Valley College it continues its mission to teach gardening through its Horticulture and Ornamental Horticulture Departments.

Formal advanced education in the art and science of horticulture was first made available to women at the Pennsylvania School of Horticulture for Women, established in 1891. For several decades this school offered career opportunities to liberate women from household drudgery and dependence on male breadwinners. Under the direction of women of superb capability such as Louise Bush-Brown, it attracted bright, highly motivated women into careers in horticulture. After World War II, its mission and role as a teaching institution and landscape were taken over by Temple University, which incorporated it into its suburban campus at Ambler. It was named the Temple School of Horticulture and Landscape Architecture.

Your Garden Landscape

To a large degree, gardening in Pennsylvania is like gardening anywhere. It involves choosing plants; learning techniques for planting, pruning, watering, and soil preparation; recognizing pests and diseases; choosing equipment; designing planting beds; protecting plants . . . the list goes on and on. However, these things are not difficult, and a gardener does not have to master them all before he or she can enjoy gardening. Gardening is a process rather than a product; a garden is a work of art, never quite completed.

Those of us who already garden or are starting to garden here in Pennsylvania are heirs to a rich horticultural tradition. Rather than be intimidated by it, be inspired by it. Almost nowhere else in this country are conditions so favorable and information so available. Also, perhaps not since the early Quaker days have the citizens of our Commonwealth been so acutely aware of how important it is to preserve the natural resources that we enjoy. While gardening here is a healthy pastime, a source of creative expression and personal pleasure, it is simultaneously a contribution you can make to the preservation of the legacy of Penn's "greene countrie towne" throughout Pennsylvania.

An Approach to Gardening

This book incorporates several themes. It is first a practical guide to growing 173 specific plants of various kinds that grow well and appropriately in Pennsylvania. Also, it suggests the diverse uses of plants, not just as ornamental features in a designed residential landscape, but as essential elements of a balanced, natural ecological system that is predicated on plant and animal diversity and sensitivity to the soil environment. Finally, it pays tribute to the role that passionate plantsmen and gardeners from Pennsylvania, historical and contemporary, have played in developing and maintaining our rich horticultural tradition.

This book is intended for both newcomers to Pennsylvania and longtime residents. It is for both novice gardeners and experienced gardeners who want more geographically focused horticultural information. It is also for homeowners who simply want to know how to take better care of their yards. It is not intended to replace more technical books on specific plants such as Roses and specific techniques such as pruning, which go into more depth. It does not cover ancillary topics such as landscape design or seed starting and other forms of propagation. Only a few of the hundreds of plants that do well in our state could be included. They were chosen because they are attractive, available, and relatively low main-tenance, and have successful track records here. They are garden-worthy plants that are representative of the wide range of those commonly used and available in Pennsylvania, with the possible exception of those few areas of the state in horticultural zone 4.

Gardening Guidelines

Gardening techniques and procedures recommended in this book reflect and encourage a wholistic view of the entire yard rather than a focus on individual garden beds or areas in isolation. Viewing the yard as an integrated ecosystem, where host and visitor, predator and prey—from the tiniest fungal spore or bacteria in the compost pile to the largest resident, the gardener—contribute to maintaining a self-sustaining balance, actually makes it easier to garden successfully. This book also assumes that among your goals are to do as little work as possible and to protect the environment. Because Mother Nature's system is the ultimate low-maintenance, environmentally healthy system, the following suggestions reinforce this system in your yard.

Choose appropriate plants. Lots and lots of plants are available for gardens and home landscapes. They have widely varying cultural requirements. Some are easygoing and relatively flexible about their location. Others are very demanding and require very specific conditions. Plants that are unsuitable for conditions in your yard will be miserable and have chronic problems due to stress. They will need constant attention. Therefore, be aware of your hardiness zone, and choose plants tough enough for your winters. Take time to understand your yard, its soil, its shady spots, its wet areas, and its hot spots. Choose plants that will thrive in (not just tolerate) the conditions where you plant them. The healthier and more self-reliant they are, the less you have to do to care for them.

Care for your soil. No one has perfect soil, but we can improve what we have just as the Amish do. Add organic matter at every opportunity to improve its drainage and moisture-holding capacity. Spread organic mulch (not too deeply) or plant ground cover plants over any bare soil to protect and enrich it. Healthy soil is alive. Make sure your gardening activities support rather than destroy the active micro- and macro-organisms in the soil. Take care of the soil, and it will take care of your plants for you.

Plant properly. The more we learn about plants, the more we appreciate how important correct planting is to their health. This is particularly true of trees and shrubs where planting too deeply is often a death warrant. Take the time to dig a hole of the correct depth. Do not put any loose soil in it before setting a rootball in it. (The exception is planting bare-root plants.) Do not enrich the backfill soil. Be sure newly planted plants get plenty of moisture. The sooner they become established and vigorous, the sooner you can reduce the amount of care you must provide.

Water when necessary. Like people, plants are mostly water and need constant replenishment. Those in poor soil suffer the effects of drought sooner because the soil has little organic content to absorb and hold moisture for them. Also, poor soil is usually compacted, so roots cannot penetrate very deeply. They dry out near the surface more quickly. In decent soil, most plants need about 1 inch of water a week during the growing season, less when they are dormant, more when the soil is poor. The best way to water is to use a dripping garden hose or porous, "leaky pipe" irrigation system. Both slowly deliver moisture directly into the soil for maximum absorption and minimum evaporation or runoff. A 2-inch layer of organic mulch will retard evaporation, too. How fortunate that the best way to water takes the least amount of your time!

Fertilize judiciously. Healthy, fertile soil meets the nutrition needs of most established plants. Use a slow-acting fertilizer to aid plants in mediocre soil until you can improve it. Slow-acting products are gentler on the soil and its denizens and offer more consistent nutrition for a sustained period than fast-acting, water-soluble products. They are not harmful if you accidentally overdo. Fertilize the soil around plants known to be "heavy feeders" or those that are in their young, fast-growing stage and need a rich diet for a while. Because they last from ten to sixteen weeks, slow-acting products do not need several repeat applications, saving you time and energy.

Prune plants properly. Growing plants need pruning, pinching, or cutting back occasionally for their health as well as a pleasing appearance. Prune at the correct time of year to guide the development of a tree or shrub while preserving flower buds. Cut to shape the plant or to stimulate growth. When pruning, cut at the correct place, and use sharp tools for a clean cut to assure prompt healing. Reserve shearing for special situations such as hedges and topiary. *Never* top trees. If you must cut back a tree or shrub every year or two to reduce its size, move it to a place where it has room to grow comfortably, and let it grow. This saves you time and makes the plant happier.

How to Use This Book

Each entry in this guide provides you with information about a plant's particular characteristics, habits and its basic requirements for vigorous growth as well as my personal experience and knowledge of it. I have tried to include the information you need to help you realize each plant's potential. Only when a plant performs at its best can one appreciate it fully. You will find such pertinent information as mature height and spread, bloom period and seasonal colors (if any), sun and soil preferences, water requirements, fertilizing needs, pruning and care, and pest information. Each section is clearly marked for easy reference.

Sun Preferences

Symbols represent the range of sunlight suitable for each plant. "Full Sun" means to site the plant in a location receiving 8 to 10 hours of sun daily. "Part Sun" means to site the plant where it receives partial or bright, indirect sun all day, or mostly morning sun. "Part Shade" means dappled shade or shade at some time of the day or indirect light all day. "Full Shade" means the plant needs a shady location protected from direct sunlight. Some plants grow successfully in more than one range of sun, indicated by more than one sun symbol.

Full Sun   **Part Sun**   **Part Shade**   **Full Shade**

Additional Benefits

Many plants offer benefits that further enhance their appeal. The following symbols indicate some of the more notable additional benefits:

 Attracts Butterflies

 Attracts Hummingbirds

 Produces Edible Fruit

 Has Fragrance

 Produces Food for Birds and Wildlife

 Drought Resistant

 Suitable for Cut Flowers or Arrangements

 Long Bloom Period

 Native Plant

 Supports Bees

 Provides Shelter for Birds

 Good Fall Color

Companion Planting and Design

In this section, I provide suggestions for companion plants and different ways to showcase your plants.

Did You Know?

Some plants have interesting histories; others have important uses beyond the garden. Learn more about the life and lore of your plants in this section.

USDA Cold Hardiness Zone Map

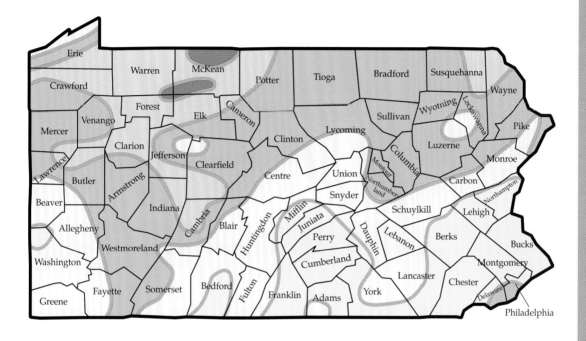

ZONE	Average Minimum Temperature		ZONE	Average Minimum Temperature
4B	-20 to -25		6A	-5 to -10
5A	-15 to -20		6B	0 to -5
5B	-10 to -15		7A	5 to 0

USDA Cold Hardiness Zones

Cold-hardiness zone designations were developed by the United States Department of Agriculture (USDA). They are based on the minimum average temperatures all over the country. Each variation of 10 degrees Fahrenheit represents a different zone, indicated by colored bands on a zone map. Because perennial plants, whose roots survive winter, vary in their tolerance for cold, it is important to choose those plants that are suitable for the zone for your region of Pennsylvania. Consult this map to learn in which zone you live. Most of the plants in this book will perform well throughout the state. Pennsylvania has zones ranging from 4b to 7a. Though a plant may grow (and grow well) in zones other than its recommended cold-hardiness zone, it is best to select plants labeled for your zone, or warmer.

Annuals *for Pennsylvania*

Annuals are the flower mainstay of most residential landscapes. How can you not love plants that knock themselves out to flower as furiously as they can for as long as they can? Annuals such as Impatiens, Cosmos, and Nasturtiums are under a biological imperative to produce as much seed as possible in one season to assure future generations. They literally burn the candle at both ends, giving their all to flower and seed production at the expense of root development and energy storage. Those that do not succumb immediately to frost soon die of exhaustion anyway.

About Annuals

Some annuals are called *hardy annuals*—seemingly a contradiction in terms—because they tolerate a bit of frost in the fall before dying. When they do die, Cleomes and Four-o'-Clocks, among others, leave behind tough seeds that can survive first winter, then cold and soggy thaws, to germinate in the spring. Other annuals, such as Geraniums, are really perennials by nature, structured to invest in root systems and store energy for the future. However, their roots are too tender to survive where there are real winters. So they are called *tender perennials*. Gardeners in Pennsylvania grow them for their wonderful flowers, then usually treat them as they would regular annuals, letting them die in the cold in the fall. In some cases, they dig them up, pot them, and grow them indoors on a windowsill over the winter.

Then there are the annuals that seem to defy their destiny and live over the winter and into the following season. *Biennials* are programmed to take their time at accomplishing their seed production and, thus, to handle one winter. Their first season they grow their foliage, but delay developing flowers and making seed until the following season. A good example of a biennial is Forget-me-not. The trick here is to avoid mistaking their foliage for weeds and pulling up the plants at the end of the gardening season.

Annual Assets

As a group, annuals are extremely versatile. Whether acting as vines, ground covers, or bedding plants, they offer just about any flower color. Because most deliver it nonstop all season, their dependability is unmatched by other flowering plants. Reliable color means the yard will have a consistent look all season. It means a steady supply of blooms for indoor arrangements. It means regular visits from butterflies, hummingbirds, and honeybees all summer, and seed-eating birds in the fall.

Caring for Annuals

Annuals require cultural techniques suited to their go-for-broke natures. Steady blooming over many, many weeks requires steady nutrition to stay healthy and stress free. Slow-acting granular fertilizer mixed into their soil at planting time assures consistent, uniform nutrition over this long period. It can be supplemented during periods of stress (such as when pinching Petunia stems back in midsummer to rejuvenate the plants) by a spray or watering of diluted liquid fertilizer for a quick energy boost.

Typically, annuals have shallow, fibrous roots that need watering more frequently than deeply rooted permanent plants. Mulching the soil over their roots to retard evaporation of moisture and to discourage competitive weeds extends the time between necessary waterings. Also, if they think they have produced enough seed to assure a new generation, annuals will stop flowering. Trimming or pinching off faded flowers interrupts seed production, stimulating them to flower again so they can produce more seed.

Annual seedlings are relatively inexpensive. Because of this and their short life expectancy, pest and disease control is less an issue than with large, permanent perennial plants. In the face of disease or insect attack, gardeners can cut back the entire annual plant and let it renew itself. It is easier, safer, and often less costly to pull up seriously affected annual plants and replace them with other annuals than to treat the ailment.

I do not discuss starting seedlings indoors in the following plant entries, for several reasons. One is that, in most cases, top-quality commercially grown seedlings are generally widely available. Another is that the seed of so many annuals germinates so easily and quickly outdoors that there is not much time to be saved by early indoor starting. The main reason, however, is that growing sturdy, healthy seedlings requires another whole set of skills and equipment to raise plants of equal quality to professionally grown ones. Starting seeds indoors under lights is a wonderful, rewarding activity that enhances—but is not essential to—outdoor gardening.

Alyssum
Lobularia maritima

Like a sprinkling of snow or a layer of lace, Alyssum covers the ground with loose mounds of tiny clusters of white florets. Their delicate presence is easy to take for granted until the subtle honey scent wafts by and announces it to passersby. Low-growing, dark-green, narrow leaves set off the flowers at the tips of soft, delicate stems. Though fine-textured, Alyssums are sturdy, their Mediterranean heritage guaranteeing them to be tougher than they look. Drought tolerant once established, they are excellent plants for bedding, rock gardens, edging, and containers. They may droop somewhat in the heat of our summers, but they recover promptly and bloom until, perhaps through, the first light frost. There are many choices of Alyssum as seeds, fewer as retail seedlings.

Other Name
Snowdrift

Bloom Period and Seasonal Color
May to October; blooms in pink, white, or lilac

Mature Height × Spread
2 in. × 18 in.

When, Where, and How to Plant
Plant seeds outdoors in late April. Seeds germinate quickly; plants bloom in seven or eight weeks. Transplant young potted plants in May. Plants with lilac flowers appreciate some shade to prevent color from fading. Although it prefers soil rich in organic matter, Alyssum accepts ordinary soil as long as it is regularly moist but well drained. Cultivate the soil down 8 to 10 in., and add a handful of a granular slow-acting all-purpose fertilizer. Mix some organic material into heavy soil to promote drainage. Plant seeds as directed on their label; do not cover with soil. For seedlings, dig planting holes 6 in. apart and as deep as their rootballs so each plant is at soil level. Set plants in their holes, press soil over each rootball, then water well.

Growing Tips
Water Alyssum well at planting time and during droughty periods. A watering of very dilute liquid fertilizer after a midseason trim encourages flowering to resume.

Care
Trim or shear lanky stems back to about 2 in. at midseason to revitalize plants. Later, leave some seedpods, and Alyssum may self-sow and appear next spring if the soil is not disturbed. Properly grown Alyssum is basically pest free.

Companion Planting and Design
Alyssum spills gently over the edges of window-boxes and softens the sides of planters. Its fine texture contrasts with larger-leafed, coarser annuals such as Geraniums and Wax Begonias. Set this old-fashioned plant between steppingstones. Use taller forms as cut flowers.

Did You Know?
Pale or white flowers reflect waning light in their luminous petals, assuring pleasure in the garden at the end of the day or in the evenings. Alyssum is a staple of evening gardens, which also feature Moonvine, Lilies, Nicotiana, night-blooming tropical Water Lilies, and silver- or gray-foliaged plants. Plants with fragrance, variegated foliage, and trees and shrubs with pale bark contribute to the wonderful experience of a glowing after-hours garden.

When, Where, and How to Plant

Plant transplants in May when all danger of frost is past and the soil has warmed. Then plant rooted cuttings or plants anytime in summer. Give dark-colored Coleus light shade; newer, brighter types do best with considerable sun. They all like average, well-drained soil of any type. Overly rich soil causes floppy stems and may affect foliage color. Dig the soil down 8 to 10 in. to loosen and aerate. Mix in granular slow-acting all-purpose fertilizer to provide consistent nutrition for the season. Add organic material to improve soil drainage if necessary. Dig a planting hole about as deep as and slightly wider than the rootball so plants are level with the surrounding soil. Backfill, firm soil gently, and water well. Space plants 1 to 2 ft. apart to allow for mature width.

Growing Tips

Spread 2 or 3 in. of organic mulch to keep surrounding soil moist and discourage weeds. Water Coleus during droughty periods. Water those in containers or in sun regularly. Limit fertilizer to the initial planting dose to avoid excess tender foliage, which attracts aphids.

Care

Pinch off flowers to encourage more foliage. Pinch long and leggy stems back to a pair of leaves to encourage compactness. Stressed plants attract mites or whiteflies. Coleus are extremely vulnerable to cold.

Companion Planting and Design

Group Coleus plants for accents or ground covers. They combine well with Snapdragons, Caladiums, Salvias, Marigolds, Zinnias, and Cockscombs in beds or containers. They grow better than most plants under trees.

Did You Know?

Scientists define plants both botanically and horticulturally. A plant's botanical definition is based on how its reproductive system is structured. Thus, Coleus is a tender perennial because it lives for more than one year where winters are warm. Horticultural definitions are based on how a plant functions in the garden. In our climate Coleus dies when frost arrives, so it is effectively an annual. For gardeners, the horticultural definition is the one that counts.

Coleus foliage contributes rich and riotous color to summer gardens. Formerly a staple of elaborate Victorian-style designs, Coleus has come into its own in this era as a versatile, contemporary plant. A bit flashy and coarse—sort of like a gaudy Hawaiian shirt at a formal party—Coleus has often been relegated to shady corners. Now, newer, sun-tolerant versions of Coleus blend better with other plants, especially tropicals. These bushy, upright plants feature foliage in an astounding variety of shapes and colors. Heart-shaped, oval, or filigreed, some leaves are fringed or toothed. They may be white, cream, yellow, chartreuse, green, bronze, purple, red, or rose, often combined or edged with contrasting colors. Many Coleus are dwarf, suitable for lush, tropical container plantings.

Other Name

Flame Nettle

Bloom Period and Seasonal Color

Insignificant blooms; colorful foliage midsummer to fall

Mature Height × Spread

6 to 30 in. × 12 to 18 in.

Corn Poppy
Papaver rhoeas

Corn Poppies are the slim, colorful Poppies in the delightful wildflower mixes that cheer drivers near turnpike interchanges, highway cloverleafs, and median strips. Their airy, fragile beauty often stops traffic wherever they grow. Domesticated for the garden, they are also called Shirley Poppies after the English town where they were painstakingly bred in the 1880s. Shirley Poppy flowers are up to 3 in. wide, featuring water-colored, tissue-paper petals. Some have distinctive black blotches in their centers; some are double petaled; others are streaked or edged in white. They float at the tips of pliable, leafless, hairy stems above their dark-green, finely divided papery leaves. They produce prodigious amounts of pollen, which their brightly colored petals boldly advertise to insects galore. They bloom only a few weeks.

Other Name
Field Poppy

Bloom Period and Seasonal Color
Late May into June; blooms in pink, red, salmon, or white

Mature Height × Spread
2 ft. × 1 ft.

When, Where, and How to Plant
Corn Poppies self-sow after blooms turn to seedpods, their seeds surviving the winter to germinate in spring. Start to sow purchased seeds in late March or early April, even before the soil warms, for blooms in sixty days. Sow seeds at two- or three-week intervals for color all season. However, late sowings are less successful in summer heat. Poppies take full sun and any well-drained soil, even alkaline soil. Sow seeds directly into the designated area. Because of their taproots, they are tricky to move later. Early-spring soil is too wet to dig without harming it; just scratch its surface to create a shallow seedbed. Sprinkle seeds, mixed with sand, on the disturbed soil. Barely cover with $1/8$-inch layer of very fine soil, and moisten. Naturalize by sowing seed randomly over mowed or bare-soil areas either after Thanksgiving or in early March.

Growing Tips
Thin seedlings to 6 in. apart. Spread a thin layer of organic mulch on the soil between young plants to discourage weeds and retain moisture. There is no need to fertilize them. Water if rain is scarce.

Care
After flowers fade, remove seedpods to encourage more flowering. Leave pods from the last flush of fall bloom to encourage self-seeding. Corn Poppies do not have significant pest or disease problems.

Companion Planting and Design
Use Corn Poppies in informal settings alone or combined with ornamental grasses, Bachelor Buttons, Daisies, and other meadow-type flowers.

Did You Know?
When John McCrae wrote, "In Flanders fields the poppies blow between the crosses, row on row . . . ," he was referring to a stunning sea of red Corn Poppies that sprang from soil trampled by embattled soldiers in World War I. Later in the area, consecrated as a cemetery for those who fell on the Western Front, the deep-red Poppies eerily symbolized the blood that had flowed there. Today, the artificial "Buddy" Poppies that veterans sell around Memorial Day commemorate the tragedy, the place, and the Flanders Poppies.

Cosmos

Cosmos bipinnatus

When, Where, and How to Plant

Plant seedlings or seeds in the spring, usually mid-May. Transplant potted plants anytime during the growing season. Site in full sun. Any average soil that drains well and is slightly acidic is fine. Cosmos accept sandy soil. Loosen the soil down 8 to 10 in., digging in organic matter or coarse sand to improve drainage if necessary. Sow seeds as directed on the seed packet. Dig holes large enough to accommodate the root systems of transplants, and set them so that the tops of soilballs are slightly deeper than the surrounding ground. New roots can form from the lower part of the stem which also help support leggy plants. Backfill, and water well. Space plants 1 ft. apart.

Growing Tips

Spread a thin layer of organic material as a mulch over the bare soil around Cosmos seedlings to keep it moist and discourage weeds. Skip fertilizer if the soil is decent because too much nitrogen makes Cosmos rangy. Water during droughty periods.

Care

Taller Cosmos will need staking unless their young stems are pinched back early on to encourage compactness. Use strong stakes, set early in the season. Try dwarf varieties for more compact plants. Deadheading stimulates new flowering all season. Cosmos are virtually pest free.

Companion Planting and Design

Fully mature plants have a blowzy, informal look that suits their roles as fencerow, open field, and median strip plants. They are also delightful at the back of a flower border, where their lack of good posture is not too noticeable, or in a cutting garden for use indoors. Standard-sized ones look best behind other plants; dwarfs in the foreground are see-through.

Did You Know?

Both Painted Lady (Cosmopolitan) and monarch butterflies visit Cosmos. Painted Ladies migrate from northern Mexico in the spring, sometimes flying in groups of thousands low to the ground. Many settle in Pennsylvania in the spring, and breed and die here. They are mostly black-patterned orange with white wing tips and black dots on the edges of their back wings.

This old-fashioned flower is enjoying something of a comeback these days. For many gardeners it has never gone away, although it may have been taken for granted. Like many annuals, it is tough, agreeable, and beautiful, and it is easy to grow. An open, branching, sturdy plant, it features pastel-colored, daisy-type flowers with yellow centers. Up to 3 to 4 in. across, the flowers bloom above airy, finely divided, ferny foliage. Sonata series are dwarf at 2 ft. tall and mixed pink and white. Versailles series are 3 ft. tall, ideal for cutting. Bicolor 'Candy Stripe' is white with red edges on petals. Seashell series have petals in a variety of colors that curve in to form tubes.

Other Name

Mexican Aster

Bloom Period and Seasonal Color

June through September; blooms in red, rose, magenta, white, or bicolor

Mature Height × Spread

4 to 6 ft. × 2 to 3 ft.

Four-o'-Clock

Mirabilis jalapa

Some people believe that a flower garden is not a true garden unless it includes Four-o'-Clocks. Once these old-fashioned flowers are planted, they are there for the duration because of their reliable self-seeding. As their name suggests, they put on their show late in the day. Their newly opened 1- to 2-in. trumpet flowers brighten the waning light and provide a last stop for local hummingbirds before the sun sets. Attuned to the sun, they do not open on cloudy or rainy days. Their tough roots and sturdy stems testify to their staying power, taking pollution, dust, and a certain amount of drought in stride. By the end of summer, they are bushes, so give them space. 'Jingles' is a smaller, denser plant with striped flowers.

Other Name
Beauty-of-the-Night

Bloom Period and Seasonal Color
July until October; blooms in yellow, rose, white, or red

Mature Height × Spread
2 to 3 ft. × 2 ft.

When, Where, and How to Plant
Four-o'-Clocks plant themselves in the garden by dropping seeds in the fall. Grow the resulting seedlings in place next spring, or transplant them elsewhere in the yard. An alternative is to collect the seeds from faded flowers in the fall and sow them directly in a bed outdoors in the spring. Four-o'-Clocks like full sun, but accept some shade. They do fine in well-drained ordinary soil. When transplanting, dig the soil down 8 to 10 in. to loosen it. A handful of a granular slow-acting all-purpose fertilizer mixed into the soil at this point will sustain Four-o'-Clocks all season. Dig a hole about as deep as and slightly wider than the seedling's rootball, and set it so that it is level with the surrounding ground. Firm soil around the stem, and water well. Plant new seedlings or thin existing ones to at least 1 ft. apart to allow for their mature size.

Growing Tips
The only necessary ongoing care for these low-maintenance plants is watering in a severe drought.

Care
If Four-o'-Clock plants flop over from the weight of their dense branching, cut them back a bit, or stake them. Pull up unauthorized seedlings before they become established. Their primary pest problem is Japanese beetles in July. Brush them off the foliage into a jar of soapy water several times daily. Cut back marred foliage.

Companion Planting and Design
Plant Four-o'-Clocks as edging along high walls, in flower borders, or in mixed borders where they can serve as temporary shrubs by late summer.

Did You Know?
Four-o'-Clocks are the ultimate passalong plant. Their seeds are large and convenient for gardeners to collect and pass along to friends and neighbors. For this reason commercially grown young plants are rarely available at local garden centers. Seeds, and sometimes root tubers, are available, though, in retail outlets and mail-order catalogs every spring.

Geranium

Pelargonium × hortorum

When, Where, and How to Plant

Plant young plants in May when the air and soil are warm. Plant full-grown plants anytime all season. Although they like full sun, they can handle part sun also. Geraniums manage fine in average garden soil as long as it drains well. They prefer a more neutral pH, but rarely get it in Pennsylvania gardens where soil is often on the acidic side. Add organic material to promote drainage and granular slow-acting all-purpose fertilizer to provide nutrition when loosening soil down about 12 in. Dig each hole as deep as and slightly wider than plant rootballs. Set plants so that they are level with the surrounding soil. Firm the soil gently, and water well. Adding granular slow-acting fertilizer to soil-less potting mixes when planting in containers will provide uniform, consistent nutrition all season.

Growing Tips

Geraniums like a wet-dry watering cycle. Allow soil to dry out a bit before each watering. If slow-acting fertilizer was not provided at planting, add diluted water-soluble fertilizer to the water every few weeks.

Care

Mulch to discourage weeds. To groom and encourage blooming, remove spent flowers by breaking off their stiff stalks at their base near the main stem. As the first fall frost nears, bring plants indoors to overwinter as houseplants or to store bare root for a source of cuttings for next spring. Those that remain in the garden will succumb to a hard frost. Stressed plants may attract whiteflies or mites. Wet soils and poor air circulation promote root rot and mildew on foliage.

Companion Planting and Design

Use groups of three plants, spaced about 1 ft. apart, for best effect in a mixed flower bed.

Did You Know?

Scented Geraniums are the lesser-known Geraniums. Usually planted in pots, their flowers are less showy, but their foliage is remarkable. Various types have curled, frilled, or finely cut leaves that smell like lemon, pineapple, coconut, rose, nutmeg, or peppermint. They are used to flavor cakes and jellies, and are dried for potpourris.

The American public votes common Geraniums into the top ten most popular annual plants every year. They show no sign of losing favor as the backbone of millions of windowboxes, hanging baskets, planters, and light post and mailbox beds. Their flowers attract all of the attention—small florets clustered in 5- to 7-in. balls of rich-hued color, large enough to be seen from a distance. They bloom at the tips of stiff, bare stalks; their crisp, upright habit lending an air of formality to the proceedings. Geranium leaves typically have reddish-colored rings or "zones," although some may be plain green or variegated green and cream. All this, and an easygoing nature that takes pollution, dry soil, and partial shade, explains why Geraniums are so loved.

Other Name
Zonal Geranium

Bloom Period and Seasonal Color
July to October; blooms in red and pink, white, salmon, or bicolor

Mature Height × Spread
2 ft. × 2 ft.

Impatiens

Impatiens walleriana

What did we do before we had Impatiens? This plant has changed the look of our residential landscapes where large, gorgeous leafy trees are common and shade is a fact of life. Impatiens, named for the tendency of its seedpod to impatiently split open at the slightest touch, offers a dazzling array of colorful flowers with five flat petals backed by a thin, spurred bract. Hybrid types offer more elaborate double-flowered, iridescent, white-edged, and longer blooms; more colors; uniform size; and variegated foliage. Some are low growing; others grow more upright. Dazzler series are 8 in. tall, with large flowers. Swirl series flowers are edged with a contrasting color. New Guinea–type hybrids feature tropical-colored and narrower foliage, and they tolerate more sun.

Other Name
Busy Lizzie

Bloom Period and Seasonal Color
June to October; blooms in red and pink, white, salmon, orange, white, or bicolor

Mature Height × Spread
6 in. to 2 ft. × 8 to 12 in.

When, Where, and How to Plant

Directly seed Impatiens into the garden in late May, or if you are impatient for Impatiens, transplant seedlings or potted plants. They can handle some (morning) sun, but Impatiens prefer bright indirect light or shade. A woodland setting with moist, well-drained soil is ideal. They like soil a bit toward neutral but manage with more acidic soil. Dig and loosen the soil down 10 to 12 in., mixing in organic material and a sprinkling of granular slow-acting fertilizer. Dig the hole as deep as and slightly wider than the rootball. Set the plant level with surrounding soil, then backfill. Water well, and spread organic mulch on the soil near each plant to discourage weeds. Set plants about 1 ft. apart in groups of three to heighten the impact of their color.

Growing Tips

Thirsty Impatiens droop alarmingly, so water them before they become stressed. Maintaining mulch retards evaporation of moisture from the soil. Impatiens in containers with soilless medium need frequent checks for moisture, especially if they receive any sun. If there is no slow-acting granular fertilizer in their planting mix, Impatiens in containers need diluted liquid fertilizer in their water every two weeks. Do not overdo fertilizing when watering.

Care

Pinched stems root readily in a glass of water. Pinch stems back to keep plants more compact. Occasionally, young Impatiens attract aphids to their tender growing tips. Pinch off the infested tips, and discard them.

Companion Planting and Design

Their shallow roots suit Impatiens for planting under trees and shrubs to brighten the landscape. Impatiens are perfect for containers in shady spots and for woodland settings among Ferns and Hostas.

Did You Know?

Catalogs sometimes use specialized terms to describe plants: *Eye*: the center of a flower blossom that is a different color from the petals. *Picotee*: flower petals edged with a strong, contrasting color. *Series*: a group of similar plants, usually hybrids, that are not identical.

Larkspur

Consolida ambigua

When, Where, and How to Plant

Larkspur does not like transplanting, so either plant very young plants in May, or sow seeds directly into the garden in late fall after frost or in the very early spring. Seeds can handle March cold if the soil is workable, taking about twenty days to germinate. Site in full sun. They do fine in well-drained garden soil of any type. Prepare the planting bed by loosening the soil down 6 to 8 in. and mixing in a handful of a granular slow-acting all-purpose fertilizer. Add organic matter to improve soil drainage and moisture-holding capacity if needed. Sow seeds as directed, or plant seedlings in holes about the size of their rootballs. Thin seedlings to 10 to 12 in. apart when they are a few inches tall.

Growing Tips

Water young plants regularly until they are established and then whenever rainfall is scarce. Slow-acting fertilizer in the soil is sufficient to maintain them for the season.

Care

Mulch the soil around seedlings to discourage weeds. Cut off faded flower heads to groom and to stimulate continued flowering or allow them to mature and form seeds to self-sow. Larkspur tends to decline and die back after flowering. Stake tall, blossom-heavy plants so that they do not fall over. Crowding and humidity promote mildew on foliage. *Note: All parts of Larkspur are poisonous.*

Companion Planting and Design

Finely divided into many narrow leaflets, the foliage of massed Larkspurs creates a misty effect that contrasts well with coarser-textured foliage of neighboring plants. Use Larkspur as a filler in a flower border for a cottage garden look or in a cutting garden.

Did You Know?

Wherever they grow, Larkspurs attract the local hummingbirds. Only ruby-throated hummingbirds visit Pennsylvania gardens. They arrive here in May and leave anytime after July. The male has the trademark ruby bib as well as iridescent olive-tinted sides. Hummers nest in Hickory, Hornbeam, Oak, Pine, and Tuliptrees.

Larkspur is the next best thing to Delphinium, which struggles in areas where summer nights are very warm. (They do best, however, before the onset of hot weather.) Larkspur, too, provides vertical interest with upright, floret-covered spires in wonderful shades of blue, pink, or white. Larkspur florets may be single or double, about 1 in. long, and spurred. They are arrayed along the upper parts of stems above feathery, soft-green, 4-in.-long leaves. Sometimes flowers are tightly clustered along the stems; other times they are widely spaced. Dwarf Rocket series have double flowers and grow 1 to 2 ft. tall. Plants of the Giant Imperial series branch readily low on 2- to 3-ft.-tall main stems; they have double flowers. Larkspurs make great cut flowers for indoor arrangements, either fresh or dried.

Other Name
Annual Delphinium

Bloom Period and Seasonal Color
June through October; blooms in blue, pink, white, or lilac

Mature Height × Spread
2 to 5 ft. × 2 to 3 ft.

Marigold

Tagetes species and hybrids

Their various common names notwithstanding, Marigolds are from Mexico. They have a long history in gardens in the United States, however. Their intense color, many forms, and reliability qualify them as dependable summer standbys, lasting well into fall when their colors coordinate beautifully with autumn hues. Marigold foliage is composed of finely cut green leaflets and is notorious for its musky smell. The flowers are from $^{1}/_{2}$ to 5 in. wide, a size for every landscape and garden use. Their hybrids, triploid types, have 4- to 5-in.-wide double blossoms and withstand heat well. The American Marigold (Tagetes erecta), Lady hybrid series, is an All-Time Gold Medal All-America Selections winner. 'French Vanilla' is the first hybrid white Marigold 24 in. tall, with flowers 3 in. wide.

Other Names
French, Signet, American Marigolds

Bloom Period and Seasonal Color
June to October; blooms in yellow, orange, mahogany, white, or bicolor

Mature Height × Spread
Species range from 8 in. to 3 ft. × 10 to 20 in.

When, Where, and How to Plant
Plant seeds or transplants outdoors in mid-May. Marigold seeds germinate in no time. The plants thrive in sun and hot, southern exposures. Plants will take any well-drained soil of poor to average fertility. With ample moisture they can handle the reflected light and heat of pavement. Dig the soil down 8 to 10 in., and add organic matter to improve drainage if necessary. Add a handful of a granular slow-acting all-purpose fertilizer. Dig holes the size of their rootballs, then set each plant level with surrounding soil. Backfill, and water well. Space taller types 15 in. apart, smaller ones 8 to 10 in. apart.

Growing Tips
Water Marigolds when rainfall is sparse. Avoid overhead watering of American Marigolds, which causes their flowers to deteriorate rapidly. Apply a 2- or 3-in. layer of mulch on the soil to discourage weeds and retain moisture. More fertilizer is not needed.

Care
Stake tall types. Clip off faded flowers to groom and to prevent reseeding. Watch for caterpillars and Japanese beetles on American Marigolds. Control aphids by pinching off infested stems or by spraying insecticidal soap. Marigold foliage may have a gray mildew coating, more unsightly than dangerous. Diseased Marigold foliage and flowers turn yellow and are stunted. Pull up plants immediately, and put them in a plastic bag in the trash. Disinfect tools in hot water and household bleach.

Companion Planting and Design
The American Marigolds are the tallest and are good for small hedges to divide the garden area, edging for walks, backdrops for shorter flowers, and cutting. Smaller French and Signet Marigolds are great for edging and containers, and for interplanting with vegetables.

Did You Know?
Marigolds are almost synonymous with the W. Atlee Burpee Seed Company in Warminster, Pennsylvania. Since 1915 the company has been at the forefront of Marigold breeding. It campaigned to have the Marigold chosen as the national flower; however, that honor was bestowed on the Rose.

Nasturtium

Tropaeolum majus

When, Where, and How to Plant

Nasturtiums are not available as garden center seedlings because they resent transplanting. Plant seeds outdoors after the last expected frost in mid-May in full sun. They like decent soil, not overly rich in nutrients, but well drained. Shore conditions are ideal. Soak seeds overnight in lukewarm water to soften their hard coatings. Then plant them in garden soil that has been loosened down 4 to 6 in. Cover seeds with soil to provide the darkness they need to germinate. Expect leaves in ten days or so, then flowers in five to six weeks. Nasturtiums will grow indoors over the winter in a cool, sunny room. Start seeds in pots of soilless mix outdoors, and then bring them inside in October before frost hits.

Growing Tips

Water as they get established and thereafter when conditions are droughtlike. Do not fertilize if their soil is decent. If flowering is sparse after several weeks, allow them to dry out a bit to stress them into production.

Care

Weekend gardeners like Nasturtiums because they need so little attention. Watch for aphids underneath leaves, a chronic problem. Pinch out the infested leaves and flowers, wash them with a forceful water spray, or spray them with insecticidal soap. Clean plants up promptly after the first dusting of frost reduces them to black mush.

Companion Planting and Design

Use Nasturtiums for edging, hanging baskets, and screens for eyesore utilities and drain pipes. As ground covers, trailing types insinuate themselves through and among other plants to weave them together or fill bare spots in vegetable beds where plants have been harvested.

Did You Know?

People have been eating Nasturtiums for ages. The first American book on gardening, *The American Gardener's Calendar*, mentions that they are excellent when garnishing dishes and that their pickled unripe seeds resemble capers. Spicy with a bit of bite, Nasturtium leaves and petals brighten salads. Use only those never treated with insecticides. Pick early in the morning.

Gardeners cannot resist planting Nasturtiums somewhere in their yards. Part of their appeal is their versatility because the dwarf-mounded, semi-trailing, and trailing forms of Nasturtiums literally cover just about any landscape situation. Their bright, zesty flowers and interesting foliage account for most of their appeal. Nasturtium flowers have creased petals with slightly frilled tips and spurred bases in exuberant jewel colors. They bloom at the tips of slim, flexible, pale-green or bluish green stems that nestle among similarly stemmed lily pad–type leaves. Newer forms of Nasturtiums feature pastel-colored flowers that rise above the foliage and have no spurs. 'Alaska' has variegated leaves, green marbled with cream, and mixed flower color. Double Dwarf Jewel series have bushy, small habits and large, double flowers.

Other Name

Indian Cress

Bloom Period and Seasonal Color

June to October; blooms in mahogany, red, orange, yellow, or white

Mature Height × Spread

8 in. to 1 ft. × 2 ft.

Nicotiana

Nicotiana species and hybrids

Nicotianas are instantly recognizable by their narrow, tubular flowers with star-shaped flaring petals at their tips. The original lanky night bloomer, whose flowers drooped during the day, then perked up at night to release a wonderful fragrance, is still available as Jasmine Tobacco. Newer, more compact versions of Nicotiana are less fragrant, bear more flowers, and are open in the daytime. There are semi-dwarf hybrids in wonderful colors that bloom all season. Flowers grow in sprays at the ends of branching stems emerging from rosettes of green leaves near the soil. They bloom all season, often tolerating the first frost to continue into early November. Some plants may survive under mulch during a mild winter. They may self-sow for next year.

Other Name
Ornamental Tobacco

Bloom Period and Seasonal Color
June through October; blooms in red, rose, pink, white, or green

Mature Height × Spread
1 to 2 ft. × 1 ft.

When, Where, and How to Plant
At the garden center purchase Nicotiana plants that do not yet have buds or blooms. Plant in May as soon as the soil is workable. Hardened off plants can handle an errant light frost. Site Nicotianas where they can receive full sun at least in the mornings. Some afternoon shade is fine and even enhances their colors. They like good garden soil that drains well. Cultivate down 8 to 10 in., digging in granular slow-acting all-purpose fertilizer to provide season-long nutrition. Dig a planting hole as deep as and slightly wider than each rootball. Set each plant so that it is level with the surrounding soil. Backfill, and water well. Space smaller hybrids about 10 to 12 in. apart, taller ones up to 2 ft. apart.

Growing Tips
Water until plants are established and when rainfall is sparse. Apply a 2- to 3-in. layer of organic mulch over their soil to discourage weeds and conserve moisture.

Care
Nicotianas are content with routine, minimal care. Cutting their flowers stimulates more flowering and provides blossoms for indoors. Nicotianas are vulnerable to mosaic virus or Colorado potato beetles, but these are not common problems in most gardens.

Companion Planting and Design
Use Nicotianas as their heights suggest—middle of borders, edging, containers, along fences, or in a cutting garden.

Did You Know?
True Tobacco (*Nicotiana tabacum*) is also ornamental. It reaches 7 ft. and has pinkish blossoms. In 1560, seventy years after Columbus encountered native people of the West Indies smoking the dried leaves of a certain plant called "Tobago," Jean Nicot, a French ambassador to Portugal, planted it in his Lisbon garden and harvested the leaves for snuff. He eventually introduced it into France. Thus, it began its commercial and ornamental life with the man memorialized in its botanical name, *Nicotiana*. He is also remembered in the name of the compound in its foliage, nicotine, eventually banned as an insecticide because it is so poisonous.

Pansy

Viola × wittrockiana

When, Where, and How to Plant

If planted in fall, young plants will have well-developed root systems by early spring. Alternatively, buy seedlings in late winter, and plant them as soon as soil is workable. Pansies do best in full sun during the cool spring and fall. To encourage continued summer bloom, put them in some shade. They are not picky about soil type as long as it is rich, cool, moist, and well drained. Dig the soil down 6 to 8 in., and add organic matter. For spring planting, mix in granular slow-acting all-purpose fertilizer. Dig planting holes about as deep as and slightly wider than their rootballs so they are at soil level. Backfill, and water well. Space transplants 6 to 8 in. apart in beds. Plant them more closely in containers with drainage holes; add slow-acting fertilizer to the soilless potting medium.

Growing Tips

Cover the soil around fall-planted Pansies with chopped leaves, straw, or evergreen boughs after a hard frost to insulate the soil. Water when the soil is dry. Delay fertilizing until early spring. Also mulch spring transplants to keep soil cool and extend bloom period. Adding slow-acting fertilizer in their soil will see them through the season.

Care

Pinch off faded flower stems to groom plants, stimulate flowering, and prevent reseeding. Pull up plants when they begin to flop in the heat. Pansies growing in somewhat shaded, moist sites may suffer slug damage.

Companion Planting and Design

The large, multicolored, clown-faced Pansies show best in containers or rock gardens or grouped as focal points and fillers. The slightly smaller, single-colored ones make great ground covers, alone or among spring bulbs such as Snowdrops or Tulips.

Did You Know?

Old-fashioned flowers evoke memories of grandmother's garden. Heirlooms from before the turn of the century suggest times when life was simpler and slower paced. A hallmark of old-fashioned flowers is fragrance, as found in Pansies. Often sacrificed by modern hybridizers in favor of other traits, fragrance turns back the clock.

There are few cool-weather flowering annuals, but Pansies save the day. Their jaunty, colorful blooms ease difficult seasonal transitions. Cousins of Violets and Johnny Jump-ups, they are tougher than they look. Mulched fall-planted ones can survive our winters with no fuss, emerging all set to bloom in early spring. Over the years breeders have developed ever-larger, more colorful flowers that face upward rather than nod and that can handle heat, too, blooming well into the summer. Hybridizing over one hundred years has yielded many kinds and colors, new ones appearing every year. Choose from among grandiflora types ('Majestic Giants') with flowers up to 4 in. across or multiflora types ('Universal' hybrids) with 2$\frac{1}{2}$-in.-wide, more numerous flowers.

Other Name
Heartsease

Bloom Period and Seasonal Color
March through June, September through December; blooms in all colors except green

Mature Height × Spread
6 to 10 in. × 1 ft.

Petunia
Petunia × hybrida

If there were no Petunias, they would have to be invented. In fact, botanically speaking, they were. Descendants of two South American species, they are the result of generations of crossbreeding. The most recent hybrids are wildly colorful and elaborate, featuring ruffled or fringed petals, edged and streaked petals, dark eyes in their centers, and very large or very small blossoms. Petunia flowers bloom at the tips of lax stems among simple, oval leaves covered with sticky fuzz. Many, especially purple ones, have a wonderful cinnamon fragrance early in the morning and late in the day. Petunias continue to top the list of most popular annuals year after year. Choose from hundreds of varieties. To narrow your choice, decide on the type, then the color.

Other Name
Garden Petunia

Bloom Period and Seasonal Color
June through October; blooms in pink, red, white, purple, lilac, yellow, or bicolor

Mature Height × Spread
6 to 18 in. × 12 to 18 in.

When, Where, and How to Plant
Plant young plants in May. They perform best in full sun. Petunias accept almost any kind of soil that drains well. They prefer, but do not insist, that it be light and pH neutral. Acclimate seedlings raised indoors by setting them out during the day for a week or two; start with a few hours each day, and gradually increase the time. Dig the soil down 8 to 10 in., and mix in granular slow-acting all-purpose fertilizer to provide steady nutrition all season. Add organic matter to improve water retention and drainage if necessary. Dig planting holes about as deep as and slightly wider than plant rootballs. Set plants to be level with the surrounding soil. Backfill, and water well. Space upright types 12 in. apart.

Growing Tips
Petunias are shallow rooted, so they need regular moisture for peak performance. Petunias in containers may need daily watering in summer. Double-flowered types are very susceptible to flower damage from overhead watering or rain. Without slow-release fertilizer in the soil, they will need a snack of diluted liquid fertilizer every month while they are in high gear.

Care
Pinch back leggy stems by half at midseason to stimulate more bloom. Do not grow Petunias near their vegetable cousins, such as Tomatoes, Potatoes, or Eggplant, because their pests—whiteflies and flea beetles—like Petunias, too. Pull up heavily infested plants and discard them.

Companion Planting and Design
Plant ground cover Petunia types on sunny slopes, and cascading ones in hanging baskets and other containers. Combine them with other sun-loving annuals such as Snapdragons, Salvias, Nicotiana, and Ageratum. The smaller the flower size, the smaller the overall plant.

Did You Know?
Hybrid plants are more expensive than others because they are painstakingly hand-pollinated to assure that the correct parents are paired. This must be done each year with the same parents under scientifically controlled conditions to assure uniformity. Hybrids typically offer more colors, fancier shapes, and enhanced disease and weather resistance.

Portulaca

Portulaca grandiflora

When, Where, and How to Plant

Plant young plants in late May. Portulaca needs heat and full sun to thrive. It actually prefers sandy, lean soil that drains well. Plant it where nothing else will grow. Dig the soil down 4 to 6 in., deeper if it needs sand or gravel mixed into it to improve its drainage. Sow seeds as directed. Or dig planting holes for seedlings about as deep as and slightly wider than transplant rootballs. Then set plants so they are level with the surrounding soil. Backfill, and water well. Space seedlings 6 to 8 in. apart.

Growing Tips

Portulaca does fine on moisture provided by rain. Use no fertilizer or mulch.

Care

A bit of weeding may be necessary until plants really spread. Portulaca has no pests or diseases.

Companion Planting and Design

Use as a filler in sunny beds where other plants go dormant by midsummer, in rock gardens, between steppingstones, and in containers. Massed as a ground cover, Portulaca will obscure embarrassing bare spots in the yard.

Did You Know?

Plants with a desert heritage are suited to life without much moisture. Some, like Portulaca, are succulent, their fleshy stems and leaves filled with moisture-retaining sap, and coated with wax to prevent drying out. Other plants have other physical characteristics that identify them as low-water-demand plants. The adaptations are most often in their foliage because that is where plants lose moisture most as they transpire. They may have small leaves or thorns instead, or finely divided leaves that reduce the surface area exposed to sun. Many have silver or gray foliage that reflects heat and light, hairs on their leaves that shade leaf surfaces and trap dew, and leaves with aromatic oils that are volatile in heat to envelop the plant in a protective haze. Low-water-demand plants often have fleshy, deep roots, or taproots, to store moisture and trailing habits to keep them close to whatever soil moisture is present.

Portulaca is the agreeable, easy-care plant that is perfectly happy decorating the hottest, most inhospitable site on your property. Its desert heritage enables it to survive with aplomb, producing waves of brightly colored flowers at the tips of its trailing stems all summer. Up to 2 in. wide, the flowers open during sunny days and close at night or on cloudy days. When they fade, they drop off, leaving behind tiny seeds for a new crop of Portulaca next year. New, fancier hybrids offer double flowers and more of them, but their self-sown plants may not resemble them. Portulaca foliage is succulent and narrow, like needles, and it and plant stems may be green or tinged with red or bronze.

Other Name

Moss Rose

Bloom Period and Seasonal Color

June through October; blooms in pink, red, orange, yellow, or white

Mature Height × Spread

6 to 10 in. × 6 to 12 in.

Red Salvia
Salvia splendens

Red Salvia is impossible to overlook in a residential garden. Its upright posture and the richness and brightness of its red flowers make it such a standout that most neighboring plants retire into the background under its intensity. A little Red Salvia goes a long way unless you want to lure hummingbirds, then plant a bed of it. This plant seems made to order for hummers, its narrow, tubular flowers crowding along tall stems and facing outward for easy access. They contrast wonderfully with the heart-shaped, medium-green foliage below. The traditional Salvias are tall and red flowered; newer, more garden-compatible varieties have more rounded habits, dwarf or intermediate height, and a range of softer colors. 'Firecracker' and 'Hot Stuff' are dwarf, under 1 ft. tall.

Other Name
Scarlet Sage

Bloom Period and Seasonal Color
May through October; blooms in red, purple, salmon, maroon, or cream

Mature Height × Spread
1 to 3 ft. × 1 to 1¹/₂ ft.

When, Where, and How to Plant
Transplant in May when all danger of frost is past. Choose an overcast day or late hour to avoid transplant stress. Full sun is best for the most intense color of the Red Salvias; those of other colors can take a bit of shade. Salvias need moist, but not soggy, soil. Dig the soil down 8 to 10 in., and mix in granular slow-acting all-purpose fertilizer to provide steady nutrition all season. Sow seeds as directed on packet. Or dig planting holes for transplants about as deep as and slightly wider than their rootballs. Set plants at the level of the surrounding soil. Backfill, and water well. Space tall Salvias about 2 ft. apart, medium and dwarf types proportionally less.

Growing Tips
With their shallow root systems Red Salvias appreciate regular moisture from rain or a sprinkler. Spread 2 or 3 in. of organic mulch on the soil to discourage weeds and help retain moisture.

Care
Deadhead spent flowers. Pinch back stems of tall varieties to stimulate branching. Newer, more compact types branch automatically. Stake tall Salvias. Stressed plants may suffer mite, aphid, or whitefly attacks.

Companion Planting and Design
Salvia's straight spikes provide vertical punctuation in beds of mounded or low-growing plants. Choose a site that takes advantage of Red Salvia's heat tolerance, for instance, poolside planters or south-facing windowboxes. Use various sizes of Salvias to line walks and walls or to fill tubs and barrels. Use Red Salvias as the centerpiece of a red, white, and blue garden. Plant them behind white Petunias, then plant low-growing blue Ageratum in front.

Did You Know?
Plants reveal many of their problems through their foliage. Is Red Salvia foliage: Drooping or wilting? *Dryness.* Yellow on lower leaves, dull on upper? *Nutritional deficiency.* All pale? *Whiteflies.* Pale or curled? *Aphids.* Ragged holes? *Slugs.* Stippled with pale dots or discolored? *Spider mites.* Black and soft all over? *Frost.* Gray blotched or coated? *Mildew.*

Snapdragon
Antirrhinum majus

When, Where, and How to Plant

Sow seeds outdoors as soon as the soil is dry enough to cultivate. Wait to plant young plants until early May. They can take some shade and any soil that drains well. Dig down 6 to 8 in, and mix in granular slow-acting all-purpose fertilizer to supply nutrition over their long bloom season. Plant seeds as directed on the packet. Dig holes for transplants about as deep as and slightly wider than their rootballs. Set them level with the surrounding soil. Backfill, and water well. Space tall plants about 1 ft. apart, dwarf ones about 8 in.

Growing Tips

Water young Snapdragons until they are well established. Then water only in the absence of regular rainfall when they are so dry that their foliage starts to droop. Add a 2- or 3-in. layer of organic mulch over their soil to discourage competing weeds and to retain soil moisture. Water in very dilute liquid fertilizer if blooming slows midseason.

Care

Stake tall varieties to assure straight stems for cutting. Pinch off stems with spent flowers to promote side branching. For return engagements, either allow Snaps to self-sow, or mulch disease-free plants to overwinter. Snapdragons are prone to rust, so choose resistant varieties, rotate plants around the yard, and avoid overhead watering. This fungal disease develops in cool, humid weather on leaves that are wet for more than six hours. Stressed plants may attract aphids or whiteflies.

Companion Planting and Design

Use dwarf-sized Snaps for edging, traditional bedding, containers, or rock gardens. Use intermediate-sized ones in mixed flower borders, tucked among shrubs, or along fences. They are also good for larger containers and cutting.

Did You Know?

Colorful and long-blooming annual flowers are a good way to introduce kids to gardening. Seeds of Sunflowers, Nasturtiums, Zinnias, and Marigolds are easy to handle and germinate quickly. Unusual flowers such as Snapdragons and Pansies appeal to the imagination. Set aside a small garden plot for the children to plant and enjoy.

Many people remember Snapdragons from childhood, but they are less frequently grown in home gardens now as in the past. That is unfortunate because these classic staples of florist bouquets are sturdy, colorful garden plants. Their distinctive flowers are 1 to 1½ in. long, with two upper petals and three lower petals forming "dragon jaws." They are compactly clustered along narrow, tall stems above fine-textured, green foliage. Snapdragons open gradually from the lower to the upper stem, creating spires of pastel colors. Newer hybrids have butterfly and double Azalea-type flowers that are more open faced with fluted edges. They are technically tender perennials and commonly survive mild winters in Pennsylvania gardens. 'Tahiti' is low growing, available as individual colors or a mixture.

Other Name

Garden Snapdragon

Bloom Period and Seasonal Color

June through October; blooms in white, yellow, pink, orange, rose, or lavender

Mature Height × Spread

6 to 30 in. × 8 to 18 in.

Spider Flower
Cleome hassleriana

Spider Flowers are a contradiction of bold structure and delicate flowers; therefore, they are interesting and attractive in the garden. They grow as tall, sturdy-stemmed, branching plants, decorated with light-green, palm-shaped foliage having five to seven narrow lobes. The flowers themselves top each branch as loose, rounded 5- to 6-in.-wide clusters of inch-wide florets, each with several extended thready stamens that suggest spider legs. Over time, the main stem grows woody and develops thorns. This plant flowers nonstop. As successive flower heads form, its branches elongate and become laddered with seedpods from previous blossoms. Permitted to dry on the plant, they will release thousands of tiny seeds. 'Helen Campbell' has all-white flowers. Burpee's Queen series offer mixed colors and separate colors.

Other Name
Cleome

Bloom Period and Seasonal Color
June through October; blooms in white, rose, pink, or lavender

Mature Height × Spread
4 to 5 ft. × 4 ft.

When, Where, and How to Plant
After planting Spider Flower the first year, just thin the resulting gazillion tiny seedlings in subsequent years in June when they are a few inches tall. Plant seeds as directed on the packet label. Transplant young plants or sow seeds directly into the garden anytime after mid-May. Spider Flowers prefer full sun; they accept some shade but may become lankier. Dig down 6 to 8 in., and mix in granular slow-acting all-purpose fertilizer that will supply consistent and uniform nutrition over their long season of bloom. Dig holes about as deep as and slightly wider than transplant rootballs. Set them in their holes level with the surrounding soil. Backfill, and water well. Space plants about 2 ft. apart.

Growing Tips
Water young plants until they are well established. A 2- or 3-in. layer of mulch discourages competing weeds and retains soil moisture. Although they can take some drought when mature, Spider Flowers do best with regular moisture. Additional fertilization is not needed.

Care
Stake fully grown plants in areas exposed to winds and storms. Cut off aging, elongated flowering stems where rows of seedpods are maturing to control rampant reseeding, make the plant more compact, and reinvigorate blooming. Spider Flowers are virtually pest free.

Companion Planting and Design
Spider Flowers are tough enough to handle reflected heat and sun from pavement and walls, poor soil, and neglect. Use these lanky, slightly cockeyed plants informally at the back of a border, along fences and boundaries, and in cutting gardens.

Did You Know?
Do not count on notorious self-sowers such as Spider Flowers to appear the next season if you spread a pre-emergent-type herbicide on the soil in the flower bed to deter weeds. These products prevent seeds from germinating and do not distinguish between desirable and undesirable ones. They do not harm plants, however, and are often used on lawns to prevent weeds from infiltrating existing turf.

Sunflower

Helianthus unnuus

When, Where, and How to Plant

Sunflower seeds sprout and grow rapidly, so sow directly in the yard in May. Plant every couple of weeks into mid-July to extend the bloom period over the summer. Sunflowers need full sun. They accept any well-drained soil, but the more fertile the soil, the bigger the flowers. Sow seeds as directed on the packet. Mix a handful of a granular slow-acting all-purpose fertilizer into the soil to sustain new young plants all season.

Growing Tips

Water seedlings if rainfall is scarce until plants are well established. Do not fertilize more; too much nitrogen delays bloom.

Care

Thin seedlings: dwarf types 1 to 2 ft. apart; taller types 3 to 4 ft. apart. Branching ones need more space unless they are to be used for cutting. Pinch the main stems of branching types to induce more branching. Stake tall ones. Some gardeners regard squirrels as a major pest. When the back of each flower head pales to yellow, then turns brown, cover the flower with a paper bag tied tightly at the stem to protect the ripening seeds. To harvest seeds, cut the flowers off, and hang them to dry. *Note: Pollenless Sunflowers do not produce seeds.* Mildew on the foliage does not harm plants.

Companion Planting and Design

Site tall Sunflowers so that they do not shade other plants in a cutting garden. Plant them in a row as a screen, along a fence, or at the back of an informal border. Sunflower roots emit a growth inhibitor to which some vegetables are sensitive, so plant them at least 3 ft. away from them. Shorter, ornamental Sunflowers integrate well into flower borders or containers.

Did You Know?

Birds prefer the smaller black seeds that are commercially raised to produce oil. They are easier for birds to manage and for most feeders to dispense. Among the numerous Sunflower seed fans in Pennsylvania are cardinals, various finches, juncoes, chickadees, titmice, nuthatches, blue jays, and grosbeaks.

It seems incredible that something so ridiculously easy to grow is also delightful and useful. There is a reason that Sunflowers have infiltrated our culture as a decorative motif on everything from napkins to shower curtains. Native to North America, their tall but gentle presence and informal, cheery demeanor are distinctively American. The wild plants that thrive on prairie farms are too tall for other than novelties in contemporary residential yards, but now there are more refined, ornamental versions of Sunflowers. They offer a wide range of colors, flower types, and sizes. Some are even pollenless, making them more welcome indoors as cut flowers. They all have the remarkable stiff, fuzzy stems, coarse, bristly green leaves, and wide flower heads ringed with petals.

Other Name

Annual Sunflower

Bloom Period and Seasonal Color

July until September; blooms in yellow, gold, mahogany, or bicolor

Mature Height × Spread

2 to 12 ft. × 2 to 4 ft.

Wax Begonia

Begonia semperflorens-cultorum hybrids

This annual is all that it can be and then some. Neat and tidy enough to excel at formal bedding designs and edging chores, it is so versatile and adaptable that it accommodates shady nooks, containers, and life indoors. Furthermore, it blooms all summer, then into fall and possibly past light frost without missing a beat. Wax Begonias have dense, crisp, rounded, or tapered foliage. Waxy and glossy surfaced, their leaves may be bright green, deep bronze, maroon, or variegated. Flowers of tall Begonia varieties are 1 to 2 in. wide; those of dwarf types are 1 in. wide. They bloom in clusters at joints in the fleshy stems where leaf stems branch off. Each has four rounded petals and two narrower, winglike ones.

Other Name
Bedding Begonia

Bloom Period and Seasonal Color
June to October; blooms in red, white, or pink

Mature Height × Spread
6 to 15 in. × 8 to 10 in.

When, Where, and How to Plant
Plant seedlings in May. Bronze- or maroon-foliaged Wax Begonias can handle full sun if the temperature is below 90 degrees Fahrenheit and they are well watered. Otherwise, they do best in some shade. Too much shade causes leggy stems. Begonias accept any soil rich in organic matter that will hold moisture, yet drain well. Loosen soil down 8 to 10 in., digging in organic matter and a handful of granular slow-acting all-purpose fertilizer. Dig a planting hole about as deep as and slightly wider than the rootball so the plant is level with the surrounding soil. Backfill, and water well. Space plants about 6 to 10 in. apart in groups of three in beds; pack them in closely in containers. Use soilless potting medium laced with granular slow-acting fertilizer in containers that have drainage holes.

Growing Tips
Water Begonias during dry periods to maintain steady bloom. Those in pots or under trees competing with their roots for moisture will need more frequent watering. Slow-acting fertilizer added at planting should last the season.

Care
Begonias drop their spent blossoms, so they do not need deadheading. Pinch back their brittle stems midseason to make plants more compact. Begonias in moist, mulched woodland settings may suffer slug damage on their leaves. Pot up Begonias in October for wintering indoors.

Companion Planting and Design
Use Wax Begonias in hanging baskets and planters alone or with other, slightly taller annuals such as Ageratum and Blue Salvia. They add color to beds of Parsley, Basil, and other herbs.

Did You Know?
Plants that have spent time indoors must be hardened off to ensure their successful transition to the outdoors. Begonias wintered over as houseplants or raised indoors from rooted cuttings need gradual acclimatizing to sun and outdoor temperatures. In the spring put plants outdoors in a sheltered area for a few hours daily, then bring them inside. Increase their time and light outside each day over a week or two, eventually leaving them out overnight. Then plant them in the garden.

Zinnia

Zinnia elegans

When, Where, and How to Plant

Sow seeds outdoors when nighttime temperatures are reliably above 50 degrees Fahrenheit. Wait to plant young plants until warm weather truly arrives in late May because they respond to heat. They do best in full sun. They accept any decent well-drained soil. It can be a bit on the alkaline side. Choose an open site where air circulation is good to minimize mildew problems. Dig the soil down 8 to 10 in., and mix in granular slow-acting all-purpose fertilizer to provide steady nutrition all season. Either sow seeds as directed on the package, or dig holes about as deep as and slightly wider than plant rootballs. Set each plant level with the surrounding soil. Backfill, and water well. Space tall Zinnias about 2 ft. apart, medium and dwarf types proportionally less.

Growing Tips

Water young plants while they get established, then they can manage with just rainfall. Regular moisture promotes better flowering. Add a layer of organic mulch to help soil retain moisture. Avoid wetting their leaves when watering.

Care

Deadhead spent flowers to keep more coming. Stake tall types. Zinnias may develop unsightly, but not fatal, mildew on their foliage as summer progresses. Sometimes Japanese beetles attack in July. Knock them from foliage into a jar of soapy water. Bag-type traps only attract more beetles.

Companion Planting and Design

Grow these tough, easy-care annuals in a garden of their own for cutting or with other flowering plants at the back of the border. The dwarf versions do well in containers and as edging.

Did You Know?

All-America Selections (AAS) tests new plant varieties for vigor, reliability, and improved performance. Professional horticulturists evaluate contenders coded by number against proven plants growing next to them in field trials all over the United States and Canada. Annual winners proudly bear the AAS logo on their seed packets and labels and in catalogs. Trial gardens are at Penn State, University Park, and Burpee's headquarters in Bucks County.

The Mexican heritage of Zinnias is reflected in their bright colors, prolific bloom, and ability to handle hot, dry weather without complaint. They are fast growers and steady bloomers. Their stiff, hairy stems are decorated with coarse, green leaves and topped by flower heads ranging from small buttons up to 6 in. across. Brilliantly colored, they are composed of flat rings of layered petals around yellow centers. Hybrid forms boast fancier flowers that resemble Dahlias or shaggy Chrysanthemums. Some are ruffled or bicolored. Some seem to be deer resistant. Members of the hugely diverse Zinnia clan are categorized by height. Consider these small members: 'Thumbelina' is only 6 in. tall; 'Dreamland' is 12 in. tall with double flowers; 'Pinwheel' has good mildew resistance.

Other Name

Youth and Old Age

Bloom Period and Seasonal Color

June through October; blooms in all colors except blue or black

Mature Height × Spread

$1^1/_2$ to 3 ft. × 1 to 2 ft.

Bulbs *for Pennsylvania*

For novice gardeners, bulbs are a good way to start gardening. For experienced gardeners, they are indispensable. No single group of plants offers so much for so little effort. Ranging from giant Cannas to tiny Crocuses, they provide color, texture, structure, and in many cases fragrance to a variety of landscape situations. Some also respond well to "forcing" for indoor blooms during the winter, and many make excellent cut flowers. Use bulbs everywhere: naturalize them in woodlands or lawns, mass them in drifts or island beds, showcase them in borders, or nestle them in rock gardens.

Bulb Biography

Characterizing all plants that grow from bulbous structures as bulbs is most convenient. Actually, in addition to true bulbs, which are essentially fully formed plants in bud stage, there are corms, tubers, and rhizomes—various types of swollen stem structures. All have in common the capacity to store nutrients and energy underground so that plants can survive drought and heat and (in the case of *hardy bulbs*) cold winters. Once planted, they quietly develop roots and bide their time. Eventually, they appear without much fuss, moisture and rising temperatures coaxing them from dormancy according to their built-in timers. They multiply by creating tiny bulblets, or offsets, attached to the main bulb or stem that are easily separated from the mother bulb and planted individually to create new plants.

Flower bulb plants are herbaceous; the foliage of most typically ripens and flops, then dries or dies back four to six weeks after they finish blooming. While many of the most common flowering ones are cold hardy in Pennsylvania and provide our stunning spring display, some cannot handle even the relatively mild winters in our "banana belt" area near Philadelphia. Called *tender bulbs,* they must wait to be planted in the spring for summer bloom. Among these tender ones are Caladiums, Cannas, and Dahlias. (Lilies, the exception that proves the rule, handle our winters, but still bloom in the summer.) Treat tender bulbs as annuals and replace them every year, or dig them up before frost and store them over the winter in a cool place indoors to replant in the spring.

The size of bulbs influences their performance. In most cases, larger is better (and a bit more expensive). Growers grade bulbs by size, which is typically measured as the circumference of the bulb at its widest point. Use the very largest for forcing; slightly smaller ones are fine for gardens. Except for Tulips, bulk purchases of smaller- or uneven-sized bulbs are ideal for naturalizing (and a bargain).

General Culture

Most bulbs have similar cultural preferences—good drainage, rich soil, and lots of sun. Hardy bulbs are available at retail outlets or are shipped from mail-order nurseries in late summer and early fall. Tender summer bloomers are available in the spring. Plant your bulbs as soon as you acquire them; they keep better in the ground than in the shed or garage where they are often forgotten. Every type of bulb has a particular optimum planting depth, but the easiest way to proceed is to use this rule of thumb: plant at a depth $2^{1}/_{2}$ times the bulb's height, measured from the bottom of the hole. For many plants, such as Tulips, it pays to plant them deeper. Deep planting keeps them stronger by delaying offshoots and protects them from digging squirrels and rodents. Plant small bulbs, such as Snowdrops and Crocuses, about 3 to 4 inches deep.

If your soil is less than wonderful, your hardy bulbs will benefit from an annual dose of fertilizer in the early fall to spur their root growth. Sprinkle a granular slow-acting product formulated for bulbs on the soil surface (never down in planting holes) as instructed on its label. The rain and snow will gradually soak it in where it will become available over time to promote strong root growth. If clumps get crowded, dig up bulbs in late summer when they are dormant, separate them, discard any damaged ones, and replant.

Finally, a word about bulb aftercare. Allow the relatively inconspicuous small flowers and fine foliage of minor bulbs like Crocus and Snowdrops to gradually die back and melt away after blooming. Cut off spent flowers from the more conspicuous large flowering bulbs such as Daffodils and Lilies. It is extremely important to allow bulb foliage to remain, however bedraggled, to soak up the sun for several weeks until it turns yellow and collapses.

Bearded Iris

Iris germanica hybrids

There is no mistaking Bearded Iris. With stiff, pointed swordlike leaves and tall, rigid stems topped by elegant blooms, they are showstoppers in a spring flower border or as a specimen clump. Iris flowers, often called Garden Orchids, are an elaborate arrangement of six petals— three erect "standards," alternately arranged with three drooping "falls." The fuzzy tuft of hairs on the falls are "beards." They bloom sequentially along the stalks over two or three weeks, each flower lasting a day or two, depending on the warmth of the weather. Some are fragrant. Grow plenty of Irises so that you will have lots to cut and enjoy indoors. Although the tall Bearded Iris is the most familiar and commonly used Iris, there are several other bearded types.

Other Name
German Iris

Bloom Period and Seasonal Color
May and June; blooms in lilac, purple, yellow, pink, or white

Mature Height × Spread
8 in. to 3 ft. × indefinite clumping

When, Where, and How to Plant
Plant the cold-hardy Iris rhizomes in August through early fall (six to eight weeks before the ground is likely to freeze). Transplant potted plants anytime. Irises like well-drained soil in a very sunny spot. They do fine in most soils except heavy clay. Planting Irises in raised beds facilitates drainage. Dig and loosen the soil down 8 to 10 in., simultaneously mixing in bulb fertilizer. Dig in organic matter to improve clay soil if necessary. Make a narrow, shallow furrow, and lay the rhizomes horizontally so that the roots nestle into the soil indentation. Cover the rhizome with sufficient soil to bury its roots, but leave its top surface partially exposed. Water well. Space about 12 in. apart, pointing the ends with the fan of foliage in the direction the clump is to spread.

Growing Tips
Fertilize every fall with slow-acting fertilizer or specially formulated bulb fertilizer. Water if the weather conditions are droughty.

Care
Iris stems may need staking. Cut off faded blooms and stems, but leave the foliage so it continues to absorb sunshine. If foliage flops and looks ratty, cut it back to 2- or 3-in. fans in the fall. After three to five years, divide crowded clumps of rhizomes in midsummer. Discard rotted rhizomes. Dust an insecticide containing pyrethrum to protect bulbs in beds where there has been borer activity. Borers are the most serious pest. A systemic insecticide product listed for this problem will control borers. Wet streaks on foliage signal the presence of a virus; remove affected plants.

Companion Planting and Design
The stiff vertical profile of clumps of Irises contrasts nicely with Coralbells and Peonies that bloom about the same time. Bearded Irises grow well in containers that are 1 to 2 ft. wide and at least 1 ft. deep.

Did You Know?
Because they come in a rainbow of wonderful colors, Irises are aptly named from the Greek word *iris*, meaning "rainbow." In Greek mythology, Iris was the goddess of the rainbow and a messenger of the gods whose path was a rainbow.

Canna

Canna × generalis

When, Where, and How to Plant

Plant these tender rhizomes in the spring after the soil has warmed to about 65 degrees Fahrenheit. To get a jump on the season, plant them first in pots indoors four weeks before the last expected spring frost for your region of Pennsylvania. Cannas thrive on full sun and fairly rich, slightly acidic, well-drained soil of any type. Cultivate the soil down 8 to 10 in., adding a generous dose of a granular slow-acting all-purpose fertilizer. Plant 3 to 4 in. deep and 18 to 24 in. apart. Cover with soil, and water well.

Growing Tips

Water Cannas during drought periods; they can handle fairly damp soil. Slow-acting fertilizer added to the soil when planting is sufficient for the season.

Care

To groom and stimulate lush flowering, pull off each faded bloom immediately. Cut just below each faded flower cluster—cutting farther down may cut off potential secondary flower stalks. Stake tall types. Japanese beetles may be a problem from early July until mid-August. The best control is to pick or knock beetles off into a jar of soapy water. For a heavy infestation, spray foliage with a pyrethrin insecticide.

Companion Planting and Design

Cannas love the company of other tropicals such as Elephant Ears and Ornamental Bananas. Relegate tall, stately ones to the back of the garden as a backdrop or along fences. Smaller types mix well with annuals in garden beds or containers around a patio or pool. Many Cannas grow well in pots sunk in water-filled barrels and jars.

Did You Know?

A native species of Canna was first spotted by Pennsylvania's own William Bartram in 1777 on an exciting trip to Louisiana. In his *Travels* printed in London in 1792, he described the plant as "presenting a glorious show, the stem rises six, seven and nine feet tall, terminating upward with spikes of scarlet flowers." Thus began the American gardener's on-again, off-again affair with Cannas.

Because one gardener's "bold" is another's "brazen," more traditional gardeners are ambivalent about Cannas. These summer bloomers boast colorful, long-lasting flowers atop equally showy red, green, blue-green, bronze, or striped foliage. Canna leaves are typically 1 to 2 ft. long, with blunt edges and prominent veins, so they are ornamental in their own right. Cannas were the rage in 1893 after being showcased at the World's Columbian Exposition at Chicago. Their reputation waned until the 1950s when a breeder in Germany, Wilhelm Pfitzer, developed dwarf Cannas that are much more adaptable to typical residential landscapes. 'Pretoria', 'Mohawk', and 'Durban' are becoming readily available. Versions of Canna that grow from seed include 'Seven Dwarf Mixed' and 'Tropical Rose'. Canna glauca is aquatic.

Other Name

Hybrid Canna

Bloom Period and Seasonal Color

Mid- to late summer, early fall; blooms in pink, salmon, yellow, orange, or red

Mature Height × Spread

3 to 6 ft. × as permitted

Crocus
Crocus vernus

Most of the so-called minor bulbs such as Snowdrops and Squill are dainty and unassuming. Many Crocuses are, too. Dutch Crocuses, however, are in your face with their large-sized (3 in.) and richly colored blooms with striped petals. What they lack in subtlety or humility, they more than make up for in emphatic presence. The latest of the spring-blooming Crocuses to bloom, they are the least bothered by squirrels and voles. Their flowers open wide in bright sun and close tightly among their bundled, grasslike leaves at night. Count on them to multiply and spread if they like their location. Thomasini's Crocus (Crocus tommasinianus), *one of the smaller earliest Crocuses, is ideal for naturalizing in the lawn and will spontaneously multiply over the years.*

Other Name
Common Crocus

Bloom Period and Seasonal Color
April; blooms in white, lavender, or bluish purple

Mature Height × Spread
5 in. × as permitted

When, Where, and How to Plant
Crocuses are cold hardy, so plant corms in the late summer or early fall. Site them in well-drained soil in full sun. Plant each corm 4 in. deep in ordinary soil cultivated down 8 to 10 in. Mix into the soil some slow-acting granular all-purpose or bulb fertilizer. Plant them in groups in individual holes, or cluster three or five corms in a single large hole. If voles are a problem, line the planting holes with wire mesh or fine gravel to protect the corms. Water the area.

Growing Tips
Crocuses require no special watering other than what you will do for the rest of the garden in early spring. Dormant Crocuses can take dry conditions. Additional fertilizer is not needed if Crocus foliage is left on each year to collect sunshine to store energy for the following year. But, Crocuses in the lawn benefit from lawn fertilizer.

Care
Crocuses seem to flourish with benign neglect. Their faded blooms sort of melt away, so they do not need deadheading. Allow the foliage to ripen and die back, even if it means delaying mowing the lawn. If flowers are targets of rodents, cover them with a low cage of wire mesh. Spread a light mulch of chopped leaves or pine needles on the soil to buffer temperature extremes during the winter.

Companion Planting and Design
Plant Crocuses among surface roots under the branches of deciduous trees and shrubs. Poke them into the soil among evergreen ground covers such as Sweet Woodruff, Ajuga, English Ivy, or even turf-grass. Plant Crocuses in outdoor containers in the fall either alone or among dwarf evergreen shrubs. Try forcing Dutch Crocuses into preseason bloom indoors. Nestle bulbs closely in a shallow, flat-bottomed bowl filled with wet gravel. Set in a dark, cool area, then bring into a warm room as buds show.

Did You Know?
In some Middle Eastern cultures the starchy Crocus corms are made into flour. Saffron Crocus (*Crocus sativus*) has a distinctive reddish-orange, three-branched stigma in its center. When dried, it becomes the expensive, exotic spice saffron. Saffron Crocus is not dependably hardy in most of Pennsylvania. It is grown from southern Europe to Kashmir to provide saffron all over the world.

Daffodil
Narcissus species and hybrids

When, Where, and How to Plant
Plant bulbs in the fall before the ground freezes hard. Daffodils prefer full sun, or part sun in a spring woodland setting before the trees leaf out. Well-drained soil is a must. Lighten clay soils with organic material. Cultivate 12 in. deep, mixing in granular bulb fertilizer. Plant standard Daffodil bulbs 6 to 9 in. deep; dwarf types 4 to 6 in. deep. Plant in clusters of three or more, spaced 4 or 5 in. apart, the pointed tips of the bulbs upward. Naturalize plantings in woodlands by randomly casting handfuls of bulbs across the area and planting where they fall.

Growing Tips
Fertilize garden-grown Daffodils each fall to encourage root growth. Naturalized ones can manage without supplemental fertilizing. Cover with 2 or 3 in. of organic mulch to insulate soil in winter and prevent splashing of mud onto flowers. Water during fall or spring drought conditions.

Care
Cut off spent flowers and stems, but allow Daffodil foliage to ripen and die back naturally. Divide overlarge clumps of Daffodils if they threaten to outgrow their space. Unlike most bulbs, they can be dug and replanted while "green" in the spring if summer is inconvenient. Daffodils are virtually pest free.

Companion Planting and Design
Daffodils bloom early, so plant them under deciduous trees and shrubs; they finish blooming before the leaves emerge and create shade. Plant them among ground covers which obscure their dying foliage. 'Paperwhites' (*Narcissus tazetta*) are the easiest to force because they do not require a long cooling period. Miniatures and dwarfs such as 'Tête-à-Tête' are particularly suited to rock gardens. Daffodils make excellent cut flowers.

Did You Know?
Narcissus, Daffodil's formal name, is almost as commonly used as its informal name. It recalls the Greek myth of Narcissus, who spent his days gazing at the reflection of his handsome face in a pool of water. He was so entranced by his reflected beauty that he failed to appreciate and respond to the nymph Echo. She punished him by turning him into a flower destined to nod beside the pool forever.

The wide appeal of all kinds of Daffodils is largely due to their bright, jaunty appearance at a time when everyone is sick of winter. Their interesting forms, their self-reliance, and in some cases their fragrance are also appealing. For some, their ultimate virtue is that deer and rodents do not disturb them. The flowers of all types feature a central tubular "cup" protruding at right angles from a ring of six petals with pointed tips. They bloom at the tops of stems among long, stiff, straplike leaves. Hundreds of hybrids of these hardy bulbs have been categorized by fanciers into thirteen divisions. For most gardeners, however, the issue is simply, "How many Daffodils can I fit into my yard?"

Other Name
Narcissus

Bloom Period and Seasonal Color
Mid-March into May; blooms in yellow, peach, white, pink, orange, or nearly red

Mature Height × Spread
4 to 18 in. × as permitted

Dahlia
Dahlia species and hybrids

Do not be daunted by the fact that there are more than two thousand kinds of Dahlias to choose from. Dahlias offer a riot of colorful flowers all summer, reaching their peak in September when the weather cools. Leaves may be bronze or purplish, although they are usually medium green. Their flower size varies from dwarfs (1 to 4 in. wide) to giants (up to 18 in.). Most commonly, flowers are 6 to 10 in. across. After setting, buds are tantalizingly slow to open—up to thirty days—but the wait is worth it. Dahlias make wonderful cut flowers, lasting seven to ten days if properly conditioned when they are picked. Some Dahlias are grown from seed rather than tubers. 'Redskin' is a popular choice.

Bloom Period and Seasonal Color
Mid-June until October frost; blooms in yellow, orange, red, pink, purple, white, or bicolor

Mature Height × Spread
1 to 8 ft. × as permitted

When, Where, and How to Plant
Plant these tender bulbs outdoors in spring after the soil has dried and warmed. Dahlias like full sun and well-drained soil. Build raised planting beds or add organic matter to lighten clay soil. Cultivate soil down 12 in., mixing in a slow-acting granular fertilizer. Dig planting holes at least 6 in. deep. Set tubers on their sides with their eyes, or buds, pointing upward. Plant them at least 1 to 3 ft. apart to assure good air circulation around mature plants, which discourages powdery mildew.

Growing Tips
Assure Dahlias regular moisture. Because they sometimes temporarily stop blooming during really hot weather, mulch to conserve moisture and cool the soil. Do not fertilize further beyond what was provided at planting time.

Care
Insert sturdy stakes into the soil near nondwarf types when planting to avoid harming tubers as the mature plants need support. Deadhead to promote heavy bloom. To encourage bushier plants with more flowers, pinch out the central stem after four to six leaves form. Allow plants to die with hard frost, or dig them up, store over the winter, and replant in spring. At that time divide the tubers to jump-start indoors in pots in early spring or plant outdoors later. Aphids or corn borers sometimes infest stressed plants. Foliage may show mildew.

Companion Planting and Design
Mass Dahlias in their own bed or integrate them into perennial borders to add texture, foliage contrast, and color. Use dwarfs as edgers; plant tall ones in rows to screen undesirable views.

Did You Know?
Both Dahlias and Garden Chrysanthemums offer a variety of similar flower shapes. *Anemone:* pincushionlike, ray petals surround a tightly clustered center tube of petals. *Cactus:* ray petals have curled or pointed tips and radiate irregularly from the center. *Peony:* one or two rows of uniform ray petals surround a central disk; some may be curled. *Pompon:* curved petals form dense balls. *Single:* a single row of petals surrounds a central disk in a flat plane.

Gladiolus

Gladiolus × hortulanus

When, Where, and How to Plant

Plant round corms in spring every ten days to three weeks in succession from March until early July to assure a continuous supply of flowers over the season. Flowers mature in eight to ten weeks. Glads like full sun and well-drained soil that is rich, sandy, and slightly acidic. Lighten clay soils with organic matter. Dig the soil down 12 in., mixing in granular slow-acting fertilizer. Planting depth varies with the size of the corm—those less than $1/2$ in. across, go 3 in. deep; 1-in.-wide corms, go down 4 to 5 in.; those more than 1 in., go to 6 to 8 in. deep. For best display, plant corms in groups of five or more, spaced 6 to 8 in. apart. Aim the pointed side of the corm upward.

Growing Tips

Mulch Glads to discourage weeds and keep soil evenly moist. Water when the soil below the mulch seems dry. There is no need to fertilize further beyond what was provided at planting time.

Care

Tall types of Gladiolus will need staking. When leaves ripen and turn yellow, dig up the corms, trim off dying stems, and allow them to dry. Gently clean off dried husks from the corms, and store them in bags of dry vermiculite in a ventilated space where temperatures are a steady 60 to 70 degrees Fahrenheit. Glads' nemesis is thrips, tiny insects that attack leaf sheaths and unopened flowers. Foliage turns silvery or brown, buds shrivel, and florets fail to open. Use a systemic insecticide product listed for thrips.

Companion Planting and Design

Lacking fragrance, but little else, Glads are useful where spring bulbs have died back in a flower border or in a cutting garden.

Did You Know?

Gladiolus is named for its distinctive swordlike leaves. The Latin word *gladius* means "little sword." An integral part of Roman culture, they were reputed to be the floral emblem of gladiators. Paintings of Glads are found in the ruins at Pompeii.

There is much more to Gladiolus than a few spikes in a florist's arrangement. They are a real asset in the garden for color, vertical accent, and summer-long bloom if plantings are staggered. Flowers in lovely colors crowd the top third of the stiff stems, opening successively from bottom to tip over several days. Stiff, swordlike leaves complete the handsome display. Grow enough Glads to have plenty for cutting. Although they are technically tender bulbs, Glads often survive winters in gardens south of Philadelphia. Butterfly hybrids are only 25 in. tall and do not need staking. Winter-hardy Gladiolus (Gladiolus byzantinus) form more delicate clumps and bloom in early summer. 'Pixiola' hybrids are specialty Glads, very tiny with 2- to 3-in. florets.

Other Name

Florists' Glad

Bloom Period and Seasonal Color

June to October; blooms in white, cream, yellow, orange, salmon, red, rose, or violet

Mature Height × Spread

3 to 5 ft. × 6 to 8 in.

Lily

Lilium species and hybrids

Lilies may have it all. They are summer bloomers but are hardy enough to overwinter in the ground. They offer stunning colors, a great range of heights, often a wonderful fragrance, and they attract butterflies and hummingbirds. Their grace and dignity add aristocracy to the landscape. Their stiff stems are laddered with short richly green leaves and topped with gorgeous trumpet-shaped flowers, sometimes in branched clusters, which open in succession from the lower to the upper buds. There are many Lily species, but the hybrids created by breeders are the easiest to grow. They fall into four categories: early-blooming small Martagons (best for shade); varied early-blooming Asiatics; fragrant, summer-blooming Trumpets (Aurelian); and fragrant, later-summer-speckled Orientals. 'Star Gazer' was the top florist Lily grown in Holland in 1996.

Bloom Period and Seasonal Color
Early summer to late summer; blooms in white, yellow, orange, pink, or red

Mature Height × Spread
2 to 8 ft. × as permitted

When, Where, and How to Plant
Plant Lilies in the fall or spring; transplant potted bulbs to the garden anytime in the spring or summer. Plant overwintered bulbs immediately because, unlike most bulbs, Lily bulbs are never completely dormant. Lilies like full sun, well-drained soil, and good air circulation. Cultivate the planting area to 12 in. deep. Add lots of organic matter to keep soil loose and well draining. Mix in slow-acting granular fertilizer. Plant Lilies at a depth three times the bulbs' diameter, measured from the bottom of the hole (roughly 4 to 6 in.). For good mass effect, plant bulbs 6 to 8 in. apart.

Growing Tips
Mulch Lily beds to assure cool, moist soil and discourage weeds. Water when your other plants need moisture in times of scarce rain. There is no need to fertilize if the bulbs are properly grown. Allow foliage to ripen after blooming so the bulbs manufacture their own food.

Care
To forestall the formation of seedpods, cut off faded flowers. Leave at least $2/3$ of the stem so that foliage remains to ripen and die back naturally. Young Lilies, those in windy sites, and those in shade that lean toward the sun may need support. Divide crowded Asiatics in four or five years. Trumpet Lilies do not truly establish until two or three years; Martagons hate to be moved at all. Occasionally, aphids introduce viruses to Lilies.

Companion Planting and Design
Try Lilies with Ferns, Campanulas, Peonies, Lamb's Ears, and Astilbes. Consider their expected height, and plant them to best advantage. They coordinate nicely with many perennials, but do not crowd them into an intensively planted bed. They make good cut flowers (trim pollen-laden anthers from flower centers to eliminate pollen stains).

Did You Know?
Images of white Lilies decorate frescoes and vases from Crete as early as 1500 B.C. They were a common fertility motif in ancient Greek art, incorporated into the Roman myth of Juno and Hercules. Somehow when Christians adopted the Lily, it came to signify virginal purity, thus becoming the symbol of the Virgin Mary.

Ornamental Onion
Allium spp.

When, Where, and How to Plant
Plant bulbs in the fall before the ground freezes. Ornamental Onions do best in well-drained, good garden soil in full sun. 'Purple Sensation', a hybrid of *Allium aflatunense* is the easiest to grow and most reliable of the large-headed ones. *A. aflatunense* types tend to self-sow, but their seedlings take many years to reach flowering size. Cultivate the soil down 8 to 10 in., and mix in bulb fertilizer. Plant individual bulbs about 6 in. deep, 12 to 18 in. apart, or closer as clusters of three, five, or seven.

Growing Tips
Alliums are one of the few summer-blooming bulbs to overwinter safely in the garden. Mulch soil to insulate it over the winter. Fertilize each fall and water when rainfall is scarce.

Care
Ornamental Onions shortchanged on sun may have weak stems that need staking. Either clip off faded flower heads and stems, or leave them to dry over the summer. 'Purple Sensation' forms bulblets over the years, eventually crowding the planting and reducing flower size. Divide large clumps, and replant them more widely spaced to bloom in one to three years, depending on their size. They do not attract pests.

Companion Planting and Design
Plant tall Ornamental Onions throughout a border; their slim stalks make them see-through plants. Use them effectively massed in large borders in drifts among perennials that have silver foliage such as Lamb's Ears and Yarrow. Smaller *Allium* cousins such as Lily Leek (*Allium moly*) are ideal for rock garden situations. Use dried flower heads in dried arrangements and floral crafts.

Did You Know?
Allium is Greek for "garlic." This clan includes many cousins, such as Bulb Onions, Chives, Leeks, Shallots, and Scallions. They share with their ornamental cousins a sturdy self-reliance, globe flowers of lilac or pinkish, twinkly florets, and a distinctive smell. Culinary use goes back to the beginning of recorded time. Late-summer-blooming Garlic Chives (*Allium tuberosum*) represent a meeting of both worlds because they are ornamental and edible.

The sight of their dramatic spheres of fuzzy lavender florets at the tips of leafless, narrow stalks rising above the other plants like visitors from another planet is unforgettable. Ornamental Onions are increasingly common in flower gardens—and no wonder. They sustain garden interest after the flush of spring bulbs passes and the summer show is yet to come. They continue to offer interest as petals drop and flowers dry to form lovely seedheads. 'Purple Sensation' has 4-in.-wide flower heads on tall stems, at the base of which rise straplike 6- to 8-in. leaves from 1 1/2 to 3 in. wide that age and disappear by the time the flower heads fade. Allium 'Globemaster' is larger at 5 ft. with 5-in.-round flower heads. Deer leave these plants alone.

Other Names
Flowering Onion, Allium

Bloom Period and Seasonal Color
May into June; blooms in reddish-purple or white

Mature Height × Spread
3 to 4 ft. × 1 ft.

Tuberous Begonia

Begonia × tuberhybrida

Tuberous Begonias are shade lovers. Sometimes pendant, usually double, their flowers resemble Roses or double Camellias in form. They are always richly colored in primary or pastel colors, their velvety petals luminous in filtered or indirect light. Flowers in the picotee lace strain have contrasting color on the edges of petals plus scalloped edges. Blossoms appear where glossy, pointed leaves join succulent stems. Upright plants sport flowers 6 to 8 in. across; flowers of pendant types are 3 to 4 in. Properly stored tubers will last years, but young one- or two-year-old ones are the most vigorous. Standard upright, multiflora type plants grow 8 to 10 in. tall, yielding many small flowers. Fragrant, pendant types 'Nectarine Rose' and 'Fragrant Lemon' are ideal for hanging baskets.

Other Name
Tuberous-rooted Begonia

Bloom Period and Seasonal Color
June to October; blooms in red, pink, orange, yellow, or white

Mature Height × Spread
8 in. × 12 in.

When, Where, and How to Plant
Plant these tender tubers outdoors in spring after any danger of frost is past and the soil has warmed. Avoid full sun; Tuberous Begonias like partial shade, either as filtered light or as early-morning sun that gives way to shade. Site them where they have good air circulation. Orient them so that their leaves receive maximum light, since they all face the same direction. Tuberous Begonias prefer soil rich in humus. Or start tubers in pots early indoors as soon as they are available (about February). Set hollow sides up, about 1 in. below the soil surface. To transplant outdoors, cultivate soil down 8 to 10 in., and mix in granular slow-acting fertilizer. Plant so that tops of soilballs are level with surrounding ground. Space 12 in. apart.

Growing Tips
These Begonias need moisture alternated with short dry periods to avoid crown rot. Water potted plants more often in summer heat. They are heavy feeders.

Care
Tuberous Begonias dislike frost, dry soil, soggy soil, wind, and too much sun. Pick off spent blossoms to stimulate flowering. Pinch to keep plants compact. Stake upright types. To prevent fungal disease, avoid wetting their foliage. Watch for the occasional aphid blitz, and pinch off stem tips where they tend to gather. Keep pots off the ground to avoid slug invasions. When the first frost kills their tops, dig up the tubers, and store in dry peat indoors.

Companion Planting and Design
Tuberous Begonias are sold at garden centers as mature plants in hanging baskets and other containers from early summer to fall. Use them to decorate a porch or shaded patio.

Did You Know?
You can enjoy Tuberous Begonias all year. Bring outdoor potted ones indoors, or pot some from the garden just before frost hits and bring them indoors. Good drainage is essential. They like a bright eastern or northern exposure and periodic watering with a very diluted liquid fertilizer.

When, Where, and How to Plant

Plant these hardy bulbs in the fall, anytime before the ground freezes. If planting is delayed, keep them cool. Bulbs exposed to heat over 70 degrees Fahrenheit produce smaller flowers. Tulips like full sun and well-drained soil. Just about any soil, except clay, is fine. Planting Tulips in raised beds or adding organic matter to the soil facilitates soil drainage. Mix in slow-acting, granular bulb fertilizer, then dig individual holes, or dig out a bed for a mass planting. Plant bulbs 6 to 8 in. deep, pointed tip up. Planting as deep as 12 in. yields bigger flowers and reduces rodent damage. Backfill, then water.

Growing Tips

To assure good repeat flowering in subsequent years, scratch fertilizer into the soil over bulb beds in early spring and fall. Water Tulips with other plants when rain is scarce. Tulips blooming in containers tend to dry out rapidly.

Care

Cut off stems and faded flowers, leaving all foliage to ripen and collapse in a few weeks. Deer love Tulips, so protect them. Also, Tulips are vulnerable to "tulipfire," a fungal blight that deforms flowers, foliage, and bulbs. It dies out if no Tulips are planted in the area for at least four years.

Companion Planting and Design

Plant Tulips among evergreen ground covers or low-growing spring annuals such as Pansies or Forget-me-nots. Grow in containers for spring display; in the fall, set bulbs with sides touching 6 in. deep in deep pots filled with soilless potting medium. Set them outdoors to chill, and keep them watered.

Did You Know?

When the first Tulip bulbs were introduced into Europe in the late 1500s, they caused a sensation. Astute Dutch businessmen recognized the commercial potential of this Tulipmania and strove to develop new and unusual types to feed the speculative market that developed among the general public. After the 1630s when the market collapsed, taking with it many fortunes, Holland remained the major producer of Tulip bulbs.

The origin of cultivated Tulips is something of a mystery. They seemed to just appear in Turkey. They spread to Europe, and after centuries of growing and breeding in Holland, they evolved into modern hybrids with the familiar solitary, cup-shaped, crayon-colored blooms at the tips of tall, straight stems. Variously described as Darwin, Darwin hybrids, Cottage, and Hybrid Tulips, these hardy bulbs have not been reliably perennial. Gardeners often treat them as annuals and discard them after a single year in the garden. Newer versions, promoted as perennial, are more likely to persist for several years, however. In addition to Tulips with classic, cup-shaped flowers, there are Water Lily types called Kaufmanniana and Greigii Tulips. The several smaller, daintier species Tulips are more dependably perennial.

Other Name
Garden Tulip

Bloom Period and Seasonal Color
Early March, April, May; blooms in all colors except black and blue

Mature Height × Spread
18 to 24 in. × 10 in.

Grasses *for Pennsylvania*

Until fairly recently, grass in residential landscapes meant turfgrass. Homes were (and are still) typically surrounded by large areas planted with turfgrass as a ground cover. A legacy from our English settlers who established grassy "commons" in the center of their villages for animals to graze on, these "lawns" became a subtle sign of status when private plots of grass were incorporated into bigger residential properties by increasingly prosperous homeowners during the nineteenth century. Lawns function today as recreation areas, unifying elements to link planted areas, and as background to set off decorative plantings.

These days grass in the landscape is just as likely to mean ornamental grass as turfgrass. As a group, these plants offer things that turfgrasses do not—drought resistance, pest and disease resistance, seasonal color, variegated foliage, showy flowers, and minimal cutting. For some, the most important virtue of all is that ornamental grasses are environmentally "correct," not needing regular applications of water, pesticides, or fertilizers.

Ornamental grasses are also part of a legacy, that of early human beings who were at home on the grassy savannas of Africa, and later, that of our ancestors who settled great prairies in this country. In the frontier era Americans lived among the tall grasses and within sod houses. We continue to incorporate grasses into our culture. They are a staple of our diet and that of the grazing animals that we raise for food.

A Common Heritage

Turfgrasses and ornamental grasses share many characteristics because they share a common heritage. They grow in two ways. Some are runners or creepers, spreading by means of horizontal stems, or

stolons, that run over or just under the soil surface, rooting as they go. Others are clumpers, spreading by means of increasingly larger clumps that sometimes give turf a tufted appearance. Both function as ground covers; both have annual or perennial varieties. Ornamental grasses, large and small, are much more versatile than turfgrasses, however. They have many landscape uses besides serving as a ground cover. They provide vertical accents in ornamental beds and borders. They substitute for shrubs, serve as focal points, and provide winter interest. Use them to make a transition to naturalized areas and meadows, to prevent erosion on stream banks, to screen views, to cover slopes that are difficult to mow, and to be an essential filler in meadow or wildflower mixes.

Although both turfgrasses and ornamental grasses have warm-season and cool-season varieties, this distinction matters most with turfgrasses because lawns are expected to be green during the growing season. Warm-season turfgrasses, such as Zoysia, are more at home in the South because they go dormant during cool weather and thrive during hot weather. Zoysia is truly happy (that is, green) here only about fourteen weeks out of the year. You always can tell a Zoysia lawn because it is brown and dormant most of the time. In Pennsylvania cool-season turfgrasses are appropriate for lawns because it is mostly cool here. We water them during the relatively few weeks in summer when it is hot and they are tempted to go dormant. They grow lushly in spring and then do very well again in fall. Sometimes a Kentucky Bluegrass lawn stays somewhat green all winter.

Turfgrass Care

Turfgrasses require more care than ornamental grasses, which are pretty self-reliant. Critical to lawn health is decent soil. The better the soil, the better it can care for the grass plants, and the less you have to do. Core aerate the lawn every year or two to prevent soil compaction, which stifles root growth and causes thatch. Top-dress annually with organic material such as compost, chopped leaves from the mulching mower, or topsoil each year so that the soil holds moisture, drains well, and supports micro-organisms that convert nutrients to a form grass plants can use. Use a granular slow-acting fertilizer in the spring to deliver consistent, uniform nutrition to the grass over many weeks. Because this type of fertilizer is gentle on soil-dwelling creatures, resident beneficial spiders and ants will maintain residence there and prey on pest insects, their eggs, and larvae. Most important, be sure turfgrass gets regular water. If rainfall is sparse, water deeply every ten days to two weeks. Frequent sprinkles only encourage shallow roots and damage grass. During severe droughts it is less stressful to allow a lawn to brown and go dormant than to try to keep it watered and green.

Blue Fescue
Festuca glauca

This attractive, colorful, low-mounding grass is easy to use. Although its name—Blue Fescue— suggests turf-grass, it is definitely ornamental. Its blue color is a glaucous coating on its narrow foliage that is similar to that on Blue Spruce needles. It is great in winter when there is so little color in the yard. The flowers are arrayed on beige spikes in late June or July, and they are easy to overlook. They are upstaged by the foliage anyway. Cut them off so they do not drain energy from the plant. As a cool-season grass, Blue Fescue may struggle a bit in full sun during our hot, humid summers, but it usually does fine if it gets enough moisture. 'Elijah Blue' is the most available.

Other Name
Sheep's Fescue

Color and Texture
Silvery blue; fine evergreen blades

Mature Height × Spread
6 to 12 in. × 12 in.

When, Where, and How to Plant
Plant Blue Fescue divisions either in spring or fall. Transplant young potted plants anytime when it is not extremely hot and humid. For best performance, plant in full sun. Plants thrive in most well-drained soils. Dig down about 6 to 8 in. to loosen soil, and mix in a handful of granular slow-acting fertilizer to provide nutrition for the whole season. Adding organic matter helps gritty soil hold moisture. Dig a planting hole about as deep as and slightly wider than the rootball. Set the grass clump at or slightly above soil level. Backfill and firm the soil, and water well. Space plants 12 in. apart, a bit closer for instant edging.

Growing Tips
Water if rain is scarce. Even drought-tolerant grasses need moisture while they struggle to become established. Mulch the soil to retain moisture and to discourage weeds. Do not fertilize further beyond what was provided at planting time.

Care
Blue Fescue foliage is evergreen, so there is no need to cut it back. Keep clumps neat by clipping unruly foliage to 4 in. Divide every three years when clumps look ratty in their centers. Dig the clump, and expose its roots. Cut chunks of fresh foliage with good roots from the clump's edges, then replant. This plant is virtually pest free.

Companion Planting and Design
Blue Fescue provides year-round interest. It is wonderful for planters and containers. Its small, neat habit and distinctive color combine well with vertical and trailing plants. Use as ground cover, in rock gardens, or as edging. It combines well with dwarf conifers.

Did You Know?
Bestowing Latin names on plants usually eliminates confusion. Common names typically change with the region or culture, but a Latin scientific name is universally recognized. Sometimes even a Latin name changes to reflect a new understanding of a plant's pedigree, however. Because a consensus has not been reached about Blue Fescue, it appears under many Latin names. It may be listed in books and catalogs as *Festuca ovina*, *Festuca cinerea*, *Festuca caesia*, and others.

Hakone Grass

Hakonechloa macra 'Aureola'

When, Where, and How to Plant

Divide and replant overlarge clumps in either spring or fall. Transplant from containers anytime during the growing season. Hakone Grass prefers the partial shade of woodland settings, but likes some morning sun. Plant in moist, well-drained soil rich in organic matter. Loosen it down 8 to 10 in., and mix in a sprinkling of granular slow-acting fertilizer to sustain new transplants over the season. Dig the planting holes as deep as and slightly wider than the plant rootballs. Set each so that it is at soil level or slightly above. Backfill, firm to remove air pockets, and water well. Space plants 2 ft. apart.

Growing Tips

Water new plantings well, especially during hot weather. Spread a 2- or 3-in. layer of organic mulch to enrich the soil and discourage weeds and the evaporation of moisture. No further fertilization is needed if soil remains rich in organic matter.

Care

Hakone Grass requires little care. By spring its foliage is scruffy, so cut it back to make way for new shoots. It is virtually pest free.

Companion Planting and Design

Use Hakone Grass as a fine-textured filler in containers with other shade-loving plants. It is also effective as a ground cover or living mulch under trees where turfgrass will not grow. It provides interesting textural contrast to a woodland planting of Astilbes, Hostas, and Coleus. It makes a good edging, too. Hakone Grass looks especially at home in gardens with an Oriental theme.

Did You Know?

A former genus name for Hakone Grass is *Phragmites*. Fortunately, its name has changed because another *Phragmites* is a horrible, invasive weed, and Hakone Grass would suffer from its notorious reputation. Common Reed (*Phragmites australis*) is choking our wetlands. It drives out native plants and fills in streams and ponds. Do not introduce Common Reed into your landscape, lest it escape and naturalize in local drainage ditches and fields.

Golden Hakonechloa, or Hakone Grass, is currently enjoying considerable popularity for good reason. Somewhat tricky to propagate commercially, it is now more available than ever before. It's easy to divide in the garden though. It is immensely useful because, unlike most ornamental grasses, it accepts shade. It grows as a low clump of glowing, arching, bamboolike leaves that turn toward the light. The more sun it receives, the more yellow the foliage becomes. Although it spreads by means of rhizomatous roots, it is not at all invasive. A warm-season grass, it is cold hardy only to zone 6. Hakonechloa macra, which has plain green leaves and is more sun, cold, and drought tolerant, is eminently suitable for colder regions of Pennsylvania, however. It grows faster and features a copper-orange color in the fall.

Other Name

Hakonechloa

Color and Texture

Variegated gold with green streaks, pinkish-red fall color

Mature Height × Spread

18 to 24 in. × 2 ft.

Kentucky Bluegrass
Poa pratensis

Traditionally, Kentucky Bluegrass has been the gold standard for Northern lawns. It is still valued for its good color, even texture, and uniform spread. A cool-season grass, it maintains some green color through the winter in the areas of Pennsylvania where winters are mild and snow cover minimal. It greens up beautifully early in the spring. It is high maintenance, however, because it requires lots of water and fertilizer during the growing season and is prone to fungal disease in hot, humid regions. Since other turfgrass varieties have improved enormously over the last decade, Kentucky Blue is best used in a mixture with them where its assets are visible and its liabilities are offset by its tougher companions.

Other Name
Kentucky Blue

Color and Texture
Rich blue-green; fine texture

Recommended Mowing Height
Mow to 3 in. in summer.

When, Where, and How to Plant
Sow seed on prepared soil just after Labor Day. Lay sod or patch lawns with seed in either spring or fall. Kentucky Bluegrass does best with a minimum of eight hours of sun daily in an organic rich soil that is neutral or slightly acidic. Do not plant turfgrass under trees where it has to compete for water, light, and nutrients. Till in organic matter, smooth soil, and when weeds erupt after a week, kill them with a herbicide. After seven to ten days sow seed as directed on the seed package in the undisturbed soil bed, and water daily to keep seed moist at all times. Fertilizing at this time is optional. Apply a mulch of white poly-spun garden fleece or straw to maintain moisture and to protect seed from heavy rains and birds.

Growing Tips
Continue to water seedlings into winter if rainfall is sparse. Once grass plants are established water Kentucky Bluegrass lawns in good soil only when the grass looks limp. In poor or compacted soils water more often. Fertilize with a granular slow-acting product formulated for lawns in spring or fall.

Care
Cut new turfgrass when it approaches 4 in. tall. Regularly cut to 3 in. height until its final cut in the late fall at 2 in. Spread lime if soil is acidic. Leave the grass clippings on the lawn to provide nitrogen and some organic matter to the turf. Aerate and top-dress with organic material such as leaves chopped fine by a mulching mower. Kentucky Bluegrass tends to get powdery mildew, fusarium, pythium, and red thread. Most infections are caused by temporary extreme weather conditions. To treat chronic problems, overseed with disease-resistant Bluegrass varieties or other types of turfgrasses.

Did You Know?
Turfgrasses develop thatch (an accumulation of tough dead grass stems and crowns) over time. Promoted by compacted soil and overfertilization, it blocks air and moisture penetration to the roots and harbors pest larvae and pathogens. Rake up thatch layers thicker than 1/4 in.

Maiden Grass
Miscanthus sinensis 'Gracillimus'

When, Where, and How to Plant

Divide large clumps, and replant in the spring. Plant potted plants anytime during the growing season. Choose a sunny site; foliage tends to flop in shade. Maiden Grasses can handle almost any type of soil, even sand. Some varieties grow in shallow water as marginal plants. Dig and loosen the soil down about 12 in. There is no need to improve it. Dig a hole as deep as and about three times as wide as the rootball. Plant so that the top of the rootball is level with the surrounding ground. Backfill, firming gently around plant stems, then water well. Set plants 3 to 4 ft. apart to allow for their gradual spread, closer to establish a hedge or screen quickly.

Growing Tips

If there is no rain, water newly planted Maiden Grass until it is established. Mulch it to keep soil moist. Maiden Grass does not need routine fertilizing.

Care

Cut back fronds with hedge shears or a trimmer in the early spring to make way for new shoots. Divide overlarge clumps every three or four years. They are extremely difficult to handle. Dig up the rootball, and then with an ax, saw, or sharp spade or knife, slice through the tough matrix of roots to dislodge chunks of rooted grass from its edges. Discard the center of the rootball if it has begun to die out. Beware of sharp edges on grass blades. Stake floppy grass that is in overrich soil or shade. Japanese Silver Grasses are virtually pest free.

Companion Planting and Design

Japanese Silver Grass varieties are useful in groups as specimens, in rows for screens, and in the middle of a mixed border. Use fronds in floral arrangements.

Did You Know?

There is some concern that certain forms of Maiden Grass are "escaping" from landscape settings and seeding into the wild. The culprit is most likely mislabeled Banner Grass or *Miscanthus sacchariflorus*, a known runner and self-sower. Purchase ornamental grasses from reliable sources where labeling may be more accurate. The best strategy is to plant sterile cultivars or plant ones that bloom later. 'Morning Light' blooms late and doesn't seed. 'Cabaret' is sterile.

Japanese Silver varieties of Maiden Grass are landscape mainstays. Their substantial presence as widely arching or upright clumps of long, pointed leaf blades about 3/8 in. wide is the very archetype of an ornamental grass. Moreover, they are grasses for all seasons. They are a ghostly presence in late winter and early spring, their beige fronds near collapse as new shoots begin to form. In season Japanese Silver Grasses sport white, silver, or yellow stripes or bands on green straplike leaves, the silvery types glowing in evening gardens. They are especially dramatic in late summer. When everything seems to disappear from the garden, their September flowers turn silvery and pinkish as they fluff and release their seeds. Then the foliage begins to bleach again for winter.

Other Name
Japanese Silver Grass

Color and Texture
Variegated silver striped, gold banded or plain green, depending on the cultivar; fine texture

Mature Height × Spread
3 to 12 ft. × 12 ft.

Perennial Ryegrass
Lolium perenne

A good-looking cool-season turfgrass, Perennial Ryegrass is most valued because it germinates quickly—only a week after sowing. Therefore, its roots get enough of a head start in the spring to assure its survival in hot, humid summers. Seedlings of other turfgrasses, slower to germinate, usually succumb to summer heat. Perennial Rye is an important component of turfgrass mixtures sown in the fall. As a "nurse" grass, it quickly provides some green, assuring us that more grass will appear. Eventually, the seed of other varieties in the mixture germinates and fills in the bare seedbed. Use Perennial Rye to patch bare spots during the summer so that weeds will not move in. In the fall overseed those spots with whatever seed or mixture constitutes the surrounding turf.

Other Name
Perennial Rye

Color and Texture
Medium green; medium texture

Recommended Mowing Height
Mow to 3 in. in summer.

When, Where, and How to Plant
Plant anytime during the growing season. Lay sod or patch lawns with seed in either spring or fall. Perennial Rye does best with at least eight hours of sun daily in rich organic soil that is neutral or slightly acidic. Do not plant turfgrass under trees where it has to compete with tree roots for water, light, and nutrients. When sowing seed, improve the soil first, then till in organic matter. Smooth and water the area to germinate weed seeds; then kill them with a herbicide. Ten days later sow seed as directed. Keep seed moist at all times. Fertilize with a seed-starter fertilizer at sowing, or wait until fall to use a regular fertilizer on established turf. A mulch of white poly-spun garden fleece will maintain moisture and protect seed.

Growing Tips
Continue to water grass seedlings into winter if there is no rain. Water Perennial Ryegrass lawns in good soil only when there has been little or no rainfall for more than two weeks and the grass looks limp. Water turfgrass in poor soils more often. Fertilize with a granular slow-acting lawn fertilizer in spring or fall.

Care
Cut new turfgrass when it approaches 4 in. tall. Regularly cut it at 3 in. until its final cut in the late fall at 2 in. Spread lime if the soil is too acidic. Aerate and top-dress with organic material such as leaves chopped fine by a mulching mower. Perennial Ryegrass is susceptible to the fungal diseases pythium, brown patch, and red thread. Although sporadic outbreaks are usually a function of hot, humid, temporary weather, overseed with seed of disease-resistant varieties for chronic problems.

Did You Know?
Here are tips to have healthier lawns. *Mow with a sharp blade.* Dull blades damage tips and promote disease. *Mow tall*—a minimum of 3 in. in summer—so foliage shades the soil and conserves moisture. *Mow frequently.* Cut only about 1/3 of the grass height each time to avoid stress. *Mow dry* for an even cut. Wet clippings clump; blades bruise when stepped on.

Purple Fountaingrass

Pennisetum setaceum 'Rubrum'

When, Where, and How to Plant

Plant grass overwintered indoors outside in late spring when the soil has warmed. Transplant plants in containers in spring when frost danger is past or anytime during the growing season. Fountaingrass does best in full sun in any well-drained soil, including clay. It likes moist soil, so it does well near streams and pond banks. It can even take 1 or 2 in. of water over its roots. Dig and loosen the soil down about 12 in. There is no need to improve the soil. Add a handful of granular slow-acting fertilizer for season-long nutrition. Dig a planting hole as deep as and three times as wide as the rootball. Set the top of the rootball level with the surrounding ground. Backfill, firm the soil to remove air pockets, then water well. Set plants 3 to 4 ft. apart to allow for their gradual spread, closer for a mass planting.

Growing Tips

Water Purple Fountaingrass well when it is first planted. Once it is established and starts to send up new shoots, it can handle typical summers. Water containers regularly. Do not fertilize further.

Care

Purple Fountaingrass roots will not survive Pennsylvania winters. Overwinter plants in pots indoors. Otherwise, cut off their disintegrating flowers, leave their dried foliage for winter interest, and pull up the dead plants in the spring. They have no pests.

Companion Planting and Design

This grass is a good color accent for small yards with limited space. Extremely drought tolerant, it looks great with Sedum 'Autumn Joy', Purple Coneflower, and conifers in the background. Purple Fountaingrass also does well in containers.

Did You Know?

If you like red grasses, try another warm-season grass, Japanese Bloodgrass (*Imperata cylindrical* 'Red Baron'). A small plant featuring vertical foliage that reddens by degrees over the season, it is a stunner. Its translucent, blood-red foliage catches the autumn light as no other plant does. It has no flowers.

Purple Fountaingrass is grown as an annual in Pennsylvania because it is not cold hardy here. Its spikes of 8- to 12-in.-long flowers nod on arching stems amid upright clumps of reddish foliage, their soft, fuzzy reddish or purplish "bottlebrushes" suggesting a spray of water from a fountain. They bloom from June to September, providing color and texture all season. Fountaingrass foliage turns rosy-gold as fall approaches and is bleached tan when killing frost arrives. Its flowers are useful for fresh or dried floral arrangements or floral crafts. The bright green blades of annual Fountaingrass (Pennisetum alopecuroides) are streaked yellow and brown in fall, then beige in winter. 'Moudry' has almost black flowers. Feathertop (Pennisetum villosum) has a shorter flowering period and habit, but smaller size.

Other Names

Burgundy or Red Fountaingrass

Color and Texture

Burgundy to bronze-red; fine blades

Mature Height × Spread

2 to 3 ft. × 2 to 3 ft.

Switch Grass

Panicum virgatum

This lovely grass is native to the tall grass prairies in the United States. It is a classic example of how we overlook, or take for granted, a wonderful plant until it is adopted by Europeans and then reintroduced to our country. It is adaptable and easy to grow just about everywhere. 'Heavy Metal' bears airy pinkish or silvery flowers in July that wave in the breeze up above the tall, upright foliage. Switch Grass seedheads last into winter. Various Switch Grasses have slender green to gray- or bluish green foliage with rough edges that narrow to a fine tip. Their fall color is legendary. 'Shenandoah' foliage turns burgundy red. It is easy to imagine endless seas of it undulating across the prairie of yesteryear.

Other Name
Panic Grass

Color and Texture
Silvery-green blades turn yellow or reddish in fall

Mature Height × Spread
7 ft. × 3 ft.

When, Where, and How to Plant
Divide and plant overlarge clumps either in spring or fall. Transplant potted plants anytime during the growing season. Full sun is best. Switch Grasses appreciate rich, well-drained soil, but tolerate a wide range of soil types. They even tolerate 1 or 2 in. of water over their roots at water's edge. Loosen the soil down about 12 in. Add organic matter to enhance its ability to hold moisture and to drain well. Dig a planting hole about as deep as and slightly wider than the rootball. Set each plant so that the top of its soilball is level with the surrounding ground. Backfill, firming soil gently around plant stems to remove air pockets, then water well. Set plants about 3 ft. apart to allow for gradual spread, closer to establish a hedge or screen quickly.

Growing Tips
Water Switch Grass well while it becomes established. It can handle some drought once it has settled in the first season. Do not fertilize routinely.

Care
Cut back dried foliage fronds in early spring to make way for new shoots. In the spring, divide overlarge clumps by digging up each rootball and slicing chunks of rooted grass from its edges. Plant divisions in new sites. Switch Grasses have no pests or diseases.

Companion Planting and Design
In today's residential landscapes Switch Grasses serve well when clustered as specimens or ground covers, or planted in rows for backgrounds or screens.

Did You Know?
Ornamental grasses, turfgrasses, Bamboos, and many other plants spread either as compact clumps by means of underground creeping roots or as irregular patches by means of vigorous horizontal rooting stems. These latter types, the runners, tend to rapidly overwhelm the yard. Rather than avoid them completely, use them judiciously in areas where they can be confined: between a building and pavement, in containers, or along banks enclosed by natural barriers of stone.

When, Where, and How to Plant

Seed new lawns around Labor Day. Lay sod in spring or fall. Keep seed and sod moist while it establishes. Tall Fescue needs at least eight hours of sun daily. It prefers neutral or slightly acidic organically rich soil. When seeding or patching, add organic material to the tilled seedbed. Smooth and water the area. When weeds erupt, kill them with a burn-down herbicide (such as Roundup™). Do not disturb the soil further. Sow grass seed seven to ten days later. Fertilize when seeding or later in the fall. A temporary mulch of white poly-spun garden fleece maintains moisture and protects the seeds until first mowing.

Growing Tips

Water seedlings if rainfall is undependable. Established in good soil, Tall Fescue has legendary drought resistance. Water mature lawns in decent soil only after two weeks or more without rain. In poor or compacted soils where roots cannot grow deep, water more often. Fertilize with a granular slow-acting lawn fertilizer in spring or fall.

Care

Cut new Tall Fescue when it approaches 4 in. tall. Maintain at 3 in. until it goes dormant in the fall, then cut at 2 in. to overwinter. Aerate and top-dress with organic material biannually. Every few years mow close and overseed with premium Tall Fescue to maintain turf density. Tall Fescue is prone to pythium and brown patch in areas with hot, humid summers. Use mixtures of several turfgrasses so that their specific resistances collectively assure that some grass stays green if a fungal disease strikes.

Did You Know?

In the past mowers left unsightly clumps of grass clippings on lawns, smothering the turf beneath them. A lot of valuable nitrogen was raked up and discarded in the trash. Now, mulching lawn mowers cut clippings into tiny pieces that disappear among the grass blades, rapidly decompose, and release nitrogen. These mowers save us time and effort while improving the health of the lawn.

Tall Turftype Fescue was originally so coarse and clumpy that its use was limited to athletic fields and expanses of public turf where constant foot traffic mandated toughness over beauty. Over time breeders have developed it into a finer-textured, more uniform turfgrass whose appearance rivals that of more elegant turfgrasses such as Kentucky Bluegrass. It can be used alone or as a welcome addition to mixes of turfgrasses intended for residential landscapes. While it is often a prominent component of mixtures labeled for play areas, its toughness and drought resistance also contribute to the sturdiness of residential lawns. Choose a premium quality seed. For areas with high use, choose a mixture of Kentucky Bluegrass and Perennial Ryegrass with a significant proportion of Tall Fescue.

Other Name
Turftype Fescue

Color and Texture
Dark green; slightly coarse texture

Recommended Mowing Height
Mow to 3 in. in summer.

Ground Covers *for Pennsylvania*

All kinds of plants can be ground covers because this label refers only to their function in the landscape, not any particular botanical trait. The universal stereotype of green, crawling plants hardly does justice to the world of ground covers. Plants that cover the soil may be annuals or perennials, shrubs or vines, predominantly flowering or foliage, evergreen or deciduous, sun or shade loving. Often familiar garden stand-bys are eminently successful and useful as ground covers. A ground cover plant is simply one that, planted *en masse*, effectively covers the soil, forming an attractive tapestry of color and/or texture. By means of slowly widening clumps or running roots or stems, plants knit together into a protective mat over the soil. As a living mulch, a ground cover planting helps soil retain moisture, resist erosion, and avoid compaction.

Ground cover plants nourish and shelter the microlife that keeps soil alive and healthy. Good ground covers also suppress weeds, contribute to plant diversity in the landscape, and look attractive. Although American homeowners most commonly use turfgrasses for ground covers (see the chapter on grasses), turfgrasses lack the versatility of ornamental plants. Many plants are more visually interesting, have lower maintenance, and are more useful in solving problems in the yard because they can handle poorer, wetter, or shadier conditions than turfgrass can. Gardeners prefer to work with a larger palette of plants and strive to achieve decorative as well as functional goals.

What makes a good ground cover? Ground cover plants described in the following pages have many desirable traits that make them useful in Pennsylvania:

- They form a thick mat over the soil fairly quickly.
- They adapt to a variety of soil types.
- They spread deliberately but not rampantly.
- They are easy to pull up to control spread.
- They have winter interest—seedheads, evergreen foliage.
- They have good foliage color, possibly variegated.
- They need little grooming or pruning.
- They hold up over many years with minimal care.
- They have a tough constitution, often belied by a fine texture.

Planting

Plant individual ground cover plants as you would any plant—in decent, prepared soil that suits its preferences. Because they are planted as mass plantings, however, spacing becomes an issue. How far apart to set them is a function of five things: the size of the transplant, the speed with which it spreads, the size of the area to be covered, the degree of your impatience for the plants to knit together, and the number of plants that you can afford to buy. Nursery stock in quart containers costs more, but establishes and spreads faster. Buy fewer and plant them farther apart, and be patient. Rooted cuttings are inexpensive, but slower to spread. Buy them by the flat, plant them fairly close together, and be patient. If the area to be covered is modest and the budget is healthy, buy the larger nursery stock, plant them closer together, and your patience will be rewarded sooner!

How to Use Ground Covers

Use ground covers as a low-maintenance substitute for turfgrass and as a way to protect soil. They solve all kinds of landscape problems—covering tree surface roots, controlling erosion, enduring shade, and obscuring eyesores such as old stumps and utility vents. They mask dying bulb foliage and provide variety and interest. In large areas plant lower, finer-textured plants in the foreground. Place taller, coarser-textured ones in more distant situations. Experiment with variegated foliage to brighten deepest shade. Use those with contrasting foliage to attract attention and divert the eye from other areas. Similar colors work well to form a backdrop for specimen plants.

Flora Non Grata

With ground covers there can be too much of a good thing. Some plants that have many of these assets have them in too great supply or are relentlessly overbearing. Although some may be virtual weeds that arrive in the yard unbidden, others are cultivated plants still sold commercially for landscape use. (See Invasive Plants of Pennsylvania, page 234.) Because these ground covers do not know the meaning of restraint, frustrated gardeners often refer to them as "thugs." Unless they are grown in a container, avoid the following:

Barren Strawberry (*Waldensteinia fragariodes*)   Goutweed (*Aegopodium podagraria*)

Chameleon Plant (*Houttuynia cordata*)   Mint (*Mentha* species)

Crown Vetch (*Coronilla varia* 'Penngift')   Purple Loosestrife (*Lythrum salicaria*)

Gooseneck Loosestrife (*Lysimachia clethroides*)

Ajuga
Ajuga reptans

As well known by its formal Latin name as by its common name, Ajuga is a useful ground cover of the first order. It is attractive, adaptable, and easy to take for granted. Its tightly packed whorls of colorful foliage are semi-evergreen during our milder winters and can withstand occasional foot traffic. Ajuga's spring spikes of tiny blue or white snapdragonlike flowers are a real ornamental bonus and an attraction for honeybees. Ajuga does not seem to interest deer. Best of all, it spreads with decorum and is easy to pull up when it goes out of bounds. Gardeners may choose from many versions. Ajuga reptans 'Burgundy Glow' has paler variegated foliage and is the most cold sensitive; 'Purpurea' has purplish foliage.

Other Name
Bugleweed

Bloom Period and Seasonal Color
May; blooms in blue, white, pink. Has green, purple, bronze, silver or pinkish variegated foliage

Mature Height
2 in.; flower spikes 6 in.

When, Where, and How to Plant
Plant rooted divisions or young plants in spring or fall. Ones in pots can go into the garden anytime during the growing season. Plant in either full sun or partial shade in very well-drained ordinary garden soil. Soggy or very rich soil promotes rot. Dig down 4 to 6 in., and add sand or gravel, if necessary, to encourage good drainage. Dig a hole the size of the roots, and set the plants so that the foliage is slightly above the level of the surrounding ground. Backfill, firming soil gently around the crown to remove air pockets, then water well. Set plants 6 to 8 in. apart.

Growing Tips
There is no need to mulch or fertilize, but since the roots are fairly shallow, water when rainfall is scarce.

Care
Ajuga needs little attention. Cut off faded flower spikes to groom plants and prevent their sowing seeds. Clip off foliage rosettes on runners that have overstepped their bounds. When the rosettes of leaves start to pile on each other, thin the planting. The only significant problem of Ajuga is crown rot. Usually a function of excessive heat and humidity, it is most common in overcrowded patches. Typically, part of a patch dies out. It may fill in again on its own over time, however.

Companion Planting and Design
Ajuga tolerates the hot sun between stones on a patio and the shade of a woodland area. Geneva Bugleweed (*Ajuga genevensis*) does not spread and is good for rock gardens.

Did You Know?
The botanical names of plants have at least two Latin words in them. This binomial epithet describes the make and model of the plant. The first word is capitalized and is the genus—*Ajuga* (or Toyota). The second word, the species—*reptans* (or Camry)—describes a trait or commemorates the person who found or bred the plant. Be aware that *reptans* or *repens* means stems that creep and root, and plant accordingly!

Barrenwort
Epimedium species and hybrids

When, Where, and How to Plant
Plant rooted divisions in spring or fall. Plant potted plants anytime during the growing season. Barrenwort can handle some sun, but it is happiest in shade or partial shade areas. Once established, it accepts mediocre soil and some dryness, but it prefers a moist, organic, rich soil. It competes well with tree roots, and it is great as living mulch around large trees with shallow or surface roots. Dig the soil down 8 to 10 in., mixing in granular slow-acting all-purpose fertilizer and organic material to improve drainage. Dig the planting hole large enough to accommodate the roots and shallow enough so that the plant is at the same soil depth that it was in its pot, but no deeper. Backfill, firming soil gently around plant to remove air pockets, and water well. Set plants about 10 to 12 in. apart.

Growing Tips
Water during dry periods. Barrenwort in good garden soil needs no supplemental fertilizer. Otherwise, a sprinkling of slow-acting granular fertilizer on the soil near each patch helps plants through the season.

Care
In early spring cut back foliage retained to provide winter interest before the tender new shoots start to unfurl. Divide overlarge clumps late in the summer when the heat subsides. Dig up a clump to expose the tough wiry roots, and cut through them with a sharp spade or knife. Replant rooted chunks. Barrenworts are virtually pest and disease free.

Companion Planting and Design
Their relatively shallow roots grip the soil tenaciously, which makes Barrenworts useful for holding the soil on slopes and tops of walls. Patches spread slowly and decorously, as permitted.

Did You Know?
The name Barrenwort reminds gardeners of the conditions that this plant can tolerate if it must. Often described as a dry shade plant, this is certainly what the word *barren* suggests. Homeowners who have lots of trees are grateful for a ground cover that can manage under trees.

Barrenworts came from Asia originally and arrived in our country by way of Japan and Europe where they have grown since the 1600s. Another common name, Bishop's Hat, is derived from the resemblance of the flowers to a Roman Catholic bishop's four-cornered hat, called a beretta. Only recently have these plants received the appreciation they deserve as stalwarts in shady landscapes. Their spring daintiness belies their toughness, but the wiry stems and stiffly textured leaves persist as winter closes in reveal it. Barrenwort foliage is not exactly evergreen, yet it adds to the winter scene if not cut back during fall cleanup. Barrenwort spreads slowly. Red Barrenwort (Epimedium × rubrum) has red flowers and heart-shaped leaves. Other good, commonly-available varieties that deserve mention are E. × versicolor 'Sulphureum', which is yellow; E. × youngianum 'Niveum', which is white; and E. × warleyense which is orange.

Other Name
Bishop's Hat

Bloom Period and Seasonal Color
Spring; blooms in yellow, pink, red, white, or orange

Mature Height
8 to 12 in.

Bellflower

Campanula poscharskyana

Dainty, but vigorous, Serbian Bellflower sprawls tidily in mounded clumps of heart-shaped, ripple-edged leaves on short stems. In late spring stems as long as 12 in. suddenly appear and are quickly arrayed with starry blue flowers having five-pointed petals. They rebloom sporadically in cool-summer regions. At this point Bellflowers' decorum slips a bit as the stems flop over with the weight of the blooms, but they are so thick that no one notices. The Campanula clan is large and diverse, and its many members are assets in residential landscapes. Most have the trademark bell-shaped flowers in shades of blue or white. Among the ground covers, there is also Dalmatian Bellflower (Campanula portenschlagiana), which grows closer to the ground with similar colored flowers that bloom in June or July, but is less of a spreader.

Other Name
Serbian Bellflower

Bloom Period and Seasonal Color
Late May or early June; blooms in lavender-blue or pale blue

Mature Height
4 to 6 in.

When, Where, and How to Plant
Plant young potted plants anytime during the growing season. Plant divisions after they bloom in early summer. Choose an overcast day or plant in the evening to minimize transplant shock from the sun. Bellflowers can take fairly harsh conditions. They do not mind full sun, and they thrive in sandy or other thin, well-drained soil. Dig down 8 or 10 in., and mix in coarse sand to promote drainage if needed. Add a granular slow-acting all-purpose fertilizer. Dig holes roughly the size of the plants' containers. Set plants in holes so that they are at the same depth in the ground that they were in their pots. Backfill, firming soil gently, and water well. Set plants 8 to 10 in. apart.

Growing Tips
Mulch new plantings of Bellflower to discourage competing weeds and maintain soil moisture while seedlings are struggling to establish. Water if rain is scarce. Do not fertilize further.

Care
After they bloom, remove the stems of faded flowers by clipping or pinching them off at their base back among the foliage clump. Intermittent repeat bloom over the summer is fairly common. Bellflower has no serious pests or diseases.

Companion Planting and Design
Use Bellflower at the front of the flower bed as edging to set off minor bulbs and blend with other ground covers such as Rock Cress. Plant along stone walls, between steppingstones, and along paved walks. Serbian Bellflower looks good under yellow Daylilies.

Did You Know?
Campanula means "little bell." Thus it makes an appropriate family name for several related groups of plants with similar characteristics—including, but not limited to, the classic bell-shaped flowers. The family is *Campanulaceae*. Confusion may arise because of the resemblance to the genus name *Campanula*. If a Latin word has *ae* or *aceae*, it is a family name. Botanists and taxonomists determine which plants belong to which families and then name them.

Creeping Juniper
Juniperus horizontalis

When, Where, and How to Plant
Plant balled-and-burlapped Juniper shrubs in spring or fall. Transplant those in containers in any cool, moist weather during the growing season. Shade new summer transplants their first day or two. Junipers love full sun and adapt to any kind of well-drained soil pH and type. Loosen soil down at least 1 ft., and mix in granular slow-acting fertilizer. Add organic material to improve soil drainage. Dig saucer-shaped planting holes exactly as deep as and slightly wider than each plant's root-ball. Cut or loosen any circling roots. Set each in its hole so that its crown is at or slightly above soil level. Backfill, firming soil gently around its stem, and water well. Set plants at least 3 ft. apart, slightly closer to encourage their knitting into a mat.

Growing Tips
While they establish themselves, Junipers need regular watering and some weeding. Spread mulch between shrubs to discourage weeds, but do not pile it against stems. After their first season they do not need fertilizer.

Care
Clip off damaged or overlong branches. Never prune back as far as the bare stem because foliage will not regenerate there. Mites may attack when the shrubs are stressed by unusually wet, dry, or hot weather. Control mites with horticultural oil. Juniper plants less than five years old are occasionally victimized by a tip blight, *Phomopsis*. Prune out the browned, dying twigs. Older plantings are prone to mice damage in winter.

Companion Planting and Design
Plant small spring-flowering bulbs among Creeping Junipers, which set off their beauty, then obscure their ripening foliage after they bloom. These Junipers are useful on slopes to control erosion.

Did You Know?
An early Juniper selection, 'Plumosa', is part of our state horticultural history. Andorra Nurseries in Philadelphia introduced it in 1907, and it became popular over the years. Because it is susceptible to blight, lower-growing, more resistant Junipers have superseded it.

For a heavy-duty ground cover one of the best choices is sturdy Creeping Juniper. This low-growing native shrub forms a clump of dense, woody branches that spread horizontally to 6 or more ft. into a roughly circular mound. Rather than root where they touch the soil, the branches just lie on it. Collectively, several shrubs will carpet the ground with a quilt of attractive bluish green foliage that acquires a purplish tinge in winter. It is just prickly enough to discourage shortcuts by people and pets across the area it covers. Moreover, Creeping Junipers tolerate all sorts of indignities such as heat, drought, seashore conditions, road salt, and mediocre soil. Female shrubs bear tiny conelike flowers that become Juniper "berries" in August.

Other Name
Carpet Juniper

Bloom Period and Seasonal Color
Evergreen; bluish green scales

Mature Height
1 to 2 ft.

Creeping Phlox
Phlox stolonifera

This native woodland plant was a hit with gardeners as soon as it became available. Not only does it creep over the ground with measured speed, but its foliage mat is fine textured and neat. In mid-spring it sends up perky 6-in. stems tipped with clusters of small florets that bloom for a week or more. The foliage carries on in style all summer, successfully avoiding the mildew problems that plague other Phloxes. There are many colors: 'Bruce's White' (white), 'Blue Ridge' (blue), 'Pink Ridge' (pink), 'Sherwood Purple' (purplish blue), and 'Irridescens' (lavender). Wild Blue Phlox (Phlox divaricata) is also native to our woodlands. More wispy and delicate looking, it dies back and disappears in the summer. 'Fuller's White' is a white-flowered version.

Other Name
Stoloniferous Phlox

Bloom Period and Seasonal Color
Evergreen foliage; May; blooms in blue, white, purple, or pink

Mature Height
2 in.; flower spikes 6 to 10 in.

When, Where, and How to Plant
Plant young potted plants anytime during the growing season. Plant rooted divisions in spring or fall when dividing an overlarge patch of Creeping Phlox. Plant in partial shade or some place where it gets spring sunshine under deciduous trees. Creeping Phlox does best in woodsy soil—moist, acidic, rich in organic matter, and well drained. Aerate and loosen soil by digging down 8 to 10 in. Add organic matter such as peat moss, compost, or chopped leaves to improve soil drainage, and mix in granular slow-acting fertilizer to give new transplants a boost during their first season. Dig planting holes about as deep as and slightly wider than the rootballs. Set plants in their holes so that their crowns are just at soil level. Backfill, firming soil gently, and water well. Set plants 8 to 10 in. apart.

Growing Tips
Water newly planted beds frequently until plants are established. Do not fertilize in the future if the soil is good.

Care
Mulch bare soil to discourage weeds until the plants knit together. Clip faded flower stems back to the foliage after bloom. Cut off unauthorized, dead, or injured runners anytime during the season. Divide overcrowded Creeping Phlox after flowering. It does not have mildew problems. Too much summer sun may cause stress, however, reducing plant vigor and causing foliage to become pale.

Companion Planting and Design
The most shade-tolerant of the Phlox clan, Creeping Phlox is ideal for edging walks and beds, and for transition areas between shade and sunny sites. This low grower also does well between steppingstones.

Did You Know?
The Perennial Plant Association selected Creeping Phlox as its Plant of the Year in 1990. This organization of plant growers and sellers is committed to promoting education and cooperation within the perennial plant and related industries. Each year the association members select a perennial plant that they believe has superior appearance, vigor, and disease and pest resistance.

Deadnettle
Lamium maculatum

When, Where, and How to Plant
Plant rooted divisions in spring or fall. Plant potted plants anytime during the growing season. Their variegation shows to best advantage in the shade, but they can handle some sun. They prefer moist, well-drained, good garden soil, but will make do with poorer, drier soil after they become established. They spread more slowly in poorer soil. Dig and loosen soil down 8 to 10 in., and add granular slow-acting fertilizer for season-long nutrition. Dig holes as deep as and slightly wider than plant rootballs, and set them so that their crowns are at soil level. Backfill, firming soil gently around plant stems, and water well. Space 6 to 8 in. apart.

Growing Tips
Water new plants well while they adjust to their site and become established. Mulch the bare soil between them the first season to control weeds and hold moisture. They require no further fertilizing.

Care
After they flower, clip or shear back stem tips to forestall reseeding and to keep plants compact. The fresh new foliage growth will hold up over the rest of summer and through winter. Divide and replant in spring or fall. If slug damage on foliage is a nuisance, remove mulch layer from the soil.

Companion Planting and Design
Plant Deadnettles under shrubs and along edges of woodland beds. Allow them to mingle freely with Hellebores, Ferns, Mosses, and other ground covers.

Did You Know?
When plantsmen discover a sturdy, adaptable, ornamental plant in the wild, they see a candidate for the garden. Many potentially good plants such as Yellow Archangel (*Lamium galeobdolon* 'Variegata') flunk the good citizenship test, however, because they are too rambunctious and invasive. Undeterred, plantsmen search for more mannerly variations of such plants. When they find promising ones, they name and develop them for garden use. These CULTIvated VARieties, or cultivars, such as 'Hermann's Pride', a clumping form of Yellow Archangel, often go on to fame and fortune.

A major asset of certain shade-loving ground cover plants is variegated foliage. Silvery or white streaks and blotches on Deadnettle foliage brighten the ground under larger green plants such as Azaleas, Rhododendrons, and Cherrylaurel while protecting the soil and providing foliage texture. Their stem runners grow energetically, but are not invasive. The many kinds of Deadnettles are quietly effective, easily controlled, and attractive. As a bonus they bear small flowers in dainty whorls at the top of leafy spikes in late spring. 'Beacon Silver' has silvery leaves edged with green, and lilac flowers. 'Shell Pink' has long-blooming pink flowers; 'White Nancy' has whitish foliage and flowers.

Other Name
Spotted Nettle

Bloom Period and Seasonal Color
Mid to late spring; blooms in pink or white

Mature Height
8 to 12 in.

English Ivy
Hedera helix

Just because it is the traditional green foliage ground cover widely used in landscapes, English Ivy is not to be ignored. There is a reason why it is so ubiquitous—the best reason of all—it is an excellent plant. Do not let familiarity breed contempt because this Ivy is not always so familiar. There are hundreds of versions with foliage in every imaginable pattern of variegation, leaf shape, and leaf size. The typical ground cover is usually a juvenile form of the plant. Encouraged to grow and spread and climb, English Ivy undergoes a transition, developing a mature shrubby form that bears flowers near the top of more rounded leaves. Its flowers attract bees. Eventually, they give way to black berries, which are poisonous. The hardiest for ground cover use includes 'Thorndale'. One of the hardiest variegated Ivy is 'Buttercup', which has golden foliage in sun.

Other Name
Ivy

Bloom Period and Seasonal Color
Fall; rounded blooms in greenish white. Evergreen foliage is green or variegated white or yellow with green

Mature Height
8 to 10 in.

When, Where, and How to Plant
Plant potted plants anytime during the growing season, but spring and fall are best. Plant rooted cuttings in spring. Ivy thrives in shade or partial shade and in almost any soil type except the truly soggy. It prefers woodsy soil that is moist and rich in humus. Dig soil down 8 or 10 in., mixing in organic material to improve drainage. Add granular slow-acting fertilizer to poor soils. Dig holes carefully between roots of existing shrubs and trees. Make them as deep as and slightly wider than Ivy rootballs. Set each plant's crown at soil level. Backfill, firming soil gently, and water well. Set plants 1 ft. apart or closer.

Growing Tips
If rainfall is sparse, water regularly until plants establish. There is no need to fertilize once English Ivy is off and running.

Care
Mulch to discourage weeds. Otherwise Ivy needs no care except to prune stems that overstep their bounds. Periodically renovate a long-established bed by mowing with the mower set at its highest setting. Planting dwarf cultivars will reduce pruning chores. Improve the exposed soil by spreading organic material. Evergreen Ivy foliage sometimes suffers from harsh winter sun and wind. Browned foliage will disappear under new spring growth. English Ivy causes dermatitis in some people, so wear gloves while handling it. Severely stressed Ivy may attract mites.

Companion Planting and Design
Plant English Ivy under trees to protect their root zones from damage by mowers and string trimmers. Allow it to climb walls or wander between and over rocks and landscape eyesores. Try 'Buttercup', a Pennsylvania Horticultural Society Gold Medal Award winner.

Did You Know?
Some plants are so beloved that they acquire fan clubs, called plant societies. These groups, such as the American Ivy Society, play an important part in developing and disseminating information about the care and use of the plant. Ivy Society members grow and study Ivy, and some seek new varieties and propagate them. For more information, go to the website (www.ivy.org).

When, Where, and How to Plant

Plant divisions in spring or early fall. Transplant potted plants anytime during the growing season. European Ginger needs shade. It is happiest in classic woodsy soil—rich in humus, acidic, moist, and well drained. Dig soil 8 or 10 in. deep, mixing in granular slow-acting fertilizer for sustained nutrition and organic matter to improve the soil. Do not plant too deeply. Planting holes should be only as deep as the Ginger is in its container so that its crown is at exactly the same soil level in the ground as it was in the pot. Backfill, firming soil gently around plant stems to remove air pockets, and water well. Set plants about 6 to 8 in. apart.

Growing Tips

Water new plantings well until they are truly established and send up new foliage. Do not fertilize further.

Care

European Ginger is virtually carefree, pest free, and disease free. Its foliage stays nice most of the year, so there is no need to shear it for extensive renewal. Just pick off ratty leaves as needed during the season. Because it spreads so slowly, plants rarely need dividing unless they are restricted to a small space. Otherwise a patch can remain in place ten years or more.

Companion Planting and Design

European Ginger foliage beautifully sets off the colorful flowers of small spring bulbs. It then obscures their dying foliage over several weeks.

Did You Know?

Here is a case where a common name is misleading. European and native Wild Gingers have nothing to do with the Ginger plant that produces the familiar spice. The real Gingers are tropical plants (*Zingiberaceae*) that can be grown in our area only indoors in greenhouses or as houseplants, or outdoors as annuals. They die when frost arrives. The rhizomes and seeds of various members of the true Ginger family provide cardamom, turmeric, and ginger for the kitchen.

The job of ground cover may not be prestigious, but some plants bring to their duty certain polish and dignity. European Ginger is such a plant. Covering the soil with a layer of its neat, glossy, deep-green kidney-shaped leaves, it spreads at a measured pace by means of underground rhizomes. Its flowers are all but invisible, crouching in the deep shade of its foliage, the color of the soil they nestle against. European Ginger is a low-profile and a low-maintenance plant that is restrained and effective. Canadian Wild Ginger (Asarum canadense) is our native version. Its large, round, deciduous leaves are a duller green, sometimes with attractive mottling. It handles heat and more alkaline soil better than A. europaeum.

Other Name
European Wild Ginger

Bloom Period and Seasonal Color
May; blooms (insignificant) are brownish; evergreen dark-green foliage

Mature Height
6 to 8 in.

Flower Carpet® Pink Rose

Rosa 'Noatraum'

In recent years interest in Roses that can be integrated into the landscape has prompted breeders to develop more useful landscape or "shrub" Roses. Flower Carpet Pink is a standout among this group of more versatile new Roses because it is unprecedentedly disease free and very tough. Dense and compact, it makes a beautiful ground cover, each plant spreading in neat, loose mounds of stems tipped with clusters of fifteen to eighteen subtly scented flowers. Properly sited and appropriately watered and fertilized, a mature plant can produce two thousand flowers per season virtually nonstop. Flower Carpet White (Rosa 'Noaschnee') has slightly larger, camellia-like scented flowers. Flower Carpet Appleblossom (Rosa 'Noamel'), a "sport" of Flower Carpet Pink, has deep-pink buds that develop into pastel-pink flowers.

Other Name
Flower Carpet Rose

Bloom Period and Seasonal Color
June to October; blooms in rose-pink

Mature Height × Spread
2 to 3 ft. × 4 ft.

When, Where, and How to Plant
Plant potted Roses anytime during the growing season, although springtime is best. Plant when the sun is not out to minimize transplant shock. While Flower Carpet Rose performs best in full sun, it still blooms freely in four to five hours of sun or all-day filtered light. It is not particular about soil as long as it is well drained. Cultivate down 12 in., and mix in granular slow-acting fertilizer. To improve drainage, mix in organic matter. Dig each saucer-shaped hole as deep as and somewhat wider than the container. Loosen any matted roots, and set rootballs level with the surrounding ground. Backfill, firming soil gently around each plant, and water well. Set two to three plants per square yard for a ground cover.

Growing Tips
Transplanted Flower Carpet Roses need regular watering to develop vigorous, strong roots. Mulch with a 2- or 3-in. layer of organic material to keep soil moist. Water and mulch well for the winter. These profuse bloomers need consistent, uniform nutrition from a granular slow-acting fertilizer sprinkled on the soil every spring.

Care
In spring prune all canes back hard to 6 in., fertilize, and renew mulch. Deadheading during the season is not necessary, but cut canes back in mid-season to shape and encourage compactness. This Rose is remarkably free of pests and diseases.

Companion Planting and Design
Flower Carpet Roses are useful massed on slopes and along walls and walkways. They do extremely well in containers and among other flowering plants in beds.

Did You Know?
In Germany, Roses are put through their paces in stringent All-Deutsche Rose (ADR) trials—one of the toughest competitions in the world. Candidates are evaluated six times annually for three years in nine test gardens with no chemical spraying or dusting. They are evaluated for general appearance, ease of growing, and disease resistance. Flower Carpet Pink won the 1990 ADR Gold Medal with the highest rating for natural disease resistance ever given.

Foamflower
Tiarella cordifolia

When, Where, and How to Plant
Plant rooted divisions in spring or fall. Transplant young potted plants anytime during the growing season. Foamflower needs shade. It does well under trees because it is shallow rooted and does not compete with them or disturb their roots. It does best in classic woodsy soil—rich in organic matter, acidic, and well drained. Once established, it can handle mild drought and more light. Dig and loosen the soil down 8 to 10 in., mixing in granular slow-acting fertilizer to provide season-long nutrition for the transplants and organic material to promote soil drainage. Dig holes as deep as and slightly wider than the rootballs. Set each plant so that its crown is at soil level. Backfill, firming soil gently around plant stems, and water well. Space plants about 10 in. apart to allow for their gradual spread.

Growing Tips
Water newly planted areas well until plants are established. No additional fertilizer is necessary.

Care
In the spring deadheading spent flower spikes makes the patch look more attractive, but is not practical for extensive areas. The flower stems are thin and relatively inconspicuous after blooms fade. There is no need to clip faded foliage; the new leaves will cover it. To acquire more plants, clip off rooted pieces of runners, and replant them anytime during the season. Typical of native plants, Foamflower does not have serious pest or disease problems. Occasionally, areas die out, but surrounding plants spread to fill the space.

Companion Planting and Design
Intermingle Foamflower with wild Phlox. Plant patches of it near Ferns, Common Bleeding Heart, and spring-blooming hardy bulbs.

Did You Know?
What is better than two great plants? A plant breeder's answer to this question is: a third one that combines them! Thus × *Heucherella*, a hybrid of Foamflower (*Tiarella*) and Coralbells (*Heuchera*). Varieties of *Heucherella* have the charming Foamflower foliage and long, airy stems of tiny bell-shaped flowers of Coralbells.

It is always magical when Foamflower does its spring thing. The woodland floor or shade garden suddenly is carpeted in dainty, upright flower spikes. After about two weeks they fade, and the fresh, new replacement foliage is revealed. Foamflowers carpet the area by sending out runners along the soil surface. They trail and tumble over rocks and logs and between stones with abandon, but are easy to clip off when they overstep their bounds. 'Rambling Tapestry' has maroon veins in its leaves. Wherry's Foamflower (Tiarella wherryi or T. cordifolia 'Collina') grows in clumps. Its pink-tinged flowers tend to last longer than those of regular Foamflower. It has purple-tinged foliage. 'Oakleaf' has green leaves that resemble Oak tree leaves.

Other Name
Allegheny Foamflower

Bloom Period and Seasonal Color
May; blooms in white

Mature Height
6 in.; flower spikes to 12 in.

Japanese Painted Fern
Athyrium nipponicum 'Pictum'

Perhaps because their delicate, lacy fronds give Ferns a fragile look, gardeners often shy away from using them generously in the landscape. In fact, they are enormously useful as ground covers, and none more so than the Japanese Painted Fern. It has all the virtues of other Ferns, plus extraordinarily silvery-reddish-colored foliage that relieves the unremitting greenness of other plants in shady sites. It forms handsome clumps of airy fronds, with no two plants alike. The colors appear to vary subtly from one plant to another and in varying light conditions. In optimum conditions clumps double or triple their size in one growing season, but always avoid undignified spread. Lady Fern (Athyrium filix-femina) is easy to grow and slow spreading; it has classic green foliage.

Other Name
Painted Fern

Bloom Period and Seasonal Color
Blended reddish, lavender, and silvery-green fronds

Mature Height
12 to 18 in.

When, Where, and How to Plant
Plant potted plants or divisions from overlarge clumps in late spring. Japanese Painted Fern can handle morning or late-day sun, but it prefers dappled shade. It needs soil rich in organic matter that retains moisture, yet drains well. Dig 10 to 12 in. deep; mix in organic matter and granular slow-acting all-purpose fertilizer. Dig each planting hole as deep as the rootball so that its crown is at soil level. Backfill, firming soil gently around stems, and water well. Set plants about 2 ft. apart.

Growing Tips
Ferns are shallow rooted; water if conditions become too dry (fronds collapse when a Fern is thirsty). There is no need to fertilize more if the plants are mulched occasionally with compost or chopped leaves.

Care
Japanese Painted Fern is quite self-reliant once it is established. When the fronds die back after frost, allow them to remain on the soil as mulch. Clip them off when new fronds unfurl in the spring. When Fern clumps grow too large for their space, dig up and divide them in spring. Painted Fern is virtually pest free.

Companion Planting and Design
Plant this Fern in a woodland setting under shrubs such as Rhododendron and Azalea, near rocks or stone walls alone or with other ground covers such as Foamflower, Anemones, and Sweet Woodruff. It also coordinates with other Ferns and spring bulbs. Its relative, Alpine Lady Fern (*Athyrium distentifolium*), is ideal for rock gardens.

Did You Know?
Along with Algae and Moss, Ferns such as Japanese Painted Fern represent prehistoric plant life that has adapted to our modern world. Lacking typical flowers, they rely on a primitive two-step method of reproduction. First spores (tiny dark spots) develop under the leaflets. They are released into the air and eventually settle to earth where they form a special flat structure that supports the development of male and female organs. Fertilization takes place, and new Fern plants develop.

Lamb's Ears
Stachys byzantina

When, Where, and How to Plant
Plant divisions in the spring, potted plants anytime during the growing season. Lamb's Ears plants prefer full sun and must be in soil that has good drainage to avoid foliage rot. Once established, they can handle significant drought. Loosen soil down 8 to 10 in. If necessary, mix in organic material such as peat moss or chopped leaves to improve drainage. Dig a hole as deep as and slightly wider than a plant's rootball. Set it in the hole so that its crown is at or slightly above soil level. Backfill, firming soil gently around plant stems, and water well.

Growing Tips
Water new plantings until they are established. Do not fertilize.

Care
Cut off flower spikes to neaten the ground cover patch. Thin overcrowded plants in midsummer to improve air circulation. Clip off stem sections to control spread. If the center of the patch gets ratty, dig up that section, and discard it. Clean up rotted foliage at the end of winter. Lamb's Ears have a tough constitution, and their fuzzy leaves are unappetizing to most pests, crawling or four footed. Their foliage is vulnerable, however, to some rots that flourish when humidity is high. Avoid overhead sprinkling. Cut off affected leaves, clean up soggy interior foliage, and wait for better weather.

Companion Planting and Design
Use Lamb's Ears in inhospitable areas in the landscape. Plant them between stones, as borders of annual beds, in containers of flowering plants, and around lamp and mailbox posts with Petunias and Geraniums.

Did You Know?
Lamb's Ears, like so many silvery-foliaged plants, is a low-water-demand plant. Planted with others that need minimal moisture, they constitute a Xeriscape, a landscape area that needs less watering. Gardeners in Pennsylvania are acutely aware that the availability of water is an important issue. Designating areas for low-water-demand plants in the home landscape (especially useful where the hose does not reach) conserves water.

Lamb's Ears generously blanket sunny, poor soil sites with narrow, perky silver-gray foliage that so resembles a bunny's ears that it begs to be stroked. Although this plant produces striking tall flower spikes, the foliage is more ornamental than the flowers. Lamb's Ears contributes a lot to a landscape, such as tenaciously gripping poor, thin soil to prevent erosion, adding texture and light to the scene, and filling hot spots where virtually nothing else will grow. A bonus is that it manages to survive the heat, the humidity, and the deer (usually not guaranteed!) that plague parts of Pennsylvania. 'Big Ears' has very large foliage and seems to handle heat and cold well. 'Big Betony' (Stachys grandiflora) has pretty violet flowers on tall spikes.

Other Name
Woolly Betony

Bloom Period and Seasonal Color
June; blooms in magenta, known for its fuzzy silvery foliage

Mature Height
8 in.; flower spikes to 15 in.

Lily-of-the-Valley
Convallaria majalis

Lily-of-the-Valley first seduces by its incredible fragrance, then when plantings spread, it proves itself as a tough, attractive ground cover. Perfect for woodland and other shady sites, it carpets the area with rich, broad, elongated green leaves rising from tiny bulblike stems called pips. After three years, the graceful, arching stems arrayed with tiny, nodding, waxy bell-shaped flowers appear each spring. Sheltered by the leaves, they infuse the area with fragrance for a week or two before fading away. Later in the summer the foliage ripens, yellowing and melting back to the ground. 'Fortin's Giant' has larger leaves and flowers. 'Rosea' has pink flowers; 'Flora Plena' has larger, double flowers. 'Striata' has white-striped foliage; 'Aurea-variegata' has yellow-striped foliage. Note: All parts of this plant are poisonous!

Bloom Period and Seasonal Color
May; blooms in white or pink. Some have striped yellow or green foliage

Mature Height
6 to 8 in.

When, Where, and How to Plant
Plant pips in the spring. Transplant plants in containers or divisions anytime. Lily-of-the-Valley tolerates poor soil, but prefers moist, woodsy, well-drained soil on the acid side. They tend to be invasive, so give these plants a shady bed of their own. Cultivate down 8 to 10 in. when spring soil warms and dries out a bit. Mix in granular slow-acting all-purpose fertilizer to provide nutrition for this first year. Set pips 1 to 2 in. deep, buds facing upward, spaced about 6 to 8 in. apart; cover them; water well. Mulch the soil to discourage weeds.

Growing Tips
Lily-of-the-Valley needs no care except possibly watering during a major drought. To encourage profuse flowering, use a sprinkling of slow-acting granular fertilizer on their soil each spring.

Care
In the spring dig up crowded clumps, and pull apart from them healthy-looking pips that have good roots and at least one bud. Replant them, and discard others. After their foliage dies back, clean it up, and set potted annuals in the bare spots. Handle any mite problems with a forceful spray of water or a spray of insecticidal soap.

Companion Planting and Design
Alone or among other shade lovers (even dry shade) such as Hostas, Lily-of-the-Valley is excellent for areas under trees where grass refuses to grow and near walls, especially when they have a northern exposure. Lily-of-the-Valley does well in containers such as patio planters and windowboxes as long as they are in the shade. Use flowers in bouquets with other dainty flowers that bloom about this time, such as Johnny Jump-ups, Creeping Phlox, Columbine, Pansies, and Sweet Woodruff.

Did You Know?
Lily-of-the-Valley Factoids:
• its fragrance is the essence of the perfume Joy,
• Christian tradition dedicated it to Mary, and it was also known as Ladder to Heaven and Virgin's Tears,
• it symbolized humility and chastity because the white flowers bow modestly,
• thus, it became a traditional part of brides' bouquets.

Lilyturf
Liriope spicata

When, Where, and How to Plant

Plant young plants or rooted divisions in the spring. Plant potted plants anytime during the growing season. Lilyturf prefers full sun, but tolerates light shade. It likes moist soil of almost any type that is rich in organic matter, but once established, it does fine in poorer, drier soil. Cultivate the soil down 8 to 10 in., and add a handful of a granular slow-acting fertilizer. Dig planting holes about as deep as and slightly wider than plant rootballs. Set each plant in its hole, its crown at soil level. Backfill, firming soil gently around plant stems, and water well. Set plants about 8 to 10 in. apart to allow for their spread.

Growing Tips

Water new beds regularly until the young plants are established. There is no need to encourage Lilyturf by annual fertilizing; it knows what to do.

Care

There is no need to cut off flower spikes because they are somewhat obscured by foliage. Leave foliage to provide winter cover. To make way for new shoots, mow it to about 2 or 3 in. when it gets ratty near springtime. Unless it is planted between paved walks, Lilyturf inevitably spreads beyond its bounds. Periodically dig up the encroaching plants, and replant elsewhere. Lilyturf in particularly moist, acidic soil sometimes has slug problems. A few strategically placed shallow plates of beer or baker's yeast in water will attract the slugs, and they will drown. Empty and refill traps often, especially after a rain.

Companion Planting and Design

Lilyturf's uniform foliage makes a neat appearance, especially on banks where erosion control is needed or under trees where grass will not grow.

Did You Know?

Mondo Grass (*Ophiopogon* spp.) is often mistaken for Lilyturf because its foliage is so similar. Various types grow in clumps of green straplike leaves from the dwarf, 2-in. 'Compactus' to others 18 in. tall. 'Ebony Knight' (*O. nigrescens*) has blackish foliage.

This is one tough ground cover. Lilyturf does a wonderful job covering large areas with a sea of neat, dark-green, grassy foliage, resembling dark, overlong turfgrass. It spreads by underground roots and runners and needs a controlling hand from the outset to direct and restrain its energy. Often, its late-summer flower spikes are barely visible above the arching leaves, so they cannot be counted upon for ornamental interest. The small, dark berries that subsequently appear are inconspicuous. Blue Lilyturf (Liriope muscari) forms well-behaved clumps of narrow, straplike foliage. Lilyturf may be green, or green variegated with yellow, or silver variegated such as 'Silvery Sunproof'. Its flower spikes rise above the foliage and are useful as cut flowers. 'Big Blue' has lilac-blue flowers.

Other Name
Creeping Lilyturf

Bloom Period and Seasonal Color
August; blooms in lilac to white

Mature Height
8 to 12 in.

Moneywort

Lysimachia nummularia 'Aurea'

The more sun, the brighter the yellow foliage on this little creeper. Moneywort usually has green leaves, but those on 'Aurea' are much more striking in shades of chartreuse to bright gold. Moneywort's flat, creeping stems root frequently at nodes where their coin-shaped leaves grow. They proceed to insinuate themselves between stems of larger plants in beds forming a golden living mulch. Stems encroach onto the lawn like rivulets of melted butter but are easy to lift and snip off. In the summer tiny flowers bloom on threadlike stalks at leaf nodes, visible only to the close observer. Moneywort can take some foot traffic now and then. It will also grow in a pot sunk into a pond or decorative water-filled container.

Other Name
Creeping Jenny

Bloom Period and Seasonal Color
Early summer; blooms in yellow

Mature Height
1 to 2 in.

When, Where, and How to Plant
Plant young plants or rooted cuttings anytime during the growing season. Plant on an overcast day or in the evening to minimize stress. Moneywort does equally well in any type of average soil, including boggy pond edges. Dig the soil down 4 to 6 in. If it is poor and thin, mix in organic matter to improve its texture and some granular slow-acting fertilizer to help new transplants establish over their first season. Create an indentation in the loose soil the dimensions of plant rootballs. Set plants so that each crown is level with the soil surface. Press soil over plant roots, and water. Space plants 8 to 10 in. apart.

Growing Tips
Water Moneywort well until it starts sending out new stems. Then water only during periods of drought. Do not fertilize further beyond what was provided at planting time.

Care
Monitor its progress overland, and clip off overambitious stems when necessary. If they have roots, press them into soil elsewhere to start new ground cover patches. Moneywort has no significant pest or disease problems.

Companion Planting and Design
Moneywort is wonderful for rock gardens, spaces between patio stones, edging, and containers. This golden plant was available just in time to jump on the chartreuse-and-maroon color combo bandwagon in garden design. It looks great with the purple foliage of Bugleweed (*Ajuga reptans*) or black Mondo Grass. It echoes the yellow-green variegation in the foliage of many Coleus varieties that can be planted nearby.

Did You Know?
Why do otherwise charming plants so often have such unlovely common names? Mugwort, Barrenwort, Liverwort, Moneywort . . . Well, many common names were bestowed in England during medieval times when the vernacular was Middle English (Latin being the language of the educated scholars). *Wort* was an Anglo-Saxon four-letter word for "plant." Typically, plants were named for some particular physical trait or use, and then wort was attached to that word. Thus "Moneywort" because its foliage resembles coins.

Ostrich Fern
Matteuccia struthiopteris

When, Where, and How to Plant
Plant offshoots in the spring, or transplant potted plants anytime during the growing season as long as it is not too hot and dry. Plant when the sun is not out. Ostrich Fern tolerates some sun, but it prefers shade. It likes damp, woodsy soil, but it does fine in ordinary garden soil if provided with year-round moisture. Loosen soil down 1 ft., and add organic matter. Dig holes about as deep as and slightly wider than plant rootballs, 3 ft. apart. Keeping as much moist soil around roots as possible, set each plant so that its rhizome is oriented horizontally, but with its growth tip almost vertical. Backfill, firming soil gently around the growing tip of the rhizome. Trim broken fronds, and mulch.

Growing Tips
Brown frond tips signal thirst. Water during dry periods in the summer. Do not worry about overdoing. It takes two seasons for Ostrich Ferns to establish. They do not need supplemental fertilizer.

Care
Leave dead fronds to mulch plants over the winter. Clean them up in the spring. Harvest small offshoot plants to control the spread of the ground cover planting and to minimize crowding. Ostrich Ferns are virtually pest free.

Companion Planting and Design
Ostrich Ferns make a stunning foundation planting near buildings. Use them to line driveways, to hold sloping creek banks, to be a woodland understory, and to effect a transition from the landscape to the woods.

Did You Know?
In the spring, the new, young fronds of Ostrich Ferns are edible. Collect them when they are only 2 or 3 in. tall and tightly furled. Store them in a plastic bag in the refrigerator until you accumulate enough. Then wash off their scaly tan coating, and boil them for three or four minutes. Drain and serve hot as a vegetable or in broth as a soup, cold in a salad, or with a dip.

There is a good reason why Ostrich Fern is the most widely used Fern in residential landscapes. A moderately-slow spreader by means of rhizomes, it has a unique clumping habit because the rhizome rests somewhat vertically in the soil. The stately dark-green, slightly leathery fronds grow in a vase shape from its upper tip, which constitutes a crown. They appear a bit later than those of other types of Ferns and are followed by new, shorter fertile fronds in late summer. Their undersides covered with spores, these fronds eventually dry and turn brown, persisting all winter before discharging their spores. During the growing season, subsidiary plants pop up 1 or 2 ft. from the mother plant from runners that issue in all directions from each rhizome.

Other Name
Shuttlecock Fern

Bloom Period and Seasonal Color
Deciduous; medium- to dark-green lacy fronds

Mature Height
4 to 6 ft.

Pachysandra
Pachysandra terminalis

Whoever coined the term low-maintenance ground cover *had to be thinking of good old Pachysandra. It is everywhere, and there is a reason for that. It is versatile, neat, evergreen, and easily disciplined. Furthermore, its flowers support honeybees and other beneficial insects. Pachysandra knits rapidly by underground roots into wide patches. In only one or two years it creates an effective year-round ground cover, even accommodating shallow tree roots. In winter its foliage tends to flop and fade to yellowish, but it recovers nicely every spring. More upright, 'Green Carpet' grows closer to the soil and sports glossy, deep-green leaves. 'Green Sheen' has truly shiny foliage. Leaves of the less vigorous 'Variegata' or 'Silver Edge' are edged with white and show best in shade.*

Other Name
Japanese Spurge

Bloom Period and Seasonal Color
April; blooms in off-white, known for foliage

Mature Height
6 to 10 in.

When, Where, and How to Plant
Plant in spring or summer if it is not too hot and dry. Pachysandra can handle bright light or sun, but prefers light to medium shade. Provide it with well-drained, moist, woodsy soil. Dig soil down 8 to 10 in., mixing in organic material to promote drainage. Add granular slow-acting fertilizer. Dig holes 5 to 10 in. apart and as deep as plant roots. Set each plant so that its crown is at soil level. Backfill and firm soil around plants, and water well. Transplant large mats by pulling them up gently, roots intact, and laying the entire mat in a prepared trench. Press loose soil in and among roots, and water well.

Growing Tips
Pachysandra does fine pretty much on its own. Once established it needs water only in severe drought. Do not fertilize further. Allow fallen leaves to provide a necessary mulch layer.

Care
Rejuvenate established patches every few years in spring. Shear plants by mowing them, with the mower blade on its highest setting. Top-dress the bed with organic material or slow-acting fertilizer, and water well. Yellowish foliage may mean Pachysandra is getting too much light. In winter, exposure to sun may burn the foliage. It is vulnerable to a fungus that causes dark blotches on leaves. Cut off the infected leaves and stems, and throw them in the trash.

Companion Planting and Design
Use this well-behaved ground cover to mask the ripening foliage of bulbs planted throughout the area. Pachysandra's foliage sets off the stunning flowers of Azaleas, Rhododendrons, Lilac, and Spirea. This plant makes an excellent living mulch in shade or on a steep bank where mowing is dangerous.

Did You Know?
Allegheny Spurge (*Pachysandra procumbens*) is our native Pachysandra. It has duller, slightly puckered gray-green foliage. Slow growing, it is semi-evergreen in warmer regions of Pennsylvania, the leaves becoming tinged with red in the fall. Frost mottles it with silver. Showy flowers emerge in spring. It prefers shade. It has no pests or diseases.

When, Where, and How to Plant

Plant in spring before the summer becomes too hot and dry. Sweet Woodruff does best in partial shade or areas that receive just a little sun each day. It prefers moist, well-drained soil rich in organic matter. Cultivate the soil down 8 to 10 in., and add organic matter if necessary. Sprinkle granular slow-acting fertilizer to provide season-long nutrition for transplants. Dig planting holes deep and wide enough to accommodate plant root systems. Set plants at the same depth they were in pots or flats. Backfill, firm soil gently around each plant, and water well. Space plants 6 to 10 in. apart.

Growing Tips

Water newly planted patches if rainfall is scarce to help them through their first season. Keep moist well into summer to delay decline. No further fertilizing is necessary.

Care

As the summer progresses, stems elongate and flop. Shear foliage back to 2 or 3 in. to extend its attractiveness. Rake up dead foliage in fall, and spread 1 or 2 in. of chopped leaves over the beds as winter mulch. If Sweet Woodruff spreads beyond its allotted space, slice the soil with a spade to sever the wiry roots, and pull up extra growth. It is pest and disease free.

Companion Planting and Design

Sweet Woodruff does well in windowboxes and planters where there is not too much sun. Use it is a living mulch under shallow-rooted shrubs such as Azaleas and Rhododendrons. Its foliage provides a wonderful backdrop for spring bulbs, and it gets along well with Ferns and Hostas, which like similar conditions.

Did You Know?

Sweet Woodruff flowers play a modest role in the culinary world as a flavoring in May wine. In Germany they prepare and consume *Maiwein* to observe May Day. They add flowering sprigs of Waldmeister (Sweet Woodruff) to wine, allow it to steep awhile, then drink up to celebrate the arrival of May.

The name Sweet Woodruff suggests all the nice things about this ground cover. It is tidy, dainty, and deer resistant. In the spring its stems are arrayed with whorls of fine-textured, deeply cut foliage and topped by delicate white, lightly scented flowers. Dried, they are described as vaguely vanilla or hay scented. Throughout the first part of the summer, Sweet Woodruff moves quickly by means of shallow, fibrous roots to cover any and every available area of bare soil. It combines well with shallow-rooted trees because its matrix of fine roots forms just below the soil surface. In very hot, dry summers the foliage tends to melt away. It is easy to pull up mats of Sweet Woodruff to control its spread or replant elsewhere.

Other Name

May Flower

Bloom Period and Seasonal Color

May; blooms in white

Mature Height

6 to 8 in.

Vinca
Vinca minor

Vinca is on everyone's list of reliable ground cover stand-bys. Its small, glossy, dark-green oval leaves have a refinement lacking in others. Its measured progression across the ground by means of gracefully arching low stems that root along the way sets it apart from other, coarser ground covers. Lovely blue five-petaled flowers punctuate Vinca plantings in spring. Energetic without being pushy, it is fairly common for a single plant to send out one hundred stems in early spring. Flowers last about a month. Vinca roots are so shallow that it is easy to pull up when it overreaches its allotted space. In recent years variegated forms of Vinca have become available, so that now it offers foliage color to its list of virtues. A good low-growing cultivar is 'Gertrude Jekyll' which has white flowers.

Other Name
Periwinkle

Bloom Period and Seasonal Color
April into May; blooms in lilac, purplish blue, or white; some have variegated foliage

Mature Height
6 to 8 in.

When, Where, and How to Plant
Plant rooted cuttings in spring or fall. Transplant potted plants anytime. The less light Vinca receives, the darker green its foliage, and the slower its growth. It accepts any type soil, preferring it to be woodsy and well drained. Loosen the soil down 8 to 10 in., and mix in granular slow-acting fertilizer for season-long nutrition. Dig holes as deep as and slightly wider than the plants' root systems, and set plants so that they are at soil level. Backfill and firm soil around them, and water well. Space plants from pots 1 ft. apart. Space smaller ones 6 to 8 in. apart. Mulch between them to control weeds.

Growing Tips
Water new plantings during the first year if rain is scarce. Once established, Vinca is amazingly drought resistant. It does not need supplemental fertilizer.

Care
Snip off trailing stems that overstep their bounds. To encourage density, clip stems back to about 4 in. in early spring. Mow or shear the bed every few years to revitalize the planting. Spread compost or other organic material over the stubby plants and exposed soil, and water well. Vinca has no significant pest or disease problems.

Companion Planting and Design
Vinca sets off minor bulbs such as Crocus, Snowdrops, Squill, and Snowflake, and then helps obscure their ripening foliage after they bloom. Then it blooms for a prolonged show. Vinca's handsome foliage and trailing stems look good in planters and hanging baskets.

Did You Know?
Q: When is a Vinca not a Vinca?
A: When it is a Madagascar Vinca!
Madagascar Vinca/Periwinkle (*Catharanthus roseus*) is a different plant altogether, but because its flowers and leaves resemble Vinca/Myrtle/Periwinkle (*Vinca minor*), it has acquired the same common name. It is tropical, however, so it is used as an annual in our state. It is more upright and bears flowers in white, red, or shades of pink. They bloom off and on over the season.

Wintercreeper
Euonymus fortunei

When, Where, and How to Plant
Plant rooted cuttings in spring. Transplant balled-and-burlapped or containerized stock anytime during the growing season when it is not too hot. Wintercreeper prefers partial shade, but it can handle shade. It makes do in almost any soil as long as it is not soggy. A hot, dry western exposure will stress it. Dig the soil to 1 ft.; add granular slow-acting all-purpose fertilizer and organic material if the soil lacks organic matter. Dig the hole exactly as deep as and slightly wider than the plant rootball. Set each transplant so that its crown is at or slightly above soil level. (If it is present, cut away all burlap you can reach.) Backfill, firm soil gently, and water well. Set plants about 2 ft. apart.

Growing Tips
In decent soil there is no need to fertilize once plants are established. This avoids excessive stem and leaf growth, which attracts aphids.

Care
Prune back unruly stems to keep plants neat and inbounds. Every few years shear Wintercreeper in spring by hand or by mowing at the highest mower setting. Severe wind chill may desiccate foliage in winter, so erect a low burlap screen to shelter it. Wintercreeper is vulnerable to scale (white specks) on its leaves and stems. Spray scale bumps with light (superior) horticultural oil in March, June, or September.

Companion Planting and Design
Long-lived and very hardy, Wintercreeper obscures utility boxes, rocks, and stumps. Its variegated versions brighten darker areas under trees and building eaves.

Did You Know?
Most introduced (non-native) garden plants were discovered in Europe and Asia by intrepid nineteenth-century botanists who trekked the wilderness in search of potentially desirable garden specimens. The efforts of these plant hunters are often memorialized in the names of the plants. *Euonymus fortunei* was brought back from China by Robert Fortune, as its name indicates.

Tough and versatile, this handsome shrub readily adapts to any situation. It opportunistically trails, tumbles, and climbs, depending on its site, by means of tiny rootlets that develop on its flexible stems. Over a season stems can grow 4 to 5 ft. Sometimes Wintercreeper morphs into a vine and crawls up walls and tree trunks that interrupt its horizontal progress. Like English Ivy, it has both a juvenile and a mature form. The latter flowers and bears fruits and is marked by a variety of leaf shapes. The fruits are orange-red capsules that are poisonous. Wintercreepers labeled Euonymus fortunei 'Coloratus' are especially well adapted to ground cover duty. Their deep-green foliage turns purple in the winter, and they are vigorous growers.

Other Name
Creeping Euonymus

Bloom Period and Seasonal Color
Evergreen; some with variegated foliage

Mature Height
8 to 12 in.

Perennials *for Pennsylvania*

Perennials are plants that bloom season after season. Technically, woody-stemmed trees and shrubs and hardy bulbs fit this definition, but the term *perennial* usually refers to herbaceous flowering plants. Their soft stems wither or dry and die back with frost, but their roots are cold hardy. They send up new stems the next spring when the weather warms.

Unlike annuals, which are programmed to produce copious flowers to make seed for next year in anticipation of sudden death at the end of the season, perennials pace their blooming and seed setting. They allow plenty of time over the summer for their foliage to collect energy from the sun and nutrition from the soil and build roots to support life the following season. Therein lies the big difference for gardeners. Because they have this larger agenda, perennial plants do not bloom very long. Integrating them into a garden bed means accepting that all they contribute to the scheme of things for much of the season is foliage.

For this reason gardening with perennial flowering plants is regarded as requiring more sophisticated knowledge than gardening with annuals. The interplay of foliage color and texture becomes almost as important as that of flower color, size, and height. Plants with variegated or unusually colored foliage are highly valued. Unusual plants become collectibles in an effort to enliven a perennial border that may be largely foliage a good bit of the time.

More or Less Work?

At the same time, gardening with perennials is sometimes regarded as easy when one thinks about the labor involved in digging and planting flowering annual plants every year. The perception is that perennials just pop up year after year, growing gratifyingly larger clumps to fill in the bed until, at some point, there is an automatic garden. The truth is that perennials require quite a bit of maintenance to look their best. Keeping them happy, therefore stress free, is also the best way to keep them healthy and beautiful.

Placing Perennials

Try to match up each plant's cultural needs with an appropriate site on your property to assure that it will be happy. Here is where an understanding of the specific environmental conditions in the various areas of your yard really helps. Every landscape actually has many different environments—called *microclimates*—where air flow, humidity, available light, reflected heat, and other conditions deviate from the prevailing conditions in most of the yard. Knowing the sheltered pockets of warmth, the boggy spots, or the shallow dips where frost persists helps you choose a spot that suits the needs of each individual plant. A struggle to adapt to inhospitable conditions takes a toll on a plant's vigor because the stress compromises the ability to fend off the insects and diseases that plants are heir to.

Soil Is the Key

While planting in the right place is fundamentally important, good soil is the key to perennial happiness ever after. Yet it is difficult to work the soil to maintain the drainage, organic content, and nutrients that most plants desire where the plants are always in the way. Some perennials such as Peonies and Hostas do not need to be divided and moved and are often resident for decades.

Mulching perennial beds year-round with organic matter such as chopped leaves or compost is the best way to improve and protect the soil over time. Mulch protects its surface from compaction from hard rains and harsh sun. It retards evaporation of its moisture, too. As it continually decomposes, organic mulch introduces chunky, spongy organic particles into the upper levels of the soil, which maintain its texture by creating air spaces and storing moisture. The microbial organisms that accompany the organic matter into the soil convert its nutrients into a form that plant roots can absorb. As the saying goes, "Take care of the soil, and it will take care of your plants."

Keeping perennials happy takes time and skill. The following plant entries prescribe mulching, fertilizing, and watering as well as pruning tailored to each plant's particular nature, staking for support, and dividing when they become too big. Because each plant responds to slightly different approaches to these tasks, experience plays a part in getting it right in each case. Fortunately, plants are forgiving, learning is fun, and next year provides another chance for the gardener.

Artemisia
Artemisia species and hybrids

Every yard needs silver foliage to punctuate the green and set off individual plants and their flowers. For this reason, members of the large clan of Artemisias are important to a garden. Although they bear deep-yellow, buttonlike flowers, it is their foliage that is ornamental. Artemisias feature fine-textured, silvery or gray-green leaves, which are sometimes slightly woolly. Some plants are a bit shrubby, the base of their stems becoming woody over the season. Their foliage and stems have a distinctive resinous or medicinal smell, likely the reason why they have virtually no pests—not even deer. Silver Mound Wormwood (Artemisia schmidtiana 'Silver Mound') is fine textured and only 12 in. tall. White Sage (Artemisia ludoviciana) 'Silver King' and 'Silver Queen' grow 2 to 3 ft. tall.

Other Name
Wormwood

Bloom Period and Seasonal Color
August to October; silver foliage, yellow blooms

Mature Height × Spread
12 to 36 in. × 12 to 36 in.

When, Where, and How to Plant
Plant divisions in spring or fall. Transplant potted plants anytime during the season. Artemisias require good sun and average, well-drained soil. (Soils that are sandy or gravelly, as in a rock garden, are ideal.) They can tolerate alkaline soils. Dig the soil down 10 to 12 in., and mix in organic matter to improve drainage. Dig holes about as deep as and slightly wider than plant rootballs, and set each in its hole so that its top is level with or a bit higher than the surrounding ground. Backfill, then firm soil gently, and water well. Space plants 18 in. apart for good air circulation and room to grow.

Growing Tips
If rain is scarce, water newly planted Artemisias until they put out new growth. Once established they will be quite drought tolerant. Avoid frequent watering and heavy mulch which promote rot. Fertilizing or rich soil makes stems floppy.

Care
Pinch stem tips to encourage denser growth as transplants grow. Most Artemisias respond enthusiastically to a more severe cutback to about half their height in June to assure compactness. Do not cut back to where stems are woody and have no leaf buds. Unless the flowers are useful, cut them off to keep foliage looking its best. Stake tall Artemisias. Divide overlarge clumps in the fall. Artemisias have no pests.

Companion Planting and Design
Artemisias start the season by obscuring ripening bulb foliage and are still present to set off Chrysanthemums in the fall. They do well in containers with good drainage; containers are perfect for the rampant spreader 'Silver King'.

Did You Know?
French Tarragon (*Artemisia dracunculus* 'Sativa') is an edible Artemisia. Its narrow foliage has a slight Anise flavor with a touch of sweetness and is useful in vinegars, soups, marinades, and sauces (it is the star of Bearnaise sauce). Crumbled fresh or dried, its leaves enhance roasted chicken, fish, and salads. A little goes a long way.

When, Where, and How to Plant

Plant divisions in the spring. Transplant potted plants anytime during the growing season. To minimize transplant shock, plant on an overcast day or in the evening. Asters prefer full sun. They accept almost any type of soil of average fertility as long as it is moist and well drained. Cultivate the soil down 12 in., and mix in a handful of a granular slow-acting all-purpose fertilizer. Dig the hole as deep as and slightly wider than the rootball. Set the rootball so that its top is level with the surrounding ground. Backfill, firm soil around plant stems, and water well. Set plants about 2 ft. apart.

Growing Tips

Water transplants if rain is scarce. Spread a 2- or 3-in. layer of organic mulch on the soil to discourage weeds and maintain soil moisture. There is no need to fertilize Asters in decent soil that is mulched year-round. Too much nitrogen promotes excessive foliage growth and floppy stems.

Care

Pinch stem tips of tall New England Asters from June to late July to reduce legginess. Unpinched plants or those in shade (which makes them grow taller to reach light) will definitely need staking. Cut plants to the ground after blooming to prevent seeding. Divide overlarge clumps after a few years. Asters may develop mildew or rust in humid weather. Thin out crowded stems, and divide overlarge clumps to promote good air circulation. Asters have no significant insect pests.

Companion Planting and Design

Use Asters with other seasonal plants such as Goldenrod, Chrysanthemums, and fall-blooming bulbs in borders or as edging, or naturalize them in fields.

Did You Know?

In the Victorian language of flowers, Asters, or Michaelmas Daisies, represented "afterthought" because they bloom so late. They are named for St. Michael's Day, which falls on September 29, relatively late in the season for flowering plants. The Michaelmas Daisy has charmingly come to symbolize "cheerfulness in old age."

For the best fall garden, look to nature. Out in the fields and along the roadsides are billows of tall wild Asters and their Goldenrod companions smothered in butterflies. Long-blooming and self-reliant, native Asters such as the New England and New York ones offer small, colorful daisylike flowers that come on strong just when summer annuals are giving up. Now that hybridizers have tamed their weedy look, these tough, colorful plants attractively hold the fort in the garden until frost. New England Aster (Aster novae-angliae) 'Purple Dome' makes a 2-ft. mound of semi-double, purple flowers, and 'Alma Potschke' is hot pink at 3 to 4 ft. tall. New York Aster (Aster novi-belgii) dwarfs are 'Jenny' (red) and 'Professor Kippenburg' (lilac-blue).

Other Name
Native Aster

Bloom Period and Seasonal Color
August to October; blooms in white, pink, or purple

Mature Height × Spread
2 to 6 ft. × 2 to 3 ft.

Astilbe

Astilbe × arendsii

Astilbes are summer bloomers, providing color in the garden long after the riotous spring-flowering season has passed. The ferny texture of their finely cut, green or somewhat bronze leaves creates a slightly blowzy, informal effect. Astilbes' main appeal is their flexible, dense plumes of small florets at the tips of their upright stems. In many colors and sizes, Astilbes are available for almost every home landscape situation. Several types have been hybridized to produce dozens of excellent garden plants: 'Deutschland' (white), 'Fanal' (red), 'Peach Blossom' (pale pink), and 'Rheinland' (pink). Fall Astilbe (Astilbe chinensis var. taquetii 'Superba') grows to 4 or more ft. and has purplish blooms later in the summer; Sprite Astilbe (Astilbe simplicifolia 'Sprite') is 1 ft. tall and blooms in midsummer.

Other Name
False Spirea

Bloom Period and Seasonal Color
Late June to early July; blooms in white, pink, lavender, peach, or red

Mature Height × Spread
1 to 4 ft. × 1 to 2 ft.

When, Where, and How to Plant
Plant divisions in spring or fall. Transplant potted plants anytime during the season. Astilbes prefer indirect light or dappled shade. They can take full sun only if their soil is constantly moist as in a stream-side situation. They do best if the soil is also rich in organic matter and slightly acid. Shallow-rooted, they are very sensitive to drought conditions. Loosen the soil down 12 in., and dig in organic matter plus a handful of a granular slow-acting all-purpose fertilizer to sustain them all season. Dig a hole about as deep as and slightly wider than the rootball. Set the rootball so that its surface is exactly level with the surrounding ground. Backfill, firm soil around the plant, and water well. Space plants about 2 ft. apart.

Growing Tips
Mulch soil around transplants to keep it moist and rich. Water regularly, especially in summer, whenever rainfall is scarce. Fertilize every spring with a granular slow-acting lawn fertilizer that is rich in nitrogen.

Care
If their soil dries out, Astilbes shrivel and quit for the season. Cutting off browned foliage may generate a flush of green when moisture is available later. After frost, leave dead foliage to provide winter protection, then cut it back in spring. Divide Astilbes every three or four years either after flowering or in the spring. They occasionally develop harmless mildew on their foliage.

Companion Planting and Design
Astilbes brighten shady woodland areas. They are dependable, attractive background and filler plants for a border. Dwarf Chinese Astilbe (*Astilbe chinensis* 'Pumila') blooms midsummer and has thick ferny foliage for a great ground cover.

Did You Know?
Goat's Beard (*Aruncus dioicus*) resembles a giant Astilbe and likes the same growing conditions. A shrublike 4 to 6 ft. tall plant, it bears plumes of tiny, creamy-white florets earlier in the summer. It has a more commanding presence than an Astilbe. Use it as a specimen in a partially shady site.

Baby's Breath
Gypsophila paniculata

When, Where, and How to Plant

Transplant potted plants anytime during the growing season. Baby's Breath likes full sun and average garden soil that is not too rich in organic matter and is on the alkaline side. Soil must drain well. Sandy soil is fine. Choose the site well because Baby's Breath roots resent being moved once they are established. Loosen the soil down 8 to 10 in. Add coarse sand to improve drainage if necessary. Dig a hole about as deep as and slightly wider than the rootball. Set it in the hole so that the top of its rootball is exactly at soil level. Backfill, then firm the soil gently around the plant, and water well. Space plants 2 to 3 ft. apart.

Growing Tips

In Pennsylvania where soil is typically on the acid side, add lime in the fall or wood ashes in the spring to raise the soil pH a bit. Water when rainfall is scarce. There is no need for more fertilizer.

Care

Cut off branches when their flowers brown to stimulate renewed flowering and compactness. Stake Baby's Breath that has not been cut back. A thin mulch will control weeds and keep dirt from splashing onto the flowers. Do not pile it against the crown and stems. Baby's Breath does not divide well. Avoid possible crown, root, and stem rot problems with well-drained soil.

Companion Planting and Design

Use Baby's Breath as a filler or as a foil to coarser, green-foliaged plants in a border or even rock gardens. Pink-flowered types harmonize with silver- or gray-leafed plants such as Lamb's Ears and Artemisias. Try it at the front of a border as a see-through plant.

Did You Know?

To air dry Baby's Breath, pick stems when flowers have just reached their peak. Strip off the leaves. Fasten several together with a rubber band, and hang them upside down in a warm, dry, ventilated room. When stems become brittle and break easily, they are dry. Spritz flowers with hair spray to preserve their petals.

Baby's Breath is full of contradictions. Its dainty appearance belies a hardy, versatile character. It is airy and insubstantial, yet it achieves the size of a small shrub. Its flowers are tiny, yet they bloom for several weeks and make a distinct impact on the landscape. Baby's Breath foliage is inconspicuous, its leaves resembling tiny Carnation leaves—linear and gray-green. They are easily overlooked on the wiry, branching stems because of the galaxy of tiny, round, white florets that cover their tips. Examples of Baby's Breath are 'Bristol Fairy' (white), 'Pink Fairy' (pink), 'Flamingo' (mauve), and 'Perfecta' (white). Creeping Baby's Breath (Gypsophila repens) is dwarf, at 6 in. tall. Annual Baby's Breath (Gypsophila elegans) looks similar but is short-lived, blooming only six weeks.

Other Name
Perennial Baby's Breath

Bloom Period and Seasonal Color
June to August; blooms in white,or pink

Mature Height × Spread
2 to 3 ft. × 3 to 4 ft.

91

Bee Balm
Monarda didyma

An Eastern native, Bee Balm is at home in both herb gardens and perennial borders. Wherever it is, butterflies and hummingbirds have no trouble finding its brightly colored mophead flowers, which are actually rounded whorls of droopy tubular florets gracing the tops of square stems. Bee Balm's leaves are on the coarse side, with fuzzy undersides, and they smell like Mint when crushed. Bee Balm is not as invasive as Mint, but it is a bit pushy, especially in optimum conditions. Examples include 'Cambridge Scarlet' (red), 'Croftway Pink' and 'Marshall's Delight' (pink), 'Snow Queen' (white), and 'Mahogany' (deep red). 'Marshall's Delight' and 'Jacob Kline' show some mildew resistance. Wild Bergamot (Monarda fistulosa) is native to Pennsylvania; it can handle drier, poorer soil.

Other Name
Bergamot

Bloom Period and Seasonal Color
Late June through July; blooms in pink, red, lavender, and white

Mature Height × Spread
2 to 4 ft. × spreading

When, Where, and How to Plant
Plant rooted divisions in spring. Plant potted plants anytime during the growing season. Lavender- and white-flowered Bee Balms do best in full sun, but red-flowered varieties like some shade. They are not fussy about soil type as long as it is moist and well drained. Truly damp sites make their stems taller and floppier. Dig soil down 12 in., and mix in organic matter and granular slow-acting fertilizer. Dig the hole as deep as and a bit wider than the plant's rootball. Set it in the hole so that its top is level with the surrounding soil. Backfill, firm soil, and water well. Space plants about 2 or 3 ft. apart.

Growing Tips
Bee Balm's creeping roots are shallow, so water when rainfall is scarce. Maintain a layer of organic mulch over the soil to keep it moist. In mulched, decent soil Bee Balm will not need further fertilizing.

Care
Stake taller plants. Pinch young stems to encourage branching and more compact plants. Deadhead spent blossoms. After three or four years dig up large clumps, and replant chunks of healthy-rooted plants. Mildew sometimes coats foliage with an ugly, but not life-threatening gray film by midsummer. Cut back stems to the ground. Plants stressed by drier soil seem to have worse mildew problems.

Companion Planting and Design
Plant Bee Balm in natural settings in large drifts or groupings of several plants to make it more attractive to the honeybees that make delicious honey from it. Their weedy, coarse texture also suits informal settings such as fence rows and wildflower plots.

Did You Know?
Bee Balm provided a tea substitute during the colonial boycott of English tea. Today Bee Balm's flowers and foliage are recognized as a source of antioxidants. To make tea, crush $1/2$ cup fresh or $1/4$ cup dried leaves, add to regular tea in a bag or teaball, and steep in boiling water up to five minutes.

Black-Eyed Susan
Rudbeckia fulgida var. *sullivantii* 'Goldsturm'

When, Where, and How to Plant
Plant rooted divisions in spring or fall. Transplant container plants anytime during the growing season. Though they can handle some shade, Black-eyed Susans prefer full sun. They accept any average well-drained soil. Once established, they are fairly drought tolerant, especially if their soil is rich in organic matter that holds moisture. Dig soil down 12 in. Mix in organic material especially if it is clay. Add granular slow-acting all-purpose fertilizer. Dig the hole about as deep as and slightly wider than the rootball. Set the rootball so that its surface is level with the surrounding ground. Backfill, firm soil gently, and water well. Plant in groups of three, about 2 ft. apart.

Growing Tips
Mulch to discourage weeds and help the soil retain moisture while plants get established. Mulched plants do not need routine fertilizing. Water transplants during droughty periods. Mature Black-eyed Susans can handle some drought.

Care
Stake large clumps vulnerable to heavy rainstorms. Either deadhead to prevent seeding, or leave spent flowers for birds. Cut back dead stems after frost, and spread a winter mulch over the area. Divide clumps every three or four years in spring or fall. Dig up a clump, and cut off several smaller-rooted chunks to replant. Black-eyed Susans may seed themselves and turn up anywhere around the yard. 'Goldsturm' has no pests or diseases.

Companion Planting and Design
Black-eyed Susans' informal look combines well with other meadow plants such as ornamental grasses, Goldenrod, Purple Coneflower, and Wild Asters. They brighten semi-shady areas and are well mannered enough for the flower border.

Did You Know?
Gaudy Gloriosa Daisies (*Rudbeckia hirta*) are also called Black-eyed Susans. Noted for their huge 5- to 9-in.-wide yellow daisy flowers splashed with red, they bloom all summer as typical annuals. 'Indian Summer' has semi-double flowers. 'Sonora' has a wide band of mahogany across its gold petals. 'Green Eyes' has green centers. 'Toto' is a compact dwarf.

'Goldsturm' Black-eyed Susan, the glory of summer gardens, is a cousin of the native annual of the fields and farms of the Eastern United States. It blooms beautifully over a long period with virtually no maintenance. Who could not love the classic daisylike flower with ray petals of rich yellow that ring its dark "eye"? Each literally glows at the tips of heavily branching stiff stems above mounds of coarse dark-green leaves, blooming dependably, regardless of what kind of summer weather has transpired. Allowed to mature, their petals fade and their centers swell as seeds develop and become a magnet for goldfinches. 'Goldquelle' has double, paler-yellow flowers and grows only to 3 ft. tall. It is a cultivar of R. laciniata. Ragged Coneflower (Rudbeckia laciniata) is 6 ft. tall; it is droopy petaled; its yellow flowers have green centers.

Other Name
Orange Coneflower

Bloom Period and Seasonal Color
July through September; blooms in golden-yellow

Mature Height × Spread
2 to 3 ft. × 2 ft.

Blazing Star

Liatris spicata

Native Blazing Star is becoming increasingly popular for many reasons, not the least of which is the colorful vertical accent it provides in the flower border. Beginning as tufts of narrow, grassy leaves, this plant responds to hot July temperatures by producing a flower spike from each tuft. The fifty or so little fuzzy florets arrayed along the spike open gradually from the top of the spike downward, creating a bottlebrush likely to be covered with butterflies on sunny days. The seedheads provide winter interest and attract birds. 'Kobold' has deep-rosy-purple flowers and is a bit more compact. Suited to beds and borders, it is the most satisfactory Blazing Star for the garden. 'Floristan White' has cream-colored flowers and grows to 3 ft.

Other Name
Spike Gayfeather

Bloom Period and Seasonal Color
July and August; blooms in mauve, purple, or white

Mature Height × Spread
2 to 3 ft. × 2 ft.

When, Where, and How to Plant
Transplant Blazing Star grown in containers into the garden anytime during the growing season. Plant corms (roots) or divisions in spring. Plants prefer full sun. Ordinary moist, well-drained soil is fine. They hate soggy winter soil. Because their tuberous roots store moisture, they can handle heat and a degree of drought. Loosen soil down 12 in., digging in organic material to improve drainage. Plant corms 2 in. deep and 1 to 2 ft. apart. Dig holes for potted plants as deep as and slightly wider than their containers. Set each in the hole so that its crown is at soil level. Backfill, firm soil gently to remove air pockets, then water well. Space plants 2 ft. apart.

Growing Tips
In good soil Blazing Star does not need routine fertilizing. In fact, a rich diet makes the flower stems floppy, and they will need staking. Water them during prolonged dry periods.

Care
Cutting back flower spikes to the basal foliage after 3/4 of the florets have died may promote rebloom in September. Do not cut back foliage until it is brown and dead. Dig and divide overlarge clumps and corms every four years. Blazing Stars have no significant pests or diseases. Foliage may show powdery mildew late in the summer. Thin plants to improve air circulation.

Companion Planting and Design
Blazing Star's rose colors are most compatible with plants which have blue-based, lilac, or magenta flowers, or those in yellow tones, such as its meadow neighbors wild Black-eyed Susans, Goldenrod, Coneflowers, Bee Balms, and Shasta Daisies. Ornamental grasses make good neighbors as well.

Did You Know?
Blazing Star is another example of how our native plants are often overlooked at home and are appreciated only after enthusiastic Europeans adopt them, improve them, and reintroduce them to the United States. Blazing Star became a staple of the florist industry abroad. Only recently have American gardeners embraced this sturdy plant that has been under their noses all along.

Bleeding Heart
Dicentra spectabilis

When, Where, and How to Plant

Transplant potted plants in spring. Plant roots in spring or fall. Plant divisions after their leaves die back in late summer or fall. Bleeding Heart can take some bright, indirect morning light, but the more shade they get, the longer they last. They are woodland dwellers that need to be sheltered from wind; they like acidic woodsy soil, moist, rich in organic matter, and well drained. Loosen the soil down 12 in., simultaneously mixing in organic matter. Add a bit of granular slow-acting all-purpose fertilizer. Dig the hole as deep as and slightly wider than the rootball. Set it in the hole so that the soil at the top of the rootball is level with the surrounding ground. Plant packaged roots at the depth suggested on the label. Backfill, firm soil gently, and water well. Space plants 2 ft. apart.

Growing Tips

Water transplants if spring rains are sparse. Spread a 2- or 3-in. layer of organic mulch to keep the soil cool and moist. Provide Bleeding Hearts with some granular slow-acting fertilizer every spring.

Care

Clean up yellowed, ripened foliage when it collapses on the ground. After several years dig up the fleshy, brittle roots of overlarge dormant clumps. Divide into chunks, each with a growing bud or "eye." Then replant. If slugs attack foliage, temporarily remove mulch.

Companion Planting and Design

Bleeding Heart looks great with Hostas and Ferns, spring bulbs, and other ground covers such as Sweet Woodruff.

Did You Know?

Many garden plants are unable to cope with heat and droughtlike conditions. Paradoxically, they often come from regions where this climate is the norm. They have adapted to it by developing the capacity for storing moisture to tide them over until temperatures cool. Common Bleeding Heart has deep tuberous roots, which soak up water and nutrients during the spring. Then when harsh summer weather approaches, it dies back and rests underground until next spring.

This gentle woodland charmer evokes fascination and delight each spring from even the most experienced gardener. It is impossible to take these graceful, ephemeral plants for granted. Bleeding Heart plants send up shiny, reddish shoots that become deeply cut, fragile, light bluish green foliage. Then arching, leafless stems emerge, their tips drooping with the weight of a row of exotic heart-shaped, deep-pink lockets. These namesake flowers form pale, droplet-shaped petals at their lower tip, which look for all the world like teardrops. Bleeding Heart foliage browns, withers, and melts away after flowering as temperatures rise, choosing to go dormant rather than face summer. Fringed Bleeding Heart (Dicentra eximia) is native to Pennsylvania and is more compact. It seeds readily and blooms dependably all season.

Other Name
Lyre Flower

Bloom Period and Seasonal Color
April and May; blooms in pink or white

Mature Height × Spread
2 to 3 ft. × 3 ft.

Candytuft
Iberis sempervirens

Candytuft is amazingly low maintenance, its Mediterranean ancestry having accustomed it to heat and drought. Its soft, needled evergreen foliage lines its flexible stems, creating a dark-green backdrop for the domed clusters of white florets that bloom at their tips. Planted along walls and allowed to grow extended stems, Candytuft will spill over to soften their edges. Because it is long-lived and slow-growing, Candytuft brightens the yard for many seasons as long as there are no deer visitors. 'Alexander's White' blooms earliest. 'Autumn Beauty' flowers in the fall, too. 'Snowflake' grows up to 10 in. tall with larger, brilliant-white flowers and larger leaves. 'Little Gem' is upright, bushy, and dwarf at 6 in. tall. Annual Candytuft (Iberis umbellata) blooms in pink, white, or lilac all summer.

Other Name
Evergreen Candytuft

Bloom Period and Seasonal Color
Late May; blooms in white

Mature Height × Spread
8 to 10 in. × indefinite

When, Where, and How to Plant
Plant rooted divisions in spring or fall. Transplant potted plants anytime during the growing season. Candytuft likes full sun. It does fine in any well-drained ordinary soil. Choose the site carefully; Candytuft is not crazy about being moved. Dig the soil down 8 to 10 in. Mix in organic material to improve drainage, and add granular slow-acting all-purpose fertilizer for season-long nutrition. Dig each hole as deep as and slightly wider than the plant rootball. Set it in the hole so that the rootball surface is level with or slightly above the surrounding soil. Backfill, firm soil gently, and water well. Space plants 1 ft. apart.

Growing Tips
Water transplants if rainfall is sparse. Once it is established, there is no need to fertilize Candytuft. A rich diet makes the stems limp and floppy.

Care
Clip off only winter-damaged or semi-bare stems in early spring prior to flowering. After spring flowering, shear all stems back to half their height. This limits their tendency to sprawl and get woody, and encourages repeat fall bloom. Lay evergreen boughs over Candytuft to shield evergreen foliage from winter sunburn and its buds from tip dieback. Candytuft occasionally suffers from humidity and poor air circulation, which cause a fungal rot in the summer. Sometimes slugs bother it.

Companion Planting and Design
It is often massed as a ground cover, yet Candytuft's tidy habit and tough constitution suit it equally well to a flower border or rock garden. Use Candytuft for edging or as fillers for containers. It is a good companion for Bleeding Heart, Creeping Phlox, and small bulbs.

Did You Know?
Embedded in their botanical names, and sometimes in their common names, are all kinds of information useful in identifying plants. For instance, *Iberis* means "Iberia," as in the Iberian Peninsula of Spain and Portugal whose classic Mediterranean climate is Candytuft's favorite. *Sempervirens* means "always green," or "evergreen," referring to its foliage.

Columbine
Aquilegia species and hybrids

When, Where, and How to Plant
Transplant potted plants in spring. Columbines develop deep taproots and are difficult to transplant unless they are young or dormant in the fall or early spring. They like sun, but flowering lasts longer in light shade. They are not fussy about soil as long as it is moist and well drained. Soggy soil promotes rot. Cultivate soil down 8 to 10 in. Add organic matter to heavy or clay soil to promote drainage. Mix in granular slow-acting fertilizer to sustain plants all season. Dig holes as deep as and slightly wider than plant rootballs. Set them level with the surrounding soil. Backfill, firm soil, and water well. Space tall Columbines 1 ft. apart, and dwarf types at 6 in. apart. Sow seeds as directed on seed packet.

Growing Tips
Water Columbine transplants during dry periods. Spread organic mulch to discourage weeds and keep soil moist. No further fertilizer is needed.

Care
Stake tall Columbines. Deadhead hybrid blooms before they can form and release seeds. Columbines have chronic problems with leafminers. Sometimes they develop powdery mildew. In both cases cut off infected leaves to stimulate new, healthy foliage. When Columbine foliage dies or is cut back in midsummer, plan for substitute plants in their garden space to finish the season.

Companion Planting and Design
Use dwarf Columbines in rock gardens. Grow others with Ferns, Hostas, grasses, and Sweet Woodruff. Columbines are short-lived but replace themselves constantly by reseeding, hybridizing freely into new color combinations. Their effect is delicate and airy, qualifying Columbine as a see-through plant, as at home near the front of the border as in the middle.

Did You Know?
Columbine represents "folly" in the Victorian language of flowers, probably because the nectaries within its flower structure resemble the pointed caps of medieval court jesters. In Latin *columba* means "dove." Early fanciers saw the similarity between the arrangement of spurred petals of the flowers and a ring of doves.

Columbines appear as a flurry of color—soft pastels or brighter, richer tones, such as yellow, red, or purple. Nodding at the tips of slim stems above pale-green or gray-green foliage, their flowers are uniquely shaped. They have five petals, each with a narrow spur, or extension, projecting from its base toward the back. There are Eastern and Western native Columbines, and others from Europe and Asia that grow well here. Music series grow to 18 in. tall with large flowers for four to six weeks; McKenna hybrids grow more than 2 ft. tall; 'Nora Barlow' has double magenta and lime flowers. Species include Wild Columbine (Aquilegia canadensis) with small, red and yellow flowers, and Japanese Fan Columbine (Aquilegia flabellata). 'Cameo' is dwarf at 18 in.

Other Name
Granny's Bonnet

Bloom Period and Seasonal Color
May; blooms in blue, violet, white, yellow, red, or bicolor

Mature Height × Spread
1 to 3 ft. × 1 ft.

Coralbells

Heuchera species and hybrids

First, there were simply Coralbells, charming plants from the West whose slender, dainty stalks branched into sprays of thready stems tipped with tiny bells. Then in the mid-1980s, there were Heucheras from the East. They boasted striking foliage variously lobed or scalloped and marbled with green, bronze, purple, and silver. Now gardeners have the luxury of choosing from an enormous number of variations of this tough, versatile plant that offers both charming flowers and stunning leaves. Modern Coralbells have it all—disease resistance, hardiness, shade and drought tolerance, colorful foliage, and delicate but showy flowers. Heuchera americana, our native species, has greenish silver foliage. 'Garnet' features deep-red-purple foliage. 'Pewter Veil' has silvery leaves with purple undersides. Heuchera micrantha 'Palace Purple' has purplish bronze foliage.

Other Names
Alumroot, Heuchera

Bloom Period and Seasonal Color
May and June; blooms in pink, red, coral, green, or white

Mature Height × Spread
2 ft. × 2 ft.

When, Where, and How to Plant
Plant divisions or young plants in spring or fall. Transplant potted plants anytime during the growing season. Coralbells prefer full sun for best flowering, but some foliage colors show best in partial shade. They like any organic rich, well-drained soil. Dig down 8 to 10 in., and mix in granular slow-acting all-purpose fertilizer and organic material. Dig a hole large enough to accommodate the root system. Set the plant so that its crown is at soil level. Backfill, firm soil gently, and water well. Space plants 12 to 18 in. apart, closer for edging.

Growing Tips
Water transplants if rainfall is scarce. Spread 1 or 2 in. of organic mulch over the soil to discourage weeds and retain moisture. No further fertilizing is needed.

Care
Coralbells virtually care for themselves. Cut off dying flower stems to neaten the plant and stimulate repeat bloom over the entire season. Plants are shallow rooted and benefit from a year-round organic mulch. Divide plants in the fall every three or four years. Replant clumps that have some roots. Coralbells are pest resistant except for black vine weevil that chews notches in leaf edges. In spring drench the soil with a biological insecticide product containing beneficial (or predatory) nematodes to kill weevil larvae.

Companion Planting and Design
Coralbells are good citizens in outdoor containers, surviving over several years as various annuals come and go. Used as edging, they are see-through plants. Use bunches of cut-flower stems indoors in flower arrangements.

Did You Know?
Pennsylvania nurseryman Dale Hendricks spotted a Coralbells with silver tracings on the foliage growing wild in the mountains of North Carolina and brought it to the attention of Allen Bush at Holbrook Farm nursery in that state. Dubbed "Dale's Strain," it was crossed with the pioneering 'Palace Purple' to yield 'Montrose Ruby'. This plant set a new standard for complex coloration and elaborate, elegant venation in *Heuchera* foliage.

Coreopsis
Coreopsis grandiflora

When, Where, and How to Plant

Plant divisions in spring or fall. Transplant potted plants anytime during the growing season. Plant on an overcast day or in evening to avoid transplant shock from the sun. Coreopsis does best in full sun and ordinary well-drained soil. Dig down 8 to 10 in. Improve the drainage of clay soil by mixing in organic material. If the soil is decent, do not add any fertilizer. Coreopsis prefers lean soil. Dig the hole as deep as and slightly wider than the rootball, and set it so that its top is level with the surrounding ground. Backfill, firm soil gently, and water well. Space plants 2 ft. apart.

Growing Tips

Water transplants if rainfall is sparse. Spread mulch on the soil to discourage weeds while plants become established. No fertilizer is needed.

Care

Cut dead flower stems to groom, prevent reseeding, and stimulate continued bloom. Flowers will self-seed; however, resulting plants are generally not true to type. Divide these fast spreaders every three or four years to get identical plants. Stake taller types or those with floppy stems due to rich soil. Coreopsis has an unusually long bloom season and resists disease and drought. Remove mulch if slugs are a problem.

Companion Planting and Design

The wide, fluted, fringed flower petals of Coreopsis are standouts in meadow wildflower mixes. It is best suited for informal, naturalized areas of the yard. Dwarf types such as *C. lanceolata* 'Goldfink' are ideal for rock gardens, containers, and edging. Coreopsis looks great with seasonal contemporaries such as Blazing Star, Purple Coneflower, Tithonia, Black-eyed Susan, Sneezeweed, and Blanket Flower.

Did You Know?

The distinctive seeds of Coreopsis are responsible for its botanical and common names. Because they have two little protuberances, their shape suggests an insect. Thus the Greek words *koris*, meaning "bedbug," and *opsis*, meaning "resemble." Prairie pioneers dubbed the plants Tickseed because they thought the horned seeds resembled ticks.

All Coreopsis are native to the United States, sharing a prairie heritage of versatility and durability over the season. They feature cheerful daisylike flowers in various shades of gold and yellow at the tips of wiry stems with narrow, pointed leaves. Bigflower Coreopsis is tall, relatively short-lived, and somewhat weedy. The delightful, more domesticated cultivated varieties are excellent garden plants. 'Early Sunrise' grows easily from seed and yields semi-double flowers that bloom dependably its first year. 'Sunray' is more compact with double blooms. Threadleaf Coreopsis (Coreopsis verticillata) has thin, ferny foliage and daintier flowers. 'Moonbeam' has a soft creamy-yellow color and grows to 12 to 18 in. tall. 'Golden Showers' grows to 2 ft. tall and 'Zagreb' to only 12 in. They are the most drought resistant of all. Coreopsis rosea has pink flowers and threadleaf foliage.

Other Name
Bigflower Coreopsis

Bloom Period and Seasonal Color
June through September; blooms in yellow

Mature Height × Spread
6 in. to 2 ft. ×

Cottage Pinks

Dianthus plumarius

Cottage Pinks do well in Pennsylvania, despite their reputation for sulking in hot, humid summers. In early summer flower stems emerge and bear charming 1¹/₂-in.-wide blooms at their tips. They are so modest that sometimes their arrival goes unnoticed until their spicy fragrance wafts across the yard. Long-lived, and drought resistant once established, Pinks are garden stalwarts. 'Kelsey' is sturdy with double, pink flowers and holds up to humidity. 'Spring Beauty' has double flowers in a variety of colors. Cheddar Pinks (Dianthus gratianopolitanus) are good low-growing, petite perennials. 'Bath's Pink' is 10 in. tall and heat and humidity tolerant. Allwoodii hybrids are short-lived perennials with showy flowers in red, pink, white, yellow, cream, and bicolors. D. alpinus is good for rock gardens.

Other Name
Grass Pinks

Bloom Period and Seasonal Color
June; blooms in white, red, pink, or bicolored

Mature Height × Spread
10 to 12 in. × 2 ft.

When, Where, and How to Plant
Plant rooted divisions in spring or fall. Transplant potted plants anytime during the growing season. Site Pinks in full sun. They do fine in average well-drained soil that may be a bit alkaline. Plant in gravelly or sandy soil, raised beds, or containers to assure good drainage. Dig down 8 to 10 in., adding granular slow-acting all-purpose fertilizer. The planting hole should be as deep as and slightly wider than the rootball. Set each plant so that its crown is just slightly above soil level. Backfill, firm soil gently around and over their roots, and water well. Space plants 2 ft. apart.

Growing Tips
Water transplants during droughty periods. Since they prefer lean soil, there is no need to fertilize Pinks once they are established.

Care
Shear back foliage after bloom to remove flower stems and rejuvenate foliage in the center, which tends to flatten. To groom a large patch, lift its edges and trim off a few inches. Do not mulch. Divide every few years in the spring or fall. Dig down through the foliage clump, pry up and detach a section with its roots and soil attached. Sprinkle lime in the fall on acidic soil (the presence of moss is a clue). Rodents and deer are sometimes nuisances.

Companion Planting and Design
Pinks' soft mat of grassy, gray-green foliage softens rocky walls, stone pathways, rock gardens, and edges year-round. 'Tiny Rubies' has deep-pink, double flowers and is 4 in. tall; it is ideal for rock gardens and edging.

Did You Know?
The common name of Pinks is not from their color. It is from the flower petals that have distinctively fringed or "pinked" tips as if they were trimmed by pinking shears. In fact, the color might have been named after the flower. The first known recorded use of the word *pink* to describe a color was in 1720. Before that, what we call pink was labeled blush, flesh, or carnation.

Daylily
Hemerocallis hybrids

When, Where, and How to Plant
Plant or transplant Daylilies anytime the ground is not frozen. Cut back foliage to 4 in., and plant when there is no sun. Daylilies are at their best in full sun, but they can handle some shade. Almost any type of well-drained soil is fine as long as it is not very rich. Cultivate down 8 to 10 in., digging in organic matter and granular slow-acting fertilizer. Dig the hole slightly larger than the plant rootball. Set it so its top is at soil level. Backfill, firm soil gently, then water well. Space standards 2 ft. apart and dwarf types 1 ft. apart.

Growing Tips
If rainfall is sparse, water transplants until they establish. Mulch soil to discourage weeds. A mid-season watering with dilute fertilizer sustains energy for rebloomers.

Care
Remove each stem when all flowers have died to groom and stimulate repeat flowering in rebloomers. Divide hybrids every three or four years in the spring. Dig up large clumps, separate rooted chunks having at least one "fan" of leaves, and replant them. After frost clean up mushy foliage, and mulch the area. Deer have a special fondness for Daylilies; the plants have no other significant problems.

Companion Planting and Design
Daylilies grace flower borders or serve as ground covers to combat soil erosion. Individual specimens are focal points in the garden. Smaller types do well in containers. Some bloom at night for an evening garden.

Did You Know?
Daylilies belong in the kitchen, too. Early spring shoots make tasty greens; fresh flower buds are delicious lightly battered and fried. Steam or dry the flowers (minus stamens) for use in soups and stews. Stuff the flowers with cream cheese, laced with smoked salmon. Sauté seedpods in butter, or pickle them. High in vitamins A and C, they have almost as much protein as spinach. Remember the basic rule of edible flowers: be sure they have not been exposed to pesticides.

Wild roadside and meadow Daylilies offer wonderful color in early summer plus great genes for toughness, drought tolerance, and disease resistance. From them plant breeders have developed modern hybrids that send up dozens of stems, each topped with multitudes of flower buds. Each trumpet-shaped flower blooms for a day, those on a stem opening in succession over several days. Flowers may be single or double; they may have ruffled or crimped edges, rippled texture, iridescence, and fragrance. Their stems stretch above clumps of arching, narrow, green straplike foliage, which arch up from the soil. There are more than 40,000 named cultivars on record. Dependable rebloomers that do well in Pennsylvania are 'Stella de Oro' (golden yellow) and 'Happy Returns' (lemon yellow).

Other Name
Hybrid Daylily

Bloom Period and Seasonal Color
June through September; blooms in red, yellow, orange, lilac, or cream

Mature Height × Spread
1 to 4 ft. × 2 to 4 ft.

Garden Chrysanthemum
Chrysanthemum × grandiflorum

Gardeners have always been able to rely on Chrysanthemums. The traditional backbone of the fall flower border, windowbox, and patio planter, Mums have only gotten better over the years. Choose from a rainbow of flower colors and wonderful flower shapes that belie their toughness. Daisy-, decorative-, pompom-, spoon-, or spider-shaped blooms top bushy, gray-green foliage with its distinctive scent when crushed. These plants are so tough that they transplant in full bloom without missing a beat. Dendranthema zawadskii 'Clara Curtis', a current favorite of gardeners in parts of Pennsylvania, has salmon-pink daisylike flowers with yellow centers. It is long blooming and tolerates more shade than most Mums. Study the photographs on plant labels to choose your favorites from among the enormous number of choices.

Other Name
Hardy Chrysanthemum

Bloom Period and Seasonal Color
August to November; blooms in red, pink, white, yellow, or lilac

Mature Height × Spread
1 to 3 ft. × 1 to 3 ft.

When, Where, and How to Plant
Plant divisions or rooted cuttings in spring. Transplant potted plants anytime during the summer into fall. Mums can handle any type of soil as long as it is in sun and well drained. Loosen soil down 8 to 10 in. Mix in granular slow-acting all-purpose fertilizer, and add organic material to improve drainage in heavy soil. Dig holes as deep as and slightly wider than plant rootballs so that they sit at the same depth that they were in their pots. Backfill, firm soil gently, and water well. Space young plants about 2 ft. apart. Space fall-planted, mature, ready-to-bloom plants as desired.

Growing Tips
Mulch with 2 or 3 in. of an attractive organic material to discourage weeds and retain soil moisture. No further fertilizer is needed the first season. If you intend to grow them as perennials, fertilize them early each season with a slow-acting, granular fertilizer as directed by the label.

Care
Pinch tips of young plants back by about half their new growth every few weeks after they reach 6 in. to delay blossoming and promote branching. Repeat this process until mid-July for early-fall bloom. Continue until mid-August for late-fall bloom. After a hard frost, cut back and mulch for winter, or treat plants as annuals and pull them up. Divide large overwintered clumps in spring. Aphids may cluster at tender stem tips early in the season. Pinch them off, stem tips and all, and discard them in a plastic bag. Insecticidal soap will handle aphids and the occasional mite infestation, too.

Companion Planting and Design
Plant Mums in containers, or use them to fill in garden spaces vacated by tired summer annuals.

Did You Know?
Mums were grown as early as 500 B.C. in China. Their cultivation spread to Japan, and the Mikado adopted them as his personal emblem. They were exhibited there as early as A.D. 900. They were subsequently integrated into the art and culture of Japan as symbols of a long and happy life. The rising sun in the Japanese flag actually represents a Mum.

Goldenrod
Solidago species and hybrids

When, Where, and How to Plant
Transplant Goldenrod anytime, even when it is in bloom. Plant rooted divisions in spring. Fall planting allows plenty of time for transplants to develop strong root systems before they must put energy into foliage and flower production. Goldenrod's prairie heritage has accustomed it to full sun and ordinary well-drained soil. It can handle some shade at the woodland edge. Plants spread by roots and self-sown seed. Cultivate soil down 8 to 10 in. to loosen and aerate. Dig holes as deep as and slightly wider than plant rootballs. Set them in holes, adjusted so the top of the rootball is level with the surrounding ground. Backfill and firm the soil around the plant, and water well. Space 1 ft. apart.

Growing Tips
Water until Goldenrod is established, then it is quite drought resistant. Mulch to maintain soil moisture. These plants do not need fertilization.

Care
For more compact plants and later bloom, cut stems back by half in early June. Stake tall types and those with softer stems growing in rich soil. Hybrid Goldenrod grows in fairly disciplined clumps. Divide large hybrids every three or four years in spring or fall immediately after flowering. Leave dried seedheads for winter interest, or cut them off to forestall self-seeding. Goldenrod may suffer from downy mildew under stressed conditions.

Companion Planting and Design
Naturalize Goldenrod with Asters and Black-eyed Susans, or integrate tall types into the back of a flower border. Seeds of several types are often included in meadow mixes. Intended for the "wild" planting, they are more blowzy in habit and more unruly.

Did You Know?
Goldenrod is not responsible for the annual hay-fever attacks that many people experience in late summer. The true culprit is ragweed, which blooms and produces pollen about the same time as Wild Goldenrod, its companion in open fields and along roadsides. Goldenrod is visited by zillions of tiny insects and butterflies, which are needed to assure pollination. Wind-pollinated plants, such as ragweed, cause allergies.

Goldenrod is another prairie plant high on the list of low-maintenance natives that are easy on the environment. After domestication by European breeders, many interesting versions of Goldenrod are now available for adoption into American gardens. Goldenrod flowers bloom as tight bunches of tiny, yellow florets at the tips of strong, flexible stems laddered with lance-shaped leaves. They are in plumed clusters or strung along narrow branchlets in horizontal tiers. The golden florets of 'Crown of Rays' are arrayed along plume-like stems. 'Golden Dwarf' is only 12 in. tall. Solidago sphacelata 'Golden Fleece' grows in shade to 18 in. tall and spreads freely. Rough-leafed Goldenrod (Solidago rugosa 'Fireworks') is 4 ft. tall and can handle moist soil. Canada Goldenrod (Solidago canadensis) is the native version.

Other Name
Hybrid Goldenrod

Bloom Period and Seasonal Color
Midsummer to fall; blooms in yellow

Mature Height × Spread
2 to 6 ft. × 2 to 4 ft.

Hardy Geranium
Geranium species and hybrids

Hardy Geraniums are easily distinguished from tender (or annual) Geraniums, which are more properly called "Pelargoniums." Besides being perennial, the more than five hundred kinds of Hardy Geraniums typically grow as mounds of low, multilobed or divided leaves in shades of dull green or gray-green. Their 1- or 2-in.-wide flowers appear at the tips of branching stems and have five rounded petals, sometimes streaked with color. Some types bloom lightly all season, but most put on a big show from May through June and then rebloom intermittently over the summer. They are endowed with tough constitutions and great adaptability. Many grow from rhizomes, which enable them to withstand harsh summers, but also help them spread vigorously. Some have scented foliage; others, fall color.

Other Name
Cranesbill

Bloom Period and Seasonal Color
May to July; blooms in magenta, pink, blue, violet, or white

Mature Height × Spread
6 in. to 4 ft. × 1 to 2 ft.

When, Where, and How to Plant
Plant divisions in the spring. Transplant potted Geraniums when they are available at the garden center. They prefer morning sun and afternoon shade. Most accept average, reasonably moist, well-drained soil. Cultivate soil down 8 to 10 in., and mix in granular slow-acting all-purpose fertilizer. Dig a hole as deep as and slightly wider than the rootball. Set it so that its top is level with the surrounding soil. Backfill, firm soil gently, and water well. Plant Geraniums in clusters of three for best effect, spaced about 1 ft. apart. Plant small ones for edging in rows 6 to 8 in. apart.

Growing Tips
Water Hardy Geraniums when rainfall is scarce during the two years they take to become fully established. Mulch the soil around them to discourage weeds and keep soil moist. In decent soil they need no additional fertilizing.

Care
After their main bloom period, cut back Geranium flower stalks to groom plants. Cut back ratty foliage of large varieties to renew it and encourage rebloom. Divide overlarge plants in early spring. Dig the rootball, and separate rooted stems to replant elsewhere. Hardy Geraniums have occasional problems with Japanese beetles in July. Handpick as many pests as possible. Cut back marred foliage at the end of July. Sometimes mildew affects foliage in late spring, disappearing later in the summer.

Companion Planting and Design
There is a Geranium variety to suit almost any landscape situation. 'Ingwersen's Variety' can take dry shade under trees. Some do well in woodland settings; others, in full sun as ground covers. Six-inch-tall *Geranium sanguineum* 'Striatum' makes an excellent ground cover.

Did You Know?
Hardy Geranium appears on many lists of perennials to which deer are indifferent. Unless they are starving, deer show distinct preferences for certain plants, ignoring others. Some others on the list of relatively safe perennials are Bellflower, Black-eyed Susan, Bleeding Heart, Columbine, Fern, Hellebore, Poppy, and Peony.

Hosta
Hosta species and hybrids

When, Where, and How to Plant

Plant divisions in spring or fall. Transplant potted plants anytime during the growing season. Yellow-foliaged Hostas such as 'Sum and Substance' like more sun; blue-foliaged Hostas prefer less sun. Most like some bright, indirect morning light, followed by mostly partial shade. Give them moist, woodsy, organic rich soil that is slightly acidic. Dig it down 8 to 12 in., and mix in granular slow-acting all-purpose fertilizer and organic matter. Dig the hole as deep as the rootball and a bit wider so that the top of the rootball is level with the surrounding ground. Backfill and gently firm the soil, and water well. Allow plenty of space between plants because foliage splays a bit in mid-summer heat.

Growing Tips

Provide regular moisture over the first two seasons until plants fully establish. Maintain a 2- or 3-in. layer of organic mulch on soil to discourage weeds. Sprinkle slow-acting fertilizer on it each spring.

Care

Hostas do not need routine division, but sometimes plants overgrow their space. In spring when the new leaf buds appear, slice away a pie-shaped chunk of roots with a sharp spade without disturbing the main plant. Then fill the space with soil. Unfortunately, deer love Hostas! If necessary, grow them in pots out of deer reach.

Companion Planting and Design

Use Hostas to hide ripening bulb foliage, in woodland settings, around trees as a living mulch, or as substitutes for foundation shrubs around the house. Long-lived, they brighten dark corners, edge borders, and star as specimens all season until their leaves collapse with frost.

Did You Know?

Hostas are favorites of slugs! They chew holes in the smoother, more delicate, and lower-growing leaves first. Leaves skeletonized by slugs will be replaced by new leaves. Some slug controls include spreading diatomaceous earth, sand, or ashes on the soil; fastening copper strips to edges of boxed beds; using spiky sweetgum balls for mulch; setting beer or yeast traps; handpicking; or renting a toad.

King of the shade garden, Hosta is the ultimate foliage plant. Yes, Hostas have flowers, lovely clusters of small trumpets arrayed along the upper part of stems that rise high above mounds of leaves. It is Hosta's regal, infinitely variable foliage that commands attention, however. Leaves may be any shade of green or even blue, plain, or with cream, yellow, or gold edges or streaks. Measuring from less than 1 in. to 22 in. long, they may be rippled, ruffled, or deeply textured with prominent ribs. August Lily (Hosta plantaginea) has white, fragrant flowers in late summer. Siebold's Hosta (Hosta sieboldiana 'Elegans') grows up to 4 ft. tall and across with huge blue leaves and white flowers. Fortune's Hosta (Hosta fortunei) has variegated foliage.

Other Name
Plantain Lily

Bloom Period and Seasonal Color
July to September; blooms in white, lavender, or purple

Mature Height × Spread
6 in. to 4 ft. (foliage height) × 1 to 3 ft.

Lenten Rose
Helleborus hybridus

Lenten Rose and its relatives have come into their own. Now recognized as a superior garden plant, it is all the more appreciated because it sustains the garden during the bleak days of winter with its handsome foliage and lovely blossoms. Its open mounds of glossy, leathery, deeply divided leaves harbor slightly nodding flowers that seem shy about blooming so early while it still seems like winter. Creamy, pink, and maroon-toned, the five-petaled flowers rise from the crown, often acquiring a pinkish tinge as they age over ten weeks. First sightings may be in February, thus the Lenten name, but even after their peak, flowers persist as colorful sepals with a swollen seedpod in the center. Long-lived, old clumps produce up to one hundred flowers.

Other Name
Hellebore

Bloom Period and Seasonal Color
March to April; blooms in cream, maroon, pink, or purple; some blooms are speckled

Mature Height × Spread
15 to 20 in. × 15 to 20 in.

When, Where, and How to Plant
Plant potted plants in spring or early fall. Transplant the seedlings in spring. Lenten Roses can handle sun or shade; however, in sun they require moister soil. Site them under deciduous trees for winter light. The leaf canopy protects them from hot summer sun. They prefer woodsy soil, rich in organic matter and well drained. Soil can be a bit on the alkaline side. Dig down 1 ft. to loosen and aerate. Mix in organic matter to enrich it and improve drainage. Dig the hole deep enough to accommodate the rootball, set so its top is level with the surrounding ground. Backfill and gently firm the soil, and water well. Set plants 18 in. apart. They flower after three years.

Growing Tips
Maintain a 2- or 3-in. layer of organic mulch year-round to keep soil moist and discourage weeds. Water during droughty periods. Heavy feeders, Lenten Roses appreciate fertilizing with a slow-acting product in late spring.

Care
Clip off ratty leaves in the spring. Deadhead plants to prevent self-seeding. Hellebores do not like to be disturbed, but they will tolerate early-spring transplanting or dividing better than others. Stressed plants become susceptible to aphids or leaf spot. Slugs may cause minor problems.

Companion Planting and Design
Lenten Rose makes a good ground cover. It combines well in a winter garden with Snowdrops and other early bulbs, then later with various Ferns, Hostas, and Bleeding Hearts. It will grow in containers.

Did You Know?
Hellebore is an unfortunate name for such a benign plant. The *hell* syllable conveys the sense of darkness and witchery with which medieval society connected it. The botanical name is from the Greek words *helein* ("to injure") and *bora* ("food"). Perhaps "injurious food" is not such a misnomer after all, since Hellebore roots contain toxic substances that are extremely irritating to internal and external tissues. Wear gloves when handling to avoid dermatitis.

Peony
Paeonia hybrids

When, Where, and How to Plant
Plant divisions in fall. Transplant potted plants in spring or anytime during the growing season. Peonies appreciate full sun but will accept partial shade. Give them good, well-drained garden soil rich in organic matter. It can be slightly alkaline. A somewhat sheltered spot is ideal. Loosen and aerate soil by digging down 12 in. and as widely as possible. Incorporate organic material and granular slow-acting all-purpose fertilizer. Proper planting depth is critical, or Peonies will not bloom. Dig just deep enough so that growing buds end up 1 in. below ground level when covered. Set potted plant roots so that their soil surface is exactly at ground level. Backfill, firm soil gently, and water well. Space 3 ft. apart.

Growing Tips
Water regularly and mulch around, but not on, Peonies to discourage weeds during the two to three years it takes them to establish. Fertilize with slow-acting fertilizer in late fall or early spring. Regularly mulched Peonies eventually do not need annual fertilizing.

Care
Stake or support large-flowered types at bloom time. Cut back discolored ripening foliage in early fall. Peonies resent being disturbed, so dig and divide in fall only. Each division must have three to five buds. Common reasons for no blooms are too much shade, planted too deeply, a cold spring, overfertilizing, competition with tree roots, too young, waterlogged, or too dry. Peonies get botrytis if stressed by dampness and lack of air circulation. Clean up spent flowers and foliage promptly.

Companion Planting and Design
Incorporate Peonies into a mixed border, or use in a row as an informal hedge.

Did You Know?
Ants and big, fat Peony buds seem to go together like ham and eggs. There is no need for alarm. The presence of ants is a sign that the Peonies are in great health—so great that they are brimming with sweet juices. The ants are there for the treat.

Lush, fragrant Peonies are joys of late spring. Long-lived and relatively carefree, they are beloved through many generations. Some of these bushy plants, more than one hundred years old, are still blooming happily in fields that were once front yards of long-abandoned Pennsylvania farms. Peony flowers are 6 or more in. across, a flutter of tissue-paper petals around yellow centers. Sweetly fragrant, they bloom in yellow, white, and shades of pink, at the top of branched stems featuring dark-green, coarse, lobed foliage. Some Peony blossoms are so top-heavy that the stems flop under their weight, especially when it rains. Blossoms typically last four to seven days. Choose early-, mid-, and late-flowering types for a longer season. "Estate"-labeled Peonies have extra-large flowers.

Other Name
Garden Peony

Bloom Period and Seasonal Color
May to June; blooms in yellow, rose, red, or white

Mature Height × Spread
2 to 3 ft. × 3 ft.

Phlox

Phlox paniculata

A native wildflower that is at home along roadsides and streambeds, Phlox has made the transition to residential gardens without missing a beat. In its new, improved, hybrid incarnation it is slightly shorter with larger flowers. These domes of tightly clustered florets crown the straight stems for many summer weeks, and many colors are available. Some have contrasting colored "eyes," or centers; some even have maroon or variegated foliage. Protect them from deer; the butterflies will be grateful. Reputed to be mildew resistant are 'David' (fragrant, clear-white flowers on sturdy stems), 'Bright Eyes' (pink with red eyes), 'Eva Cullum' (pink), 'Franz Schubert' (lavender), and 'Sandra' (scarlet). 'Nora Leigh' grows to 3 ft. with variegated, striped, gray-green-and-cream foliage with magenta flowers. 'Harlequin' also has variegated foliage and pink flowers.

Other Name
Garden Phlox

Bloom Period and Seasonal Color
July and August; blooms in white, pink, rose, or lilac-blue

Mature Height × Spread
3 to 4 ft. × 2 ft.

When, Where, and How to Plant

Transplant potted plants anytime during the growing season. Transplant divisions in the spring or fall. Phlox require full sun, although blue- or lilac-flowered ones color best in light shade. Phlox are flexible about soil as long as it is moist and well drained. It can be a bit alkaline. Dig down 8 to 10 in., and mix in granular slow-acting all-purpose fertilizer. Add organic material to clay, silty, or compacted soil for drainage. Make the hole as deep as and slightly wider than the rootball, so its top is level with the surrounding ground. Backfill, firm soil gently, and water well. Space plants 18 to 24 in. apart.

Growing Tips

Sprinkle slow-acting fertilizer on their soil each spring to sustain Phlox all season. Water if rainfall is scarce, preferably at soil level so that foliage remains dry. Mulch to keep soil moist.

Care

Stake plants so that heavy flower heads do not flop in the rain, then cut off dead flowers promptly to promote rebloom and prevent seeding. Cut back stems entirely in the fall. Put them in the trash to minimize reseeding. Divide clumps every four or five years. Replant, liberally spaced. Garden Phlox has problems with powdery mildew. It mars their appearance, but is not fatal. Use resistant varieties, provide good air circulation, and avoid overhead watering.

Companion Planting and Design

Showcase Phlox as vertical accents in the middle of flower borders, in cutting or butterfly gardens.

Did You Know?

Phlox 'David' was discovered by F. M. Mooberry, former coordinator of horticulture at the Brandywine Conservancy and designer of the native plant garden at the Brandywine Museum in Chadds Ford, Pennsylvania. In her ongoing search for plants she acquired some magenta-colored Phlox. In 1987, a lovely white one turned up among the many self-sown seedlings. Cuttings were taken, raised, and introduced by area nurseryman Dale Hendricks. When invited to name the new Phlox, F. M. promptly pronounced it 'David', her husband's name. It is the Perennial Plant Association's Plant of the Year for 2002.

Primrose

Primula × polyantha

When, Where, and How to Plant

Transplant potted plants in the spring. Plant rooted divisions after bloom is finished. An ideal Primrose site gets little wind, some morning sun, and bright light or partial shade in the afternoon. Any soil (even clay), neutral or slightly alkaline, enriched with lots of organic matter to hold moisture will do. Thoroughly dig organic material (avoid peat moss, which tends to increase soil acidity) into the top 12 in. of the soil. Add sand to improve drainage, and also add granular slow-acting all-purpose fertilizer. Dig a hole large enough to accommodate each rootball, then set it in the hole so that its crown is exactly at soil level. Backfill, and water well. Space plants 6 to 8 in. apart.

Growing Tips

Primroses need constant moisture to prevent bud drop. In truly boggy areas, gravel mulch will drain excess water away from plant crowns to prevent rot. Fertilize each spring with a sprinkle of granular slow-acting fertilizer. Maintain rich soil by mulching beds. A thin layer of organic mulch improves soil texture and fertility as it decomposes over time.

Care

To forestall fungal disease, remove dead leaves before new growth begins. Deadhead spent flowers to groom and prevent self-seeding. Divide crowded plants in spring just after they bloom. Slugs may chew holes in leaves. Bait shallow traps with beer or yeast, or sprinkle diatomaceous earth (DE) on the soil around Primroses. The sharp particles cut slugs when they try to crawl over them.

Companion Planting and Design

Group Primroses at the edge of a bed of spring flowers, in the light shade of a spring woodland garden, or in decorative containers. Japanese Primrose (*Primula japonica*) holds its flowers candelabra style on tall stems and loves pond-side conditions.

Did You Know?

It is easy to confuse common names. Primrose is also the common name of certain plants in the *Oenothera* genus. When in doubt, always check Latin botanical names.

In return for their welcome spring show of extraordinary crayon or pastel colors, Primroses demand specific garden conditions. Humidity is easy—that is plentiful in our state—but the constantly moist soil may be harder to provide. It is worth the trouble to try Primroses, however, and the polyantha types are a good place to begin. Their perky, colorful, 1-in.-wide blooms boast some of the brightest, richest colors in the floral world. They cluster at the ends of straight stems that rise above whorled clumps of paddle-shaped, often crinkly textured, yellow-green leaves. 'Pacific Giants' is widely available with flowers up to 2 in. wide in many colors, but the plants are not long-lived perennials. Siebold's Primrose (Primula sieboldii) is reputed to be the easiest to grow but loses its foliage in summer, making it more drought tolerant.

Other Name

Polyantha Primrose

Bloom Period and Seasonal Color

April into May; blooms in pastels and crayon colors

Mature Height × Spread

6 to 12 in. × 8 to 10 in.

Purple Coneflower

Echinacea purpurea

Purple Coneflower, a sturdy native of the Midwestern United States, is a welcome addition to informal yards and gardens in Pennsylvania. Its jaunty, colorful, lax-petaled, midsummer flowers persist over many, many weeks when most other perennials are idle. Once established, it is very self-reliant, spreading slowly, cheerfully accommodating the vagaries of soil, light, and weather. Purple Coneflower is a great plant for the support of wildlife. Like most daisy-flowered plants, it hosts all kinds of beneficial insects. Its dark, swollen seedheads attract finches. 'Magnus' is a deep-rose color. 'Crimson Star' is a truer red. Among the more recently developed white versions, 'Alba', 'White Swan', and 'White Lustre' are generally available at garden centers. White types are not as sturdy as the purplish-red ones.

Other Name
Purple Echinacea

Bloom Period and Seasonal Color
July to August; blooms in deep pink or white

Mature Height × Spread
4 ft. × 2 ft.

When, Where, and How to Plant

Plant divisions in spring or fall. Transplant potted plants anytime during the growing season. Purple Coneflowers prefer full sun. They are not particular about soil type as long as it is reasonably well drained. Average garden soil is preferable to rich soil, which makes their stems floppy. Loosen and aerate the soil down about 12 in. Dig a hole as deep as and slightly wider than the rootball. Set the plant so that the top of its rootball is level with the surrounding ground. Backfill, firm soil gently around plant, and water well. Space plants 2 ft. apart.

Growing Tips

Water transplants during droughty periods. Spread a 2-in. layer of mulch to keep soil moist and discourage weeds. Do not fertilize established plants.

Care

Once established, Purple Coneflowers need little attention. Stake those in a more formal garden setting. Deadhead early blossoms to promote repeat bloom and to discourage self-seeding. Allow the last flush of blooms to develop into their namesake bristly raised cones. Left to ripen on the plant, the seeds attract finches. Harvested, the seedheads are useful for floral crafts. Divide in spring or fall. Purple Coneflowers are notably heat and drought tolerant, virtually pest and disease free, and last for years. Their foliage may develop unattractive powdery mildew late in the season, but it does not seriously harm the plants. Thin plants to improve air circulation.

Companion Planting and Design

Essentially a tamed wildflower, Purple Coneflower is low maintenance and attractive in the middle of the flower border, in meadow areas, or front and center as a specimen.

Did You Know?

Purple Coneflower has attracted the attention of doctors as well as gardeners. Extracts from the roots and flowering tops of *Echinacea* have become one of the best-selling herbal remedies in U.S. health food stores and drugstores. It is reputed to stimulate the body's immune system to ward off colds and speed healing of infections.

When, Where, and How to Plant

Plant divisions in spring. Transplant potted plants anytime during the season. Longer stems wilted from transplant shock retain that posture all season. Stems are okay the following season. 'Autumn Joy' loves sun—even hot spots near walls and pavement with severe reflected sun and heat are fine. Any type of well-drained soil will do, including clay. Average or lean soil assures that the stems do not flop. Dig soil down 8 to 10 in.; improve drainage if necessary, and add a handful of a granular slow-acting all-purpose fertilizer. Dig a hole as deep as and slightly wider than the root-ball, then set it so that its surface is level with the surrounding ground. Backfill, firm soil gently, and water well. Space plants 1 to 2 ft. apart.

Growing Tips

Water transplants when rain is scarce until they become established. There is no need to fertilize 'Autumn Joy'.

Care

Support flowering stems to prevent their splaying outward. Pinching stems back by half when they are about 8 in. tall (in June) makes a more compact clump. Flowers are more numerous, but later blooming. Cut back dried stems in the spring when new stems show at the base of the plant. Divide in spring when the center buds of large clumps of Sedums get woody and flower stems are spindly. Dig the clump, cut off rooted chunks having four to six buds, and replant. Sedums have no significant pest or disease problems.

Companion Planting and Design

Plant 'Autumn Joy' alone or with Black-eyed Susans, Mums, Asters, and ornamental grasses in garden beds or borders. Sedums also do well in outdoor containers.

Did You Know?

Sedums such as 'Autumn Joy' host hoards of miniscule beneficial insects that covet the nectar in the tiny florets in their flower heads. Encouraged by the availability of this food, they stay in the area to prey on pest insects, the other part of their diet.

Many gardeners regard 'Autumn Joy' as one of the ten best perennials grown in the U.S. It is a tall Sedum, or Showy Stonecrop, as distinguished from ground cover Sedums. Foolproof to grow, it takes in stride all the misfortunes that may befall plants in our state. Its succulent, light-green foliage stores moisture to withstand humid summer heat and drought without complaint. Its late-summer flower heads of tightly clustered, tiny, star-shaped florets age from a pale greenish white to light pink to rich salmon-rose, then burgundy as the season progresses. Up to 6 in. across, they dry to a rusty maroon, persisting to spark the bleak winter landscape. Showy Stonecrop (Sedum spectabile) has bluish green leaves. 'Matrona' is a choice new tall Sedum favored by perennial gardeners.

Other Name
Showy Stonecrop

Bloom Period and Seasonal Color
August to October; blooms in greenish white to russet

Mature Height × Spread
2 ft. × 2 ft.

Shasta Daisy
Leucanthemum × superbum

Everyone loves Daisies. In fact, they are often the first flower that children learn to recognize. They are called composite flowers because they are composed of many small, individual flowers and they have two types. White ray flowers, or petals, ring clusters of tiny yellow disk flowers at the center of the Daisy. These 2-in. blossoms grow singly at the tips of wiry stems above dull-green, coarse, toothed, narrow leaves. A classic, the Shasta Daisy is beloved for easygoing egalitarianism and generosity of bloom. 'Alaska' and 'Polaris' have very large single flowers. 'White Knight Hybrid' has 4-in.-wide flowers on sturdy 20-in. stems. 'Thomas Killen' has thick stems for cutting. 'Aglaya' has frilled double flowers. 'Becky' has very strong stems and blooms later.

Bloom Period and Seasonal Color
June and July; blooms in white

Mature Height × Spread
1 to 3 ft. × 2 ft.

When, Where, and How to Plant
Plant Shasta Daisies in the spring to enjoy the current season of flowers. Plants in pots can be planted anytime during the growing season. Most love full sun; however, double-flowering ones appreciate some shade. Any good, moist, well-drained garden soil is fine. Dig down at least 12 in., simultaneously incorporating granular slow-acting fertilizer and organic material into it. Dig the hole deep enough to accommodate the rootball; set so that it is level with the surrounding soil. Backfill, firm soil gently, and water well. Plant Shasta Daisies in groups of three, spacing them about 2 ft. apart.

Growing Tips
A year-round, 2- or 3-in. layer of organic mulch keeps soil moist, weeds down, and winter soil temperatures even. Water in the absence of rain because Shasta Daisies are somewhat shallow rooted. Sprinkle slow-acting fertilizer on their soil every spring before they flower.

Care
Pinch back emerging flower stems to force branching. Stake taller stems. Cut back the stems after flowering to generate renewed foliage at their base. Shastas spread, but clumps are short-lived if not divided every two or three years. Stems or foliage of stressed plants is sometimes bothered by aphids, easily pinched off and discarded.

Companion Planting and Design
Naturalize Shasta Daisies in informal meadow areas, or include them in the middle of a flower border or cutting garden. They are particularly useful with foliage plants and those with hot-colored flowers. Shorter plants in front will screen their ragged lower stems. The dwarf Shastas do well as edging and in containers.

Did You Know?
In the floral lexicon of Victorian times Daisies communicated Secret Love and coy courtship. We still acknowledge their power to convey sentiment when we pull petals from a Daisy in rhythm to "He loves me; he loves me not." A white Daisy has traditionally signified Innocence; a double-flowered one, Participation. Consider the implications when you give a bouquet of Shasta Daisies to someone!

Veronica
Veronica spicata

When, Where, and How to Plant
Plant rooted divisions in spring or fall. Transplant potted plants anytime during the growing season. Veronicas accept shade, but their stems may flop. They accept any type of average well-drained garden soil. Loosen it down 8 in., and mix in a little granular slow-acting fertilizer. Add organic matter to improve soil drainage if necessary. Dig a hole as deep as and slightly wider than the rootball so its top is level with the surrounding soil. Backfill, firm soil gently, and water well. Space plants 1 to 2 ft. apart.

Growing Tips
Spread a 2- to 3-in. layer of mulch over the soil around newly planted Veronicas to discourage weeds and maintain soil moisture. Water well if rain is sparse until they establish. No further fertilization is necessary.

Care
Cut off spent flower spikes to stimulate plants to flower again. Young plants may bloom all summer with faithful deadheading. Shear low-growing, or prostrate, Veronicas down to the soil after their second flush of bloom. Cut stems of taller Veronicas back by 6 in. in June so that plants become more compact. Bloom time is delayed a bit, but plants may not need staking. Divide overgrown Veronicas after three or four years in spring or fall. They have no significant pests or diseases, but sometimes foliage becomes coated with mildew during wet weather. Cut back blackened stems, and wait for dry weather.

Companion Planting and Design
Use Veronicas of various sizes as edging, fillers, and ground covers. Include them in cutting gardens.

Did You Know?
The second part of a plant's botanical two-word name (binomial) is descriptive. It usually reveals an important fact about the plant. Sometimes it is a person's name, such as *douglasii*, which indicates that the plant was discovered by someone named Douglas. Often the second word describes a prominent physical trait of the plant. *Macrophylla* means "large leafed." *Spicata* refers to the fact that flowers grow as spikes.

This plant is a garden standby. Respected for its self-reliance and long bloom period, Veronica is attractive, versatile, and adaptable. First, there are the narrow, rich-green, sometimes grayish green, leaves. Then for four to eight weeks, there are the slim, unassuming flower spikes loaded with tiny florets of shades of blue or pink. They just keep coming, punctuating the flower border or rock garden with low- or medium-height, colorful, vertical interest. Pinching off the spent ones encourages more. 'Blue Fox', 'Blue Peter', and 'Blue Spires' have flowers in various shades of blue. 'Red Fox' has long-blooming, rosy-pink flowers. 'Icicle' has white flowers. 'Sunny Border Blue' boasts long-blooming, deep-blue-violet flowers; and 'Goodness Grows' is low growing with violet-blue flowers until November.

Other Name
Spike Speedwell

Bloom Period and Seasonal Color
June and July; blooms in blue, pink, or white

Mature Height × Spread
$1\frac{1}{2}$ to 3 ft. × $1\frac{1}{2}$ to 2 ft.

Yarrow

Achillea species and hybrids

Yarrow is easy to take for granted. Because it is easy to grow and has attractive green or grayish green, aromatic foliage that blends well with many other plants, nearly everyone includes its excellent hybrids in the flower border. Whereas Common Yarrow, found naturally along roadsides and in fields, is best suited for areas that are informal and meadowlike, the new hybrids have neater, more compact shapes and more interesting flower colors. They bloom almost all season long if their spent blossoms are cut off. In between flushes of bloom their foliage adds texture and variety to the garden. Best of all, deer ignore them. Multicolored 'Summer Pastel' is an All-America Selections winner. Fernleaf Yarrow (Achillea filipendula) flowers are shades of yellow.

Other Name
Milfoil

Bloom Period and Seasonal Color
June through August; blooms in yellow, gold, white, red, pink, rust, or salmon

Mature Height × Spread
1 to 4 ft. × 3 ft.

When, Where, and How to Plant
Plant divisions in spring or fall. Potted plants can go in the garden anytime during the growing season. Site it in full sun. Yarrow is not particular about soil as long as it drains well. Even thin, poor soil is tolerable. Loosen the soil down 8 to 10 in., and add coarse sand or gravel to improve drainage if necessary. Make the hole as deep as and slightly wider than the rootball. Set it in the hole so that its top is level with the surrounding ground. Backfill, firm soil gently, and water well. Plant Yarrow in groups of three, spaced 1 ft. apart.

Growing Tips
Water Yarrow until it is established. Then it rarely needs watering unless there is a severe drought. Plants that are faithfully deadheaded and that get more water tend to bloom more prolifically. Do not fertilize.

Care
Stake stems of leggy, shaded or overfertilized Yarrows. Cut off flowers when they fade to encourage repeat bloom and to control self-sowing and stem height. In the fall, cut all stems to the soil. Divide rapidly spreading Common Yarrow every year or two. Yarrow is basically pest free but may develop mildew on its foliage in particularly damp and humid summers. Thin out plants, and remove affected stems, then discard in the trash. Be sure soil drains well.

Companion Planting and Design
Plant Yarrow in informal beds and borders or with other cutting flowers. Dried flowers such as those of 'Coronation Gold' hold their color and are useful in arrangements and crafts.

Did You Know?
Achillea is a healing herb. Its foliage has antiseptic and astringent qualities. It is named after the Greek hero Achilles, who used it to staunch the wounds of his soldiers at the siege of Troy. It has since acquired common names such as Soldier's Woundwort, Carpenter's Weed, and Nosebleed for its medicinal properties. It is still used in modern-day homeopathic practice.

When, Where, and How to Plant

Plant rooted Yucca offshoots in spring. Transplant plants in containers anytime during the growing season. Wear protective clothing and glasses to avoid injury from sharp foliage. Yuccas love full sun, but they will take some shade. Any type of decent soil is fine as long as it is well drained year-round. Loosen the soil down 8 to 10 in., and mix in gravel or coarse sand to improve its drainage if necessary. Mix in a handful of a granular slow-acting all-purpose fertilizer. Dig a hole as deep as and slightly wider than the rootball. Set it in the hole so that its top is level with, or just slightly above, the surrounding ground. Backfill, firm soil gently, then water well. Space plants 2 to 3 ft. apart.

Growing Tips

Yuccas take two or three seasons to settle in and start blooming. During this time water them during dry periods. Once established, they are extremely drought resistant. Sprinkle slow-acting fertilizer on the soil the first spring or two. Established plants do not need any fertilizer.

Care

Cut back flower stalks after flowers have faded to groom plants. Divide overlarge clumps into new plants in the spring by removing the rooted offsets they develop at the edges of the clump and replanting them. Yuccas have no significant pest problems.

Companion Planting and Design

Use Yuccas as accents in mixed borders or as landscape focal points. They do well on slopes or flat ground.

Did You Know?

Butterflies seem to get all the attention. Moths deserve some attention, too. Because most are nocturnal, their beauty and contribution to plant pollination are overlooked. Moths are distinguished from butterflies by their plumper, furrier bodies and feathery antennae. When at rest, their wings lie flat or folded like roofs over their backs. Their attraction to light is legendary and explains why they visit pale and white nighttime flowers such as Yucca for nectar.

Yuccas are an acquired taste. For some, they are exciting; for others, they are visitors from an alien climate. With their sharp-tipped, stiff, swordlike leaves and no-nonsense flower spikes, they have a coarse toughness that suggests desert survival. The thin, wispy threads that split from the edges of their leaves hardly soften their profile. Yet Yuccas are perfectly at home here, contributing a strong sculptural element to the landscape and holding soil on slopes with their thick roots. Their sturdy rosettes of gray-green, green, or yellow-and-green variegated, 1-in.-wide leaves are attractive. Yucca takes on a whole new personality when it bears its waxy, creamy, fragrant bells that nod demurely in the sun and then tilt upward when night falls to await visits by moths.

Other Name
Adam's Needle

Bloom Period and Seasonal Color
June to August; blooms in cream

Mature Height × Spread
3 to 5 ft. × 3 to 4 ft.

Shrubs *for Pennsylvania*

Shrubs are the glue that holds a home landscape together, giving it coherence. Builders put them next to new homes even before there is a lawn to announce that "this is a livable place." From the beginning we take shrubs for granted, often to the point that we do not notice that the original low foundation shrubs now cover the second-floor windows!

Shrubs in the Landscape

Of course, in addition to their design role as a landscape's vegetation infrastructure, shrubs play a decorative role. As the understory layer in the landscape—the transition between the taller trees and the low-growing ground cover plants—they provide variety with their different heights, shapes, and textures. Collectively, shrubs offer flower color, fragrance, cones or berries, wonderful bark, needled or broadleaf foliage, and bare stems and branching silhouettes against sheltering walls or the open winter sky. As ornamental as any herbaceous perennial, flowering shrubs extend these smaller plants' scale, magnifying their impact with their *gravitas*. Shrub foliage also provides a rich, textural backdrop to showcase perennial and annual flowering plants.

As a group, shrubs are extremely versatile. In the ground or in containers they decorate doorways, pools and patios, property lines, and flower beds. They are also functional, solving a landscape's problems as they contribute to its beauty. Use them to obscure unsightly utilities, to hold soil on stream banks or on slopes, or to form a screen to assure privacy and quiet, and block wind and sun. As hedges, especially thorny ones that discourage trespassers, they control foot traffic. A grove of mulched shrubs reduces lawn size considerably.

Shrub Trends

Renewed interest in shrubs is reflected in the recent increasing availability of a wider variety of them and the numerous shrub trends that are evident lately. The concept of foundation shrubs is falling by the wayside. Contemporary homes are less likely to have visible ugly cement foundations, so there is no need automatically to plant shrubs next to the house. Dwarf shrubs, especially conifers, are very popular because they are a more appropriate scale for the typical smaller home landscape. Shrubs with purple, gold, and blue foliage are perceived as more interesting and useful. Native shrubs are gaining long overdue respect for their beauty, adaptability, and low maintenance. Finally, as the relentless exurban sprawl in areas surrounding Pennsylvania's cities reduces wildlife habitat even more, shrubs are increasingly valued as key elements in creating a backyard habitat that supports songbirds, honeybees, beneficial insects, and other creatures. Because deer are not usually invited into our yard, shrubs that they ignore are becoming popular.

Buying Shrubs

Shrubs are commercially available in three ways. *Bare-root:* mail-order plants and many Hybrid Tea Roses usually come with their roots bare of soil and wrapped in damp moss, sawdust, or the like. They tend to be dormant and quite small, and they should be planted as soon as possible. *Balled-and-burlapped:* since larger shrubs, or ones that are to be moved to a new site in the yard, are recently dug from the soil where they grew, their ball of roots and soil are wrapped in burlap or similar material to hold them together. *Containerized:* shrubs raised in containers are most prevalent in garden centers. Planting them is easiest on both homeowner and plant because they are manageable and their roots are well developed and minimally disturbed in the process.

Planting Practices

Current shrub-planting practices deviate from tradition—a result of new knowledge and technology relating to shrub production. Planting holes with sloping sides encourage shrub roots to grow outward rather than sulk in a straight-sided "container" hole. Because the fill soil is not specially improved, roots are forced to adjust quickly to the local soil. Since burlap these days may, in fact, be synthetic and not biodegradable, cutting it all away is advisable. Delayed fertilizing prevents stimulation of more top growth on the shrub than roots struggling to establish can support. Sprinkling granular fertilizer on the soil surface provides more uniform distribution of nutrients than do root-feeding techniques. Also, slow-acting fertilizer offers more consistent nutrition over an extended period, minimizing plant stress and homeowner effort. Finally, a layer of mulch over the root zones of newly planted shrubs discourages weeds and grass, which compete for moisture and nutrients. Lawn mowers and weed trimmers have no excuse to get too close.

American Arborvitae

Thuja occidentalis

American Arborvitae are relatively slow-growing ever-greens, valued for their dense foliage, which grows down to the ground, and their adaptability to heat, cold, and air pollution. Their versatility and handsome forms make them useful in residential landscapes. Unfortunately, these Eastern natives also top the list of deer favorites. Soft and scalelike, rather than sharp-needled, Arborvitae leaves are arranged on the branches in flattened, parallel sprays. These shrubs bear male and female flowers (cones) in the spring, which turn brown by late summer. Although some Arborvitae are virtually trees, there are many shrubby choices. 'Emerald Green' has good color all winter. 'Green Giant', a hybrid relative of American Arborvitae, won the Pennsylvania Horticultural Society's Gold Medal Award in 1998. It is reputedly deer resistant. 'Hetz's Midget' is dwarf. 'Aurea' and others have yellow foliage.

Other Name
Eastern Arborvitae

Bloom Period and Seasonal Color
Golden-green evergreen foliage, seasonal cones

Mature Height × **Spread**
4 to 60 ft. × variable width

When, Where, and How to Plant
Plant balled-and-burlapped shrubs in spring or fall. Plant those in containers anytime during the growing season, except the hottest and driest part of the summer. Arborvitae, especially yellow-foliaged ones, do best in full sun but accept some shade. Too much shade fosters loose, open branch-ing. They prefer well-drained soils that are moist, rich in organic matter, and slightly acid. Temporarily screen Arborvitae planted in exposed sites. Do not plant under roofs where sliding snow may cause branches to break. If soil is poor, loosen and dig in organic material. Dig a hole with slop-ing sides as deep as the rootball and about twice as wide. Set the rootball so its top is level with the surrounding soil. Cut as much burlap away as pos-sible. Backfill, firm soil gently, and water well.

Growing Tips
Water regularly if rainfall is unreliable the first year and during hot, dry periods every summer. In spring sprinkle slow-acting granular fertilizer suit-able for conifers on the mulch for the rain to soak in. After a few years, annual fertilization will not be necessary.

Care
Stake columnar Arborvitae their first winter. Mulch shrub root zones with organic matter year-round. Prune out dead or broken branches. Site shrubs cor-rectly to avoid pruning to control size. Shear only to form a hedge; do not cut back to bare wood. Stressed Arborvitae will develop mite problems. Treat with a forceful spray of water several times a week.

Companion Planting and Design
Use Arborvitae as specimens, along foundations, in rows as screens and hedges, and as background for more colorful plants. Smaller shrubs do well in deep containers.

Did You Know?
Bagworm caterpillars build spindle-shaped cocoons that dangle from conifer branch tips like cones. They protect overwintering eggs laid by a moth in the fall, then shelter young caterpillars that emerge periodically to feed on shrub foliage. Pick off all bags within reach. Spray infested foliage of large shrubs with *B.t.* (*Bacillus thurin-giensis*) while the caterpillars are feeding.

Beautyberry
Callicarpa dichotoma

When, Where, and How to Plant

Plant in spring or fall. Transplant container-grown Beautyberries anytime during the growing season. They do best in full sun, but partial shade is okay. Plants will take any decent well-drained soil. Once established, they can handle dry or moist soil, as well as road salt and urban conditions. No special soil preparation is necessary. Dig a saucer-shaped hole as deep as the rootball and about twice as wide. Set the shrub so that the top of its rootball is exactly level with the surrounding soil. Cut away as much burlap, if it is present, as possible. Backfill, firm soil gently, and water well. Set plants at least 4 ft. apart.

Growing Tips

Spread a 2- or 3-in. layer of organic material as mulch to conserve soil moisture and discourage weeds. Established Beautyberries are fairly drought resistant. Water during extended dry periods. There is no need to fertilize if their soil is half decent; too rich a diet promotes excess vegetative growth at the expense of flower or fruit production.

Care

Prune to within a few inches of soil level each spring to cut off any winter dieback. Prune to keep the shrub at a compact 3 to 5 ft. and stimulate heavy fruiting. Beautyberries are virtually pest free except possibly for rabbits, which nibble on their tender new stems in the spring until the stems harden with age. To enhance fruit production, plant in groups.

Companion Planting and Design

Beautyberries are suitable for hedgerows, in front of evergreens, or in a shrub border. Or mass them for a ground cover. Site Beautyberry where it can be viewed from inside the house to enjoy the berries and the mockingbirds, catbirds, and robins that relish them.

Did You Know?

Berry-laden shrubs are the backbone of a Backyard Wildlife Habitat. The National Wildlife Federation's program began in 1973 to encourage homeowners to provide shelter, food, and water for birds and other wildlife. (See Information Resources, page 250.)

Beautyberries are unprepossessing shrubs, content to coexist with more assertive ones and wait for their magic moment at the end of the season. Multistemmed and upright to horizontal, they develop pairs of dull, medium-green leaves neatly arrayed along pale-gray stems in spring. By midsummer their tiny, inconspicuous pinkish flowers appear, giving way to showy 1/4-in. berries clustered intermittently around slender, layered, arching stems by early fall. As leaves turn purplish and drop, the luminously purple berries become more obvious. Japanese Beautyberry (Callicarpa japonica 'Leucocarpa') has white flowers and white berries. Native Beautyberry (Callicarpa americana) has larger berries. 'Alba' has white berries. Bodinier Beautyberry (Callicarpa bodinieri) 'Profusion' has clusters of deep-lilac berries numbering thirty to forty per cluster, and has slightly purple fall leaf color.

Other Name
Purple Beautyberry

Bloom Period and Seasonal Color
August; blooms, then berries in purple, magenta, or white

Mature Height × Spread
4 to 6 ft. × 4 to 5 ft.

Boxwood

Buxus hybrids

Elegant but utilitarian, Boxwood has not been widely grown in Pennsylvania for fear that it was not cold hardy here. However, there are now excellent Boxwood hybrids suitable for our winters. Branching clouds of small, fine-textured foliage and naturally rounded, formal-looking habit are Boxwood trademarks. So is the musky odor that some exude. This may be the reason deer tend to overlook Common Box. Their longevity is legendary; some at Mount Vernon are more than two hundred years old. Some dependable hybrids include 'Green Gem' (2 ft. tall and wide and ball shaped); 'Green Mountain' (5 ft. tall and somewhat narrower); 'Green Velvet' (about 3 ft. wide and tall); 'Suffruticosa' (great for edging); and 'Northern Find' and 'Varder Valley' (both extra hardy).

Other Name
Common Box

Bloom Period and Seasonal Color
Evergreen; dark-green foliage

Mature Height × Spread
3 to 15 ft. × 3 to 10 ft.

When, Where, and How to Plant
Plant burlap-wrapped shrubs in spring or fall. Transplant those in containers anytime during the growing season when it is not terribly hot and dry. Three-year-old Boxwoods transplant best. Boxwoods prefer full sun and neutral soil that is moist, rich in organic matter, and well drained. Do not crowd them. Their shallow, invasive roots compete with neighboring plants. Dig in organic matter to improve soil drainage. Dig a saucer-shaped hole as deep as the rootball's height and about twice as wide. Set it so that its top is exactly at or a bit above ground level. Cut away as much burlap as possible. Backfill, firm the soil gently around each shrub, and water well.

Growing Tips
Mulch Boxwoods with a 2- or 3-in. layer of organic material to conserve soil moisture. Water them regularly if rainfall is scarce during the first year establishment period and during times of drought. After six months, sprinkle granular slow-acting fertilizer on the mulch for the rain to soak in.

Care
Protect older shrubs from drying winter wind and sun, but maintain good air circulation. Prune out browned, winterkilled branches. Thin branches to eliminate dense twigginess. Renovate old specimens gradually, cutting back only 1/3 its size per year. Spray mites and scale with horticultural oil. Eliminate shrubs infected with root rot. Identify and correct any stressful circumstances that predispose Boxwood to these problems.

Companion Planting and Design
Dense and slow-growing, Boxwood is great for edging walks and beds, especially herb gardens. It shears beautifully for topiaries, hedges, and mazes. Boxwoods do very well in containers.

Did You Know?
Parterre gardens are popular for more formal landscapes. Originally French (*parterre* means "along the ground"), this geometric style is laid out as large, flat squares or rectangles of vegetables, subdivided by low, tidy Boxwood hedges. Sometimes a fountain, sculpture, or planted container is at the center of the design. Knot gardens for herbs or flowers are similar.

Butterfly Bush

Buddleia davidii

When, Where, and How to Plant

Plant Butterfly Bushes grown in containers anytime during the growing season, but spring is best. Site them in full sun; too much shade makes them gangly and reduces flowering. They like decent well-drained garden soil; it can be on the sandy side. Dig a saucer-shaped hole as deep as the rootball is tall and about twice as wide. Set the plant so that the top of its rootball is exactly level or a bit higher than the surrounding soil. Backfill, firm soil gently around the shrub, and water well. Space shrubs at least 4 ft. apart.

Growing Tips

Mulch Butterfly Bush root zones with a 2- or 3-in. layer of organic material. If rainfall is unreliable, water the shrub regularly until it is well established. Every spring sprinkle slow-acting granular fertilizer formulated for trees and shrubs on the mulch for the rain or snow to soak in.

Care

Although not essential, trimming off spent flowers during the season will keep the shrub shaped, groomed, and productive plus it will discourage self-seeding. In spring cut back the previous year's branches to within 6 in. of the ground to stimulate new and dense growth with lots of flowers. Stressed shrubs may attract mites.

Companion Planting and Design

While commonly used as specimens or focal points in the yard, Butterfly Bushes also make good summer hedges. Try integrating them into a mixed flower border.

Did You Know?

Attracting butterflies begins with providing food for their larvae, caterpillars. Each butterfly species has a favorite plant on which females lay eggs. Newly hatched larvae eat its leaves and sometimes its flowers. Larval host plants tend to be wildflowers, weeds, and grasses that are not usually part of a backyard. Host plants for adult butterflies often have brightly colored, daisylike flowers that produce nectar over the entire season. Concentrations of these plants with different bloom times and heights lure the greatest number of butterfly species.

Butterfly Bush tops every list of plants that attract butterflies. Actually, it should top any list of totally delightful landscape plants. It deserves its reputation for vigorous growth, easy care, and reliable season-long bloom. Its slightly coarse, pale gray-green or bluish green foliage provides contrast for green in the garden, and its upright, sometimes unruly arching branches add informality. Butterfly Bush flowers grow at the branch tips as 4- to 8-in.-long tubes of tightly packed, tiny florets that resemble narrow Lilac blossoms. They do not seem to appeal to deer. Readily available are 'Black Knight' (dark purple); 'White Profusion' (white); 'Charming' (pink); and 'Harlequin' with variegated foliage and magenta flowers. 'Nanho Purple' is a dwarf, reaching only 3 or 4 ft. tall.

Other Name
Summer Lilac

Bloom Period and Seasonal Color
June through October; blooms in lavender, purple, white, pink, or yellow

Mature Height × Spread
6 to 8 ft. × 8 to 10 ft.

Cherrylaurel

Prunus laurocerasus 'Otto Luyken'

If this shrub did not exist, someone would have to invent it. Cherrylaurel is a landscape special—growing happily in shade with virtually no care. While some Cherrylaurels are full-sized trees and others are large shrubs, the dwarf 'Otto Luyken' is the perfect size for residential yards in all but the coldest parts of Pennsylvania. A fast-growing, versatile, compact shrub, it boasts attractive lustrous, pointed, dark-green foliage year-round. In the spring it bears narrow 2- to 5-in.-long upright clusters of fuzzy, musky-smelling white florets resembling bottlebrushes. These are followed by purplish black fruits that nestle inconspicuously among the foliage. Sometimes Cherrylaurels bloom again in the fall. Its fruit and its foliage are reputed to be poisonous, which may explain why deer ignore Cherrylaurel.

Other Name
English Laurel

Bloom Period and Seasonal Color
Late spring blooms in cream-white; evergreen foliage

Mature Height × Spread
5 ft. × 5 ft.

When, Where, and How to Plant
Spring and fall are best for planting potted shrubs. Cherrylaurel prefers partial shade. It appreciates bright, indirect light for a few hours a day, but not full sun. Cherrylaurels are not fussy about soil as long as it is reasonably fertile, not too acid, and well drained. Dig a saucer-shaped hole as deep as the rootball is high and about twice as wide. Set each shrub in its hole so that the top of its rootball is exactly level with the surrounding soil. Backfill, firm soil gently around the plant, and water well. Space shrubs 5 ft. apart.

Growing Tips
Spread a layer of organic mulch over shrub root zones, not touching the stems. Water Cherrylaurels regularly in the absence of rain over the first year, then only during periods of drought. For the first two falls, sprinkle slow-acting fertilizer over the mulch for the rain to soak in. After that, decomposing mulch will add organic material to the soil, and regular fertilization is not necessary.

Care
Cherrylaurels take shearing for hedges well, although clipping individual branches in the spring after flowering creates a more natural look. Prune occasional broken branches on 'Otto Luyken'. Renew neglected, larger forms of Cherrylaurel by cutting back stems to ground level, then fertilizing. The best time to renew the shrub is just before new growth begins in the spring. Foliage of shrubs exposed to winter sun and wind may suffer desiccation. Scale attacks foliage of stressed shrubs.

Companion Planting and Design
Use Cherrylaurel for hedges and foundation plantings near buildings where sunshine is limited.

Did You Know?
Cherrylaurels are not really Laurels; they are Cherries. Their name alludes to the resemblance of their foliage to that of true Laurel. Bay Laurel (*Lauris nobilis*) is the true Laurel—its botanical name is derived from the Latin words for "praise" and "famous" (thus the practice of crowning victorious Roman athletes and generals with wreaths made of Laurel leaves). True Laurel resides in spice jars in contemporary kitchens labeled Bay Leaf.

Common Lilac

Syringa vulgaris hybrids

When, Where, and How to Plant

Buy plants grown on their own roots, rather than grafted. Plant bare-root shrubs in early spring, those in containers anytime during the growing season. For best flowering, site in full sun. They are not fussy about soil as long as it is closer to a neutral pH than to acidic. Dig a saucer-shaped hole as deep as the rootball is high and about twice as wide. Set the rootball so its top is level with the surrounding soil. Position bare roots over a cone of packed soil at the bottom of the hole, and allow the roots to drape down its sides. Backfill, firm soil gently, and water well. Space Lilacs so that they have good air circulation.

Growing Tips

Maintain a year-round 2- or 3-in. mulch layer. Water regularly if rainfall is unreliable until shrubs are well established. Every spring sprinkle slow-acting granular fertilizer on the mulch under Lilacs for the rain to soak in.

Care

Prune shrubs in flower or immediately after to stimulate new growth. Renew aging Lilacs by cutting back their thickest, oldest stems to within 6 in. of the ground. Thin new shoots to a few strong ones. Cut off suckers. Chronic mildew problems turn foliage gray in late summer; it does not harm established shrubs. Borers leave small holes in bark; prune off branches below the holes.

Companion Planting and Design

You will find Lilacs growing near old barns and front porches and along fence rows; they also anchor flower beds. They blend well into a mixed shrub border when they are not blooming.

Did You Know?

Lore has it that an English nobleman abandoned an innocent girl whom he had seduced and she died of a broken heart. Because purple Lilacs left on her grave turned white, white Lilacs have come to denote Youthful Innocence. Lilacs tend to be associated with death, as when Walt Whitman mourned the death of Lincoln in his poem "When Lilacs Last in the Dooryard Bloom'd."

Since 1700, Lilacs have enjoyed enormous popularity in America. The introduction of many hybrids from France has increased their appeal. The focus is on the flowers, of course, since the plant is an unremarkable, leggy shrub eleven months of the year. Its smooth, plain green, and heart-shaped foliage sets off the gorgeous blooms. Lilac blossoms are composed of many tiny, tubular florets, clustered in 4- to 6-in.-long sprays that feature the classic Lilac fragrance. Other species bloom at different times over five or six weeks each spring. Typical bloom periods are two weeks; Lilacs that bloom later tend to be less fragrant. If properly cared for, Lilacs live many decades. Japanese Tree Lilac (Syringa reticulata) grows to 30 ft. with malodorous white flowers in June.

Other Name
French Lilac

Bloom Period and Seasonal Color
Late April through May; blooms in purple, white, pink, or rose

Mature Height × Spread
8 to 15 ft. × 6 to 10 ft.

Common Privet

Ligustrum vulgare

Not every shrub can be a landscape star. Privet plays in the chorus line, contributing enormously to the structure and functionality of the home landscapes it graces. Its primary role is as hedging, its reliable toughness, pollution tolerance, and environmental adaptability assuring that it will be around many years. It takes shearing in stride, holds its leaves, which turn purplish in all but severest winters, manages drought, and accepts shade. Left unpruned, Privet bears clusters of musky-scented, off-white flowers that attract honeybees. The small black berries that follow persist into winter if the birds do not get them first. 'Lodense' is a dwarf form that needs less pruning but is deciduous. California Privet (L. ovalifolium) is a commonly used hedge plant in the warmer parts of Pennsylvania.

Other Name
European Privet

Bloom Period and Seasonal Color
May and June; blooms in white

Mature Height × Spread
5 to 15 ft. × 5 to 15 ft.

When, Where, and How to Plant
Transplant Privet grown in containers anytime during the growing season. Spring or fall is preferred to avoid plant stress. Privet takes any soil and thrives in full sun or partial shade. Many regard it as an indicator plant. If it does not grow on a site, nothing will. Dig individual saucer-shaped holes or dig a trench with sloping sides the length of the intended hedge bed as deep as the rootballs are high and twice as wide. Set the rootballs so that their tops are level with the surrounding soil. Backfill, firm soil gently, and water well. Space shrubs 3 ft. apart for a hedge.

Growing Tips
Mulch the soil around Privet year-round with organic material. Water regularly if rainfall is unreliable until it is established. In spring sprinkle slow-acting granular fertilizer for trees and shrubs on the mulch for the rain to soak in.

Care
Prune dead or damaged stems promptly. To establish a hedge, shear for uniform growth when privets are 18 in. tall. Maintain lower branches wider than the upper ones so that the sun can reach them. In spring shear back below the intended height to allow for a gradual seasonal height increase. Shear back only some of the new growth each pruning to assure some new leaves remain at all times. To renew an old hedge, cut back all stems to within 6 in. of the ground in spring. Remove old and dead stems. Fertilize, water, and spread new mulch. Sometimes in humid areas, older foliage may suffer from mildew in late summer.

Companion Planting and Design
Plant Privets as hedges along walks and property lines and in the lawn to divide the yard into "rooms."

Did You Know?
Hedges are barriers; however, because they are plants, they are less intimidating than fences. They mediate the contrast between the structural hardscape of buildings and walls and the natural softscape of plants in a yard. As they define and enclose space, they are more welcoming than rejecting. Certainly, that is why mazes appeal rather than intimidate.

When, Where, and How to Plant

Crapemyrtles tend to arrive at Philadelphia area nurseries later in the spring than most shrubs. Purchase specifically named shrubs, not just generically labeled "pink" or "white" ones. Plant immediately after purchase, although container-grown ones can be planted anytime during the growing season. Site them in full sun. Plant in any soil that is rich in organic matter, acidic, moist, and well drained. Choose sites with some shelter to avoid dieback in severe winters. Provide good air circulation to avoid powdery mildew. Dig a saucer-shaped hole as deep as the rootball is high and about twice as wide. Set the shrub so that the top of its rootball is exactly level with or even a bit higher than the surrounding ground. Backfill, firm soil gently around the shrub, and water well. Space Crapemyrtles at least 5 ft. apart.

Growing Tips

Maintain a year-round layer of organic mulch over each shrub's root zone. Water well the first year until the Crapemyrtle is established, then during periods of drought. Fertilize lightly; rich diets reduce flowering. Decomposing mulch aids soil fertility.

Care

Prune shrubs during dormancy in late winter or very early spring to establish the strongest stems and remove weak or winter-killed ones. Crapemyrtles are susceptible to mildew infection on their foliage. Thin dense foliage for good air circulation.

Companion Planting and Design

Use Crapemyrtles as hedges, background screening, specimens, or foundation shrubs. Pruned low, they make a good accent or anchor for a flower bed. Several semi-dwarf Crapemyrtles, such as 'Hopi' and 'Zuni', do well in outdoor containers. Provide winter insulation.

Did You Know?

Summer-blooming shrubs bridge the landscape color gap between spring Dogwood and Azaleas and fall foliage color. Consider these: Bluebeard (*Caryopteris* × *clandonensis*); Butterfly Bush (*Buddleia davidii*); Chaste Tree (*Vitex agnus-castus*); Glossy Abelia (*Abelia* × *grandiflora*); Big Leaf Hydrangea (*Hydrangea macrophylla*); Plumleaf Azalea (*Rhododendron prunifolium*); Rose of Sharon (*Hibiscus syriacus*); and Summersweet (*Clethra alnifolia*).

Crapemyrtles are traditional Southern plants, but the National Arboretum has developed cold-hardy hybrids that make it possible for residents of the warmest parts of Pennsylvania (around Philadelphia) to enjoy their considerable virtues. Rugged and versatile, these summer bloomers bear 6- to 15-in.-long clusters of flowers with crimped edges on their petals at the ends of upright, arching branches. Their foliage, which appears late in the spring as a glossy yellowish bronze color and then becomes bright green, changes again to yellow, orange, or reddish fall color. For the winter season there remains handsome bark mottled with brownish and gray patches. Some suggestions are 'Comanche' (pink); 'Natchez' (white), which is a best-seller and makes a good small tree; 'Powhatan' (purple); and 'Tuskegee' (deep rose).

Bloom Period and Seasonal Color
Late July to October; blooms in pink, lavender, white, or red

Mature Height × Spread
3 to 30 ft. × 3 to 15 ft.

Daphne 'Carol Mackie'

Daphne × burkwoodii 'Carol Mackie'

Daphne is more associated with the South than with northern states like Pennsylvania. The very name suggests a delicate Southern belle, and many Daphnes have a reputation as relatively short-lived and fussy. One that copes with our winters and represents the best that Daphnes have to offer is 'Carol Mackie'. This low-growing, densely twiggy shrub offers eye-catching variegated foliage of green margined in yellow. In spring, charming flowers are poised along its branches. These clusters of up to sixteen individual waxy, pinkish-tinged white florets are renowned for their fragrance. Fortunate is the homeowner whose Daphne repeat blooms in early fall. Any berries and all parts of all Daphnes are poisonous, which may explain why deer pass up such agreeable shrubs.

Other Name
Burkwood Daphne

Bloom Period and Seasonal Color
Late spring blooms in white; variegated foliage

Mature Height × Spread
3 to 5 ft. × 3 to 6 ft.

When, Where, and How to Plant
Plant burlap-wrapped Daphnes in early spring. Plant those grown in containers anytime during the growing season, unless it's hot and dry. Site them where they enjoy full sun in the spring and afternoon shade in midsummer. 'Carol Mackie' likes most well-drained garden soils rich in organic material. Dig a hole with sloping sides as deep as the rootball is high and twice as wide to encourage roots outward. Daphne roots tend to wrap around themselves even under the best conditions. Position the shrub so that its rootball top is level with or slightly above the surrounding soil. Cut away as much burlap as possible. Backfill, firm soil gently, and water well. Space shrubs 4 ft. apart. Balled-and-burlaped Daphnes may take awhile to establish. They do not like to have their roots disturbed, so avoid moving them.

Growing Tips
Water newly planted Daphnes when they dry out until they establish, then water only when rainfall is scarce. A year-round layer of organic mulch will retain soil moisture. Do not pile it against stems. Decomposing mulch enriches the soil.

Care
Prune any broken or rubbing branches. Shape Daphnes in spring, immediately after flowering. 'Carol Mackie' flowering is sparse the first year, but it musters a full show by its second or third year. Spray aphids or scale with horticultural oil. Do not be discouraged by the mysterious "Daphne Death," which sometimes causes unexpected demise of otherwise healthy specimens.

Companion Planting and Design
Plant Daphne near walks or doorways so that passersby can enjoy its spring fragrance. Rose Daphne (*Daphne cneorum*) grows to 12 in., and is suitable for rock gardens or as a ground cover.

Did You Know?
In Greek mythology Daphne was a river nymph whose beauty attracted Apollo. When he pursued her, she rejected him and prayed to the gods for help. Unable to deter Apollo, who was accustomed to getting his way, the gods turned Daphne into a lushly fragrant shrub. Henceforth the shrub was sacred to Apollo.

Doublefile Viburnum
Viburnum plicatum tomentosum

When, Where, and How to Plant
Plant balled-and-burlapped shrubs in early spring or early fall. Transplant those grown in containers anytime during the season. Viburnums like full sun to partial shade. They are happiest in any good garden soil that is not soggy. It should be rich in organic matter, slightly acidic, moist, yet well drained. This Viburnum has a real problem with clay; incorporate lots of organic matter into heavy clay soil to improve drainage. Dig a hole with sloping sides as deep as the rootball is high and twice as wide. Set the rootball so that its top is level with the surrounding soil. Remove as much burlap as possible, then backfill, firm the soil gently, and water well.

Growing Tips
Maintain a year-round, 2- or 3-in. layer of mulch to retain soil moisture. Water regularly until well established if rainfall is unreliable. Six months after planting, sprinkle slow-acting granular fertilizer formulated for trees and shrubs on the mulch for the rain to soak in. After one or two years when the shrub is well established, decomposing mulch will provide enough nutrition.

Care
Because they have a very symmetrical habit, Viburnums do not need pruning except to remove an occasional broken branch. To discourage rodents that gnaw on the tender bark of young shrubs during the winter, wrap stems with hardware cloth. Watch for Japanese beetles. Stressed shrubs may suffer attacks by aphids, mites, or scale.

Companion Planting and Design
Site Doublefiles at the bottom of a hill or wall or deck so that people can view the flowers from above. Use one as a specimen or focal point. Group several for informal hedging or screens, or include them in a shrub border or edge of a woodland.

Did You Know?
Here are Viburnum winners of the Pennsylvania Horticultural Society's Gold Medal Award: *Viburnum × burkwoodii* 'Mowhawk'; *Viburnum* 'Conoy'; *Viburnum dilatatum* 'Erie'; *Viburnum ×* 'Eskimo'; *Viburnum nudum* 'Winterthur'; and *Viburnum plicatum tomentosum* 'Shasta'.

Viburnums are beloved by gardeners for their multiseason beauty and especially for their fall berries. Easily identifiable during bloom time is the elegant Doublefile type. From a distance it resembles a Kousa Dogwood, but the double rows of flat, white "lacecap" flowers that march along the tops of its tiered, horizontal branches are distinctive. Their central clusters of tight fertile florets are ringed by open-petaled sterile florets, the flowers float in rows atop paired green leaves, which droop on each side of the branches as if deferring to the blossoms. It makes a stunning show. By fall when the foliage turns purplish red, the fertile flowers have become berries, first red, then maturing to black. In many areas, deer tend to ignore this shrub.

Bloom Period and Seasonal Color
May; blooms in white

Mature Height × Spread
8 to 10 ft. × 10 to 12 ft.

Dwarf Mugo Pine
Pinus mugo

Dwarf Mugo Pines are popular ornamental conifers and with good reason. They have all the virtues of pines—fine needles, aromatic foliage, plump cones, and sturdy constitutions—plus a compact form. Their irregular, rounded cushions of dense needles provide contrasting texture to broadleaf plant neighbors near the front of the border. Deer that may venture into the yard are likely to bypass them. Because Dwarf Mugo Pines are not automatically under 20 ft. tall, choose named varieties. Pinus mugo 'Mops' is very dense and globe shaped; it grows to 4 ft. Pinus mugo var. mugo has medium-green foliage in spring, lighter in summer; it tends to be twice as wide as tall. Pinus mugo var. pumilio is low growing, up to 10 ft. wide.

Other Name
Dwarf Swiss Mountain Pine

Bloom Period and Seasonal Color
Evergreen conifer

Mature Height × Spread
3 to 5 ft. × 6 to 12 ft.

When, Where, and How to Plant
Plant balled-and-burlapped Dwarf Mugo Pines in spring or fall. Plant those in containers anytime during the growing season. They need full sun or a site with light afternoon shade. They accept any type of decent well-drained soil, even a bit on the alkaline side. Add organic matter to heavy, clay soil to improve drainage. Keep Mugos away from turfgrasses, which release a growth-inhibiting substance into the soil. Dig a saucer-shaped hole as deep as the rootball is high and somewhat wider. Set the rootball in it so its top is level with or somewhat higher than the surrounding soil. Remove as much burlap as possible. Backfill, firm soil gently, and water well. Mugo Pines are very slow growing, so they will stay within their allotted space for years.

Growing Tips
Mulch surrounding soil with a 2- or 3-in. layer of organic matter. Water regularly for a year or more if rainfall is unreliable until established. In spring sprinkle slow-acting granular fertilizer for evergreens on the mulch for the rain to soak in.

Care
Clip brown or broken branches anytime. Mugos do not need pruning to control size or shape. Pine sawfly larvae are caterpillars the same color as pine needles. Pick them off shrubs, place in a plastic bag, and discard. Treat heavy infestations by spraying with *B.t.* (*Bacillus thuringiensis*) while caterpillars are actively eating. Thwart scale problems by spraying foliage with light horticultural oil.

Companion Planting and Design
Mugos are eminently adaptable to home landscapes, serving effectively as foundation plants, focal points, rock garden or container specimens, and ground covers.

Did You Know?
Buyer beware: Plants are not always what they are labeled. Sometimes plants do not mature enough to be properly identified before sale. Male and female plants are difficult to tell apart for many years. Plants grown from seed are unpredictable. Thus, Dwarf Mugo Pines may turn out not to be dwarf.

Evergreen Azalea

Rhododendron species and hybrids

When, Where, and How to Plant

Plant burlap-wrapped Azaleas in early spring or fall. Transplant those in containers anytime during the growing season, but spring is best. Most prefer sunny sites, but they also enjoy some afternoon shade in the summer. Dappled light in woodland settings is ideal as long as they are not under shallow-rooted trees, which compete with them for moisture. Azaleas like moist, woodsy soil that is acidic and rich in organic matter. Choose a site with shelter from harsh winter wind and sun. If the soil is clay, mix in organic material, or build a raised bed to improve drainage. Dig a saucer-shaped hole as deep as the rootball is high and about twice as wide. Set the plants in the hole so that the top of the rootball is exactly level with the surrounding soil. Cut as much burlap away as possible. Backfill, firm soil gently, and water well.

Growing Tips

Mulch year-round with 2 or 3 in. of organic material to keep the soil moist. If rainfall is unreliable, water regularly until shrubs are well established. In spring, sprinkle slow-acting granular fertilizer formulated for acid-loving plants on the mulch for the rain to soak in.

Care

Renew old Azaleas by cutting back dead or tired branches to within 6 in. of the ground to stimulate new, dense growth. Cut back immediately after spring flowering so you can enjoy the blooms and so the shrubs have the remainder of the season to regenerate. Lace bugs attack Azaleas that are sun stressed or in dry, compacted soil; they cause pale stippling on foliage. Deer and rabbits also have a taste for Azaleas.

Companion Planting and Design

Use Azaleas as specimens and focal points, as anchors for a mixed border, as hedges, and naturalized in woodland settings.

Did You Know?

Azaleas are technically Rhododendrons. Botanists distinguish between them because Azaleas have only five stamens in the center of their flowers, while Rhododendrons have ten or more. Azaleas are usually smaller and their leaves have hairy surfaces, whereas Rhododendron leaf surfaces are smooth. Azaleas can take more heat and drier conditions.

Starting in early May, Pennsylvania breaks out in Azalea blooms. Suddenly, nondescript, little green shrubs come alive with color and the wildlife they attract. Among the standouts are Asian Azaleas and their hybrids. Compact and bushy, they bear a profusion of flowers, sometimes double or semi-double, along their stems among rich, green, lustrous foliage. In fall they take a curtain call as their evergreen leaves turn reddish or bronze with cold weather. Azaleas are often listed in catalogs as groups of hybrids developed by a particular person. Polly Hill hybrids are tough, low-growing ground covers, blooming a month after the common ones. (Deciduous Azaleas are often fragrant, and offer a range of colors, including orange and yellow, and bloom times. Native ones do not get mildew.)

Other Name
Azalea

Bloom Period and Seasonal Color
May; blooms in red, shades of pink, or white

Mature Height × Spread
3 to 8 ft. × 4 to 10 ft.

Firethorn

Pyracantha coccinea

Firethorns are aptly named; their upright or sprawling stems are covered with thorns. Then in the fall their berries turn bright red or orange, seeming to set them afire. These tough plants show a softer side in the spring, however, when they are covered with white flowers clustered among their dense, lustrous, leathery, dark-green pointed leaves. Once established, these shrubs are self-reliant and hardy in much of Pennsylvania. It is a desperate deer that nibbles on Firethorn! 'Fiery Cascade' is noted for its cold hardiness and disease resistance. 'Harlequin' has dark-green leaves marked with creamy white; 'Lalandei' has large leaves and orange-red fruit, and grows tall for espalier. 'Mohave', a hybrid, has prolific berries; see it espaliered at the Morris Arboretum in Philadelphia.

Other Name
Scarlet Firethorn

Bloom Period and Seasonal Color
June; blooms in white

Mature Height × Spread
8 to 10 ft. × 3 to 12 ft.

When, Where, and How to Plant

For ease of handling and quick establishment, choose potted Firethorns that have healthy foliage. Plant anytime during the growing season, but spring is best. For best flower and fruit production, plant in full sun, in good, organically rich, well-drained garden soil. Be sure of the location because the large thorny plants are difficult to move. Leave enough space to permit access for pruning as it grows. Add peat moss or compost to heavy clay soil. Dig a saucer-shaped hole as deep as the root-ball is high and twice as wide. Slice partway through the rootball in several places if the shrub is terribly rootbound. Set it in its hole so that its top is exactly level with or slightly higher than the surrounding soil. Backfill, firm soil gently, and water well. Space shrubs 6 ft. apart, closer for a hedge.

Growing Tips

Maintain a 2- to 3-in. layer of organic mulch over the root zone to retain soil moisture and discourage weeds so there will be no need to work under or near this thorny plant. Water regularly in the absence of rain for the first year. After six months, sprinkle granular slow-acting fertilizer for trees and shrubs on the mulch for the rain to soak in.

Care

Prune away dead or damaged branches as they occur. In winter or spring prune back the longest branches to control shrub shape and size. Firethorn is sometimes infected by the bacterial disease fireblight. Prune out blackened, dead stems, clean up leaf debris, and disinfect tools in a solution of hot water laced with household bleach.

Companion Planting and Design

Firethorns are well suited to guard duty as barrier plants under windows and around porches, and as hedges along property lines; they are strongly ornamental, especially when trained as espalier to a trellis or wall.

Did You Know?

Shrubs that offer fall berries for wildlife are Barberry, Euonymus, Beautyberry, Firethorn, Cotoneaster, Holly, Dogwood, and Viburnum.

Forsythia

Forsythia × intermedia

When, Where, and How to Plant

Plant Forsythias in spring or fall, those in containers anytime during the growing season. Full sun is essential for bloom and compact growth. They adapt to a wide range of soil types, (including that of abandoned city housing sites), but do their best in rich, well-drained garden soil. Dig a saucer-shaped hole as deep as the rootball is high and about twice as wide. Position the rootball so its top is exactly level with the surrounding soil. Cut most of the burlap away. Backfill, firm soil gently around the plant, and water well. Space shrubs 10 ft. apart, 8 ft. for hedges.

Growing Tips

Mulch shrub root zones year-round with organic material. Water regularly if rainfall is unreliable until Forsythia is well established. In spring, sprinkle slow-acting granular fertilizer on the mulch for the rain to soak in. Forsythias are not heavy feeders, so after a year or two, depend on decomposing mulch to enrich the soil.

Care

Prune back the single stem of spring-planted bare-root Forsythia to 18 in. when planting. Renovate scraggly, neglected shrubs by cutting $1/3$ of the old woody canes back to the ground each spring after flowering to stimulate new shoots. Avoid frequent cutting back of unruly growth, and never shear. Forsythia has no significant pests or diseases.

Companion Planting and Design

Use Forsythias as foundation plants, or as part of a larger shrub border where their plain green foliage can blend in during the summer. They make good hedges if not overpruned.

Did You Know?

Enjoy spring early by forcing Forsythia, Quince, Dogwood, Magnolia, and Witchhazel to bloom prematurely indoors. Cut branches showing buds, put them in lukewarm water in a cool room, and change the water every few days. When the buds swell, recut the branch ends, arrange them in a vase with fresh water, and bring them into a heated room to show their stuff.

Originally from Asia, Forsythias have had one hundred years in this country to win their way into our hearts as annual heralds of a new spring. When their graceful, arching branches are loaded with bright-yellow flowers, who cares if they are ordinary the rest of the year? After they flower, bright-green leaves appear and age over the summer to darker green and then yellow-green and sometimes purplish red before dropping. Because Forsythias bloom on the previous year's wood, the buds for the next season form by midsummer. Forsythias tolerate city conditions and benign neglect. They have virtually no pests and diseases. With a little attention these shrubs can live more than fifty years. 'Lynwood Gold' and 'Spectabilis' have bright-yellow flowers; 'Spring Glory' is soft-yellow.

Other Name

Border Forsythia

Bloom Period and Seasonal Color

April; blooms in bright yellow

Mature Height × Spread

8 to 10 ft. × 10 to 12 ft.

Fothergilla

Fothergilla gardenii

Fothergillas are gaining popularity for yards and gardens in Pennsylvania because they are sturdy shrubs with lots of appeal and many assets. The first asset is their flowers, stubby spikes of many petal-less flowers that look like fuzzy bottlebrushes at the tips of their stems. A close second is their foliage, which usually appears after they bloom. It is toothed and a dull dark green or blue-green, which turns bright red, orange, and yellow in the fall. 'Blue Mist' has blue-green foliage and requires partial shade in the summer; its fall color is less showy. 'Mt. Airy' is a superior selection; upright, more rounded, it has great fall color. Large Fothergilla (Fothergilla major or F. monticola) grows to 10 ft. tall.

Other Name
Dwarf Fothergilla

Bloom Period and Seasonal Color
April; blooms in white

Mature Height × Spread
3 to 4 ft. × 2 to 3 ft.

When, Where, and How to Plant

Transplant Fothergillas grown in containers any-time during the growing season; however, spring is best. For best flowering and fall color, plant where they get mostly sun in the spring, but perhaps some shade as fall approaches, which reportedly improves their yellow-orange foliage color. They like moist garden soils that are slightly acidic and well drained. Dig a saucer-shaped hole as deep as the rootball is high and a bit wider. Remove the shrub from its container, and untangle or clip any circling roots. Set its rootball in the hole exactly level with the surrounding soil. Backfill, firm soil gently over the shrub's root zone, and water well. Space Fothergillas 4 ft. apart.

Growing Tips

Mulch the soil with 2 or 3 in. of organic material. Chopped leaves or wood chips are fine. Water regularly if rainfall is unreliable until Fothergilla is well established. Then water only during droughty periods. In spring sprinkle slow-acting granular fertilizer formulated for trees and shrubs on the mulch for the rain or snow to soak in. Eventually, the decomposing mulch enriches the soil, and annual fertilizer will not be necessary.

Care

Fothergillas do not need routine pruning. Clip the occasional broken branch. If it becomes thin and lanky after several years, cut back the entire shrub to ground level in spring to renew it. Like many natives, Fothergillas have few pest or disease problems.

Companion Planting and Design

Fothergillas are attractive grouped for a landscape accent or massed on a hillside to hold the soil. Use them individually to anchor a mixed border or to obscure a building foundation. They are a bit too small and drab between spring and fall to be front and center as specimen shrubs.

Did You Know?

Ironically, our native Fothergillas were named after a British physician, John Fothergill (1712–80), who grew American plants in England. The dwarf one was named for Dr. Garden who discovered this smaller version.

Hybrid Tea Rose
Rosa hybrids

When, Where, and How to Plant

Plant dormant bare-root Hybrid Teas in spring. Plant containerized ones anytime during the growing season. Give them your best soil: well drained in full sun. Keep roots moist until planting time. Dig a saucer-shaped hole as deep as and slightly wider than the rootball or bare roots. Set potted Rose rootballs so that their tops are exactly at soil level. Set burlapped rootballs with grafts 2 in. below soil level; remove the burlap. Position bare-root systems over a packed soil cone on the bottom of the planting hole, roots splaying down its sides. Backfill, firm soil gently over root zones, and water well. Allow plenty of air circulation between Hybrid Tea Roses to discourage fungal disease.

Growing Tips

Mulch soil to discourage weeds. After the ground freezes, pile mulch around stems. Water regularly in the absence of rain. Hybrid Teas are heavy feeders. Fertilize as instructed on the label of slow-acting granular fertilizer for Roses.

Care

Prune winter-killed canes in spring. Identify three to five healthy canes 12 to 18 in. tall to encourage this season's stems. Snip them at a 45-degree angle just above a leaf bud on the outside of the cane to direct growth outward. Consult a book on Rose care for treating blackspot on Rose foliage. Watch for Japanese beetles in early July; regularly knock them into a jar of soapy water.

Companion Planting and Design

Hybrid Teas prefer a bed of their own. Plant a living mulch of a dainty ground cover such as Sweet Alyssum to mask their lower stems and soften the scene.

Did You Know?

The most famous, most planted Hybrid Tea Rose is 'Peace', introduced by Conard-Pyle in Chester County, Pennsylvania. Its fate was intertwined with events of World War II. It was smuggled out of France in Robert Pyle's diplomatic pouch on the last plane from Lyons before France fell to the Germans. It won the AARS medal on V-E day in 1945.

Roses have been considered the "queen of flowers" for two thousand years, and Hybrid Tea Roses require the dutiful attention lavished on royalty. They are the classic high-maintenance plant because they are susceptible to many environmental, pest, and disease problems. They require solicitous attention and seemingly constant spraying to foster healthy foliage and the classic single flower at the tips of straight stems. Sometimes other types of Roses, such as Grandifloras and Floribundas, are included in discussions of Hybrid Teas because they have similar, although not quite so strict, cultivation requirements. They produce more than one flower per stem and are not typically grafted. Choose Hybrid Tea Roses that have AARS on their tag. It signifies an All-America Rose Selection for beauty and vigor.

Other Name
Tea Rose

Bloom Period and Seasonal Color
June through summer; blooms in all colors except blue or black

Mature Height × Spread
6 ft. × 4 ft.

Japanese Barberry
Berberis thunbergii 'Atropurpurea'

Barberries have always been a landscape standby, tough, long-lived, and accommodating of prevailing conditions. Japanese Barberries add an ornamental element with their colorful foliage. All have yellow wood beneath their bark, and the twigs of Japanese types bear tufts of neat little ovoid leaves, single thorns, and inconspicuous yellow flowers in spring. Flowers become tiny red berries dangling singly or in pairs among the foliage in late summer and fall. Japanese Barberries are preferable to European ones because they are not alternate hosts for infectious rust disease. 'Crimson Pygmy' at 2 ft. tall has deep-red leaves, and 'Rosy Glow' at 5 ft. has burgundy foliage marbled with pink. 'Aurea' has yellow foliage and red berries and grows to 2 ft.

Other Name
Red Barberry

Bloom Period and Seasonal Color
Spring bloom, then berries; foliage in maroon, mottled pink, or yellow

Mature Height × Spread
2 to 5 ft. × 2 to 5 ft.

When, Where, and How to Plant
Transplant container plants anytime the ground is not frozen. For best foliage color, plant in full sun. In too much shade, purple foliage turns green. Japanese Barberries like well-drained, decent, even poor soil of any type. Dig a saucer-shaped planting hole as deep as the rootball is high and twice as wide. Mix in a handful of a granular all-purpose slow-acting fertilizer. For a hedge dig holes 4 ft. apart; 2½ ft. apart for dwarf types. Set rootballs so that their tops are level with the surrounding soil. Backfill, firm soil gently, and water well.

Growing Tips
Provide 2 or 3 in. of mulch year-round to retain soil moisture and discourage weeds. Once established, Barberries do not need watering unless there is severe drought. Follow-up fertilizing is not necessary.

Care
Prune individual shrubs if needed or shear hedges in late spring. Rejuvenate old or neglected shrubs by cutting them back to the ground then. Verticillium wilt causes Barberry foliage to turn brown and fall off. Promptly remove infected plants and their soil to limit the spread of the infection, especially if they are part of a hedge or mass planting. Disinfect shovels and pruners by dipping them into hot water mixed with household bleach.

Companion Planting and Design
Japanese Barberries do nicely in containers on the deck or patio. Because of their thorns, they make good barrier plants under windows to thwart intruders and in areas where foot traffic is to be discouraged. They take shearing for hedges, and dwarf types look wonderful massed as a ground cover with contrasting plants or as edging for planted beds.

Did You Know?
Barberries head most lists of deer-resistant plants. Others on the lists are usually thorned or spined or have fuzzy foliage, such as Lamb's Ears, or strong, resinous odors, such as Artemisias. However, deer appetites vary from neighborhood to neighborhood. Also, deer under serious population pressure will eat almost anything.

Japanese Pieris

Pieris japonica

When, Where, and How to Plant

Transplant shrubs grown in containers anytime during the growing season. Light is a critical consideration when siting Pieris. They like woodland conditions. Provide acidic, well-drained soil rich in organic matter. If they are near a brick or stone wall, check soil pH to be sure its acidity is not neutralized by lime leached from mortar. Improve heavy clay or thin, sandy soil by digging in organic matter. Dig a saucer-shaped hole as deep as the rootball is high and somewhat wider. Set the rootball so that its top is level with or a bit higher than the surrounding soil. Backfill, firm the soil gently, and water well. Space Pieris at least 5 ft. from each other or buildings.

Growing Tips

Mulch year-round with a thin layer of organic matter. Water regularly if rainfall is unreliable until well established. Do not allow the soil to dry out in summer. In spring sprinkle slow-acting granular fertilizer formulated for acid-loving plants on the mulch for the rain to soak in.

Care

Cut back dead branches in spring to within 6 in. of the ground. Screen exposed shrubs from harsh winter wind and sun. Pieris continues to transpire moisture from its evergreen leaves during winter. It cannot take up moisture from frozen soil, so water the ground deeply before it freezes to prevent desiccation. Spray foliage with an anti-desiccant in late autumn. Proper siting will avoid chronic lace bug problems.

Companion Planting and Design

Slow-growing, Pieris is at home in woodland settings or as foundation, accent, or specimen plantings in shady areas of yards.

Did You Know?

Lace bugs are a Pieris nemesis. They target Pieris stressed by drought and too much sun. Identify and treat infestations early because lace bugs have many generations over a single season. Their damage to foliage remains visible even after they have been eliminated by repeated sprays of an insecticidal soap or encapsulated pyrethrum.

The elegance of Pieris enhances any landscape. Its compact, yet free-form, openly branching habit becomes more interesting with age. As it presides over the seasons, its rosettes of narrow, finely toothed, lustrous evergreen foliage mature from bright lime-green or reddish green to dark green just in time to showcase its flowers. Their buds develop into stunning, waxy, urn-shaped florets arrayed in 3- to 5-in. pendulous, fragrant clusters that bloom for three weeks or more. Many Japanese Pieris varieties have colored flowers, such as 'Flamingo' (rose-red), 'Dorothy Wycoff' (pink), and 'White Cascade' (white). The new foliage of 'Mountain Fire' is particularly red. 'Variegata' foliage is edged with white. Mountain Pieris (Pieris floribunda) blooms in April with smaller, upright flower clusters; it is resistant to lace bugs.

Other Name

Lily of the Valley Shrub

Bloom Period and Seasonal Color

Early April; blooms in white, pink, or rose-red

Mature Height × Spread

4 to 12 ft. × 4 to 6 ft.

Landscape Rose
Rosa species and hybrids

In response to increased interest in low-maintenance Roses that integrate well into residential landscapes, breeders have produced many sturdy, colorful, self-reliant Roses called Shrub Roses. Their easygoing, informal habits assure their versatility in home landscapes. Many have multiseason interest, offering season-long bloom, then colorful seedpods, or hips, and fall foliage color. Their flowers are lovely, abundant, and often fragrant. 'Carefree Delight'™, 'Ice and Fire', and 'The Fairy' make great hedges. Meidiland™ hybrids include 'Bonica'™, which has double, pink flowers. Many others in this series are tough and attractive for hedges, ground covers, or massing. Rugosa hybrids do well in coastal areas and tough conditions such as along major highways. They have simple flowers, wonderful hips, and leathery foliage, especially 'Frau Dagmar Hartopp'.

Other Name
Shrub Rose

Bloom Period and Seasonal Color
June through October; blooms in white, pink, or red

Mature Height × Spread
3 to 8 ft. × 4 to 6 ft.

When, Where, and How to Plant
Transplant Landscape Roses grown in containers in spring to guarantee some bloom over their first season. Like most flowering shrubs, these Roses do best in full sun, at least 6 hours daily, but can handle some shade. They like well-drained soil, rich in organic matter, but accept almost any kind. In fact, Rugosa-type Roses thrive on thin, poor soils. Dig a saucer-shaped hole as deep as the rootball is high and about twice as wide. Set rootballs so that their tops are exactly level with the surrounding soil, no lower. There is no graft to worry about. Backfill, firm soil gently over shrub root zones, and water well. Space them 5 ft. apart, slightly less for hedges.

Growing Tips
Mulch Landscape Roses year-round with a 2- or 3-in. layer of organic matter such as chopped leaves or wood chips. Water them well while they become established. Many are drought tolerant, but appreciate water when rainfall is sparse. In the spring sprinkle slow-acting granular fertilizer formulated for trees and shrubs, or Roses, on the mulch for the rain to soak in. Landscape Roses are not as heavy feeders as Hybrid Teas; once a year is fine.

Care
Most Landscape Roses are self-cleaning, so deadheading is not necessary. They need no special winter protection other than their usual mulch. Cut stems back in the spring to promote dense, new growth. Landscape Roses have few problems. Occasionally, Japanese beetles sample their foliage. 'The Fairy' shows some fungal disease on the foliage in extremely humid periods, but does not tolerate fungicidal sprays well. Let the plant handle it.

Companion Planting and Design
Landscape Roses function in yards as ground covers, barrier plants, focal points, hedges, edges, and accents. Many have the "cottage garden" look; some do well in containers.

Did You Know?
A good Landscape Rose has the following: all-season bloom; no special pruning needs; drought resistance; winter sturdiness; fungal disease resistance; and self-cleaning flowers.

When, Where, and How to Plant

Transplant Mahonias grown in containers anytime during the growing season, although spring is best. Mahonia grows shorter and fuller in sun, but appreciates some shade during summers to prevent leaf scorch. It accepts almost any kind of well-drained soil, including clay, as long as it is acidic. Provide shelter from harsh winter sun and winds to protect foliage from desiccation and puncturing. Dig a saucer-shaped hole as deep as the rootball is high and twice as wide. Set the rootball so that its top is level or a bit higher than the surrounding soil. Backfill, firm the soil gently over the roots, and water well. Space Mahonias 5 ft. from shrubs or walls.

Growing Tips

Maintain a year-round, 2- or 3-in. layer of organic mulch. Water Mahonias regularly if rainfall is unreliable until they are well established. In its first spring, sprinkle slow-acting granular fertilizer formulated for acid-loving plants on the mulch for rain to soak in. Future routine fertilization is unnecessary.

Care

To reduce clump size or gain more Mahonias, cut off and dig up rooted side shoots. In the spring cut back dead and overlong branches to within 6 in. of the ground. Trimming off spent flowers during the season will stimulate more flower growth and prevent reseeding, but it will also reduce berry production. Mahonias are remarkably pest and disease free.

Companion Planting and Design

Spreading gradually by underground roots into ever larger clumps, Mahonias maintain a strong profile in the landscape. Use them as specimens or in a shrub border. They are great barrier plants as well.

Did You Know?

Lewis and Clark most likely found Mahonia on their trip west in 1804–6. Their description strongly resembled these shrubs, which were eventually discovered growing wild all over Oregon. They were named for a Pennsylvania nurseryman, Bernard McMahon (1775–1816), from Germantown. He also produced *The American Gardener's Calendar*, one of the earliest gardening guides.

Resembling both Holly and Grapes, this Pacific Northwest native is an acquired taste. Its in-your-face, two-ranked, glossy, leathery, dark-green spined leaflets resemble giant Holly leaves. They form a dark backdrop for the multiple, upright, elongated clusters of tiny yellow bell-shaped florets that fountain out of the stem-growing tips in April. Flowers are immediately covered with foraging honeybees, attracted, no doubt, by their fragrance. By midsummer blossoms give way to grapelike, purplish edible berries that decorate the shrub as fall chill turns its foliage a rich maroon. Deer show Mahonia considerable respect by avoiding it unless they are seriously hungry. Oregon Grapeholly (Mahonia aquifolium) 'Compactum' grows 30 in. tall. Leatherleaf Mahonia (Mahonia bealei) is more heat and shade tolerant and fragrant but coarser. It blooms in late winter.

Other Name
Oregon Grapeholly

Bloom Period and Seasonal Color
Early spring; blooms in yellow

Mature Height × Spread
6 to 8 ft. × 3 to 5 ft.

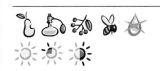

Mockorange

Philadelphus coronarius

This old-fashioned shrub evokes a bygone era when there were fewer shrubs available for the home landscape. Like others of its time, Weigela and Kolkwitzia, it tends to be overlooked and underrated in this day of designer plants and highly hybridized "stars" of the landscape. Truth to tell, Mockorange boasts only modest assets, but among them are a sturdy constitution and lovely white flowers, their citrus fragrance reminiscent of the orange blossoms that traditionally accompanied June weddings. Newer hybrids have showy, extra-large flowers, however. Philadelphus × 'Miniature Snowflake' is compact, with double flowers and dark-green leaves. Philadelphus × 'Buckley's Quill' is compact with double, white flowers, which have narrow quill-like petals. 'Aureus' has golden foliage. Partial shade promotes the best foliage color.

Other Name
Sweet Mockorange

Bloom Period and Seasonal Color
June; blooms in white

Mature Height × Spread
5 to 10 ft. × 5 to 8 ft.

When, Where, and How to Plant

Plant balled-and-burlapped shrubs in spring or fall. Transplant shrubs grown in containers anytime during the growing season. Mockorange accepts either full sun or partial shade in any decent well-drained garden soil. The richer the soil, the better the flowering. Dig a saucer-shaped hole as deep as the rootball is high and about twice as wide. Set the rootball so its top is exactly level with the surrounding soil. Cut away any burlap. Backfill, firm soil gently, and water well. It may take two or three years for Mockorange to establish and bloom profusely. Space shrubs 6 ft. apart.

Growing Tips

Mulch year-round with a 2- or 3-in. layer of organic material; do not let it touch stems. Water regularly if rainfall is unreliable until the shrub is well established. In spring sprinkle slow-acting granular fertilizer formulated for trees and shrubs on the mulch. Subsequently, the decomposing mulch will maintain soil fertility.

Care

Prune Mockorange just after blooming. At 2 ft. tall and again at 4 ft., cut 1/3 off the new growth. Each spring after cut 1/4 of its oldest, thickest branches to the ground. To renew ragged shrubs, cut all stems back to the ground in spring. Shrubs regrow within three years. They are pest and disease free.

Companion Planting and Design

Mockoranges serve basic green background duty most of the summer, fitting in with other shrubs in a border or alone near a wall or corner of a building. Carefully pruned and groomed, they have sufficient grace and form to stand alone as specimens.

Did You Know?

Mockorange is one of a handful of deciduous flowering shrubs that do not insist on full sun. Others include Burkwood Daphne (*Daphne × burkwoodii*), Doublefile Viburnum (*Viburnum plicatum tomentosum*), Dwarf Fothergilla (*Fothergilla gardenii*), Glossy Abelia (*Abelia × grandiflora*), Oakleaf Hydrangea (*Hydrangea quercifolia*), Old-fashioned Weigela (*Weigela florida*), *Rhododendron* species and hybrids, Summersweet (*Clethra alnifolia*), Winged Euonymus (*Euonymus alata*), Winterberry (*Ilex verticillata*), and Witchhazel (*Hamemelis* spp.).

Mountain Laurel

Kalmia latifolia

When, Where, and How to Plant

Transplant shrubs grown in containers in early spring or early fall. Mountain Laurel prefers the woodland conditions of its wild habitat. An understory plant, it likes dappled sun or partial shade and moist, well-drained, acidic, fertile soil. Newer varieties can handle morning sun, but appreciate some shade during hot summer afternoons. Improve heavy clay or very sandy soil by digging in organic matter such as peat moss or compost. Dig a hole with sloping sides just as deep as the rootball is high and about twice as wide. Set the rootball in the hole so its top is exactly level with the surrounding soil or a bit higher. Backfill, firm soil gently, and water well. Space 5 ft. apart.

Growing Tips

Mulch Mountain Laurel year-round with a 2- or 3-in. layer of chopped leaves or wood chips. Water regularly if rainfall is unreliable until it is well established. In spring sprinkle slow-acting granular fertilizer for acid-loving shrubs on the mulch for the rain to soak in. Thereafter, the decomposing mulch will maintain soil fertility and eliminate the need for routine annual fertilizing.

Care

In spring cut back broken or winter-killed branches to live wood. After bloom, trim off spent flowers. Renew old, gangly shrubs by cutting all stems back to within 6 in. of the ground in spring. Shrubs stressed by sun may attract scale, lace bugs, or mildew on foliage. Move the shrub to shade.

Companion Planting and Design

Use Mountain Laurels as specimens or foundation plants, or naturalize them in woodland settings.

Did You Know?

Sometimes the leaves of plants that love acid soil, such as Mountain Laurel, turn yellowish, their veins remaining green. This is called chlorosis, and it signals an iron deficiency. Because of insufficient soil acidity (high pH), they cannot access the iron in the soil. Acidify the soil with powdered garden sulfur as directed on the product label. (Used coffee grounds are a good soil conditioner and acidifier, too.)

Mountain Laurel, the lovely native shrub of our Pennsylvania forests, is our state flower. It has always been valued for its glossy, dense, dark-green foliage, its large round clusters of white flowers, and its vigor. Over the last forty years this wild beauty has undergone a transformation at the hands of plant breeders and now ranks high on every list of first-rate ornamental shrubs. Its globes of intricately formed florets come in many rich colors, the florets sometimes fancifully marked with brownish bands or splotches. Resistant to deer, it is slow growing and long lived. 'Ostsbo Red' has red buds and light-pink flowers. 'Bullseye' flowers have a cinnamon-red band on the petals. 'Elf' is dwarf, averaging half the size of standard Mountain Laurels.

Bloom Period and Seasonal Color
Late May or June; blooms in white, pink, or rose

Mature Height × Spread
8 to 15 ft. × 6 to 20 ft.

Nandina

Nandina domestica

Nandina provides unusual texture and form to residential landscapes in the warmest parts of Pennsylvania around Philadelphia (Zones 7a to 6b). Its stiff, upright, unbranched stems are reminiscent of Bamboo. Their intricately divided foliage composed of pointed leaflets creates an airy look. It progresses from young, glossy, bronzy red to summer green, acquiring a handsome red or purplish tint in autumn. Its attractive foliage provides a backdrop for its large, 6- to 12-in. upright clusters of creamy-white flowers at branch tips in spring. The subsequent large clusters of red berries develop by fall and droop on the shrub through the winter. Dwarf versions of Nandina offer glowing reddish winter foliage, but less spectacular flowers and berries. Full-sized Nandinas include 'Alba' and 'Moyers Red'. Dwarf Nandinas include 'Gulf Stream' and 'Harbour Dwarf'.

Other Name
Heavenly Bamboo

Bloom Period and Seasonal Color
Late June to early July; blooms in white

Mature Height × Spread
2 (dwarf) to 18 ft. × 2 to 5 ft.

When, Where, and How to Plant
Transplant shrubs grown in containers anytime during the growing season. Because Nandinas are not thrilled about being moved, pick a permanent site. Full sun brings out the best in flowers and foliage, especially the foliage of the red-leafed dwarf ones, although all will grow fine in some shade. They prefer good, fertile soil, but they tolerate clay or sandy soils if they get enough summer watering. Dig a saucer-shaped hole as deep as the rootball is high and twice as wide. Set the rootball so its top is level with the surrounding soil. Backfill, firm the soil gently, and water well.

Growing Tips
Mulch the root zone year-round with a 2- or 3-in. layer of organic matter to retain soil moisture and discourage weeds. Water the Nandina when rainfall is unreliable until it is well established. In the spring sprinkle slow-acting granular fertilizer formulated for trees and shrubs on the mulch for the rain to soak in.

Care
To maintain bushiness, cut back the tallest stems annually to various heights. Renew a longtime planting of Nandina by cutting out dead wood and pruning back to ground level about 1/3 of the oldest, thickest stems. Their environmental toughness notwithstanding, in the North some Nandinas lose their leaves during the winter. They are sometimes victimized by wilt and viruses, which mar their foliage. Dig up and discard affected plants.

Companion Planting and Design
A Japanese symbol of hospitality, Nandinas are a welcome addition to any yard as specimens, foundation plants, or ground covers. They are especially at home in Japanese-style gardens.

Did You Know?
Heavenly Bamboo is a lovely common name, but it may do a disservice to this fine shrub. The reputation of true Bamboos as invasive thugs whose spreading roots run rampant through yards predisposes some homeowners and gardeners to shy away from the similarly named Nandina, which is a well-mannered clumping shrub.

Oakleaf Hydrangea
Hydrangea quercifolia

When, Where, and How to Plant

Plant in spring. Transplant shrubs grown in containers anytime during the growing season. Oakleaf Hydrangeas transplant without difficulty. They can take some sun as long as the soil is woodsy—acidic, moist, rich in organic matter, and well drained. If soil is clay, dig in organic matter to improve drainage. Dig a saucer-shaped hole as deep as the rootball is high and twice as wide. Set the shrub so that the top of its rootball is level with the surrounding soil. If it is burlap wrapped, cut as much of the burlap away as possible. Backfill, firm soil gently around the plant, and water well. Oakleafs spread by means of root runners so allow at least 6 ft. between them.

Growing Tips

Maintain a 2- to 3-in. layer of organic mulch on the soil to retain moisture, discourage weeds, and improve the soil. Water when rainfall is scarce. After six months, sprinkle slow-acting granular fertilizer for acid-loving plants on the mulch for the rain to soak in. With mulched soil, there is no need for subsequent annual feedings.

Care

Prune gangly Oakleaf Hydrangea branches to control shrub width just after flowering. Do not wait too long because flower buds for next year's bloom begin to form shortly thereafter. Renew neglected shrubs by cutting stems to the ground in early spring or just after flowering to stimulate denser new growth. Watch for damage on foliage by slugs or various mildews.

Companion Planting and Design

Use Oakleaf Hydrangeas to brighten shady woodland areas, as specimens, as foundation plants, or as part of a shrub border.

Did You Know?

Dried Hydrangea blossoms are wonderful for floral crafts. Allow them to dry on the shrub awhile. Then pick blossoms over several weeks to get a range of colors. Air dry them indoors in an empty vase. Apply hair spray to preserve them. When color fades, spray with metallic paint for holiday decorations.

Oakleaf Hydrangea, a native of the Deep South, thrives in Pennsylvania as well. As its name suggests, its lobed leaves resemble those of Oaks. Coarse-textured, they emerge gray-green with felty undersides in spring. Their summer dark green turns a striking reddish purple before they fall in November to reveal richly colored, peeling tan bark on thick stems. Their early-summer flowers captivate. Cone-shaped, lacy clusters of both sterile (with "petals") and fertile (tiny and round) white florets, they grow up to 12 in. long at stem tips. With age they turn creamy beige and pink tinged. 'Snow Queen', a 1989 Pennsylvania Horticultural Society's Gold Medal Award winner, has more upright flower clusters. PeeGee Hydrangea (Hydrangea paniculata 'Grandiflora') has similar flowers, but blooms in August.

Bloom Period and Seasonal Color

July; blooms in white

Mature Height × Spread

6 to 8 ft. × 6 to 8 ft.

Pfitzer Juniper

Juniperus × *media* 'Pfitzeriana'

Good old Junipers are landscape stalwarts. These sturdy plants come in an enormous variety of sizes, shapes, and colors. They are certainly favorites of builders because they are versatile and adaptable to urban conditions. Chinese Juniper is just one of many Juniper species of diverse size. As a full-sized tree or a medium-sized shrub, it takes heat and drought in stride. Like all Junipers, the Chinese Juniper has separate male and female plants. Pfitzer types are male, and their "flowers" are inconspicuous brown cones. Berries form on female shrubs in August. Chinese Juniper (Juniperus chinensis) 'Old Gold' resembles a dwarf Golden Pfitzer. 'Torulosa' (Hollywood Juniper) is upright with deep-green foliage and twisted branches. 'Mint Julep' resembles a dwarf Pfitzer.

Other Name
Chinese Juniper

Bloom Period and Seasonal Color
Evergreen conifer

Mature Height × Spread
5 to 10 ft. × 5 to 10 ft.

When, Where, and How to Plant
Plant balled-and-burlapped shrubs in spring or fall. Transplant those in containers anytime during the season. Provide shade for new transplants their first day or two. Junipers love full sun; their branches grow loose and spindly in shade. They adapt to any soil as long as it is not soggy. They can even handle road salt. Improve soil drainage by digging in organic material. Dig a saucer-shaped hole exactly as deep as and slightly wider than the shrub rootball. Set it at or slightly above soil level. Backfill, firm the soil gently around stems, and water well. Space shrubs 6 ft. apart, closer for a hedge.

Growing Tips
Mulch soil year-round with 2 or 3 in. of organic material. Keep it at least 6 in. away from stems. Provide regular watering for the first year or two until the Juniper is established. Fertilize in fall with a granular slow-acting product for evergreens. After establishment the decomposing mulch will improve the soil, and annual fertilization will not be necessary.

Care
Routine pruning is not necessary, but clip off damaged branches promptly. Junipers less than five years old may develop a tip blight called *Phomopsis*. Prune out browned, dying twigs. Mites attack when shrubs are stressed. Use a water spray to dislodge them, or spray them with horticultural oil. Junipers under stress may also develop bagworms; pick them off.

Companion Planting and Design
Pfitzer Junipers are ideal for hedges along paved areas where reflected heat and light might stress less sturdy plants. Plant them in rows for a privacy screen or windbreak. Use them to fill bare spots where nothing else will grow.

Did You Know?
The berries of Chinese Juniper are celebrated in song and story as the key ingredient in gin. After pollination, berries take two years to ripen from green to bluish purple. Then they are ready for the distillation process. Do *not* try this at home!

Rhododendron
Rhododendron species and hybrids

When, Where, and How to Plant

Plant burlap-wrapped Rhododendrons in early spring or fall. Transplant shrubs grown in containers anytime during the growing season, but spring is best. Most Rhododendrons prefer sunny sites with afternoon shade in summer and winter. Dappled light in woodland settings suits many if they are not under shallow-rooted trees, which compete with them for moisture. They like woodsy soil, acidic, rich in organic matter, and well drained. Provide shelter from harsh winter wind and sun. Improve clay soil drainage by mixing organic material into it. Dig a saucer-shaped hole as deep as the rootball is high and twice as wide. Set rootballs so their tops are level with the surrounding soil. Remove as much burlap as possible. Backfill, firm the soil gently, and water well.

Growing Tips

Mulch year-round with 2 or 3 in. of organic matter to keep the soil moist and roots cool. Rhododendrons dry out quickly. Water regularly if rainfall is unreliable until they are established and then during hot, dry summers. In spring sprinkle slow-acting granular fertilizer formulated for acid-loving plants on their mulch for the rain to soak in.

Care

Pinch or clip faded flowers to enhance the shrubs' appearance and to prevent seed formation. Renewing old shrubs by cutting back stems to within 6 in. of the ground to stimulate new, dense growth is sometimes successful. Watch for borer holes in older stems, and prune them off below the hole.

Companion Planting and Design

Rhododendrons are understory shrubs in woodland settings, but many make fine specimens, informal hedges and screens, and foundation plantings. Pair them with Ferns and spring bulbs.

Did You Know?

Dr. John Wister, former director of Tyler Arboretum in Media and Scott Arboretum at Swarthmore College near Philadelphia, was instrumental in bringing to prominence the Dexter hybrids, some of the best Rhododendrons we have. An enthusiastic promoter of Rhodys, he bred them during the 1950s.

Rhododendron means "rose tree," and it is easy to see the connection. Rhododendrons' huge clusters of showy bell-shaped flowers framed by large, smooth, dark-green leaves add an elegant note to home landscapes. They grow all over the world, including the United States, and have been cultivated more than a century. Hybrids from native species were introduced in 1876 and represent the majority of Rhododendrons sold here. New types from Asia are proving to be popular as well. Unfortunately, the deer appreciate them as much as we do. Rosebay Rhododendron (R. maximum) is native and can handle drier soil. Rugged hybrids for sunny spots are Catawba hybrids. Fortunei hybrids bloom with the largest flowers. Yakushimanum hybrids are dwarf, compact, and do best in partial sun.

Other Name
Rhody

Bloom Period and Seasonal Color
Early April to May; blooms in red, purple, pink, white, or yellow

Mature Height × Spread
3 (dwarf) to 15 ft. × 3 to 15 ft.

Rose of Sharon

Hibiscus syriacus

A survivor from the old days, Rose of Sharon's pinkish purple flowers produce copious seeds that self-sow to assure new generations. A tough, upright shrub, she has always offered summer flowers, adaptability to any soil and temperature, and resistance to pollution and road salt. Now more civilized hybrids that do not seed promiscuously have endowed her with a new respectability. Their long-lasting flowers are bigger and are available in more colors, yet they retain their toughness. 'Diana' has clear-white flowers that stay open at night. Because it does not seed itself all over, it is recommended for landscape use. Other hybrids offering a variety of colors are 'Aphrodite' (dark pink), 'Minerva' (lilac with a red center), and 'Blue Bird' (blue with purple eye).

Other Name
Shrub Althea

Bloom Period and Seasonal Color
July into September; blooms in white, red, lavender, and pink

Mature Height × Spread
8 to 12 ft. × 6 to 10 ft.

When, Where, and How to Plant
As a summer bloomer, Rose of Sharon is better planted in spring or fall. Shrubs in containers can be planted anytime. Site them in full sun. Although it prefers moist soil, once established, it copes with almost any soil type except boggy. Well-drained ordinary soil is fine. Extra measures to prepare the soil are unnecessary. Dig a saucer-shaped hole as deep as the rootball is high and twice as wide. Set it in the hole so that its top is level with the surrounding soil. Backfill, firm the soil gently, and water well.

Growing Tips
Mulch with a 2- or 3-in. layer of organic matter. Water regularly if rainfall is unreliable until well established. Otherwise, Rose of Sharon needs no special care.

Care
Cut off spent flowers of older types to prevent reseeding. To control size and keep flowers at eye level, cut back branches by several feet during the late winter when Rose of Sharon is dormant. To renew old shrubs, in spring cut back old, thick branches to within 6 in. of the ground to stimulate new growth. Keep an eye out for Japanese beetles.

Companion Planting and Design
Use Rose of Sharon along fences, lawns, and drives, or in shrub borders. They are ideal for cottage-type gardens, screening, and even sheared hedges (usually at the sacrifice of their flowers). They grow well in containers, even trained as a standard with a single stem.

Did You Know?
In Pennsylvania, Japanese beetles emerge from lawns where they spend their white grub stage anytime after the Fourth of July weekend. They zero in on foliage food favorites where they eat and mate with abandon. They are predictable, so check Rose of Sharon and their other favorites in your yard. Begin to handpick or spray them with encapsulated pyrethrum as directed. (Do not use bag beetle traps.) Treat the lawn for white grubs for next year.

Shadblow

Amelanchier species and hybrids

When, Where, and How to Plant
Plant in spring or fall. Plant shrubs from containers anytime during the growing season. Shadblow can handle a range of light situations from full sun to shade. It produces more flowers and better fall foliage color where it gets more sun. Any well-drained ordinary garden soil on the acidic side will do. Give it room because some types expand their clumps by means of suckering roots. Dig a saucer-shaped hole as deep as the rootball is high and about twice as wide. Set it so that its top is exactly level with the surrounding soil. Remove as much of the burlap as possible. Backfill, firm the soil gently, and water well.

Growing Tips
Mulch Shadblow with a 2- or 3-in. layer of organic matter. Water regularly if rainfall is unreliable until well established. If it gets a fair amount of sun, be sure it does not dry out during summer hot spells. There is no need to fertilize decent, mulched soil.

Care
Prune only to remove old or damaged stems or reduce height. Shadblows are related to Apple trees and sometimes fall victim to their diseases. Fireblight causes twig dieback in the middle of the summer. Affected shoots look as if they were scorched by fire and develop distinctive curved ends. Prune out infected plant parts promptly, and put them in the trash to control the spread of the infection. Disinfect tools.

Companion Planting and Design
Use Shadblow in a natural woodland or streamside planting. It is also effective as a foundation or patio plant.

Did You Know?
Traditionally, early-blooming Shadblow has signaled that spring is about to arrive. For early settlers it also meant that the ground would thaw enough so that graves could be dug for those who had died during the winter. "Serviceberry" flowers marked the time to hold services for the departed and give them a proper burial.

This native woodland gem has many names. In eastern Pennsylvania it is mostly called Shadblow because it blooms very early, when the shad are running in the Delaware River. Its cloud of small, delicate white flowers clustered at its branch tips above its upright stems is visible through the still leafless forest. Just after them the down-covered new leaves arrive, maturing over three or four weeks to medium green. By June Shadblow bears edible, juicy black fruit. Its season finale is yellowish or gold foliage, sometimes tinged orange-red. In addition to its multiseason beauty, Shadblow is tough and adaptable. Downy Serviceberry (Amelanchier arborea) is more treelike at 30 ft. tall. Some hybrids are 'Autumn Brilliance', 'Cole's Select', 'Cumulus', 'Forest Prince', 'Spring Glory', and 'Tradition'.

Other Name
Serviceberry

Bloom Period and Seasonal Color
Late March, early April; blooms in white

Mature Height × Spread
6 to 20 ft. × 10 to 15 ft.

Smokebush

Cotinus coggygria

The heyday of Smokebushes was the Victorian era, but their unique flowers and accommodating nature are winning them renewed interest. The attraction is the puffy flower clusters. The hairy stalks that hold the flowers elongate as they fade and form plumes of "smoke." They turn pinkish gray and persist over the summer, this haze at tips of shrub branches upstaging the leaves. Foliage is broadly oval and usually a bluish green, but some versions have deep-purple leaves changing to reddish or orange-yellow with the approach of fall. Deer seem to leave Smokebushes alone. 'Royal Purple' has deep-purple foliage, purplish red "smoke," then red-orange-yellow fall foliage. 'Velvet Cloak' has rich, reddish purple foliage. 'Daydream' has green leaves and pale pinkish beige smoke.

Other Name
Smoketree

Bloom Period and Seasonal Color
June; blooms of tiny yellow flowers; known for pinkish gray plumes

Mature Height × Spread
15 ft. × 10 to 12 ft.

When, Where, and How to Plant
Plant shrubs grown in containers anytime over the growing season. Full sun encourages flowers and foliage color. Smokebush accepts soils from dry and rocky to moist and clayey. It even handles alkaline and compacted soils. A site somewhat sheltered from the wind protects the brittle branches. Dig a saucer-shaped hole as deep as its rootball is high and about twice as wide. Set the rootball so that its top is even with the surrounding soil. Backfill, firm soil gently, and water well.

Growing Tips
Mulch with a 2- or 3-in. layer of organic matter. Water regularly if rainfall is unreliable until well established, then Smokebush can cope with drought. A slow-acting granular fertilizer formulated for trees and shrubs sprinkled on the mulch in the spring the first year gives it a good start, but is not essential.

Care
To maintain Smokebush as a smallish shrub, cut back stems to the ground in late winter. This stimulates the production of new shoots, controls the size, and prevents overwintering scale insects. Smokebush may be pestered by rodents, which gnaw on tender bark of young transplants in the winter. Delay spreading winter mulch until the ground freezes hard to deny them a nesting place. Wrap stem bases in hardware cloth.

Companion Planting and Design
Potentially large enough also to be called Smoketree, these shrubs need pruning to maintain a good size for the residential landscape when used as foundation or mixed border shrubs. The purple-foliaged ones contrast dramatically with silver or gray plants such as Artemisias or Lamb's Ears. They also make a stunning hedge.

Did You Know?
Coppicing (also called stooling) is a pruning technique that seems drastic but improves plant health. It means cutting woody plants back to ground level in late winter or early spring. It prompts plants to send up multiple stems from the base of their former trunks. A way to renew old plants, it forces them to grow foliage on new, tender wood.

Summersweet
Clethra alnifolia

When, Where, and How to Plant
Plant in early spring for best success. Plant shrubs grown in containers anytime during the growing season. A mostly sunny understory site with some shade in the heat of the day is ideal. Moist, woodsy soil on the acidic side assures yellow fall foliage. Summersweet likes wet soil and is happy near water's edge. Improve thin or clay soils with organic matter. Dig a saucer-shaped hole as deep as the rootball is high and somewhat wider. Set the rootball so that its top is level with surrounding soil. Backfill, firm the soil gently, and water well. Space shrubs 6 ft. apart.

Growing Tips
Water regularly if rainfall is sparse over summer while Summersweet becomes established. It is particularly vulnerable to stress and drying out when flowering. Maintain a year-round, 2- or 3-in. layer of organic mulch to retain soil moisture. Fertilize with slow-acting granular fertilizer in spring.

Care
Prune Summersweet in spring; flowers form on the subsequent new growth. Clipping off spent flowers is optional. Periodically cut back any old or dead stems to the ground. Aside from occasional mites during periods of stress from dry soil, Summersweet has no insect or disease problems. Rabbits and rodents sometimes nest in thick winter mulch and gnaw on tender bark. Wrap stems temporarily with hardware cloth.

Companion Planting and Design
Summersweet's handsome, upright stems form an oval profile. It slowly widens by means of underground roots. This tendency to colonize makes Summersweet shrubs good soil holders on berms or hillsides. Individual shrubs make good specimens, anchors for a mixed border, accents, or foundation plants. Plant near a doorway, open windows, or along walkways so passersby can smell the flowers.

Did You Know?
Pennsylvania has its share of prominent plantsmen who know a good plant when they see it. Jim Plyler of Natural Landscapes Nursery popularized *Clethra* 'Hummingbird', a charming dwarf (to 4 ft.), compact shrub with dark-green leaves and white flowers.

Summersweet is a name that truly conveys the virtues and beauty of this native shrub. After its glossy, green foliage backdrops all the riotously flowering plants through spring and early summer, it is Summersweet's turn to flower. Its flowers are upright 6-in. spikes, fuzzy with tiny florets, at branch tips. They have a spicy fragrance that attracts insects galore. They bloom for more than a month, finally giving way to seed capsules that persist through winter, long after the foliage has dropped. 'Pink Spires' has light-pink flowers. 'Rosea' has dark-pink buds and paler-pink flowers, and grows to 4 ft. tall. 'Ruby Spice' has deep-pink flowers. Clethra barbinervis grows to 18 ft., has mottled bark, and bears tiny white flowers on drooping stems.

Other Name
Sweetpepper Bush

Bloom Period and Seasonal Color
July into August; blooms in white, rose, or pink

Mature Height × Spread
5 to 10 ft. × 6 to 12 ft.

Vanhoutte Spirea

Spiraea × vanhouttei

There are all kinds of Spireas these days, but the classic *Vanhoutte* is still a favorite. Featuring upright, arching branches that dip to the ground under the weight of rows of flat, round clusters of tiny white florets, it has graced American yards since the 1850s. After Spirea's brief bloom period, its small, oval blue-green leaves are more visible until they turn yellowish and drop in the fall. Often used varieties of Japanese Spirea (Spiraea japonica) are 'Little Princess' and 'Shirobana'. They are 2 or 3 ft. tall and wide, with narrow, pointed foliage and individual flat clusters of flowers in shades of pink, or pink and white. Some have chartreuse or reddish foliage. They are drought tolerant, disease resistant, and virtually pest free.

Other Name
Bridalwreath Spirea

Bloom Period and Seasonal Color
Late May; blooms in white

Mature Height × Spread
6 to 10 ft. × 8 to 12 ft.

When, Where, and How to Plant
Plant in early spring or fall. Plant shrubs grown in containers anytime during the growing season in a full-sun location. Avoid planting in periods of intense summer heat and drought. Although they prefer good garden soil rich in organic matter that is moist and well drained, Spireas accept considerably less. Mix in organic material such as peat moss or compost. Dig a saucer-shaped hole as deep as the rootball is high and twice as wide. Set the rootball so that its top is exactly level with the surrounding soil. Backfill, firm soil gently, and water well. Space 6 ft. apart.

Growing Tips
Spread a 2- or 3-in. layer of organic material over the Spirea root zone to keep the soil moist and discourage weeds. Renew mulch when the layer thins. Water regularly if rainfall is unreliable until well established. Every spring sprinkle slow-acting granular fertilizer formulated for trees and shrubs on the mulch for the rain to soak in.

Care
To revitalize older shrubs, yet maintain their fountainlike branching habit, prune out thicker, woody stems by cutting them back to ground level. To totally renovate them, cut all the stems back to near ground level in early spring. Clip stem tips off individually just after they flower for light, natural shaping. Never shear Spireas. Except for rust, a fungal disease on the foliage, Spireas are pest and disease free.

Companion Planting and Design
Use Spireas to soften corners of buildings, steps, and fences. Underplant with late-blooming spring bulbs. Spirea foliage blends in with other greenery in a shrub border over the summer.

Did You Know?
In March 1850 *The Horticulturist*, an early gardening magazine, responded to a reader's request for "the best and simplest directions for cultivating the finest of our common flowers." Among the shrubs on the list of easy-to-grow plants were Forsythia, Althea, Spirea, and Lilac. Obviously, Spirea was much loved many decades ago!

Virginia Sweetspire
Itea virginica

When, Where, and How to Plant
Plant rooted suckers from an existing plant in early spring. Plant shrubs grown in pots throughout the growing season as long as they are well watered. Virginia Sweetspires do fine as understory plants in woodland settings, but show best in full sun. They are not fussy about soil type and enjoy wet soil. Prepare sandy soil by mixing in organic matter such as peat moss, compost, or chopped leaves to help it hold moisture. Dig a hole with sloping sides as deep as the rootball is high and twice as wide. Set the rootball so it is level with the surrounding soil. Backfill, firm the soil, and water well. Space shrubs 5 or 6 ft. apart.

Growing Tips
Mulch surrounding soil with a 2- or 3-in. layer of organic matter such as chopped leaves or wood chips. Water Virginia Sweetspires regularly if rainfall is unreliable until well established. The first few springs, sprinkle slow-acting granular fertilizer for trees and shrubs on the mulch for the rain to soak in.

Care
Pull up suckering stems that are spreading beyond their authorized limits, and plant them elsewhere or give them away. Prune only to control height and only if necessary. Virginia Sweetspire tolerates drought well and is virtually pest and disease free.

Companion Planting and Design
Take advantage of Virginia Sweetspire's multi-season beauty as a specimen, foundation, or woodland plant. In rows it makes great hedges, and massed on a bank, it holds the soil well. It also grows well in a container.

Did You Know?
'Henry's Garnet' put Virginia Sweetspire on the horticultural map, and it happened in Pennsylvania. Professor Michael Dirr of the University of Georgia noticed a particularly deep-red-foliaged one on the Swarthmore College campus. Scott Arboretum correctly named and introduced the plant. Since Josephine Henry provided some seeds, the name Henry was added to "garnet," representing one of Swarthmore College's colors and its rich fall foliage color.

Virginia Sweetspire is widely grown, appreciated, and eminently satisfactory. The epitome of easy care, it has upright, slightly arching stems that get twiggy at their tops. It initiates the season with bright, shiny, light-green spring foliage on its slender reddish twigs, which turns medium green in time for the flower display. Suddenly, the Sweetspire is dripping with 2- to 6-in.-long, narrow tubes of tiny white florets. Later, the first tinges of burgundy that appear on the foliage in late August are an alert that the spectacular show of purple and bright-red leaves that lasts through most of the fall is beginning. 'Henry's Garnet' has red fall color. 'Saturnalia' is reputed to be a bit smaller with a more orangish red fall color.

Other Name
Virginia Willow

Bloom Period and Seasonal Color
June into July; blooms in white

Mature Height × Spread
4 to 8 ft. × 3 to 6 ft.

Weigela
Weigela florida

Weigela is a tough, reliable bloomer. Its inch-long, funnel-shaped flowers arrayed in clusters along arching stems are in full show when the hummingbirds arrive. Branches may be so weighed down with flowers that their tips touch and root in the soil. Weigelas have rangy, informal habits. Their foliage is a serviceable plain green. 'Briant Rubidor' has red flowers and chartreuse foliage, a striking combination! 'Bristol Ruby' has crimson flowers and a more upright posture. 'Candida' has white flowers. 'Polka' has a long bloom period and pink flowers. 'White Knight' produces white flowers through summer and is small at 5 to 6 ft. tall. 'Wine and Roses' has maroon-purple-tinged foliage and medium-pink flowers. 'Variegata' foliage has cream-colored edges and pale-pink flowers.

Other Name
Old-fashioned Weigela

Bloom Period and Seasonal Color
Late May and June; blooms in white, pink, or rose

Mature Height × Spread
6 to 10 ft. × 8 to 12 ft.

When, Where, and How to Plant
Plant in spring or fall. Plant shrubs grown in containers anytime during the growing season in full sun or partial shade. They like any type of well-drained soil. Improve thin or sandy soils by mixing in organic matter such as peat moss, compost, or chopped leaves. These shrubs can handle pollution. Dig a hole as deep as the rootball is high and twice as wide. Position the rootball so that its top is level with the surrounding soil. Backfill, firm the soil, and water well. Space standard shrubs 12 ft. apart; smaller hybrids 5 ft. apart.

Growing Tips
Mulch with a 2- or 3-in. layer of organic matter such as chopped leaves or wood chips. Water regularly if rainfall is unreliable until it is well established. Each spring sprinkle slow-acting granular fertilizer formulated for trees and shrubs on the mulch for the rain to soak in.

Care
Weigela blooms on the previous year's wood, so prune immediately after flowering. For maximum bloom, completely remove branches that have just bloomed as close to the base of the shrub as possible. Prune out dead wood on an ongoing basis. To renew, either cut entirely to the ground in early spring, or cut out the oldest, woodiest stems every couple of years. Weigela has no serious pests or diseases.

Companion Planting and Design
Paired with Mockorange, Weigela provides a flowerful transition into full summer. Older forms are content to serve unobtrusively in shrub borders or as hedges. The newer, more flamboyant compact versions are more versatile, fitting happily into mixed borders or serving as foundation plants.

Did You Know?
When hummingbirds visit flowers to obtain nectar, they pollinate their hosts. Flowers most attractive to hummers have red color, deep tubular shape, downward or sideways orientation, small petals or openings, and tough bases where they attach to their stems. Weigelas have these traits, which discourage bees and other pollinators, leaving them available to hummers.

Willowleaf Cotoneaster

Cotoneaster salicifolius

When, Where, and How to Plant

Containerized Cotoneasters transplant best. Plant them anytime during the growing season, but spring is ideal. Site them where they receive some shade during the day. Cotoneasters are not fussy about soil, but it must be well drained. Dig a saucer-shaped hole as deep as the rootball is high and about twice as wide. Set the plant so that the top of its rootball is exactly level with, or slightly above, the level of the surrounding ground. Backfill, firm soil gently around its stems, and water well.

Growing Tips

Mulch newly planted Cotoneasters, but do not pile material against shrub stems. If rainfall is unreliable, water regularly until they are well established. These shrubs are extremely low maintenance and need watering only in severe drought. They do not need fertilizing.

Care

Prune Cotoneaster only to remove brown and damaged branches and to control shape. Cut branches at their base rather than at their tips, which causes browning and dieback. Lace bugs or mites may infest stressed Cotoneasters. Spray with horticultural oil as directed on the product label, and eliminate plant stress. Occasionally, fireblight blackens stems and leaves as if they were scorched by fire. Prune out affected parts immediately, and discard. Disinfect tools after every cut to avoid spreading the infection. In serious cases dig up and throw away the shrub.

Companion Planting and Design

Cotoneasters make good screens and hedges. They are easily trained through pruning and can be espaliered against a wall. Rock Spray Cotoneaster (*Cotoneaster horizontalis*) is ideal for rock walls, banks, and similar situations.

Did You Know?

Sometimes distinguishing between a Cotoneaster and a Firethorn is difficult. Both bear whitish, smelly flowers the same time in the spring, but Firethorn flowers are more abundant and ornamental, and they grow along the stems. The presence of thorns confirms a Firethorn's identity. Other indications are that Firethorn berries are more tightly bunched and typically orange.

There is a Cotoneaster for just about every landscape situation. The tall ones, such as the Willowleaf, are large and open, some to the point of being rangy. Their narrow, leathery, textured, dark evergreen leaves provide winter interest, even though their purplish autumn tinge is not very dramatic. Willowleaf's flexible arching branches droop gracefully when covered with its musky-smelling cream flowers and later when bright-red berries take their place. Cotoneaster salicifolius var. floccosus has larger flowers; it may be semi-evergreen in severe winters or upstate. The most common is the low spreading 'Repens'. Spreading Cotoneaster (Cotoneaster divaricatus) has arching branches, red berries, and reddish purplish yellow fall foliage. Some Cotoneasters make good ground covers: Cotoneaster dammeri 'Coral Beauty' and 'Lowfast' are only 1 to 2 ft. tall and spread to 6 ft.

Other Name

Tall Cotoneaster

Bloom Period and Seasonal Color

May, June blooms in off-white; evergreen foliage

Mature Height × Spread

10 to 15 ft. ×

Winged Euonymus
Euonymus alatus

The most remarkable thing about Winged Euonymus is the peculiar ridges on its twigs that resemble flat wings. Most prominent on younger, vigorous stems, they are visible in the winter. Eventually, they are obscured by the plain, dull-green foliage that densely covers the mounded shrub. By fall, this shrub takes on a whole new personality and a name to fit its alter ego. It truly becomes a burning bush, its foliage afire with brilliant scarlet reds verging on the fluorescent, visible from great distances. Adaptable, self-reliant, low-maintenance, Winged Euonymus is so popular that it verges on overused. This may not be the case much longer, though, because it holds a prominent place on the short list of plants that deer love to eat. A popular form is 'Compacta', which is denser growing with less prominent wings.

Other Name
Burning Bush

Bloom Period and Seasonal Color
Brilliant red fall foliage

Mature Height × Spread
8 to 15 ft. × 10 to 18 ft.

When, Where, and How to Plant
Plant balled-and-burlapped Winged Euonymus in spring or fall. Plant those grown in containers anytime during the growing season. The more sun, the better the scarlet fall foliage. It accepts just about any type of well-drained soil except alkaline or salty. Improve sandy or thin soil by adding organic matter. Dig a saucer-shaped hole as deep as the rootball is high and twice as wide. Set the rootball so its top is level with the surrounding soil. Cut away as much burlap as possible. Backfill, firm soil gently, and water thoroughly.

Growing Tips
Mulch Winged Euonymus year-round to prevent shallow surface roots from drying out. Renew the 2- or 3-in. layer of organic matter periodically as it decomposes. Water if rainfall is unreliable until the shrub is well established. In spring sprinkle slow-acting granular fertilizer for shrubs on the mulch for the rain to soak in. After one or two years, the decomposing mulch will enrich the soil.

Care
Winged Euonymus grows very large without pruning. It takes shearing for a hedge very well. Cut out broken or dead stems promptly. It does not get scale or any other pests and diseases. Seeds, stems, and foliage cause stomach upset if ingested.

Companion Planting and Design
Most of the year Winged Euonymus is simply a neat, somewhat horizontally branching, basic green shrub, content to bide its time unobtrusively among other shrubs in a border, as a hedge, or as a foundation plant near the house during the summer. Its fall color is spectacular when backed by dark evergreens.

Did You Know?
The beautiful foliage colors that many trees and shrubs develop in the fall are really there all along. They are not evident because the green chlorophyll pigment obscures them. But as winter approaches, reduced daylight ends its role of manufacturing energy from the sun, and chlorophyll is no longer produced. Then the reds, yellows, and oranges glow.

Winterberry Holly
Ilex verticillata

When, Where, and How to Plant

Plant balled-and-burlapped Winterberries in early spring or early fall. Plant those grown in containers anytime during the growing season. To be sure of getting a female, buy named selections or mature shrubs whose sex can be confirmed. Site Winterberries in full sun for best berry production. They prefer moist, acid, woodsy soils that are rich in organic matter and well drained, although they do not mind wet or clay soils. Dig a saucer-shaped hole as deep as the rootball is high and twice as wide. Set the rootball in the hole so that its top is level with the surrounding soil. Cut as much of the burlap away as possible. Backfill, firm soil gently, and water well. Space shrubs 8 ft. apart from each other or from buildings.

Growing Tips

Water newly planted Winterberries during dry periods until they become established. Don't let them totally dry out. Mulch their root zones year-round with a 2- or 3-in. layer of organic matter to retain soil moisture, discourage weeds, and condition the soil. In spring fertilize with slow-acting granular fertilizer formulated for acid-loving trees and shrubs.

Care

In the spring cut back old branches to ground level to stimulate new and denser growth that will produce lots of berries. Aphids may attack new shoots. *Beware, the berries are poisonous.*

Companion Planting and Design

Use Winterberries as focal points or accents in the winter landscape, in a shrub border, or near streams or ponds. Plant them as understory shrubs, backdropped by larger broadleaf or needled evergreens, and in view of a window to enjoy from indoors and with a male Holly nearby. Berry-laden branches are great for fall and holiday dried arrangements. They have a different look from evergreen Holly boughs. They last indoors about a week. Winterberry grows well in containers.

Did You Know?

Birds that eat Holly berries include bluebirds, catbirds, cedar waxwings, mockingbirds, robins, and thrushes.

Winterberry Holly is another sturdy native shrub at home in residential landscapes. It is a Holly and has berries, but instead of the classic spined, dark evergreen foliage, it has simple, oval, medium- to dark-green, finer-textured leaves that often turn yellowish or black after frost before they drop in the fall. Winterberry's glory is berry-encrusted bare branches on female shrubs that are exposed when the leaves drop. Usually red, sometimes orange or yellow, they light up the winter landscape. These multistemmed, upright shrubs gradually spread into a thicket by means of suckering roots, but are easily controlled by pruning. 'Scarlett O'Hara' and 'Winter Red' are winners of the Pennsylvania Horticultural Society's Gold Medal Award. ('Rhett Butler' is the male pollinator for 'Scarlett', of course!)

Other Name
Coralberry

Bloom Period and Seasonal Color
June blooms in white; scarlet berries in fall

Mature Height × Spread
6 to 10 ft. × 6 to 8 ft.

Witchhazel
Hamamelis mollis

From a distance its vaselike shape, many stems, and tufts of yellow flowers along bare branches resemble Forsythia, but up close there is no mistaking Witchhazel. First the fragrance, then the unique spiderlike flowers with twisting, inch-long, narrow petals confirm its identity. Over several weeks flowers gleam in the winter sun, curling up when it is cold and expanding with milder temperatures. Chinese Witchhazel is a handsome large shrub, with the largest, most colorful flowers and longest bloom period of all the Witchhazels. When its dull green leaves appear in spring, it blends into the landscape until they turn yellow in fall and drop, exposing dried seed capsules, which shoot their two black seeds as far as 20 ft. away with a loud snap. Hybrid selections offer other colors such as 'Jelena', which has orange flowers and 'Diane', which has red flowers. Both have orange-red fall color.

Other Name
Chinese Witchhazel

Bloom Period and Seasonal Color
Late January through March; blooms in yellow

Mature Height × Spread
10 to 15 ft. × 12 ft.

When, Where, and How to Plant
Plant balled-and-burlapped Witchhazels in spring. Plant those grown in containers anytime during the growing season. For best bloom and display, plant them in full sun or under deciduous trees. They can take some shade and do well in almost any soil that is acidic, rich in organic matter, and well drained. They do not mind urban conditions. Allow them about three years to fully establish and bloom well. Dig a saucer-shaped hole as deep as the rootball is high and somewhat wider. Position the rootball so that it is level with the surrounding soil. Cut away as much burlap as possible. Backfill, firm the soil gently, and water well. Typically wider than they are tall, Witchhazels tend to spread even more with age. Space them at least 15 ft. apart.

Growing Tips
Mulch Witchhazels year-round with a 2- or 3-in. layer of organic matter such as chopped leaves or wood chips. Water regularly if rainfall is unreliable until well established, then only during droughts. Fertilize in spring with slow-acting granular fertilizer for trees and shrubs. Decomposing mulch will enrich the soil, so regular fertilizing is not necessary.

Care
Prune occasional broken branches promptly. Most named Witchhazels are grafted; cut off suckers that branch out below the graft. The shrubs have no significant pest or disease problems.

Companion Planting and Design
Use Witchhazels as focal points in the winter landscape or in shrub borders and woodland settings. Plant drifts of small spring bulbs such as Crocus or Squill under them.

Did You Know?
Native Americans and early settlers used the bark of fall-blooming native Witchhazel (*Hamamelis virginiana*) for medicine. An astringent, Witchhazel is still available in pharmacies for first aid to halt minor bleeding and reduce inflammation. It is used in commercial eye drops, skin creams, ointments, and tonics. The "witch" in its name suggests the wood's occult powers. It has long been used to make divining rods to find water.

When, Where, and How to Plant

Plant balled-and-burlapped Yews in spring or fall. Plant those grown in containers anytime all season. Yews adapt to full sun or shade, but they prefer some shade. They accept any fertile, well-drained soil. Overly wet soil turns needles brown. They do not like very acid soil, so do not plant them near Azaleas or Hollies. Dig in organic matter to improve drainage in clay soil. Dig a hole with sloping sides as deep as the rootball is high and twice as wide. Set the rootball so that its top is level with the surrounding soil. Cut away as much burlap as possible. Backfill, firm soil gently, and water well. Space shrubs 5 ft. apart.

Growing Tips

Mulch year-round with a 2- or 3-in. layer of organic material. Water regularly if rainfall is unreliable until well established. In the spring sprinkle slow-acting granular fertilizer for trees and shrubs on the mulch for the rain to soak in.

Care

To renew old Yew shrubs, cut stems back to within 6 in. of the ground in early spring. Prune to shape or control their size in the spring before growth starts by clipping individual branches for a soft, natural effect. Do not shear into rigid shapes except for topiary. Clip hedges hard before May to maintain a maximum width of 2 ft. and height of 6 or 8 ft. Stressed shrubs may attract mites or scale. *All parts of Yews contain the toxic substance taxine.*

Companion Planting and Design

Yews are useful as foundation plantings and backgrounds for colorful flowering plants. They take shearing well to create hedges and topiary and they tolerate dry shady conditions.

Did You Know?

Taxol, a drug derived from the bark of the Pacific Yew, is a potent weapon in treating cancer. It is estimated that 600,000 Yews would be needed to make enough taxol to treat a wide population of patients. Because harvesting the bark kills so many trees, every effort was made to synthesize taxol.

According to the fossil record, Yews boast an ancient history. They continue to offer long life, rich color, needled foliage, and varied sizes for use in gardens. The best are hybrids that combine the cold hardiness of Japanese Yews and the dark-green foliage of the English Yew. They have lustrous, soft, short, flat needles that are initially a bright green, turning dark green and paler beneath with age. Female Yews bear red, fleshy fruit with a seed within that is poisonous to people but does not seem to deter deer from eating foliage with gusto. 'Brownii' and 'Brownii Globe' are rounded. 'Hicks' is narrow and upright. 'Densiformis' grows to 4 ft. as a low spreader. Spreading English Yew (Taxus baccata 'Repandens') has arching branches.

Other Name
Intermediate Yew

Bloom Period and Seasonal Color
Evergreen

Mature Height × Spread
10 to 15 ft. × 15 ft.

Trees *for Pennsylvania*

Handsome shade trees and decorative flowering trees are significant elements in a residential landscape. Not only do they contribute aesthetically by defining its space—establishing scale, delineating borders, and roofing it with their canopies—but they also enhance its livability in numerous ways. They moderate the climate in the yard by transposing and filtering light and air, and creating shade and privacy. They provide habitat for wildlife—shelter and food—and add to the diversity of plants that interrelate to create a healthy ecosystem on the property. Deciduous trees reduce energy use indoors when carefully sited in the yard to block sun from windows and the roof in summer, and then permit it to shine on them after they drop their leaves in the fall. Trees are also economic assets. A healthy, mature shade tree can contribute up to $1,500 to the value of the property.

Trees Defined

Trees are typically defined as single-stemmed plants that are 25 ft. or taller. They are usually categorized as small (less than 30 ft.), medium (30 to 60 ft.), and tall (more than 60 ft.) to facilitate their selection

and use. Small trees are usually most appropriate near the house to frame it attractively. They are suitable for use under most utility wires and as understory plantings beneath taller trees. Medium trees do well in open areas a short distance from the house in typically suburban-sized properties. Tall trees are appropriate for very spacious lawns or along property boundaries where they are at least 35 ft. from the house to allow for root growth. Traditionally, tall deciduous shade trees have lined the streets of Pennsylvania towns. They do not belong between the curb and the sidewalk, however, where their confined roots eventually become swollen and injured, distorting their growth and shortening their lives. Before purchasing a tree, decide whether its purpose is to shade, to decorate, to screen a view, or to control erosion on a bank.

Buy locally, if possible, to assure that the tree is grown from local stock. It has a better chance if planted in familiar conditions. Nurseries and garden centers will often provide a warranty for trees; some

will plant them, too, for an extra fee. When trees are young, you can do the work, but it is safer for you and the tree to hire a professional to move or plant large trees. Also consider hiring a professional, a certified arborist, for any pruning job that requires a chain saw and a ladder, and for spraying insecticides or fungicides on large trees.

Modern Tree Care

In the last decade new insights into how trees grow have affected how we plant and care for them. A newly planted tree's job is to grow roots outward into the soil as quickly as possible so it can access nutrition and fuel the development of its branches and, in spring, foliage. New planting practices reflect the understanding that a tree's feeder roots exist within the top 12 in. of soil and spread much farther than the leaf canopy is wide. So, when planting, every effort is made to urge roots outward into the new soil environment at the site. That is why the planting hole should have sloping sides, and the fill soil should be the real thing (no pampering with special amendments that tempt roots to grow in circles to stay where it is comfortable). Also, offering fertilizer—a slow-acting type to provide nutrients gradually and uniformly—is delayed until after the roots get established and are able to take advantage of it.

Fall planting provides several weeks of valuable root-growing time before the ground freezes hard. Trees do not have to produce foliage as well. Watering the first year is critical as young, transplanted trees work overtime to get established. In heat all trees (and shrubs) lose enormous amounts of moisture through their foliage. Spreading a relatively thin layer of organic material over tree root zones year-round is important. Mulching eliminates turfgrass and weed competition for water and nutrients and provides a steady infusion of moisture-retaining organic matter to condition the soil so that it holds air, too. It also keeps lawn mowers and string trimmers at bay. They injure the tender bark of young trees. Never pile mulch up against tree trunks because the bark there is not able to handle the moisture and becomes prone to insect and disease problems.

Contemporary pruning techniques recognize that trees have special tissues that seal wounds. Cutting a branch to preserve this "collar" of bark, leaving a small protrusion at its base, speeds healing there. Painting wounds is no longer recommended, since trees can take care of this job themselves. Also, it is now understood that the topping, stubbing, or "heading back" of the trunk or limbs of a tree is at best futile and at worst a crime. Trees maimed in this manner always struggle to regenerate the limb to the length it was destined to be. The multiple weak, thin replacement suckers they produce are damage prone and unattractive. The stress these trees suffer in the process jeopardizes their health and reduces their life span considerably. Avoid all this by selecting trees whose mature size fits the site you choose.

Finally, staking newly planted trees is no longer routine. Experts have come to appreciate the importance of movement to developing strength in stems of all kinds of plants. Young tree trunks need

to flex a bit near their tops. Staking is now recommended for special situations only, and for only six months to one year. Stake newly planted trees that are in sites exposed to wind. A full foliage canopy acts as a sail, catching the wind and possibly toppling the tree. Also, certain trees are fairly shallow rooted, and temporary staking stabilizes them during the all-important time when roots struggle to penetrate the soil. Attach supporting lines down low on the trunk—about 18 in. from the ground—to stabilize it, but allow upper flexibility.

Deer Danger

In recent years a major factor influencing the selection and planting of trees in Pennsylvania landscapes is their vulnerability to deer. Residential landscapes (and forests) throughout the Commonwealth have been ravaged by browsing deer, young trees being the major casualties. While deer tastes vary from place to place, certain trees and shrubs seem to be widely favored by deer.

*American Arborvitae	*Crabapple	*Korean Lilac
Atlantic White Cedar	*Eastern Redbud	*Norway Maple
*Azalea	European Mountain Ash	*Rhododendron
Balsam Fir	Fraser Fir	*Winged Euonymus
Buckeye	*Hybrid Tea Roses	*Yew
Cornelian Dogwood		[*Included in this book.]

American Holly

Ilex opaca

Our native American Holly is a stunning, extremely hardy landscape star. Its leathery, spined foliage is a lustrous medium green and paler beneath. Its handsome pyramidal shape with branching to the ground is undeniably elegant. If there is a male Holly nearby, female trees bear bright-red, orange, or yellow fall berries, beloved of birds. While the prickly foliage is daunting, in some areas deer have nevertheless developed a taste for it. 'Jersey Knight' is a good male pollinator. 'Jersey Princess' has good form, dark-green foliage, and generous fruit. As her name suggests, 'Old Heavy Berry' bears copious fruit set off by dark-green foliage . An American Holly recently won the Pennsylvania Horticultural Society's Gold Medal Award for outstanding trees and shrubs for Pennsylvania landscapes.

Other Name
Christmas Holly

Bloom Period and Seasonal Color
Fall berries in bright red, orange, or yellow

Mature Height × Spread
30 to 40 ft. × 10 to 20 ft.

When, Where, and How to Plant
Plant balled-and-burlapped American Hollies in spring. Plant container-grown ones anytime during the growing season. They have maximum berries and more compact habits in full sun. Holly prefers light, sandy, well-drained soil on the acidic side. Mix organic material into clay soil to improve drainage. Plant a male tree nearby to assure good pollination and berries on female trees. Protect trees from harsh winter wind and sun. Dig a saucer-shaped hole just as deep as and somewhat wider than the rootball. Set the rootball so its top is level with the surrounding ground. Remove as much burlap as possible. Backfill with plain soil, firm gently, and water well.

Growing Tips
American Hollies up to five years old need plenty of moisture. Water regularly if rainfall is sparse, but do not soak excessively. Water well in fall before the ground freezes. Maintain a 2- or 3-in. layer of organic material over their roots. Six months after planting, fertilize lightly with granular slow-acting fertilizer for acid-loving trees. Hollies are sensitive to overfertilization. Eventually, well-mulched Hollies will not need fertilizing.

Care
Trim the tips of open and irregular branches of aging trees to maintain a uniform shape. Prune in winter. Never top trees to reduce their height. When shearing Hollies into hedges, keep lower branches wider than the upper ones so that they receive sunlight. Aphids, scale, or leafminer may attack foliage of stressed young trees. Maintain tree vigor.

Landscape Merit
Hollies are striking as individual specimens, in groups to screen a view or noise, or as background for other, smaller shrubs and ornamental plants.

Did You Know?
To medieval monks, English Holly, or "Holy Tree," was symbolic of Christianity. The sharp leaf spines recalled the crown of thorns, the white flowers symbolized purity and the virgin birth, and the red berries represented drops of blood. Thus, Holly boughs became a part of Christmas celebrations throughout England in the 1500s.

American Sycamore
Platanus occidentalis

When, Where, and How to Plant
Sycamores transplant easily. Plant young balled-and-burlapped trees in spring or fall. Plant container-grown American Sycamore hybrids or London Planetrees anytime during the growing season. Sycamores like full sun and moist soil along streams, typical of their native habitat. In moist soil, they can handle dry air, pollution, and soil compaction. They tolerate neutral or somewhat alkaline soil if it's well drained. Give them lots of room. Dig a saucer-shaped hole just as deep as and two or three times wider than the rootball. Position the rootball so its top is at soil level. Remove as much burlap as possible. Backfill with plain soil, firming it gently around the rootball. Fashion a moat to hold water, then water well.

Growing Tips
Water transplants when rainfall is limited. Maintain a year-round 2- or 3-in. layer of organic mulch over the root zone, but not against the trunk. It retains soil moisture, discourages weeds, and protects the tender trunk from mower injury. After six months, sprinkle granular slow-acting fertilizer for trees and shrubs on the mulch for the rain to soak in. After two or three years, the decomposing mulch will enrich the soil, replacing fertilizer.

Care
Sycamores self-prune, periodically dropping their dead branches. Watch for uninvited seedlings. American Sycamore is notoriously susceptible to anthracnose, a fungal disease. Large trees take this in stride, but young ones need treatment. Consult a certified arborist.

Landscape Merit
Use London Planetrees, available in nurseries, near ponds or streams, or as specimens in large yards. They make lovely street trees.

Did You Know?
How to tell the difference between London Planetrees and Sycamores? London Planetrees are deliberately planted, whereas Sycamores are typically self-sown and randomly occurring. London Planetrees are usually smaller and less wide-spreading than Sycamores. Their bark is more olive green, and they usually bear two fruits per stalk. Their leaves are more maplelike and deeply cut, but straight across the bottom.

A list of Pennsylvania trees would be incomplete without including these shade trees with massive trunks and huge gnarled branches that are ubiquitous in our parks, on campuses, and in our yards. They grow rapidly, shedding their bark in large patches, creating mottled cream, red, and gray-brown-green trunks. New bark gleams almost white in winter. Among their large, coarse, gray-green maplelike leaves, inconspicuous late-spring flowers give way to fuzzy balls that dangle from twigs, one to a stalk, through fall and winter. When they drop, they release wind-borne hairs that may cause minor respiratory problems. London Planetree (Platanus × acerifolia) 'Bloodgood,' a hybrid, is a more civilized version of American Sycamore although its trunks are less strikingly colored. More suitable for home landscapes, it is also more disease resistant.

Other Name
Buttonwood

Bloom Period and Seasonal Color
Gray-green deciduous foliage; colorful shedding bark in cream, red, and gray

Mature Height × Spread
100 ft. × 40 to 80 ft.

Bald Cypress
Taxodium distichum

This East Coast native has long been regarded as a Southern tree, its adaptability to swamps being the stuff of lore and legend. It likes conditions in the North equally well, and it is now commonly planted as a landscape or a street tree in Pennsylvania. A conifer that is not evergreen (thus the sobriquet "bald"), it offers early appeal as soft, pale-green needles flush out on branches late in the spring. Nestled among them on delicate twigs are small, 1-in. cones that eventually turn brown. In fall Bald Cypress foliage turns red-bronze and drops, branchlets and all, revealing similarly colored, fibrous bark and a uniformly dense, narrow, pyramidal architecture. Visit this tree at your local arboretum, and consider planting one at home.

Other Name
Swamp Cypress

Bloom Period and Seasonal Color
Green deciduous foliage; russet in fall

Mature Height × Spread
50 to 70 ft. × 30 to 40 ft.

When, Where, and How to Plant
Plant balled-and-burlapped trees in spring. Plant container-grown trees anytime during the growing season. Bald Cypresses like full sun, but they can take some shade. They are flexible about soil—accepting dry to downright boggy. They can handle some wind in exposed sites and are ideal for floodplain areas. Dig a saucer-shaped hole just as deep as and somewhat wider than the rootball. Set the rootball so that the root flare shows at or slightly above soil level. Remove as much burlap as possible. Backfill with plain soil, firm gently. Form a soil berm just beyond the edge of the root zone for a water-holding moat, then water well. Allow plenty of space to accommodate this tree's potential size.

Growing Tips
Water newly transplanted trees if rainfall is sparse. Spread 2 or 3 in. of organic material over the root zone, but not against the trunk. Six months after planting, sprinkle granular slow-acting tree fertilizer on mulch for the rain to soak in. After a year or two the constantly decomposing mulch will maintain the soil.

Care
Prune only to remove injured or overcrowded branches. The natural symmetry of this tree would be ruined by attempts to control its size or shape. Bald Cypress may lose needles prematurely during drought, but it is not dead. Consult a certified arborist if bark beetles or leaf spot disease appears.

Landscape Merit
Place Bald Cypress so that the color and shape are shown to best effect in a spacious area. The trees are most effective when planted in groves on large properties.

Did You Know?
Why do Bald Cypresses in swamps have knees? Knees grow only on these trees when they are in water or soggy soils. Since they protrude as far as 2 or 3 ft. above the water, traditional wisdom was that they accessed oxygen from the air. However, recent tests indicate that they are not necessary for oxygen-carbon dioxide exchange. The mystery remains.

Blue Atlas Cedar

Cedrus atlantica 'Glauca'

When, Where, and How to Plant

Young container-grown trees accept transplanting best and fill out soon. Fall is the first choice for planting; spring is second. Blue Atlas Cedars prefer full sun, but tolerate very light shade. They like well-drained soil rich in organic matter, but readily adapt to sandy or neutral soil. Provide a roomy site protected from strong winds and storms. Dig a saucer-shaped hole just as deep as and two or three times wider than the rootball. Set the rootball so that its top is level with or slightly above the surrounding ground. Backfill with plain soil, and firm gently. Form a soil berm just beyond the edge of the root zone to hold water, then water well.

Growing Tips

If rainfall is unreliable, water young trees regularly until they are established. Spread 2 or 3 in. of organic material over the root zone, but never against the tree's trunk. After six months, sprinkle granular slow-acting fertilizer on the mulch for the rain to soak in. Repeat every year for four or five years. Eventually, decomposing mulch will improve soil, and annual fertilizing will be unnecessary.

Care

Prune only to remove broken, rubbing, or awkward branches. Occasionally, rodents nest in winter mulch and gnaw at tender trunk bark. To deny them a nest, wait until the ground freezes hard before spreading winter mulch. Wrap vulnerable Cedar stems with hardware cloth.

Landscape Merit

Plant Blue Atlas Cedar individually as specimens in the lawn to show off their virtues, or use them nearer to the house to accent an architectural feature. Young Atlas Cedars do well in deep, drained containers.

Did You Know?

Many other conifers are called Cedar, but they are not true Cedars because the first part of their Latin names is not *Cedrus*: Alaskan Cedar is *Chamaecyparis nootkatensis*; Western Red Cedar is *Thuja plicata*; Incense Cedar is *Calocedrus decurrens*; and Eastern Red Cedar is *Juniperus virginiana*.

The only conifers that bloom in the fall, Blue Atlas Cedars are always elegant, dominant landscape features. They have angular, spurred branches adorned with tufted bunches of stiff, bluish, 1- to 2-in.-long needles and decorative 3-in. cones. Younger trees have an open, irregular, erectly pyramidal shape. More mature ones become more flat topped with distinctly tiered horizontal branches suggesting years of resistance to wind and weather challenges. Fast-growing in youth, Blue Atlas Cedars slow as they age and may live three hundred years or more. 'Argentea' has silvery-blue needles. 'Aurea' has yellowish needles and a narrow, stiff form. 'Glauca Pendula' has weeping branches and can be espaliered. A cousin, Deodar Cedar (Cedrus deodara) has a softer and more graceful appearance, but is less cold hardy. Of the Deodar Cedars, 'Shalimar' is the most cold hardy and better for colder regions of Pennsylvania.

Bloom Period and Seasonal Color
Blue-green evergreen foliage

Mature Height × Spread
40 to 60 ft. × 40 to 60 ft.

Colorado Blue Spruce

Picea pungens glauca

Colorado Blue Spruces are Rocky Mountain sized, their towering pyramidal maturity dwarfing the average residential yard. Yet because of their beauty, they preside over home landscapes everywhere in Pennsylvania, and they are popular as Christmas trees. Blue Spruce limbs are rigidly horizontal, turning up slightly at their tips. Stiff, stout, sharply pointed, sort of squarish needles grow at right angles all around the twigs. Their prickliness seems to deter deer in many areas. To take advantage of their best appearance, grow Blue Spruce about twenty-five years, then cut them down and replace them before they get too big and scraggly. 'Fat Albert' is semi-dwarf, pyramidal, and bushy. 'Glauca Pendula' has a sprawling habit with drooping branches. 'Montgomery' is silver-blue, cone shaped, and dwarf.

Other Name
Colorado Spruce

Bloom Period and Seasonal Color
Bluish evergreen needled foliage

Mature Height × Spread
30 to 60 ft. × 10 to 20 ft.

When, Where, and How to Plant
Plant balled-and-burlapped trees in early spring in full sun. Blue Spruce prefers moist, slightly acidic, well-drained soil of almost any type. It dislikes soggy or very dry soil. Plant away from buildings where there is space to grow. Keep soil around the roots moist until planting time. Dig a saucer-shaped hole just as deep as and somewhat wider than the rootball. Set the rootball so its top is level with or a bit higher than the surrounding ground. Remove as much burlap as possible. Backfill with plain soil, firm soil gently. Fashion a water-holding moat over the root zone, and water well.

Growing Tips
Water transplants regularly if rainfall is sparse. Mulch each root zone year-round with 2 or 3 in. of organic material. After at least six months, sprinkle granular slow-acting fertilizer for conifers on the mulch for the rain to soak in. Do this for three or four years if a tree is in poor soil. Adequate nutrition is essential to assure good blue color. Eventually, the decomposing mulch provides soil enrichment.

Care
If you anticipate that your Colorado Blue Spruce will grow too large for its space, start annual shearing of young trees during active growth over three or four weeks in late spring. When it achieves its allowed height, shear more closely each year. Cut off the ratty lower branches that develop on older trees. Snip off galls caused by spruce gall aphid infestation. On older trees, fungal dieseases often cause the loss of lower branches. Replace seriously disfigured trees with younger specimens.

Landscape Merit
Use mature trees as individual specimens and in rows as windbreaks or screens. Young Colorado Spruces do well in containers.

Did You Know?
Spider mites are an occasional nuisance on young Colorado Spruces. Their feeding causes needles to turn a sickly yellow and drop off. Sometimes fine webbing is visible. Spray mites with insecticidal soap. Horticultural oil is *not* recommended for use on Blue Spruces because it destroys the blue color, which is a coating on the foliage.

Eastern Redbud
Cercis canadensis

When, Where, and How to Plant

Plant container-grown trees, raised in the North from Northern seed, anytime during the growing season. Plant in full sun or in the light shade of understory sites. Redbuds accept any well-drained, fertile soil from sand to clay. Dig a saucer-shaped hole just as deep as and somewhat wider than the rootball, and set it so that its top is level with or slightly above the surrounding ground. Backfill with plain soil, firm gently. Create a water-holding moat over the root zone, and water well.

Growing Tips

Water regularly over the first year in the absence of rain. Maintain a 2- or 3-in. layer of organic mulch year-round on the soil (not the trunk). Mulch helps retain soil moisture, discourage weeds, and protect against mower damage. After six months, sprinkle granular slow-acting fertilizer on the mulch for the rain to soak in. Then, after two or three years, decomposing mulch will enrich the soil.

Care

Prune Redbud in spring after flowering to remove low or excess branches. Train to a single trunk, or cut back to the ground after flowering to make a multistemmed tree. Remove all but the sturdiest stems that sprout from the stump. Prune fungal canker infection, which enters through wounds in the bark, by cutting off the entire affected branch below where unaffected wood starts, so it can generate new, healthy growth. Afterward, sterilize tools in a solution of hot water and household bleach.

Landscape Merit

Redbuds are ideal for small yards. Plant them in the protective lee of larger Pines, Maples, or Oaks or at the edge of woodland settings.

Did You Know?

Redbud flowers are edible—either as buds or fully opened. They make a colorful, crunchy addition to salads. Buds can be pickled or sautéed in butter or included in mixed vegetables. Their flavor is slightly tart and beanlike. (Information courtesy of Cathy Wilkinson Barash, *Edible Flowers from Garden to Palate*, Fulcrum Publishing, 1993.)

Eastern Redbuds, native to Pennsylvania, introduce the beauty of the flowering forest into the landscape. Four- or five-year-old trees start to flower along still-leafless branches and sometimes even their trunks. The spring blooms resemble Sweet Peas and are lilac-pink or white. Flat tiers of heart-shaped leaves up to 5 in. long eventually develop on the long, dipping branches, then flat brown seedpods appear as summer progresses. Their season finale is yellow fall foliage. Older trees show architectural character when open branches and knobs or burls develop on their trunks, making them visually interesting in winter. Relatively short-lived, Redbuds often survive only twenty years, but they are a delight to have in the yard. They may be victimized by browsing deer when young.

Other Name

Judas Tree

Bloom Period and Seasonal Color

Late April, early May; blooms in white or lilac-pink; yellow fall foliage color

Mature Height × Spread

30 ft. × 25 to 30 ft.

Eastern White Pine
Pinus strobus

Although it grows quite large, our native White Pine is so beloved that it is included in even modest residential yards. Its soft, 5-in.-long needles, bundled in fives, add colorful grace to any landscape, especially in the winter. As a bonus, in June and early July, White Pines produce male and female flowers, actually soft cones, which turn brown by fall and produce seeds for wildlife. When they are young, these pines are Christmas tree shaped, but they become lanky and flat topped with distinctive horizontal branching in old age. In many areas the deer seem to leave them alone. 'Pendula' is a weeping variety with arching branches. 'Fastigiata' is narrow, columnar, and best for hedges and screens. 'Nana' is dwarf and mounded.

Other Name
White Pine

Bloom Period and Seasonal Color
Bluish green evergreen conifer

Mature Height × Spread
80 to 100 ft. × 20 to 40 ft.

When, Where, and How to Plant
Plant balled-and-burlapped trees in early spring or fall. Plant container-grown trees anytime during the growing season. Plant in a sunny, but sheltered spot. Winds break their brittle branches. Since White Pines cannot handle salt and car exhaust, avoid roadside sites. They like fertile, well-draining soil. Choose young trees raised in the North from Northern stock. Keep the rootball moist. Dig a saucer-shaped hole as deep as and somewhat wider than the rootball. Set the rootball so that its top is level with or even a bit higher than the surrounding ground. Remove as much burlap as possible. Backfill with plain soil, firming it gently over the root zone. Form a water-holding moat over the root zone, then water well.

Growing Tips
Water White Pines regularly in the absence of rain for one or two years. Maintain a 2- or 3-in. year-round layer of organic mulch on the soil. In poor soils, sprinkle granular slow-acting fertilizer formulated for conifers on the mulch for the rain to soak in about six months after planting, then annually for one or two years.

Care
Temporarily stake young, fall-planted trees only if they are exposed to winter winds. Prune to remove broken branches anytime. To encourage compactness or to form a hedge, prune in spring before their new, soft "candles" appear at branch tips. Watch for sawfly caterpillars in spring; treat with *Bacillus thuringiensis*.

Landscape Merit
White Pines do best in woodland settings or pruned as a hedge or screen. It is not a good idea to use them as windbreaks. Their brittle wood is easily damaged in winds and storms.

Did You Know?
White Pines are fellow members with Firs, Spruces, and others of a 225 million-year-old group of needled trees, usually evergreens, called conifers. They produce cones instead of conventional flowers. These elongated clusters of dense scales are either male or female, which bear seeds.

European Beech

Fagus sylvatica

When, Where, and How to Plant

Plant balled-and-burlapped trees in spring. Plant container-grown trees anytime during the growing season. Beeches do best in full sun, and moist, slightly acidic, organically rich soil. They accept any soil, even alkaline, however, as long as it drains well. They need a roomy site. Beeches transplant best if as much soil as possible remains on their roots. Dig a saucer-shaped hole just as deep as and two or three times as wide as the rootball. Set it so that its root flare is visible at or slightly above soil level. Remove as much burlap as possible. Backfill with plain soil, firm gently. Form a water-holding moat over the root zone from excess soil, then water well.

Growing Tips

Water new transplants if rainfall is scarce. Maintain a 2- or 3-in. layer of organic material over the root zone (but not up against its trunk). After six months to one year, sprinkle granular slow-acting tree fertilizer on the mulch for the rain to soak in. Do this for a year or two until the tree is well established.

Care

Prune in winter when the tree is dormant. Cut out any second leader (trunk). Prune injured branches promptly. For a hedge cut young trees back by 1/2 initially, then trim a full season later. Trim as needed to establish the desired height, then allowing 1/4 of the newest growth to remain when shearing for maintenance. Powdery mildew may develop on dense foliage during periods of extreme summer weather.

Landscape Merit

Plant small spring bulbs among exposed Beech roots. Evergreen ground covers protect and mask roots year-round.

Did You Know?

European Beech is often confused with our native American Beech (*Fagus grandiflora*), which also has smooth gray bark and dark-green, somewhat coarse foliage. One way to tell the difference is to count the pairs of veins in the leaves. European has five to nine pairs of veins; American has eleven to fifteen pairs.

European Beeches are not for the average-sized residential yard. These slow-growing, long-lived shade trees dominate any landscape, their towering canopies eventually casting a huge sheltering shadow over what might once have been a generous lawn. Beech leaves are typically 2 to 3 in. long, shiny gray-green in spring, turning dark green in summer, then bronze or yellow in fall. The smooth gray bark that is revealed when they fall is reminiscent of an elephant's hide. Gorgeous examples quietly preside over parks, spacious yards, and estate gardens all over Pennsylvania. 'Asplenifolia' has green, cutleaf foliage. 'Atropunicea' is the true deep-purple form. 'Tricolor' foliage is purple edged in cream and pink but it tends to scorch in summer heat. Weeping Beech (Fagus sylvatica 'Pendula') has drooping branches. 'Fastigata' is narrow.

Other Name

Common Beech

Bloom Period and Seasonal Color

Green deciduous foliage; bronze, yellow fall color

Mature Height × Spread

60 ft. × 45 to 60 ft.

Flowering Crabapple
Malus species and hybrids

Because Flowering Crabapples deliver gorgeous spring flowers, we forgive them their many problems, including nudity by midsummer in older more disease-prone varieties. Technically Apple trees, they have more and better flowers, smaller fruit, and narrower leaves that may color in fall. Crabapple flower buds are typically deep pink, opening to white, and are sometimes fragrant. Depending on the variety, they may be single, semi-double, or double, and the 1/2-in. fruits that follow in August or September may be red or yellow. Some trees bear lots of flowers one year, fewer the next. Select carefully for disease resistance. Among the more disease-resistant selections are award winners 'Donald Wyman' (with single, white flowers and red fruit), 'Jewelberry' (a bit smaller, with flowers with pink edges and slightly larger red fruit) and 'Adirondack', the 2002 Gold Medal winner.

Other Name
Flowering Crab

Bloom Period and Seasonal Color
Late April to June; blooms in pink, white, or red; red or yellow fruit into winter

Mature Height × Spread
15 to 25 ft. × 18 to 30 ft.

When, Where, and How to Plant
Crabapples establish with little fuss. Plant them in early fall or early spring in full sun for maximum flowering. Plant container-grown trees anytime during the growing season. They accept most soils, even poor ones, that are slightly acid and well drained. Choose a site sheltered from strong winds. Dig a saucer-shaped hole just as deep as and about twice as wide as the rootball. Set the tree in its hole, and remove as much burlap as possible. Assure that the top of the rootball is exactly level with the surrounding ground, backfill with plain soil, firming it gently. Then water well.

Growing Tips
Water newly planted trees when rainfall is irregular. Maintain a 2- or 3-in. layer of organic material over the tree root zone, not touching the trunk. Six months after planting, sprinkle granular slow-acting fertilizer for trees and shrubs on the mulch for the rain to soak in. Repeat for a year or two until the tree is established. Then decomposing mulch will nourish the tree.

Care
Prune Crabs when they are dormant. Remove damaged limbs anytime. Prune lightly to guide shape, and cut out branches that rub against others. Prune off suckers. If gnawing rodents damage bark, provide tree guards. Buy varieties resistant to apple scab, cedar apple rust, fireblight, and various rots.

Landscape Merit
Crabapples' small but wide-spreading size is in scale with most residential landscapes. Site them as specimens in the lawn to be viewed from indoors, or along fences and boundaries.

Did You Know?
Much smaller than Orchard Apples, Crabapples are generally sour and juiceless. They make great jelly, however, because they are mostly pectin. Simmer fruits in water to create a mush, press it through a food mill to remove the skins, and strain it for a clear liquid. Use for pectin in other recipes, or add sugar to produce a jelly with much more personality than apple jelly.

Flowering Dogwood

Cornus florida

When, Where, and How to Plant

Plant container-grown trees in early spring while still dormant. Never transplant Dogwood from the wild since that is the suspected source of dieback disease. Give Dogwoods moist, well-drained, organically rich, acidic soil. They are woodland edge plants, preferring their roots to be in the shade and their canopy in the sun at least six hours daily. Provide good air circulation. Most nursery-grown trees bloom by the third spring. Dig a saucer-shaped hole just as deep as and wider than the rootball. Set the rootball so that its top is level with or slightly above the surrounding ground. Backfill with plain soil, firm gently. Form a water-holding moat over the root zone; water well.

Growing Tips

Dogwoods are susceptible to drought, so water anytime rainfall is scarce. Mulch soil (not the trunk) year-round with 2 or 3 in. of organic material to keep the soil moist and discourage weeds. The first spring after planting, sprinkle granular slow-acting fertilizer for trees on the mulch for the rain to soak in. Thereafter, decomposing mulch will enrich the soil.

Care

Prune to shape or remove rubbing branches right after flowering, before the next year's flower buds form in late summer. Inspect Flowering Dogwood trunks for borer holes as they age. Provide air circulation to prevent mildew on foliage

Landscape Merit

Plant Flowering Dogwoods in woodland settings among spring bulbs, Ferns, Mosses, and shade-loving perennials.

Did You Know?

The cause of the dieback disease plaguing native Dogwoods was elusive for a while. It creates purple-edged brown spots on leaves, starting on the lower branches. Eventually, whole twigs die back. Infected trees struggle on, looking more sickly and losing more branches yearly. They produce water sprouts along branches in a vain effort to overcome the disease. Energy reserves exhausted by the output of foliage, infected trees soon die. A fungus called *Discula* has finally been identified as the culprit.

No list of wonderful Pennsylvania trees can omit our native Flowering Dogwood. Until it began to disappear from our woods and yards due to a dieback disease, we tended to take for granted its four seasons of beauty. Its flowers, with their trademark notched petals (actually bracts), are white, sometimes tinged with pink, and they appear before its rich-green leaves. Crunchy red berries beloved by wildlife appear as the leaves turn merlot red in September before falling. Then the dark, deeply chiseled bark and horizontal branching winter silhouette remain for winter enjoyment. 'Cherokee Chief' has deep-reddish pink flowers. 'Rainbow' has yellow-and-green variegated foliage. 'Welchii' has narrow, pink, cream, and green leaves. Rutger's hybrids of Japanese Flowering Dogwood, Aurora® and Ruth Ellen®, feature disease resistance. Other disease-resistant cultivars include 'Cherokee Princess' and 'Plena'.

Other Name

Native Dogwood

Bloom Period and Seasonal Color

Late April to May; blooms in white or pink; red berries in fall

Mature Height × Spread

20 ft. × 20 ft.

Fringe Tree
Chionanthus virginicus

Fringe Trees are an ideal size for the residential yard, so shrublike that they easily fit under utility wires. Native to the Southeast, their Northern form has acclimated to Pennsylvania. Fringe Trees may be either male or female, and both are necessary to produce black fruit. Both have interesting fluffy clusters of thready-petaled white flowers, the male ones being slightly longer and showier. To be sure of their sex, purchase young plants in flower. Medium-green leaves appear late in spring and develop yellowish tones in fall. Fringe Trees are variable in shape, some shrubby, others lanky. Chinese Fringe Tree (Chionanthus retusus) is smaller. Similar flowers and fruit bloom on new wood. Its fruit are more obvious and ornamental, and its gray, diamond-patterned bark peels.

Other Name
Old Man's Beard

Bloom Period and Seasonal Color
Late May into June; blooms in white; yellow fall color

Mature Height × Spread
12 to 20 ft. × 12 to 20 ft.

When, Where, and How to Plant
Plant balled-and-burlapped Fringe Trees or container-grown ones in early spring. They accept just about any soil type that is rich in organic matter to hold moisture. They like damp soil and are ideal for streambanks, but they do fine in drier spots if watered during droughts. Site in full sun or part sun. Fringe Trees are not crazy about being transplanted, so plant a young tree. Dig a saucer-shaped hole just as deep as and somewhat wider than the rootball. Set the rootball so that its top is even with or slightly above the level of the surrounding ground. Remove as much burlap as possible. Backfill with plain soil, firm gently. Form a berm just beyond the edge of the root zone to create a moat to hold water, then water well.

Growing Tips
Water Fringe Trees regularly if rainfall is scarce for one or two years until well established. Maintain a year-round 2- or 3-in. layer of organic mulch over its root zone, but never against its trunk. After six months, sprinkle granular slow-acting fertilizer for trees and shrubs on the mulch for the rain to soak in.

Care
Prune after bloom in the spring. Buds for next year's flowers set later in the season and will be lost to a fall pruning. To establish a single trunk, clip off suckering stems that make Fringe Tree bushy. Serious pests and diseases rarely bother this tree.

Landscape Merit
Showcase Fringe Tree as a specimen in a sunny lawn. Use shrubby forms as anchors for a flower border or as part of a mixed shrub border.

Did You Know?
Fringe Tree's scientific name is very descriptive. *Chio* means "snow," and *anthos* means "flower." Fringe Trees grow in the wild from Pennsylvania all the way to Florida. John Bartram offered them for sale in his early plant catalog, and Thomas Jefferson grew them at Monticello.

Ginkgo
Ginkgo biloba

When, Where, and How to Plant

Spring is optimum for planting Ginkgo, although young container-grown trees transplant well anytime during the growing season. Older transplants take several years to recover. Plant in full sun. They prefer moist, well-drained soil rich in organic material, but are amazingly tolerant of a wide variety of conditions. They can handle clay or sand and a range of pH. Dig a saucer-shaped hole as deep as and considerably wider than the rootball. Position the rootball so its top is at the same level in the soil as it was in its container. Remove as much burlap as possible. Backfill with plain soil, firming soil gently. Create a water-holding moat over the root zone, then water well.

Growing Tips

Water newly planted trees regularly for one or two years when rainfall is unreliable. Maintain a year-round 2- or 3-in. layer of organic mulch over tree root zones. It helps soil stay moist, discourages weeds, and improves the soil as it decomposes. Never pile mulch against the tree trunk. After the first six months, sprinkle granular slow-acting fertilizer formulated for trees and shrubs on the mulch for the rain to soak in. Repeat for one or two years while the roots become established.

Care

Prune to improve branching in spring when trees are young. They are extremely resistant to pests, even Japanese beetles. Their branches are brittle and may suffer storm damage. A male Ginkgo is preferable, but choosing from among young trees is a gamble.

Landscape Merit

Ginkgoes enhance Japanese-style gardens, and pools. They make great street trees, males preferably, because they do not produce the malodorous fruit that females bear.

Did You Know?

Taken internally, Ginkgo is reputed to inhibit allergic responses and improve blood circulation, thus improving memory. Ginkgo is reported to be effective in treating asthma, poor circulation in the elderly, and varicose veins. Therapeutic preparations are made from dried and processed foliage.

Ginkgos existed throughout the world millions of years ago. Today's trees are descendants of trees that survived the dinosaur period and they greatly resemble their ancestors. Although almost all Ginkgoes eventually disappeared from the wild, some were grown and preserved in the temples of China, Japan, and Korea. They are the source of all present-day Ginkgoes. Related to conifers, they have distinctive fan-shaped leaves that turn golden in the fall. Their similarity to Maidenhair Fern leaflets explains their common name. Mature trees are slow growing, tough, and tolerant of most urban stresses except smog. Good male Ginkgoes are 'Autumn Gold', which starts upright, then spreads; 'Fairmount', which was selected from a tree in Philadelphia; and 'Princeton Sentry', which is narrow and dense.

Other Name
Maidenhair Tree

Bloom Period and Seasonal Color
Golden fall foliage color

Mature Height × Spread
80 ft. × 30 to 40 ft.

Goldenrain Tree
Koelreuteria paniculata

A tree that flowers in the summer is always welcome. The 12- to 15-in. clusters of thin, small yellow flowers that halo the domed canopy of Goldenrain Trees are eye-catchers. They develop into green, lantern-shaped pods that turn yellow, then brown, and eventually release black seeds the size of peas. Goldenrain Trees have a coarse, open structure, abetted by exotic-looking leaves composed of up to 15 coarsely toothed leaflets, which are reduced in size as the tree grows older. The leaves turn orange-yellow in fall. 'September' is a 1997 Gold Medal Award winner from the Pennsylvania Horticultural Society; it flowers into September. Chinese Flame Tree (Koelreuteria bipinnata) is a bit less cold hardy and flowers into September. It has rosy-pink fruit capsules.

Other Name
Varnish Tree

Bloom Period and Seasonal Color
July; blooms in yellow; orange-yellow fall foliage color

Mature Height × Spread
30 ft. × 30 ft.

When, Where, and How to Plant
Choose trees grown in the North from Northern seed. They plant and transplant easily in the spring. Young trees look a bit gaunt at first, but fill out quickly. They appreciate full sun and decent soil, but are tolerant of poor soil as well as drought, air pollution, and wind. Dig a saucer-shaped hole as deep as and somewhat wider than the rootball. Set the rootball so that its top is level with or just slightly higher than the surrounding ground. Backfill with plain soil, form a berm beyond the edge of the root zone to create a temporary moat to hold water, then water well. Space 15 or 20 ft. apart.

Growing Tips
Water regularly if rain is sparse until the tree is established. Maintain a year-round 2- or 3-in. layer of organic mulch over the root zone (not against the tree trunk). Six months after planting sprinkle a granular, slow-acting fertilizer made for trees and shrubs on the mulch around it. If kept well-mulched, trees only need fertilizer for the first few years.

Care
Prune damaged branches promptly. Prune for shape, or cut crowded or rubbing branches during dormancy in late winter. Always cut back branches to the nearest crotch where the branch is attached. Goldenrain Tree self-sows, so lots of seedlings pop up in the area. They pull up easily before they get too woody. Stressed trees develop dieback or wilt disease.

Landscape Merit
Fast growers initially (10 to 12 ft. the first seven years), these trees stay relatively small and are suitable for lawns under utility wires or nearer the house to provide some shade. They do well in cities as street trees. They also work in smallish yards, and they do not overpower one-story homes.

Did You Know?
The other small "golden" tree with which Goldenrain Tree is sometimes confused is Golden Chaintree (*Laburnum × watereri*). It grows only 12 or 15 ft. tall with a narrower profile. Its glory is the scented yellow flowers that literally drip from its branches in late spring. It struggles a bit in hot, humid climates.

Green Hawthorn

Crataegus viridis 'Winter King'

When, Where, and How to Plant

Spring is the best time to plant, although container-grown Hawthorns can be planted anytime during the season. Hawthorns do best in full sun, but some shade is fine. They agreeably tolerate any soil and can handle air pollution. Dig a saucer-shaped hole just as deep as and about twice as wide as the rootball. Set the rootball so that its top is at the same level as the surrounding ground. Backfill with plain soil, firming it gently around the rootball to remove air pockets. Form a soil berm just beyond the edge of the root zone as a moat to hold water, then water well.

Growing Tips

Water newly planted trees when rainfall is sparse for a year or more until established. Mulching the soil over the root zone year-round with 2 or 3 in. of organic material such as chopped leaves or wood chips helps keep soil moist. Over the years the decomposing mulch will enrich the soil.

Care

Small trees may need temporary staking in sites exposed to wind. 'Winter King' is grafted onto rootstock of the Washington Hawthorn. Stem suckers will develop from below the graft; prune them promptly. Prune off water sprouts if they appear along the branches. Caterpillars, scale, or borers attack stressed trees.

Landscape Merit

Use 'Winter King' as a specimen, and site it for viewing from indoors, too. Give it plenty of room for its spread.

Did You Know?

Cedar-hawthorn rust plagues Hawthorns, which are generally highly susceptible to it. Rust needs two kinds of plants to survive, so chances of its being around are increased if there are Eastern Red Cedars (*Juniperus virginiana*) in the area. The disease starts on the Hawthorn leaves—red or brown spots ringed with yellow. The spores then infect nearby Junipers, which host them over the winter. The following spring they pop over to the Hawthorn again to cause further harm.

Their beauty notwithstanding, most Hawthorns are, as their name suggests, thorny. The thorns can be easily overlooked among the lustrous green leaves, especially when foliage turns to purplish scarlet in fall and the stems sport bright-red fruit the size of marbles. 'Winter King' overcomes the typical fungal diseases of Hawthorns. It has a broad vase shape and bears clusters of delicate white flowers each spring. After a show of bronze, red, and gold fall foliage, it reveals silvery bark patched with orange-brown and develops orange-red fruits that persist through winter. Its sparse thorns are smaller. Native Washington Hawthorn (Crataegus phaenopyrum) grows to 20 ft. tall and wide. It flowers later, bears red fruit into winter, and has thorns 1 to 3 in. long!

Other Name
Winter King Thorn

Bloom Period and Seasonal Color
Mid-May; blooms in white; bronze, red, and gold fall foliage color

Mature Height × Spread
20 to 30 ft. × 20 to 30 ft.

Hinoki Falsecypress
Chamaecyparis obtusa

Hinoki Falsecypresses are stately, slow-growing trees. Their foliage grows in drooping branchlets of flat sprays of needles that resemble those of Arborvitae. Their blunt needles have pale lines or patches beneath, and come in shades of green, yellow, or blue. Hinokis produce male flowers (cones) that shed pollen in April on their bluish, eight-pointed, scaled female cones. As our native Hemlocks succumb to an unrelenting infestation of woolly adelgid aphids, Hinoki Falsecypress may be a good substitute. They like humidity and are shade tolerant. Colorful varieties are available in a range of sizes but the dwarf ones are the most commonly available. 'Crippsii' at 10 to 20 ft. is a slower-growing, full-sized version with golden foliage. Sawara Falsecypress (Chamaecyparis pisifera) is a bit narrower and potentially taller than Hinoki with fine-pointed needles.

Bloom Period and Seasonal Color
Dark-green evergreen foliage

Mature Height × Spread
50 to 75 ft. × 10 to 20 ft. (Dwarf cultivars are smaller.)

When, Where, and How to Plant
Hinoki Falsecypress trees transplant well. Plant container-grown trees anytime during the growing season. They need sun to best show off their foliage color. Shade during hot summer afternoons is ideal. They are flexible about soil as long as it is reasonably fertile and well drained. Protect them from strong wind. Dig a saucer-shaped hole just as deep as and about twice as wide as the rootball. Position the rootball so that its soil is level with or a bit higher than the surrounding ground. Backfill with plain soil, firm gently. Form a water-holding moat over the root zone, then water well.

Growing Tips
Continue to water over the next year when rainfall is unreliable. Spread a 2- or 3-in. layer of organic material over the root zone (not against the tree trunk). Year-round mulch helps soil stay moist, discourages weeds, and improves the soil as it decomposes. After six months, sprinkle granular slow-acting fertilizer for evergreens on the mulch for the rain to soak in. Do this again for a year or two. Thereafter, decomposing mulch will improve the soil to sustain the tree.

Care
Hinokis have lovely natural shapes, so they do not need routine pruning. To control the size of large varieties, clip branches individually before new growth starts in spring. Do not shear. Cut out damaged limbs promptly. Wash off mite infestations with a forceful water spray. Deny gnawing rodents a nesting place by delaying winter mulching until after the ground freezes and by wrapping trunks with hardware cloth.

Landscape Merit
Full-sized Falsecypresses show to best advantage in large open spaces. Use dwarf shrubby types for small spaces and rock gardens.

Did You Know?
To the average homeowner, needled evergreen shrubs look alike. Sometimes only a practiced eye can easily distinguish some types of Falsecypress from Juniper. Try the touch test. Juniper foliage tends to be prickly; Falsecypress foliage is softer and smoother.

Japanese Maple
Acer palmatum

When, Where, and How to Plant

Plant balled-and-burlapped Japanese Maples in early spring immediately after winter dormancy. Transplant container-grown trees anytime during the growing season except during heat and drought. Most do best in full sun, but some shade enhances the color on the deep-red ones. Protect them from sun scorch and winter frost. Any well-drained soil is fine. Improve clay or sand with organic matter. Dig a saucer-shaped hole just as deep as and somewhat wider than the rootball. Straighten circling roots if present. Set the rootball so that its top is exactly at or slightly higher than soil level. Remove any burlap. Backfill with plain soil, firm gently. Create a water-holding moat over root zone, then water well.

Growing Tips

Water new transplants when rain is sparse until trees are established. Provide a year-round 2- or 3-in. layer of organic mulch. After at least six months, fertilize with granular slow-acting fertilizer formulated for trees. Fertilize annually for a few years; then decomposing mulch will enrich the soil.

Care

Prune Japanese Maples to remove suckers, rubbing branches, and excess twigs in mid- to late summer. Clip damaged branches anytime. Japanese Maples are susceptible to verticillium wilt. Foliage on one or more branches may suddenly wilt, shrivel, and die. Prune away infected branches. Then fertilize to encourage new sapwood growth. Do not plant a Japanese Maple where one has died.

Landscape Merit

Use Japanese Maples alone as specimens or as focal points anchoring an island bed or Japanese-style garden. Weeping types integrate easily into small yards in containers or rock gardens.

Did You Know?

Bonsai is the ancient art of dwarfing normal trees and shrubs so that they age as miniatures of their potential selves over decades, even centuries. It is possible to achieve something similar faster by using dwarf Japanese Maples. Choose a container that is wider than tall, has a drainage hole, and can take winter outdoors. Consult a book on bonsai for techniques.

In their myriad forms and colors Japanese Maples commonly grace suburban yards in Pennsylvania. Their flowers hang as small, purplish red clusters that develop into the classic maple winged seeds. Their leaves are 1 to 3 in. across, and depending on the variety, each has five to eleven lobes. Some are so deeply cut that they seem lacy. The most highly prized Japanese Maples are the many named cultivars, and their price reflects their value. 'Bloodgood' is red all season; 'Versicolor' has green leaves variegated with pink and white. Threadleaf Japanese Maple (Acer palmatum var. dissectum) has finely dissected foliage; 'Tamukeyama' is the best of the purple-leafed cutleafs, and 'Waterfall' has green foliage that turns yellow. Both are Gold Medal Award winners.

Bloom Period and Seasonal Color
Red, green, variegated deciduous foliage with yellow or orange fall color

Mature Height × Spread
3 to 20 ft. × 3 to 20 ft.

Japanese Zelkova
Zelkova serrata

Japanese Zelkovas, first recognized as good substitutes for the dying American Elms on streets and campuses in the East, have earned a reputation as versatile, attractive trees. Their moderate size suits them to residential yards. They grow rapidly, doubling their height in four to six years, to provide welcome shade. Since their flowers and fruit are inconspicuous, their dark-green foliage that turns reddish purple in the fall and their interesting patchy mature bark are their most compelling attributes. Zelkovas do fine in suburban and coastal environments where, properly sited and cared for, they thrive. 'Green Vase' features rapid growth, good form, and fall color. 'Village Green' has rusty-red fall foliage color and a broader crown.

Other Name
Zelkova

Bloom Period and Seasonal Color
Bright-green deciduous foliage; reddish purple fall foliage color

Mature Height × Spread
60 to 70 ft. × 50 to 55 ft.

When, Where, and How to Plant
Zelkovas transplant well. Plant container-grown trees anytime during the growing season. They are agreeable to any well-drained soil except sand. They tolerate a range of pH, compacted soil, pollution, and even drought, once they are established. Site in full sun. Do not plant where a diseased Elm may have been located. Dig a saucer-shaped hole just as deep as and twice as wide as the rootball. Position the rootball so that its top is even with or slightly above the surrounding ground. Remove as much burlap from a wrapped rootball as possible. Backfill with plain soil, firming it gently around the rootball. Form a water-holding moat over the root zone; water well.

Growing Tips
Water new transplants when rainfall is sparse. Spread a 2- or 3-in. layer of organic material over the root zone (not the trunk). After six months, sprinkle granular slow-acting fertilizer on the mulch for the rain to soak in. Repeat yearly for two or three years. Thereafter, decomposing mulch will nourish the soil.

Care
Stake newly planted Zelkovas their first year. Prune young trees to establish a single stem and branching framework and to remove rubbing branches. Zelkovas are highly resistant to Dutch elm disease, but they have occasional problems with Japanese beetles.

Landscape Merit
Use Zelkovas wherever shade is desired—over porches and walks. Their vaselike profile of fanning upright branches above a short trunk makes them good street trees.

Did You Know?
Dutch elm disease was introduced here from Europe in the 1930s. Logs intended for manufacture were infested with bark-eating beetles carrying the fungal disease. The epidemic's toll was an estimated 77 million dead Elms. Among the many lessons learned were these: Sterilize pruning equipment after use on diseased plants; time pruning to avoid aggravating the situation; and limit the population of any tree species in an area to only 10 percent of total trees there to maintain diversity and avoid a monoculture.

Littleleaf Linden
Tilia cordata

When, Where, and How to Plant

Lindens transplant easily. Plant larger balled-and-burlapped trees in spring or fall. Plant container-grown trees anytime during the growing season. Lindens do best in full sun, although they accept some shade. They prefer a good well-drained soil rich in organic matter. Dig a saucer-shaped hole just as deep as and twice as wide as the rootball. Set the rootball so that its top is at or slightly above the soil level. Remove as much burlap as possible. Backfill with plain soil, firming it gently over the rootball. Form a water-holding moat over the root zone, then water well. Space street trees 40 ft. apart.

Growing Tips

Water Lindens if rainfall is unreliable over the one or two years it takes them to become established, and then during droughty periods. Maintain a year-round 2- or 3-in. layer of organic mulch over the soil (not against the trunk). After six months, sprinkle granular slow-acting tree fertilizer on the mulch for rain to soak in. After three years, annual fertilization will not be necessary; decomposing mulch nourishes the soil.

Care

Lindens accept pruning well and can be hedged. Prune suckers that appear below the graft. Handpick Japanese beetles off small trees; discard into a jar of soapy water. Treat the lawn for white grubs of future populations of Japanese beetles. Older, established trees can withstand defoliation by these pests every year.

Landscape Merit

Plant Littleleaf Lindens as specimens in the lawn or along the street. Underplant with an evergreen ground cover rather than turfgrass.

Did You Know?

The bounty of the Littleleaf Linden cousin, our native American Linden, *Tilia americana,* is generous. Called Bee Tree because of the copious nectar its flowers produce, it is one of the best honey trees in the world. Herbalists use its foliage in tea for throat and voice problems, and as an appetite stimulant. Also known as Basswood, this tree's light, straight-grained wood is ideal for carving, joinery, and cabinetry.

Littleleaf Lindens abound in yards and along streets in many Pennsylvania communities—and for good reason. Their dense foliage canopy of medium-sized, toothed, heart-shaped, dark-green leaves is neat and attractive. It shelters copious clusters of fragrant, small pale-yellow flowers that dangle on thin stalks beneath a single leafy bract. By late summer the flowers become tiny dried fruits that persist after the foliage turns yellow and drops. Among other virtues, Lindens count a sturdy tolerance for pollution and shallow, disciplined root systems that make them good neighbors to buildings and other plants. 'Greenspire' is a fast grower, and its dense canopy and upright, straight trunk are the standard of comparison among Lindens. 'Glenleven' is vigorous, with a more open-leaf canopy and more informal branching.

Other Name

Small-leafed Lime

Bloom Period and Seasonal Color

Late June into July; blooms in pale yellow

Mature Height × Spread

60 ft. × 30 ft.

Northern Catalpa
Catalpa speciosa

Because of their coarse, rangy look, Northern Catalpas are an acquired taste. Native to the Midwest, they are easily spotted in vacant lots in the city, and in the exurbs on former farm properties. Their fast-growing frames, festooned with huge, heart-shaped leaves that form a broad, oval leaf canopy, have a special appeal. They have late-spring flowers, composed of clusters of 2-in.-long, tubular white blooms featuring frilled edges and yellow or purple tinges and spots. The upright clusters on 4- to 8-in. stalks are visible from a distance. The 8- to 20-in.-long seedpods that develop later and ridged, furrowed gray bark provide another season of interest. For the pioneer farmers Catalpas provided durable wood suitable for fence posts because it resists rot.

Other Name
Cigar Tree

Bloom Period and Seasonal Color
Late spring; blooms in white

Mature Height × Spread
60 ft. × 20 to 40 ft.

When, Where, and How to Plant
Plant young balled-and-burlapped trees in spring. Catalpas prefer deep, moist, fertile soil, but they can handle alkaline soil, either wet or dry. Give them full sun and plenty of space. Dig a saucer-shaped hole just as deep as and twice as wide as the rootball. Set the rootball so that its top is at or slightly above the soil level. Remove as much burlap as possible. Backfill with plain soil, firming it gently around the rootball to remove air pockets. Form a soil berm just beyond the edge of the root zone to create a moat to hold water, then water well.

Growing Tips
Water when rainfall is sparse until the Catalpa is established. Maintain a year-round 2- or 3-in. layer of mulch over the root zone of the tree to protect from mower or trimmer injury, keep soil moist, and discourage weeds. Increase the mulched area as the tree canopy spreads. Do not pile mulch up against the tree trunk. Catalpas can handle considerable heat and drought once they are established.

Care
Catalpa's brittle wood may break in storms or wind. Prune injured branches promptly, cutting them off cleanly at the branch collar, to facilitate healing. Powdery mildew on foliage may be a temporary problem.

Landscape Merit
Because they drop their pods, do not plant Catalpas near streets, walks, and gutters. Site individual trees as novelty specimens in open areas, or put them near back property lines or in undeveloped areas of the yard.

Did You Know?
If you like Catalpa, you will love Paulownia (*Paulownia tomentosa*), or Empress Tree. Paulownias are found in similar situations and also have big, coarse leaves, rangy habits, and drop-dead gorgeous flowers. Pale purple, the flowers appear in May and have a light scent. Like Catalpa trees, Empress Trees can be cut back to the ground every year and maintained as a large, shrubby foliage-only accent in smaller residential yards.

Oak

Quercus spp.

When, Where, and How to Plant

Plant Oaks when they are young. The best time is early spring, although container-grown trees can be planted anytime during the growing season. Site Oaks in full sun. They like soil that is loose, well drained, and organically rich. Dig a saucer-shaped hole just as deep as and twice as wide as the rootball. Set the rootball so its top is at or slightly above soil level. Remove as much burlap as possible. Backfill with plain soil, firming it gently around the rootball. Create a water-holding moat, then water well.

Growing Tips

Water young Oaks when rainfall is sparse until they become established. Maintain a year-round 2- or 3-in. layer of organic mulch on their soil. After six months, sprinkle granular slow-acting fertilizer for trees on the mulch for the rain to soak in. After a few years the decomposing mulch will enrich the soil, and regular fertilizing is not necessary.

Care

Prune damaged branches anytime. Prune during winter dormancy to shape, to establish a single trunk, or to remove rubbing branches. Oaks that are relatively free of stress and injury escape serious pests and diseases. Gypsy moths, their nemesis, defoliate full-grown trees in no time. Control infestations with *Bacillus thuringiensis*.

Landscape Merit

Use Red and White Oaks as street trees, but not between curbs and sidewalks. They make stunning specimens in spacious lawns. Red Oaks are best for cities; they tolerate air pollution and grow faster.

Did You Know?

It is easy to grow large Oaks from acorns. Collect blemish-free acorns in the fall, and put them in pots of moist planting mix. Sink pots in the soil over the winter, protected from rodents with hardware cloth. White Oaks germinate almost immediately in the fall, whereas Red Oaks wait until spring. Then leave the seedlings in pots for another year, or plant them inground in a protected sunny location.

Their presence echoing the hardwood forests that once covered this region, stately Red Oaks (Quercus rubra) and White Oaks (Quercus alba) are familiar, native shade trees that grace churchyards, old properties, and winding streets in Pennsylvania. Red Oak's foliage has pointed lobes, while that of White Oaks has rounded lobes. Both deliver deep, rich color in the fall. Neither produces acorns until trees are about twenty-five years old. Because they are extremely long-lived trees, attentive care bestowed on them as young trees (including protection from deer) is vital to their future. Old trees are extremely sensitive to damage to their wide spreading roots by nearby construction projects and heavy machinery. A cousin, Pin Oak (Quercus palustris), is fast growing, with a uniform shape, and tolerates wetter soil.

Bloom Period and Seasonal Color

Dark-green deciduous foliage turns red or golden-yellow in fall

Mature Height × Spread

40 to 80 ft. × 60 ft.

179

Ornamental Cherry
Prunus species and hybrids

Ornamental Cherry is a catchall label for several decorative Cherry trees from Japan that flower in spring. Common in home landscapes over most of Pennsylvania, they play a major role in our state's gorgeous springs. They all offer a blizzard of pink or white, single or double, flowers and sometimes fragrance. They have a relatively short life span, about twenty years. Okame Cherry (Prunus × 'Okame') features long-lasting, early-season pink flowers and orange and yellow fall foliage. Weeping Higan Cherry (Prunus subhirtella 'Pendula') has weeping branches and pink flowers. Kwanzan Cherry (Prunus serrulata 'Kwanzan') is vase shaped and produces loads of large, double, pink cotton candy flowers. 'Mt. Fuji' has scented, double, white flowers. Yoshino Cherry (Prunus yeodensis) bears white flowers in early April.

Other Name
Japanese Flowering Cherry

Bloom Period and Seasonal Color
April through June; blooms in white, shades of pink

Mature Height × Spread
15 to 25 ft. × 15 to 25 ft.

When, Where, and How to Plant
Plant container-grown trees in early spring or fall. Full sun prompts the best flowering. Ornamental Cherries can handle almost any kind of well-drained soil. Add organic matter to soil that is primarily clay to improve its drainage. Dig a saucer-shaped hole just as deep as and twice or more as wide as the rootball. Set the rootball so that its top is even with or a bit above the surrounding ground. Backfill with plain soil, firming it gently around the rootball to remove air pockets. Form a berm just beyond the edge of the root zone to hold water, then water well.

Growing Tips
Water transplanted trees if rainfall is sparse. Spread 2 or 3 in. of organic material over root zones but not against trunks. It helps retain soil moisture, discourage weeds, and protect young tree trunks from injury from lawn-care equipment. Six months after planting, sprinkle granular slow-acting nursery fertilizer on the mulch for the rain to soak in. After three or four years, constantly decomposing organic mulch will nourish the tree.

Care
Prune suckers that emerge below the graft on grafted trees. Prune off caterpillar tents at the tips of branches as soon as possible. Guard against tree borers in young saplings. Cherry foliage is susceptible to Japanese beetles, so control grubs in the lawn with milky spore.

Landscape Merit
Japanese Cherries are effective planted alone as specimens, in rows to line walkways and boundaries, or grouped in threes on spacious properties.

Did You Know?
For more than ten years the Pennsylvania Horticultural Society (PHS) has sponsored a Gold Medal plant award program to select and promote woody plants that perform exceptionally well in Philadelphia area gardens. A distinguished committee evaluates nominated plants for several years for their hardiness, pest and disease resistance, and durability. Initiated by the late J. Franklin Styer, the award has the goal of getting superior plants into Pennsylvania gardens. (See page 237.) In 1998, *Prunus* 'Okame' earned this medal.

Ornamental Pear

Pyrus calleryana

When, Where, and How to Plant

Plant dormant balled-and-burlapped trees in spring. Plant container-grown Ornamental Pears anytime during the growing season in full sun. Trees planted in shade lose their shape. They accept almost any kind of reasonably fertile, well-drained soil, even clay. Dig a saucer-shaped hole just as deep as and somewhat wider than the rootball. Set the rootball so that its top is exactly at soil level or even slightly above. Remove as much burlap as possible. Backfill with plain soil, firming it gently over the rootball. Form a water-holding moat, then water well. Reserve an open space of 30 ft. around the tree to accommodate its mature size.

Growing Tips

Water new transplants whenever rainfall is sparse. Maintain 2 or 3 in. of mulch over the root zone (not the trunk) year-round to retain soil moisture and discourage weeds. After six months, sprinkle a little granular slow-acting fertilizer formulated for trees on the mulch for the rain to soak in. Do this annually for two or three years. Avoid excessive fertilizer to discourage foliage disease. Thereafter, the decomposing mulch will nourish the soil.

Care

Ornamental Pears do not need shaping because their habit is so uniform. Prune only to remove damaged or rubbing branches. Occasional scale, aphid, and mildew problems occur on foliage of stressed trees. To deter chewing rodents, delay winter mulching until the ground has frozen; cover trunks with hardware cloth or tree wrap.

Landscape Merit

Showcase Ornamental Pears as specimens in open lawn and garden areas. Plant a row along a property boundary for dramatic effect.

Did You Know?

Ornamental Pears make attractive espalier specimens. Plant so that their straight trunks grow close to a wall trellis or a sturdy wire and post support. Prune to establish strong lateral branches, then train them to grow horizontally, flat against the support. With this pruning and support, any tendency to split with age is no longer a problem.

Ornamental Pear trees have become fixtures in residential landscapes because of their uniform shape, rapid growth, and white spring flowers. Relatively carefree, they do not develop edible fruit, just inconspicuous little dried knobs. Their leaves turn wine red before dropping in October. A few have thorns, but many are thornless. Once established, they are somewhat drought tolerant. The most popular has been 'Bradford'. It offers good flowers, disease resistance, and fall color. Its brittle dense branches, narrowly crotched, tend to split from wind or weight of snow, however. Thus, its effective life span is generally less than twenty years. Compared to 'Bradford', 'Aristocrat', with glossy leaves, no thorns, and upcurving branches, has stronger wood and is less likely to split.

Other Name
Callery Pear

Bloom Period and Seasonal Color
April; blooms in white; red fall foliage color

Mature Height × Spread
30 to 45 ft. × 20 to 25 ft.

Red Maple

Acer rubrum

Red describes them best. Swamp Red Maples have red buds in winter, red flowers and winged seeds in spring, red leaf stalks in summer, and red foliage in fall. This excellent native tree is fast growing, yet has strong wood. Females have more conspicuous flowers, and the day when their seeds cover the lawn is a delight for people and squirrels. 'Autumn Flame' colors earliest in the fall. It has smaller leaves and is slower growing than most Red Maples. 'October Glory' turns color the latest—a display of crimson red to orange. An early hard frost sometimes preempts the color. 'Red Sunset' is highly rated; it holds its red fall foliage longest and has a narrower canopy than many.

Other Name
Swamp Red Maple

Bloom Period and Seasonal Color
Green deciduous foliage; red fall color

Mature Height × Spread
40 to 60 ft. × 30 to 50 ft.

When, Where, and How to Plant
Plant in the spring. Transplant container-grown trees anytime during the growing season. Avoid grafted trees. Red Maples do best in full sun. They tolerate all soils, including wet ones. Their shallow, wide-ranging roots tend to surface when crowded, so site them well away from buildings and curbs. Dig a saucer-shaped hole just as deep as and twice as wide as the rootball. Position the rootball so its top is even with or slightly above the surrounding ground. Remove as much burlap as possible. Backfill with plain soil, firm soil gently. Form a water-holding moat, then water well.

Growing Tips
Water newly planted trees regularly for one or two years whenever rainfall is sparse. Mulch root zones year-round with 2 or 3 in. of organic material to maintain soil moisture and protect trunks from injury by mower or weed trimmer. After six months, sprinkle granular slow-acting fertilizer for trees on the mulch for the rain to soak in. Repeat annually three or four years. In the future, the decomposing mulch will enrich the soil.

Care
Sometimes two leaders develop in young trees. Prune one off early on to establish a single trunk. Trees pruned in late winter will leak sap but suffer no harm. June pruning avoids this. Prune diseased or injured branches immediately. Stressed transplants may attract aphids, scale, caterpillars, or fungal leaf spots on foliage. Maintain tree vigor.

Landscape Merit
Use Red Maples as specimens in a large yard or to line drives or border the property. Flaunt that fall color! Avoid sites close to the house or near utility wires.

Did You Know?
Norway Maples (*Acer platanoides*) are among several brightly fall-colored foliage cousins of Red Maples. Norways have earned themselves the opprobrium of most local arborists, horticulturists, and environmentalists. More and more gardeners and homeowners are realizing the nuisance that they represent as they seed everywhere, driving out native plants and hogging soil moisture. 'Crimson King' is an exception.

River Birch

Betula nigra 'Heritage'

When, Where, and How to Plant

Plant larger balled-and-burlapped trees in spring; plant container-grown ones anytime during the growing season until mid-August to assure that roots have time to establish before winter. River Birch loves full sun and moist, acidic, organically rich soil. It can also handle drier soil and even quite wet acidic soils. Dig a saucer-shaped hole just as deep as and considerably wider than the root-ball. Set the rootball so that its top is exactly even with or slightly above the level of the surrounding soil. Remove as much burlap as possible. Backfill with plain soil, firming it gently around the root-ball. Form a soil berm beyond the root zone to create a moat to hold water, then water well.

Growing Tips

Water regularly if rainfall is scarce for a year or two until the tree establishes. Maintain a year-round 2- or 3-in. layer of mulch spread over its root zone, but not against its trunk. Six months after planting, sprinkle granular slow-acting fertilizer for trees over the root zone. Repeat for a year or two.

Care

Check deep in the canopies of older River Birches for dead or injured branches; prune them promptly. To create a multistemmed tree, cut back the original leader to nearly soil level when it is one or two years old to stimulate new stem growth. The clump tree will be a bit shorter than a typical single-stemmed one. River Birches may suffer wind and ice damage.

Landscape Merit

Use 'Heritage' as a specimen in the lawn, naturalized along stream banks, or grouped in groves. Underplant with Narcissus, Ferns, or evergreen ground cover.

Did You Know?

Birches get their name from the ancient Sanskrit language. "Birch" evolved from *Bhurga*, which signifies "a tree whose bark is used for writing upon." A distinguishing feature of most Birches is their peeling, curling bark, which it is easy to believe, especially with white-barked ones, could serve as paper.

Fine-textured, slender Birches are wonderful additions to home landscapes. In Pennsylvania the perfect choice is the native River Birch because it is not susceptible to the bronze birch borer. River Birches are fast growing under preferred conditions—up to 5 ft. in one year, 30 to 40 ft. in twenty years. Columnar when young, their shape becomes rounded as they age. Their toothed leaves are dark green with tiny hairs on the midrib beneath. Young trees have thin bark that peels to reveal reddish or tan and brown underneath. 'Heritage', the most available variety, has paler bark color and more closely resembles the classic white-barked birches. It has slightly pendulous branches and larger leaves. It is listed among the top ten trees for U.S. landscapes.

Other Name
Heritage River Birch

Bloom Period and Seasonal Color
Medium-green deciduous foliage; yellow fall color

Mature Height × Spread
40 to 60 ft. × 40 to 60 ft.

Saucer Magnolia
Magnolia × soulangiana

Saucer Magnolias, bred from Japanese and Chinese Magnolias, provide a reliably cold-hardy version of Magnolia for Pennsylvania yards. They cover themselves with glory every spring before their leaves emerge with 5- to 8-in.-wide, fragrant, saucer-shaped blossoms. Usually white with a pink or purplish blush on the undersides of their outer petals, they hold an annual contest with the last frost. More often than not they lose, their petals turning to brown mush within hours of opening. Oh, but the years when they win! Magnolia × 'Galaxy' blooms in April. Its dark-pink flowers usually escape early frosts. Star Magnolia (Magnolia stellata) 'Centennial' has smaller, white, double, fragrant flowers. 'Elizabeth' bears lovely soft-yellow blossoms. All three have received the Pennsylvania Horticultural Society's Gold Medal Award for exceptional merit as landscape plants.

Bloom Period and Seasonal Color
April; blooms in white with pink

Mature Height × Spread
30 ft. × 30 ft.

When, Where, and How to Plant
Magnolias' fleshy roots are tender and sparse. Damage delays recovery from transplant shock. Plant balled-and-burlapped trees in March or April. Smaller, potted ones transplant best, especially early in the season. They start flowering when they are 4 ft. tall. Saucer Magnolias do best in full sun out in the open. Sheltered sites heat up too soon, encouraging flower buds to open early and risk premature death from frost. Provide soil that is slightly acidic, organically rich, and well drained. Dig a saucer-shaped hole just as deep as and about twice as wide as the rootball. Set the rootball so that its top is exactly at the level of the surrounding ground, no lower. Remove as much burlap as possible. Backfill with plain soil, firming it gently around the rootball. Create a water-holding moat over the root zone, and water well.

Growing Tips
Water when rainfall is sparse during the first year or two. Maintain a year-round 2- or 3-in. layer of organic mulch on the soil. Six months after planting, sprinkle granular slow-acting fertilizer for trees on the mulch for the rain to soak in.

Care
Prune the occasional damaged branch promptly. Cut off any branch that crosses and rubs another and any vertical water sprouts or suckers along branches. Prune for size and shape immediately after flowering because new buds form over the summer for next year's show. Stressed trees may experience various leaf spot diseases. Maintain tree vigor. Deer generally ignore Magnolias.

Landscape Merit
Site Saucer Magnolias front and center in a spacious yard. Plant small, hardy bulbs such as Snowdrops, Squill, or Grape Hyacinth under Magnolias. Cultivating the soil for annual plants damages their shallow roots.

Did You Know?
Saucer Magnolias are named for Chevalier Etienne Soulange-Bodin, a French soldier. A veteran of the Napoleonic Wars, he devoted his retirement to gardening, becoming the director of the Royal Institute of Horticulture in France. Around 1820 he crossed a white Yulan Magnolia with a purple lily one, and the Saucer Magnolia resulted.

When, Where, and How to Plant

Plant balled-and-burlapped Sourwoods in spring. Transplant container-grown trees anytime during the growing season. Young trees up to 3 ft. tall transplant easily. Their coarse, deep, lateral roots make them trickier to transplant when older. Plant in sun or in their familiar understory sites at woodland edges. They appreciate rich, acidic, moist, well-drained soil. Once established, they can handle dry soil. Dig a saucer-shaped hole just as deep as and two or three times wider than the rootball. Set the rootball so its top is exactly at soil level or even slightly above. Remove as much burlap as possible after it is in the hole. Backfill with plain soil, firming it gently over the root zone. Fashion a water-holding moat over the root zone, and water.

Growing Tips

Water newly planted Sourwoods regularly for a year when rainfall is sparse. Maintain a year-round 2- or 3-in. layer of organic mulch over the root zone (not the trunk) to retain moisture, discourage weeds, and protect the bark. After six months, sprinkle granular slow-acting fertilizer for trees on the mulch for the rain to soak in. After three or four years, the decomposing mulch will enrich the soil, and the tree will not need annual fertilizing.

Care

Prune competing leaders to establish a single trunk. Cut off injured or rubbing branches, cutting smoothly at the branch collar to promote healing. Provide temporary staking the first winter to protect from winter wind. Prune out nests of fall webworms before the caterpillars venture forth to eat the leaves.

Landscape Merit

Use Sourwoods as specimens to display their multiseason virtues. They are a good substitute for Dogwood.

Did You Know?

Multiseason Hall of Fame—Sourwood tops any list of landscape trees offering ornamental features virtually year-round. Here are others not covered in this book: Katsura (*Cercidiphyllum japonicum*); Japanese Clethra (*Clethra barbinervis*); Franklin Tree (*Franklinia alatamaha*); Pagoda Tree (*Sophora japonica*); and Japanese Stewartia (*Stewartia pseudocamellia*).

Native to Southwestern Pennsylvania and the South, Sourwoods are ornamental in every respect, their unflattering name deriving from the sour taste of their foliage. Sourwood leaves resemble Peach foliage in shape and are a bit leathery. Shiny green in spring, they become a glossy red or burgundy starting in September. Meanwhile, branches drip with clusters of 6-in. strands of tiny, white, drooping urn-shaped florets most of the summer. Later, they give way to tan fruits that contrast with the green foliage. Typically upright and narrow when young, Sourwoods' irregular branches sometimes get distracted, and they form a rounded or flattened top as the tree ages. Sourwoods are slow growing, so they are shrubby for their first decade or so.

Other Name
Sorrel Tree

Bloom Period and Seasonal Color
July; blooms in white; red fall foliage color

Mature Height × Spread
25 to 30 ft. × 15 to 20 ft.

Sweetgum
Liquidambar styraciflua

The tall trunks and shapely foliage canopies of Sweetgum are easily overlooked in their native Pennsylvania woodland settings, but they are standouts in spacious home landscapes. Their leaves resemble those of Maples, but a closer look reveals a more lustrous, smoother surface and three to seven starlike points. They emerge later than most in the spring on branches that bear inconspicuous flowers and, eventually, their trademark prickly fruit. In fall the leaves turn shades of yellow, orange, and red to purple. Fast-growing in moist soils, Sweetgums grow more elongated as they age. 'Gumball' is a rounded, fruitless, large shrub. 'Variegata' has green foliage marked with yellow streaks and blotches. 'Rotundiloba' is fruitless; the tips of the lobes on its foliage are rounded.

Other Name
Gumball Tree

Bloom Period and Seasonal Color
Green deciduous foliage; yellow, orange, purple, or red fall color

Mature Height × Spread
60 to 75 ft. × 30 to 50 ft.

When, Where, and How to Plant
Plant young balled-and-burlapped Sweetgums in early spring. Container-grown trees have the best chance because their coarse, fleshy roots are more compact. Be sure your tree is grown from seed from the North. It may take one or two years to establish. Plant in full sun and in any organic rich soil that is slightly acidic and well drained. They do well in wet soil. Site them at a distance from buildings and sewer lines. Dig a saucer-shaped hole just as deep as and twice as wide as the rootball. Position the rootball so its top is even with or slightly above the surrounding ground. Remove as much of the burlap as possible. Backfill with plain soil, firming it gently around the rootball, then form a water-holding moat over the root zone. Water well.

Growing Tips
Water regularly in the absence of rain for one or two years while the roots become established. Maintain a year-round 2- or 3-in. layer of organic mulch on the root zone. Expand the mulch area as the tree canopy grows wider. After six months, sprinkle granular slow-acting fertilizer for trees on the mulch for the rain to soak in. Repeat annually for three or four years in mediocre soil. Thereafter, the decomposing mulch will enrich the soil.

Care
Prune broken branches promptly. Prune out any secondary leaders to establish a single, strong trunk. Watch for caterpillar tents, and cut them out of branches immediately. If borer holes are visible, cut off branches below them.

Landscape Merit
Add Sweetgums to woodland plantings for diversity and fall color. Site fruitless varieties (which have no prickly balls) to shade drives and walkways.

Did You Know?
Creative gardeners and Sweetgum fans have struggled to find a use for the interesting, but prickly, gumballs. Collect them for slug barriers. Spread them as a mulch around plants vulnerable to slugs. There are no guarantees, but give it a try. They may think twice about crawling over the gumballs to get to the plants. Sweetgum ball mulch also repels other critters from shrub beds.

Thornless Honeylocust

Gleditsia tricanthos inermis

When, Where, and How to Plant

Plant container-grown Honeylocusts anytime during the growing season. Plant larger balled-and-burlapped ones in spring in full sun. They are not fussy about soil type as long as it is well drained. Dig a saucer-shaped hole just as deep as and somewhat wider than the rootball, and set the rootball so its top is level with the surrounding soil. Planting too deeply fosters disease. Backfill with plain soil, firming it gently around the rootball. Form a temporary water-holding moat over the root zone, then water well.

Growing Tips

During the time that Honeylocusts are becoming established, they need regular moisture over their root zone and adjacent soil. Maintain a year-round 2- or 3-in. layer of organic mulch to retain soil moisture, discourage weeds, and improve the soil.

Care

Prune young trees to curb their potential for erratic shape and to establish a single leader for a trunk. Prune damaged branches promptly. Cut off suckers growing from below the graft. Prune out nests of webworms (caterpillars), which may produce brown patches of foliage or defoliate the tree.

Landscape Merit

Honeylocusts' lovely fine-textured foliage is a main attraction, especially in the fall, so they deserve an open spot in the lawn. If that is not possible, plant them along fence lines or property boundaries to view from the house.

Did You Know?

Honeylocusts may be victims of their own success. Originally prized for their dearth of serious pest and disease problems, they were frequently planted along streets and in parks in the East and Midwest. They seemed the perfect plant to fill the gap left by the loss of the American Elm to rampant disease. This frequent civic planting may be causing a significant increase in the incidence of many minor problems that affect Honeylocusts. Their ubiquity seems to be making them more vulnerable to webworm, borer, plant bugs, spider mite, and leaf canker. These are less of a problem in home landscapes.

Their fine texture, salt tolerance, drought resistance, and adaptability to a range of city and suburban conditions account for Honeylocusts' huge popularity as street trees and yard specimens. Breeders have developed thornless versions of the wild Honeylocust that abounds in Pennsylvania forests. They have nice proportions and light, airy foliage. Featuring twenty to thirty small leaflets, the green leaves turn pale yellow in autumn. In early summer, the scented flowers bloom an inconspicuous green, then give way to brown, twisted, strappy pods up to 8 in. long later in the summer. These have no pods or thorns: 'Halka' (compact and rounded); 'Moraine' (deep-green foliage to yellow in fall); 'Shademaster' (good form with ascending branches); and 'Sunburst' (golden spring foliage).

Bloom Period and Seasonal Color
Inconspicuous green flowers, followed by yellow fall foliage color

Mature Height × Spread
30 to 50 ft. × 30 ft.

Tuliptree
Liriodendron tulipifera

Tuliptrees are often described as majestic. They are the tallest Eastern deciduous tree growing in the wild—as tall as 200 ft. Shorter in the landscape, they retain their ramrod-straight trunks, branchless for the lower two-thirds. They are one of the earliest trees to leaf out in spring. Tuliptrees are recognizable by their distinctive leaves, equally broad as they are long with shallow lobes, their squarish shape suggesting a cat's head. Their 2- to 3-in. flowers are tuliplike, greenish yellow with an orange blotch in the center. They are typically obscured by the leaves high in the canopy of mature trees. Tuliptrees are drought indicators, being the first to show stress—in August and September—from lack of rain. 'Aureo-Marginata' (Majestic Beauty™) has yellow-and-green variegated foliage. 'Fastigiatum' is narrow.

Other Name
Yellow Poplar

Bloom Period and Seasonal Color
Late May; blooms in yellow

Mature Height × Spread
70 to 90 ft. × 40 to 50 ft.

When, Where, and How to Plant
Plant young container-grown Tuliptrees carefully in spring. They are a bit difficult to transplant because their fleshy roots break easily. Site in deep, rich, moist, well-drained soil in full sun. They prefer acidic soil but can handle higher pH. Dig a saucer-shaped hole just as deep as and two or three times as wide as the rootball. Position the rootball so its top is at soil level or even slightly above. Remove as much burlap as possible. Backfill with plain soil, firming it gently around the rootball. Fashion a water-holding moat. Water well.

Growing Tips
Water as often as necessary to keep the soil moist while Tuliptrees establish over their first year or two. Maintain a 2- or 3-in. layer of organic mulch over their root zone year-round to retain soil moisture, discourage weeds, and protect the tender bark from mower injury. Because mulch improves the soil as it gradually decomposes, a Tuliptree in moist, decent soil will not require annual fertilization after one or two years.

Care
Prune damaged branches promptly. Tuliptrees are not without their drawbacks. Their leaves attract aphids which produce sugary honeydew; this in turn causes unsightly, but harmless, sooty mold Their tendency toward self-cleaning means that they readily drop twigs and branches, leaves, flower petals, and hard seeds. Yet all is easily forgiven.

Landscape Merit
Tuliptrees are ideal for floodplains and woodland settings, growing up to 3 ft. per year when young and happily situated. Keep them away from the house because they are brittle and lightning prone.

Did You Know?
Daniel Boone used Tuliptree for his 60-ft. canoe. Tuliptrees indicated to pioneers the location of the best farming soils. Thomas Jefferson planted thousands at Monticello; today only about a half-dozen remain. Tuliptrees have fine-textured, light-grained wood that is easy to work, but difficult to split. Within is a compound called hydrochlorate of tulipiferine, which is a heart stimulant.

Weeping Willow

Salix species

When, Where, and How to Plant

Plant dormant bare-root Willows in early spring. They are among the first trees to leaf out in spring, so plant promptly. Plant container-grown trees anytime during the growing season. They need full sun. The soil type is less critical than its moisture. However, the richer it is in organic matter, the more moisture it will hold. Dig a saucer-shaped hole just as deep as and somewhat wider than the rootball. Set the tree so that its rootball is at soil level. Support bare-root trees at the correct height in the hole with a cone of packed soil. Backfill with plain soil, firming it gently around the rootball. Fashion a water-holding moat, water well.

Growing Tips

Follow up planting with regular watering whenever rainfall is scarce. Maintain a year-round 2- or 3-in. layer of organic mulch. After six months, sprinkle granular slow-acting fertilizer for trees on the mulch for the rain to soak in. Stop annual fertilizing after a year or two.

Care

Routine pruning of Willows is not needed. Their brittle wood is prone to storm damage, however. Promptly prune broken branches with smooth cuts to promote healing. Stressed Willows may attract aphids, borers, scale, or caterpillars.

Landscape Merit

Site Weeping Willows at the edge of a stream or pond, or in boggy areas and floodplains, well away from wells and septic systems. Their notorious extensive root systems will search widely for water. Plant away from buildings or parking areas because older trees sometimes fall over. Many shrub versions are decorative and appropriate for small yards.

Did You Know?

Weeping Willows have contributed their flexible branches to many cultures for weaving baskets, mats, and wattle fences. Arguably, their greatest gift has been the compound salicin, found in their bark and tender branches. Used by Native Americans for treating inflammations and fevers, it has been synthesized in modern times as salicylic acid, or aspirin.

To many, Willow may automatically mean the good old Weeping Willow whose graceful, drooping branches seem to have sheltered our childhoods. It is easy to forgive its brittle wood, its tendency to drip twigs and leaves onto the ground, its susceptibility to pests and diseases, and its need for extra watering during periods of drought. After all, its yellow-green halo of new twigs signals spring for us. Then narrow, pointed, fine-textured leaves emerge to clothe curtains of long, thin, flexible branches. It retains its wonderful winter silhouette long after the leaves yellow and drop late in the season. Babylon Weeping Willow (Salix babylonica) is the most "weeping" of all. Golden Weeping Willow (Salix alba 'Tristis') has an upright habit and yellow bark on young branches.

Other Name
White Willow

Bloom Period and Seasonal Color
Green deciduous foliage; yellow fall color

Mature Height × Spread
30 to 40 ft. × 15 to 20 ft.

Vines *for Pennsylvania*

Surely the Garden of Eden must have had lots of vines. Their vertical stems draw the eye to Heaven while a bounty of wonderful foliage, colorful, sometimes fragrant, blossoms and unique fruits evoke the lushness of an earthly garden. Today, through a sort of cultural osmosis the Romantic ideal of a "vine covered cottage" continues to appeal. It is no accident that the hallmark of this emotional haven is vines, which link the pleasures of the earth and the sky, while providing shelter.

Underused in recent years, vines are making a comeback in residential landscapes everywhere, as many beautiful, interesting plants become more available to gardeners. In addition to beauty, upwardly mobile plants offer a third spatial dimension to the landscape. By taking advantage of airspace, vines and other climbers increase the size of a garden while defining it in new ways. By taking advantage of airspace, vines and other climbers increase the size of a garden while defining it in wonderful new ways. Their various features add color and texture to the scene, while contributing to plant diversity, so important to healthy ecosystems.

Vines also solve landscape problems. Their foliage tapestry cools bare walls exposed to summer sun. It muffles street noise, ensures privacy, and obscures eyesores such as utility meters and old stumps. Clambering over pergolas or arbors, vines provide a transition between hardscape (walls, steps, light posts, and fences) and softscape (lawns, planted beds, trees, and shrubs). They will even substitute for trees in small spaces to create shade for other plants. Planted as specimens on trellises, they become focal points. Of course, they are ideal for small properties where planting ground is at a premium, requiring just a few square inches of soil. Many will grow happily in containers. Tender tropical vines in pots are easily transported indoors for the winter. Outdoors the twisted ropes of woody stems of perennial vines such as Wisteria or Autumn Clematis add drama and structure to an otherwise bleak winter landscape.

About Vines

Vining and climbing plants may be annuals or perennials. The annual ones grow each year from newly planted seed or seedlings, starting slowly in the cool spring, then climbing with gusto and exploding with bloom when the heat arrives. They produce until frost kills them back. Many, such as Hyacinth Bean, are inclined to generously self-sow their seeds, assuring their return to the same place next season. Perennial vines tend to proceed more decorously, taking time their first season to develop strong roots and sturdy stems that will hold them up over the long

term. Most are deciduous, and many benefit from pruning back in the fall or late winter so that they can bloom on new wood next year.

A vine's distinction is its willingness to grow vertically by means of flexible stems that attach opportunistically to any nearby support. Vines and other climbers achieve this in one of several ways. Some, like Ivy, are *clingers*. They fasten themselves directly to a surface with sticky rootlets similar to suction cups on their stems. Others, like Wisteria, are *twiners*. They wrap their stems around whatever is handy for support. Because of this climbing method, they are capable of inadvertently strangling living trees. Still others, such as Clematis, are *grabbers*, latching onto the nearest structure with special curling tendrils that they produce from their leaf stems. Finally, there are *sprawlers*, such as climbing Roses. Their stiff, elongated branches lean on whatever is convenient and stretch up or across it.

Pruning

While young vines may need guidance toward their intended support, they literally catch on quickly and begin to climb. Typically, they grow at will, their upward and outward progress limited only by the length of the growing season or pruning. Many, like wayward children, need judicious discipline to achieve their potential and look their best. Be prepared to prune and pinch wayward stems periodically all season. Supervise Ivy closely as it climbs toward windowsills, gutters, and shutters. Be sure to trim it back before it insinuates itself under roof shingles.

Choosing the Right Support

Obviously, appropriate and sufficient support is an important consideration in growing healthy vines and climbers. Be sure to choose a support that accommodates a specific vine's growing style and its future size.

Otherwise there may be a disastrous collapse midway into the season. Mount trellises a few inches away from walls that will need maintenance over the years.

Clingers, such as Ivy, will adhere directly to a smooth surface; usually, no harm is done to it. They may damage walls where mortar or stucco is deteriorating or soft, however. Grabbers do best with thin supports such as wire, lattice, or netting that their tendrils can easily grasp. The long canes of sprawlers must be tied because they have no special fastening features of their own. Use soft twine or "twist-ties" to attach them to a sturdy trellis or arbor that can hold their mature weight. Twiners are the biggest challenge. Perennial ones such as Kiwi and Wisteria last many years, their woody stems growing ever thicker and tougher, so their support must be very strong. They do best on arbors and pergolas firmly set with cement footers. Annual twining vines have thinner stems, but lots of them, so provide a secure fence, sturdy trellis, or an established nearby shrub for them to scale. Predictably, they collapse and go mushy with frost at the end of the season.

In recent years it has become the fashion to use other plants, usually shrubs, to support vines. A supporting plant is softer and more informal than a rigid, constructed arbor or trellis. The effect is more naturalistic. The idea is to encourage vines and trailing plants such as Nasturtium to thread their way among the stems and twigs of shrubs that have had their bloom period and have only foliage to offer the rest of the season. A typical pairing might be summer blooming Clematis clambering over a Forsythia or Lilac shrub. Of course it is important to be sure the size and scale of the vine is proportional to that of the shrub, lest it overwhelm it.

Overachievers

Vines, like ground covers (which are sometimes, as with Ivy and Wintercreeper and others, the same plant), earn their keep by spreading. In fact, we count on them to

develop lots of stems with foliage and flowers. Some are so vigorous, however, that the words *rampant* and *invasive* come to mind. Only faithful pruning qualifies them as garden assets. Virginia Creeper is a good example; it roams at will up phone poles and over utility lines if permitted. Because this rowdiness is balanced by the fact that it is relatively easy to pull up and it offers food and shelter to wildlife, it earns a place in a residential landscape. Alan Lacey points out that there is a bargain required with rampant vines—to have the beauty, you must be willing to do the pruning.

Sometimes it is a close call as to whether a particular vine can truly be controlled enough. Many lovely vines pose an environmental problem when they escape from backyard cultivation into the wild. Their uncontrolled spread suffocates natural vegetation and degrades the health of the forest. Although plants introduced into the area from elsewhere are often the worst culprits, sometimes native plants are a problem, too. The best way to avoid aiding and abetting this ongoing environmental disaster is to avoid acquiring and planting known offenders. If you have some of them on the property already, dig them out and put them in plastic bags and discard them in the trash. Or guard against their spread by cutting off their berries before they are ripe and attract birds and other animals that might carry them off.

Flora Non Grata

Because they have certain ornamental value, some of these vines are still offered in the trade for landscape use. They are generally regarded as having more vices than virtues, however, and should not be planted in residential gardens in Pennsylvania. (For a more complete list see Invasive Plants of Pennsylvania on page 234.)

- Fiveleaf Akebia (*Akebia quinata*)
- Hall's Honeysuckle (*Lonicera japonica* 'Halliana')
- Kudzu (*Pueraria lobata*)
- Leatherleaf Clematis (*Clematis terniflora*)
- Mile a Minute Vine (*Polygonum perfoliatum*)
- Oriental Bittersweet (*Celastrus orbiculatus*)
- Porcelainberry (*Ampelopsis brevipedunculata*)

Boston Ivy
Parthenocissus tricuspidata

Boston Ivy enjoys a certain distinction because it is the "Ivy" of Ivy League colleges. It is well represented on the stone walls of highly respected Pennsylvania institutions where it confers a similar aura of tradition. Its dense, glossy, trilobed leaves reflect heat, cooling courtyards and walkways. They do the same in residential landscapes where they provide a stunning fall show of deeply red leaves and blue berries. 'Beverly Brooks' has large leaves; 'Fenway' has yellow-green to gold foliage; 'Lowii' has smaller, multilobed leaves. 'Purpurea' has reddish-purple foliage all season; 'Veitchii' has smaller, finer-textured leaves. Small-leafed types are less hardy than Boston Ivy. Our native Virginia Creeper (Parthenocissus quinquefolia) has shiny, rich-green leaves, five lobes, and long-lasting fall color.

Other Name
Japanese Creeper

Bloom Period and Seasonal Color
Mid-June; blooms (insignificant); scarlet fall foliage color

Mature Height × Spread
60 ft. × as permitted

When, Where, and How to Plant
Transplant vines grown in containers anytime during the growing season. Though Boston Ivy can handle full sun, it is sensitive to bright light and extreme heat, so an eastern or northern exposed wall is best. It does well in almost any type of well-drained soil, but prefers it to be woodsy, moist, and slightly acidic. Cultivate soil down 8 to 10 in., mix in granular slow-acting fertilizer, and add organic matter if the soil is thin or clay. Dig the hole about as deep as and somewhat wider than the plant's root system, about 1 ft. from its intended support. Set the rootball so that its top is level with the surrounding ground. Backfill, firm the soil, and water well.

Growing Tips
Water transplants well until they become established. Mulch around stems to hold soil moisture and to protect against damage. Once established, Boston Ivy does not need fertilizing.

Care
Prune away broken or discolored stems. Control overambitious vines by pruning lightly and frequently, or by cutting back hard occasionally. Foliage of stressed vines may show scorch, mildew or leaf spot disease, or scale insects.

Companion Planting and Design
Train Boston Ivy on trellises or lattice panels for a screen. It dresses up chain-link fencing and looks handsome climbing up trees. (It will not harm them.) It is not suitable on wood buildings; the humid environment among dense leaves promotes rot and interferes with regular painting. Because it is a clinger, this Ivy leaves rootlet marks on walls from which it is removed.

Did You Know?
Boston Ivy's juvenile foliage closely resembles poison ivy. The leaves of Boston Ivy seedlings also have three leaflets, and the admonition "leaves of three, let it be" seems appropriate. A close look confirms that mature leaves of Boston Ivy are actually single with three lobes at their tips. While its foliage is safe, Boston Ivy's berries are poisonous if eaten.

When, Where, and How to Plant

Plant container-grown Clematis anytime during the growing season; however, spring is best for bare root plants. Plants often take two seasons to get up to speed. They like full sun for their flowers and foliage, but cool soil for their roots. Clematis prefer rich, well-drained garden soil. Cultivate the soil down 12 to 16 in. and over a 2-ft.-wide area. Mix in granular slow-acting fertilizer and organic matter. Dig the hole deeper and slightly wider than the plant's root system. Set its crown 4 in. below soil level. Set the crown of bare-root plants on a cone of packed soil in the bottom of the hole, so the roots fall down its sides. Backfill, firm soil gently, and water well.

Growing Tips

Spread organic mulch over the soil (but not against plant stems) to keep it cool and moist. Water if rainfall is sparse. Well-mulched vines need no further fertilizing.

Care

Provide temporary support for young plants until they reach their permanent support. Guide stems to encourage them to grab on and climb. Flowers bloom on old and new growth, so prune dead stems in spring. Cut back to new leaf buds. Cut nearly to the ground to revitalize plants. Unhappy plants may be attacked by aphids, scale, or whiteflies. Foliage may show rust or mildew. Cut back stems with severely damaged foliage. Address the causes of stress.

Companion Planting and Design

Let Clematis climb traditional vertical supports or grow horizontally on a fence. Encourage it to scramble informally over shrubs.

Did You Know?

Pronunciation of plant names is always fraught with uncertainty. Clematis is a perfect example. *CLEM-a-tis* is the way the British pronounce it. Many horticulturists say it that way because classical horticultural training is steeped in British tradition. *Clem-A-tis* is the way everyone else says it because in the United States we tend to emphasize the second syllable in three-syllable words. Either pronunciation is correct.

Clematis vines look so exotic that the assumption is only the gifted gardener can manage them. In recent years their progress from estate gardens to neighborhood mailboxes testifies to their increased popularity and availability as people realize they are not a big deal to grow. Hybrids deliver the biggest color splash, their broad, flat flowers—often as large as 4 or 5 in. across—featuring four to six beautifully colored petals. Their fancy seedheads of curved filaments are a continuing decorative feature through summer into fall. Among the large-flowered types, Jackman Clematis (Clematis × Jackmanii) has showy flowers and is among the easiest to grow. Clematis 'Betty Corning' (a viticella hybrid) has fragrant, bell-shaped summer flowers. Clematis 'Duchess of Albany' (a texensis hybrid) produces charming upright pink tulip-shaped flowers.

Other Name
Large-flowered Clematis

Bloom Period and Seasonal Color
May, intermittently through summer; blooms in white, shades of purple, pink, or rose

Mature Height × Spread
15 ft. × as permitted

Climbing Hydrangea
Hydrangea anomala ssp. *petiolaris*

This vine signals substance and permanence. Essentially an elongated, vertical shrub, a mature Climbing Hydrangea becomes a dominant landscape feature through the seasons. But it takes several years before these slow starters catch on, climb, and deliver on the promised layers of faintly scented, lacy, flat spring flowers among rich green, textured leaves. Clinging by means of holdfast rootlets, the woody stems of Climbing Hydrangea develop a rough, cinnamon-colored bark that becomes a landscape feature after the leaves drop late in fall or early winter. Plant one if you plan to stay on the property for several years or want to give a gift to future owners. An alternative Climbing Hydrangea is Japanese Hydrangea Vine (Schizophragma hydrangeoides 'Moonlight').

Bloom Period and Seasonal Color
Late May through summer; blooms white florets in flat clusters

Mature Height × Spread
15 ft. × as permitted

When, Where, and How to Plant
Plant container-grown Climbing Hydrangea almost anytime that it is not very hot and dry. Overcast days or late afternoons are the best planting times to minimize transplant shock. For best flowering, locate vines in full sun. They can cope with shade, but growth will be slower. A site sheltered from winter winds is ideal. Climbing Hydrangea likes moist, well-drained garden soil. Dig down at least 12 in., mixing in granular slow-acting fertilizer. Add organic matter to improve drainage in clay soil. Dig the hole about as deep as and slightly wider than the container. Climbing Hydrangea roots are fragile; untangle them very gently. Set the rootball so that its top is exactly level with the surrounding ground. Backfill, firming soil gently, and water well. Place at least 1 ft. out from its intended support.

Growing Tips
While it recovers from transplanting, keep Climbing Hydrangea moist, but do not overwater. Be patient while it establishes and grows. Fertilize its first few springs, after that decomposing organic mulch will provide sufficient nutrition.

Care
Pruning is unnecessary the first few years. Then prune the vine after flowering to train it to grow as desired. Periodically, in its fullness of years, Climbing Hydrangea will need thinning to improve air circulation and appearance.

Companion Planting and Design
Its vertical progress against a building eventually turns Climbing Hydrangea into an architectural element, softening corners, delineating adjacent stairways, and defining patio spaces to create an entirely original profile. Climbing Hydrangea looks especially good on stone or brick walls. It grows up trees without hurting them.

Did You Know?
Another Climbing Hydrangea lookalike is Wood Vamp (*Decumaria barbara*). This easy-care vine likes shade and moist soil. It has flat, white, lacy flowers and glossy green foliage, which turns yellow in fall. Despite a wild pedigree and faster growth, it has a controlled habit, evident as it happily ladders up large tree trunks. It is remarkably free of pests and diseases.

Hardy Kiwi
Actinidia kolomikta

When, Where, and How to Plant
Plant container-grown Kiwis anytime during the growing season on an overcast day or in the evening. For best foliage color, site in full sun. They prefer average soils that are well drained. Dig down 8 to 10 in., and add organic matter to improve drainage. Mix in a trace of granular, slow-acting fertilizer. Dig holes about as deep as and slightly wider than rootballs. Set crowns exactly at soil level. Backfill, firm soil gently around stems, and water well. Set each plant about 1 ft. from its support to allow room for roots to grow.

Growing Tips
Water transplants if rainfall is sparse. Spread organic mulch on the soil around, but not touching, the stems to help soil retain moisture and to discourage weeds. Once established, Kiwi vines are fairly self-reliant. They will not need annual fertilizing.

Care
Prune vines in late winter to establish a few main stems and to control the number of subsidiary stems. Cats love the taste of Kiwi foliage. Spray young vines with pet repellent, or surround stems with a chicken wire cage for protection. Once vine stems turn woody, remove the barrier. Plants are vulnerable to fungal disease due to insufficient sunlight or other environmental conditions.

Companion Planting and Design
Hardy Kiwi turns an ordinary wall into a showpiece. It needs a sturdy trellis set solidly in the soil a few inches out from the wall surface or a wire grid fastened to hooks embedded in wood or masonry.

Did You Know?
Hardy Kiwis produce edible fruit if certain conditions exist. Plant both a male and a female vine within 15 ft. of each other to assure good pollination. Site them where they get at least five hours of sun daily. Kiwis are ready to pick when they feel slightly soft, usually in September. Yields will be sparse until the vines are seven or eight years old.

Hardy Kiwi is renowned for its unusual calico foliage rather than its fruit—although by the end of summer, mature female vines drip with sweet, yellow-green berries smaller than the subtropical Kiwis at the grocery store. This ornamental vine twines its way to the top of a trellis or arbor with woody stems. The variegated 4- or 5-in.-long leaves on both male and female Hardy Kiwi vines are blotched with white and pink. They look like a painter has dripped white paint on them. These markings are reputedly a bit more striking in male plants and grow richer in color as the vine matures. Silver Vine (Actinidia polygama) has white-tipped leaves, but is less energetic. Bower Actinidia (Actinidia arguta) features glossy deep-green leaves and edible fruit.

Other Name
Kolomikta Vine

Bloom Period and Seasonal Color
May; blooms in white

Mature Height × Spread
30 ft. × as permitted

Hyacinth Bean
Lablab purpureus

Hyacinth Bean, or Lablab vine, is decorative and fun. Like most annual vines, it is a vigorous grower and prolific bloomer once it gets started and the season's heat arrives. It produces purplish-tinged leaves in threes on reddish stems that are willing to climb up anything handy. Lablab blossoms are upright clusters of small lilac-purple flowers that resemble Sweet Peas. In no time they give way to flat, shiny maroon bean pods, which dangle from the vine as new flowers, then more pods, form in lush succession over the summer. The seeds within the pods are black with a curious white line on them. They are responsible for this vine being the ultimate pass-along plant. When visitors admire and inquire, hand them some seeds.

Other Name
Lablab

Bloom Period and Seasonal Color
Midsummer to fall; blooms in lavender

Mature Height × Spread
10 ft. × as permitted

When, Where, and How to Plant
Plant Hyacinth Bean seeds outdoors in May. If the pods are left on the vine the previous season until they dry and open, it is likely to self-sow. This vine loves sun. It tolerates virtually any soil, but it is most vigorous in well-drained garden soil near a post, trellis, or other intended support. Loosen the soil down a few inches, and add granular slow-acting fertilizer. Set seeds, the white "eye" facing upward, 1 or 2 in. deep, 2 or 3 in. apart. Cover with soil, then water. Expect germination in two weeks. Transplant seedlings grown in pots into soil dug down 6 to 8 in. Set so that their rootball top is level with the surrounding ground. Space 1 ft. apart. Water well, and mulch.

Growing Tips
Water when rainfall is particularly scarce. Provide a place to climb, or Lablabs will find one themselves. When seedlings are several inches tall, thin to the desired number and spacing, then mulch to keep down weeds and retain soil moisture. No further fertilizing is needed.

Care
Hyacinth Bean needs no special pruning; the lusher the foliage and flowers, the better. Pick off bean pods when they start to dry up. They are virtually pest free.

Companion Planting and Design
Use Hyacinth Bean vines on fences to mask chain-link types, to create decorative enclosures around vegetable gardens, and to screen out noise and views. Plant them in children's gardens.

Did You Know?
Was Hyacinth Bean the "purple bean" that Thomas Jefferson mentioned in the journals he kept on his wonderful garden at Monticello? He recorded planting more than forty-four varieties of garden beans. An entry for April 17, 1812, which mentions "Arbor beans white, scarlet, crimson, purple at the trees of the level on both sides of terrasses, and on long walk of garden," suggests that he used colorful beans as decorative features. Perhaps the tropical Lablabs were among them.

Moonflower

Ipomea alba

When, Where, and How to Plant

Because seedlings are tricky to transplant, sow Moonflower seed directly into the garden. Wait until the weather has turned warm, around the middle of May. Choose well-drained, average garden soil in a sunny site. Soil that is too rich in nutrients will stimulate foliage at the expense of flowers. If it is near a doorway or an arbor so that passersby can enjoy the scent, all the better. Dig 6 to 8 in. deep to loosen and aerate soil. Mix in organic material to improve drainage if necessary. Cut or scrape the hard coating on the seeds before planting to encourage germination. Plant seeds in groups of two or three, 1 in. deep. Lightly tamp the soil over them, and water well. Expect sprouts in about two weeks.

Growing Tips

Moonflower takes care of itself very well once it is established. Water only during periods of extended drought. Do not fertilize.

Care

Prune only if vine has exceeded its bounds and engulfed the lawn furniture. In the fall when the frost kills it, pull down the dead stems. Tough Moonflower rarely has insect pest or disease problems.

Companion Planting and Design

Moonflower twines with abandon on fences, arbors, and trellises. It may be the only plant needed on an apartment balcony or patio. It will grow in a container and climb the nearest vertical support. It is useful for covering landscape eyesores such as decaying stumps, drainpipes, and utility boxes. Plant it with white Morning Glory to enjoy continuous bloom, day and night.

Did You Know?

Sweet Potato Vine (*Ipomea batatas* 'Blackie') is a member of the same family as Morning Glory and Moonflower. It is ornamental and edible. Extremely vigorous, it bears large, three deeply lobed leaves colored deep black-purple on tender, trailing stems. Its flowers are lavender and tubular, but are small and take a backseat to the foliage. The tuberous roots are the Sweet Potatoes.

Moonflower is not just another twining Morning Glory, although it is a member of that family. This exotic, sophisticated cousin stays up all night and closes the next day. Its white flowers are a spectacular 6 in. across where fluted petals come to points, forming a starlike face. The show actually begins on hot evenings with coiled, pointed buds that unfurl before your eyes among oversized, heart-shaped, rich green leaves. Moonflower is the centerpiece of an evening garden. Common Morning Glory (Ipomea purpurea) has similar, but smaller leaves and flowers (blue, white, pink, and bicolor). Morning Glory (Ipomea tricolor) 'Heavenly Blue' is an All-America Selections winner; 'Pearly Gates' is a white-flowered form. There is also a red-flowered version with white trim.

Other Name
Moon Vine

Bloom Period and Seasonal Color
Midsummer to fall; blooms in white

Mature Length × Spread
15 ft. × as permitted

Rose
Rosa hybrids

Climbers are distinguished from Bush Roses by their arching canes that, if permitted, will grow more than 10 ft. long. They are the Roses celebrated in the romantic notion of the Rose-covered cottage. Among Roses that have aerial ambitions are old-fashioned Roses, large-flowered climbers, and ramblers. Traditional ramblers are more informal, bloom only once, and have more flexible canes. Large-flowered climbers and their kin, pillar Roses, appear more formal with stiffer canes. 'New Dawn' is a large-flowered climber featuring copious semi-double, pale-pink flowers on thorny stems in the spring, and then sporadically over the summer; it is among the most disease-resistant. The red 'Blaze Improved' blooms continuously. 'Golden Showers' bears large, fragrant, double, yellow flowers all summer; almost thornless, it has good disease resistance and is very hardy.

Other Name
Climbing Rose

Bloom Period and Seasonal Color
Spring; blooms in white, red, yellow, pink, or apricot

Mature Height × Spread
10 to 15 ft. × as permitted

When, Where, and How to Plant
Plant dormant bare-root climbers when danger of frost is past. Keep roots moist until then. Transplant container-grown Roses anytime all season. Roses need full sun and good organic-rich garden soil that is slightly acid and well drained. Dig the soil down 2 ft., and add organic material and granular slow-acting rose fertilizer. Dig a saucer-shaped hole about as deep as and twice as wide as the root-ball. Set the Rose at the same level that it was in its container. Support the crowns of bare-root plants on a hump of packed soil in the hole so roots can extend downward. When planting bare-root Roses, locate the swollen graft union just below the soil level. Backfill, firm soil, and water well. Provide plenty of air circulation around each plant.

Growing Tips
Spread a 2- or 3-in. layer of organic mulch over the root zone, slightly thicker in winter. Provide consistent moisture and nutrition. Water early in the day to avoid encouraging fungal disease. Fertilize annually with a granular slow-acting product.

Care
Fasten Rose canes to sturdy supports with soft material. Prune dead canes anytime, but wait two or three years to begin maintenance pruning. Prune after flowering to control the direction of growth or to thin for better air circulation. In the fall cut back the oldest canes to their base. Train at least four healthy, younger canes securely tied to the support to replace them. Roses are victimized by Japanese beetles. Fungal leaf diseases are less troublesome in locations of good air circulation where foliage dries quickly.

Companion Planting and Design
Climbing Roses soften buildings, smother derelict trees with color, and curtain a pergola with beauty. Ramblers are particularly effective spilling over a wall or down a steep hill.

Did You Know?
The ubiquitous Multiflora Rose that rambles all over Pennsylvania is a menace. While its clusters of small white flowers look lovely along roadsides and in abandoned fields, the plant is an invasive nuisance, choking fields with brambles and overwhelming indigenous plants. Do not encourage it to grow on your property.

Scarlet Honeysuckle

Lonicera sempervirens

When, Where, and How to Plant

Plant bare-root Honeysuckle in the spring. Plant container-grown plants anytime during the growing season. Scarlet Honeysuckle flowers best in full sun. It likes moist, good garden soil but accepts almost any type and pH, even limestone. Because it has sparse roots, this Honeysuckle is a bit tricky to transplant. Choose 1- to 2-ft.-tall plants. Loosen soil 8 to 10 in., and add granular slow-acting fertilizer and organic matter. Dig the hole to accommodate the rootball. Set it so its top is level with the surrounding ground. Backfill, firm soil gently around stems, and water well. Space plants 2 ft. apart, 1 ft. from their support.

Growing Tips

Water when first planted and during periods of severe drought. Spreading organic mulch around the roots will help the soil retain moisture. Annual fertilization is unnecessary. A rich diet only stimulates excess foliage.

Care

Train vines by pruning stems just after flowering or in winter after foliage has dropped and the stems are visible. Provide supports at least 8 ft. tall. Tender new stems, tips, and flower buds may attract aphids. Dislodge them with strong water spray every day or two. Honeysuckle has a phytotoxic reaction to insecticidal soaps, so spot treat severe infestations with a product featuring pyrethrins. Foliage sometimes develops powdery mildew. Thin out branches to provide better air circulation.

Companion Planting and Design

Use Honeysuckle trained to a fence or trellis to be a garden backdrop or to mask landscape eyesores such as derelict trees, abandoned sheds, or rock piles. Watch for hummingbirds!

Did You Know?

A rowdy cousin of Scarlet Honeysuckle, Hall's or Japanese Honeysuckle (*Lonicera japonica* 'Halliana') bears white-and-yellow flowers that smell deliciously fragrant on hot summer nights along roadsides where it was originally planted to control erosion. Now a weedy nuisance, it has invaded woodland areas, climbing over trees and shading native understory plants, killing them. It is not a good garden plant.

Scarlet Honeysuckle is hardy, dependable, and drought resistant. Its bright-red 2-in.-long tubular blossoms cluster at the tips of stems from the previous year during its peak bloom period in late spring and early summer. Subsequently, flowers appear sporadically on new wood until fall when reddish orange berries develop. Left to its own devices, this vine will flop on the ground and twine around whatever is nearby. Lonicera sempervirens *'Sulphurea' has deep-yellow flowers. 'Magnifica' has deeper-red flowers, and 'Superba' has larger red ones. 'Manifich' flowers are lighter tangerine. 'Cedar Lane' is resistant to aphids. Goldflame Honeysuckle (*Lonicera × heckrottii *'Goldflame') has red flowers that turn to pink highlighted by a yellow throat; it blooms May through midsummer, then intermittently until fall and is fragrant at night.*

Other Name

Coral Honeysuckle

Bloom Period and Seasonal Color

Late spring to fall frost; blooms in red, orange, or yellow

Mature Height × Spread

15 ft. × as permitted

Wisteria
Wisteria species and hybrids

The drooping cascades of Wisteria's lilac pea-type flowers are worth the wait and the effort to control the vine. Its numerous foliage leaflets along thin stems turn yellow in fall before frost. Furry green seedpods that persist into winter complete the show. Wisteria can be trained as a shrub with a single stem, but is most effective as a vine. It is potentially invasive, and it appears on some lists of nuisance plants. Beware of allowing this twiner to climb trees; it may strangle them. Japanese Wisteria (Wisteria floribunda) has 2- to 3-ft.-long flowers. Chinese Wisteria (Wisteria chinensis) has smaller flower clusters and leaves, and blooms before leaves emerge. Two lovely native Wisterias, W. frutescens and W. macrostachys, are less spectacular but are also less aggressive and bloom May to June.

Bloom Period and Seasonal Color
May; blooms in lavender, pink, or white; yellow fall foliage color

Mature Height × Spread
40 ft. × as permitted

When, Where, and How to Plant
Transplant container-grown vines anytime during the growing season when it is not extremely hot or dry. Plants need a minimum of six hours of sun daily. Avoid the north side of a building or under trees or roof overhangs that may obstruct light or rainfall. Wisteria tolerates almost any well-drained soil. Already-blooming grafted stock in containers is most dependable. Loosen soil down 12 in., and mix in organic matter to improve drainage. Add slow-acting granular fertilizer. Dig the hole out 1 ft. from its support as deep as the plant's rootball. Backfill with plain soil, and water well. Mulch to keep soil moist.

Growing Tips
Skip fertilizing if the soil is fairly decent; deprivation may promote flowering. Once it is established and new leaves appear, water Wisteria only when rainfall is scarce.

Care
Train vines to a very sturdy support at least 6 in. from a wall to assure air circulation. Attach the strongest shoot to a vertical support. Clip off all other tendrils. Shoots that form flower buds grow from horizontal side branches; the flower buds from near the base of the shoot. Prune off all others. When the vertical leader reaches desired height, clip off its tip. Severely cut back all main branches by half in late winter. Trim flower-producing spurs to only two or three buds at the base of the shoots where they are close together. Stressed young vines may show scale, aphids, Japanese beetles, viruses, or leaf spots on foliage.

Companion Planting and Design
Train Wisteria vines over a sturdy arbor or pergola for display and shade. They are lovely near porches, pools, and patios.

Did You Know?
The similarity of the plant name Wisteria to the old Philadelphia-area family name of Wister (or Wistar) is not coincidental. The plant was named for Caspar Wistar, professor of anatomy at the University of Pennsylvania in the early nineteenth century.

Water Plants *for Pennsylvania*

Gardening in water represents another dimension in gardening. It is possible because certain plants are hydrophytic, able to live in water. Their roots are specially adapted to wet environments, either soggy soil or outright water, so that they do not suffocate for lack of air as terrestrial plants would. In nature these aquatic plants inhabit oceans, lakes, streams, tidal marshes, swamps, and floodplains, adjusting as well to man-made drainage ditches and retention basins. Tamed by hybridization or cultivation in pots, which curbs their natural tendency to run rampant and controls their overall size, many qualify as lovely ornamental plants. When they are planted in containers before they are set in the water, they are easy to arrange, maintain, and remove from a water garden.

Once cultivating aquatic plants in water gardens was limited to the very rich who could afford to build expensive concrete or tile ponds and pools and acquire numerous exotic-looking plants. Thanks to modern technology, however, in recent years water gardening has become accessible to almost everyone.

Relatively inexpensive flexible liners, preformed fiberglass pools, and interesting tubs and kettles are widely available. Residential scale filters, pumps, fountains, and pre-fab waterfalls are available too. New water-loving plants are being discovered and developed daily. Happily, dwarf and miniature versions of familiar aquatic plants make it possible to garden in water almost anywhere—in a tiny yard, on a balcony, or even on the dining room table!

Growing Water Plants

Water plants are no more difficult to grow than terrestrial plants. Some are frost tender and are therefore treated as annuals in Pennsylvania. Many others are cold hardy in our state and are therefore perennial, growing year after year in the water garden. According to their habit, size, and nature, water plants play various roles in a pond, just as terrestrial plants do in a garden bed. Some function as specimens or focal points, others as ground(water) covers (floater plants), and still others as screens at the edge of the water garden. Certain ones live totally below the water surface (submerged

plants) and specialize in maintaining a healthy water environment. Some plants feature foliage; others flowers, fragrance, decorative seeds or pods. Their containers are set at different levels in the water garden pond depending on whether they prefer to have just their roots wet (bog or marginal plants) or their roots and their stems wet.

In the wild, water plants root and grow in the soil at the bottom of natural lakes and streams. They get their nutrients from this soil, and they freely send out roots and runners and spread at will. In a cultivated water garden setting this is not feasible. Residential ponds typically have liners rather than soil bottoms, thus plants have nowhere to root. Also, it is important to be able to work with the plants without joining them in the water. So planting water plants in soil in pots enables gardeners to control their spread and lift them from the pond to groom or move them when necessary.

Plants that grow in water require the same type of maintenance that terrestrial ones do. They need periodic fertilization, deadheading of faded blossoms, and removal of yellowed leaves and stems over the growing season. Some especially tall ones may need staking to keep them from flopping over into the water. Perennials may need cutting back at the end of the season. They occasionally come down with a case of mildew or rust, or attract aphids and caterpillars and need attention. Perennial aquatic plants spread and crowd their pots after a season or two, and they need to be divided (and repotted), usually in the spring, just as terrestrial perennials do. Water gardens do not need to be weeded exactly, but sometimes overenthusiastic submerged or surface-floating plants need to be scooped or hauled out to make clear water space for spreading Water Lily foliage.

A Healthy Water Environment

A healthy water environment is as important for aquatic plants as good soil is for terrestrial plants. Oxygenating (submerged) plants, waterfalls, and fountains aerate the water, just as tilling and digging in organic matter aerate the soil. Microbial life in the form of brown, furry algae that covers pots, liners, roots, and stems underwater provides balanced nutrients and the correct pH in water, just as microbial life does in soil. Water gardens do not have earthworms, but they have fish and snails to do housekeeping chores.

The biggest chore, however, is left to the water gardener. Even though the water may be pumped through a filter during the season and a net cover prevents falling leaves from fouling the water every autumn, organic debris builds up over time in the bottom of a water garden pond that has a liner. Every fall or two it needs to be cleaned out before too much accumulates, turns anaerobic, and begins to suck the oxygen from the water. Some years dredging the bottom of the pond after temporarily shifting or lifting out the plants does the trick. Use a sturdy long-handled net or another device that will not tear or puncture a flexible liner to scoop up gunk from the bottom and deposit it in a pail. (Spread this organic material on a garden bed or put it in the compost pile.) Periodically, nothing less than draining the pond in the fall and scrubbing the sides and bottom of the liner, then refilling it, will assure healthy water and plants for the next season.

Starting a Water Garden

Traditionally, water garden supplies and aquatic plants have been sold by mail order, and they still are. It is possible to have the entire garden—liner, containers, plants, fish, food, snails, fertilizer, pump, filter, tubing, and assorted other peripherals—delivered to the front door. These days, however, with the increased interest in aquatic plants, many garden centers and home centers carry these supplies, a selection of aquatic plants, and books on water gardening.

The few water plants included in this book are suggestions to get you started. Talk with friends and neighbors who garden in water. Visit a local botanic or display garden to become familiar with more plants. During the warm summer months, water gardens come alive with color and even fragrance. The sound of trickling waterfalls or fountains and the movement of the darting fish under the water and the dragonflies, bees, butterflies, and other insects in the air above make a water garden an oasis of peace in a troubled world.

Anacharis

Egeria densa

Although they are not considered ornamental features of water gardens, submerged plants such as Anacharis have a delicate beauty as they float just under the surface of the water. They are assets, integral to the healthy functioning of the aquatic ecosystem that a water garden represents. Anacharis stems resemble seaweed laddered with small dark-green leaves that create an efficient water filter. Later in the season their stem tips at the water surface bear tiny white flowers that have three petals with yellow centers. Anacharis's main job as an oxygenator is to maintain water quality. It replenishes the oxygen in water, and it absorbs excess nutrients such as nitrates, ammonia, and phosphates that promote the development of stagnant water. Anacharis is hardy in the warmer parts of Pennsylvania.

Other Name
Elodea

Bloom Period and Seasonal Color
Summer; blooms in white

Mature Dimensions
Indefinite spread

When, Where, and How to Plant

Introduce submerged plants such as Anacharis first into a *new* water garden. Set potted stems into *existing* ponds in spring. Anacharis likes full sun but can manage in incidental shade. Set pots so plants are visible while covered by 1 or 2 ft. of water, not shaded by foliage of surface plants. Anacharis and other submerged plants are packaged as bunches of 6-in.-long foliage-covered stems. Use one bunch, or six stems, per 2 square ft. of pond surface, more if there are many fish. Plant two or three bunches together in an 8-qt. pot filled with clean sand. Insert each stem end 1 in. or more in the sand, then cover the sand with gravel to prevent fish from stirring it up and dislodging the Anacharis. Soak the container with water to remove any air bubbles, then sink it in the pond.

Growing Tips

Submerged plants do not need any routine care. Do not fertilize submerged plants.

Care

Thin excessively crowded stems later in the season. Clip off and pull up as many stems as necessary to restore some open water. Swish foliage coated with fine, brown silt around a bit to wash it off. Submerged plants are potentially invasive. Do not plant them directly in soil at the bottom of a natural pond. Take care when discarding stems that they do not "escape" into natural waterways. Fish may occasionally nibble Anacharis. Otherwise, it has no pests or diseases.

Companion Planting and Design

It is okay to use other oxygenating plants such as Cabomba with Anacharis.

Did You Know?

Fish are ornamental and practical additions to a water garden. Part of the natural housekeeping staff, they eat mosquito eggs and algae. Be aware, however, that their waste adds nutrients to the water and fosters excess algae production if there are no oxygenating plants to absorb them. Fish depend on these submerged plants to protect them from bird predators and to provide a thicket of undulating fronds in which to lay eggs.

Cattail

Typha angustifolia

When, Where, and How to Plant

Plant Cattails anytime up to a month before expected first frost in October. Set out young plants in spring when water temperature is over 50 degrees Fahrenheit. Cattails like full sun but accept light shade. Set pots of mature plants on a submerged shelf so no more than 12 in. of water covers their soil. Plant rhizomes in containers that hold a minimum of $3^1/2$ qt. of heavy soil to anchor the plant securely when submerged. A mulch of washed gravel or decorative stones over the soil keeps it settled. When new shoots appear, set them in only 1 in. of water at first, lowering the pots as plants grow. Maintain several inches of water above the top of the pots. Make holes in the bottom of each container so that the roots stay wet if the pond water level drops below the edge of the pot.

Growing Tips

Cattails are hardy in Pennsylvania; they can spend the winter pondside. Add slow-acting fertilizer to the soil when repotting them in the spring.

Care

Over the season cut back ratty foliage, but do not cut below the water line or it will kill them. Cut back in spring to prepare for the emergence of new shoots. Divide crowded clumps in spring. Take care when discarding roots after dividing. Cattails can be invasive nuisances if they find their way into natural wet areas. They have no significant pests or diseases.

Companion Planting and Design

Narrowleaf Cattails provide vertical interest at the edge of a water garden that contrasts with its horizontal surface. They frame large ponds as a background. Use their smaller cousins in containers.

Did You Know?

Cattails are useful for floral crafts if they are cut at the correct time. Harvest in July when the male flowers—which have gold tassels on the top part of the flower stalk—are still blooming. Set long stems in empty containers for air drying.

Native Cattails (Typha latifolia) are easily recognized by their distinctive seedheads, resembling velvety brown cigars at the tops of slender stalks. Abounding in roadside drainage ditches and water retention basins, they are ideal for stabilizing stream banks but are too large and invasive for garden situations. Narrowleaf Cattails (Typha angustifolia) are similar, having more slender leaves and a finer texture. They catch the breeze and provide sound and movement through the entire year. Their flowers are densely packed spikes of tiny beige florets, male and female on the same stalk, clustered at the top of stems rising amid long, narrow-pointed green leaves. Graceful Cattail (Typha laxmannii) is 4 ft. tall and forms seedheads sooner; it has good proportions for small ponds. Dwarf Cattail (Typha minima) is only 30 in. tall, ideal for a container water garden.

Other Name

Narrowleaf Cattail

Bloom Period and Seasonal Color

Late summer; blooms in beige

Mature Dimensions

2 to 7 ft. tall; spreading clumps

Lotus
Nelumbo nucifera

Lotus is the ultimate water garden plant. With its dominating size and exotic appearance, it is a commanding specimen. The rounded bluish green saucer leaves, 10 to 30 in. across, glisten with beads of water trapped on their waxy surface. Lower ones float Water Lily style on the surface of the water, and upper ones float in the air on tall stems. The incredibly fragrant 6- to 12-in.-wide Lotus flowers open from pointed buds at the stem tips. Resembling Water Lilies in shape, they open early and close at midday, their petals falling after three days. In their wake they leave their trademark flat pods. The good news is that Lotus is winter hardy in Pennsylvania; the bad news is that deer like it. Two excellent dwarfs for small ponds or containers are 'Momobatan' which has double pink flowers, and 'Chawaubasu' which has white flowers edged with pink.

Other Name
Sacred Lotus

Bloom Period and Seasonal Color
Mid-July through August; blooms in yellow, cream, pink, or rose

Mature Height × Spread
1 to 7 ft. × 2 to 6 ft.

When, Where, and How to Plant
Pot Lotus tubers in the spring. Runners will then develop for summer, tubers forming again in fall. Set pots in the water garden when frost danger is past and water temperature exceeds 50 degrees Fahrenheit. Plants bloom after three or four weeks of sunny, warm (80 degrees Fahrenheit) weather. Lotus needs a minimum of five to six hours of direct sun. Site in still water. Plant full-sized Lotus in 30-qt. containers that are 16 in. or more across and at least 10 in. deep. Miniatures take pots half that size. Orient tubers horizontally on heavy soil, 2 to 4 in. below the pot rim, so that the growing tips protrude $1/2$ in. when covered with more soil. Insert fertilizer pellets deep into soil but not touching the tuber, then water. Submerge the pot so the soil level is 4 to 12 in. below the water surface. Shallower is better the first year. Gradually lower the pot as shoots grow. Lotus takes one or two years to establish, blossoming the second summer.

Growing Tips
Fertilize twice a month until early September.

Care
Routinely clip off limp, faded foliage and flowers. In fall cut back the stems, and sink the pot in 3 ft. of water, safely below the frost line. An alternative is to wrap it and store indoors in a cool area. In spring, divide the tubers so each has two joints and a growing tip, and repot. Wash mites or whiteflies from foliage by dunking it in the water.

Companion Planting and Design
Plant Lotus alone in a barrel or tub, or as part of a community of plants in a water garden. Miniature Lotus is suitable for a 10-by-10-ft. or less pond.

Did You Know?
American Lotus (*Nelumbo lutea*) grows to 5 ft. tall and produces single, 5- to 7-in. light-yellow flowers and huge 2-ft.-wide leaves. Native Americans called it Chinquapin or "pond nuts" because its starchy tubers were useful for food.

Papyrus
Cyperus prolifer

When, Where, and How to Plant

Set out seedlings or rooted divisions whenever air temperatures are reliably warm and water temperature is around 70 degrees Fahrenheit. Papyrus thrives in full sun at pond's edge or in pots in water about 6 in. deep. Plant in containers that hold a minimum of 3$^1/_2$ qt. of heavy soil. Slightly acid garden soil with a bit of organic matter or clay soil is ideal. Avoid soilless potting mixes because its lightweight components will not anchor plants. A mulch of washed gravel or decorative stones over the soil keeps it settled. Set pots in only 1 in. of water at first, lowering the pots as the plants grow to maintain several inches of water over their edges. Use pots that have holes in their bottoms so the roots are always in water whatever the water level.

Growing Tips

A handful of granular slow-acting fertilizer in the potting soil will sustain Papyrus all season.

Care

Trim flopping stalks to groom Papyrus. At season's end, cut back all brown, flopping Papyrus stems. Papyrus will not survive outdoors during winter. Either let it die, or bring it indoors to overwinter as a houseplant in a container of water. Divide and repot in spring. Wash off aphids or spider mites under the faucet, or spray with insecticidal soap.

Companion Planting and Design

Use any Papyrus as a vertical accent or screen at the edge of a water garden, similar to an ornamental grass. Grow Dwarf Papyrus as a houseplant indoors. Use its dried stalks in arrangements.

Did You Know?

Egyptian Paper Reed or *Cyperus papyrus* grew as marginal plants along the Nile, the resource upon which the ancient Egyptian culture was built. Among other uses, its huge 14-ft. reeds were processed for paper and woven into baskets. It is likely that Moses was hidden among Papyrus reeds. Because Papyrus was unfamiliar to English translators of the Bible, however, they used the word *bulrushes* instead.

Forms of Papyrus that grow naturally from Egypt to tropical Africa and elsewhere reach 6 ft. tall. This interesting marginal plant also comes in dwarf form, an appropriate scale for most backyard ponds and container water gardens. For a tropical plant Dwarf Papyrus can handle fairly cool temperatures, staying evergreen when air temperatures remain over 59 degrees Fahrenheit. Its three-angled, leafless stems stand upright in crowded reedlike clumps, each one topped with a 2- to 3-in.-wide tuft of radiating spiky, grassy foliage that resembles a Fourth of July sparkler. Leaves bear little green seedpods at their tips that eventually turn brown. As the season wanes, older stalks bend and flop, the brown seedpods dipping into the water to root in the soil of an adjacent potted plant.

Other Name

Dwarf Papyrus

Bloom Period and Seasonal Color

Summer; brown spikelets

Mature Height × Spread

2 to 3 ft. × 1$^1/_2$ to 2 ft.

Parrot's Feather
Myriophyllum aquaticum

Parrot's Feather, part oxygenator, part floater, is the aquatic equivalent of a ground cover. Although parts of the stems are submerged, trailing thin rootlets and sparse, yellowish hairlike foliage below the water, their top 4 or 6 in. protrude above the water surface. These stem tips are whorled with lovely fine-textured, feathery, pale-blue-green foliage, and they emerge farther out of the water as the summer progresses. Generally hardy, over-achieving Parrot's Feather stems rapidly form crowded, tangled masses by midseason and will literally crawl out of a kettle or tub water garden, draping themselves down its side. Other small-leafed floating plants that act as "ground covers" in a water garden are Four Leaf Water Clover (Marsilea mutica), Yellow Fringe (Nymphoides germinata), and Winter Snowflake (Nymphoides cristatum). Both Yellow Fringe and Winter Snowflake have small but attractive flowers.

Other Name
Diamond Milfoil

Bloom Period and Seasonal Color
Summer; blooms in yellow-green (insignificant)

Mature Height × Spread
Tips are 6 in. above water surface × trailing

When, Where, and How to Plant
Immerse potted cuttings in ponds in spring. Parrot's Feather likes full sun, but does fine in light shade part of the day. Set the pots under open water at the bottom of the pond so that the sun reaches the plants. Use one bunch, or about six stems, per 2 square ft. of pond surface. Use more if there are many fish. Their roots are primarily to anchor themselves in the soil at the bottom of a natural pond and to winter over. Instead anchor them in the soil in pots. Insert stems at least 1 in. deep in heavy soil or washed sand in 1 qt. container. Cover its surface with gravel to prevent fish from stirring up the soil. Water thoroughly, then immerse in pond so that the soil level is 2 to 6 in. under the water surface.

Growing Tips
There is no need to fertilize Parrot's Feather. It gains nutrition by removing excess nutrients from the water.

Care
Trim or thin Parrot's Feather as the season progresses. If it gets crowded, its stems will rise practically upright several inches above the water. Parrot's Feather is potentially invasive. Do not plant directly in soil at the bottom of a natural pond. Take care when discarding stems that they do not "escape" into the wild. Occasionally caterpillars may eat leaves that protrude above the water's surface, or fish may nibble on it.

Companion Planting and Design
Parrot's Feather fills in the open water spaces between the other plants, its soft tufts weaving a tapestry of floating water foliage. Its leaves open and close each day, their soft, fine texture contrasting with the round, flat surface foliage on neighboring Water Lily or Lotus.

Did You Know?
Aquatic plants have their share of pests, among them aphids and corn earworm. Aphids infest lily pads, speckling the leaves. Caterpillars chew holes in foliage surfaces. Either pinch off infested leaves, or dunk them in the water to wash off the pests. Fish in a water garden make short work of the dunked insects or caterpillars.

Pickerel Rush

Pontederia cordata

When, Where, and How to Plant

Plant rooted sections of Pickerel Rush in pots, and immerse them in the water garden pond anytime from spring until a month or so before frost is likely in October. Water temperature should be above 50 degrees Fahrenheit. Pickerel Rush, especially the white-flowered type, likes full sun. Blue types can take some shade. Set pots so that 2 to 10 in. of water cover their rims. Plant seedlings or rooted divisions in containers that hold a minimum of $3^1/2$ qt. of heavy soil. Slightly acid garden soil that has a bit of organic matter is ideal. Avoid fluffy soilless potting mixes because they do not anchor the plant securely in the pot. A mulch of washed gravel or decorative stones over the soil in the pot settles it. Make holes in the bottom of the container so roots are always in water.

Growing Tips

Set each pot in very shallow water at first, lowering the pots as the plants grow to maintain several inches of water over their edges. Mix slow-acting fertilizer into the soil in spring; it will last all season.

Care

Cut back dead stems after frost to within 1 or 2 in. of the pot surface, then lower the pot to the deepest part of the pond. Divide clumps, and repot in spring. Take care when discarding Pickerel Rush that plants do not "escape" into local waterways. Put them on a compost pile or in a plastic bag in the trash. Pickerel Rush has no significant pests or diseases.

Companion Planting and Design

Confined to a pot and planted as a marginal plant to frame the edge of the water garden, Pickerel Rush plays an ornamental role. Cut its flowers for arrangements.

Did You Know?

In the South where it chokes lakes and streams Pickerel Rush is called, aptly, Pickerel Weed. It tends to be rangy and floppy, the attractiveness of its flowers obscured by its crowded foliage. This is often the case with wild versions of domesticated plants. Controlled breeding and careful cultivation tame plants.

Native to Pennsylvania, Pickerel Rush grows wild in tidal marshes. Tamed in pots for water gardens, medium-sized clumps send up clusters of bare stems with waxy, arrowhead-shaped leaves branching off just below their flowered tips. The mid- to late-summer flowers are spikes of clustered tiny florets in blue, white, or pink. Each floret has two petals per flower, the upper one having two yellow dots. Pickerel Rush dies back in fall, but its roots are cold hardy. Hardy Thalia (Thalia dealbata) is bolder than Pickerel Rush and less hardy. Its stiff, slender stems are 4 to 6 ft. tall with narrow-tipped, oval, 20-in.-long leaves jutting from them at right angles. Delicate, deep-purple florets tip flexible stems that protrude another 1 to 5 ft. taller.

Other Name

Pickerel Weed

Bloom Period and Seasonal Color

Spring through summer; blooms in blue, white, or pink

Mature Height × Spread

3 to $4^1/2$ ft. × 2 to $2^1/2$ ft.

Taro
Colocasia esculenta

Although typically used as a marginal plant, Taro is handsome and dramatic enough to be a featured foliage specimen in a water garden. It is available in both regular and dwarf sizes, and its distinctive leaves may be green, purple, or variegated, many marked with indented, pale veins that accentuate their texture. Taro usually bears two leaves per stem at any one time, each up to 2 ft. long. Acutely angled downward, their surfaces are practically vertical, resembling Elephant Ears. A tropical plant, Taro cannot handle Pennsylvania winters outdoors. 'Hilo Beauty' has green leaves mottled with white. 'Fontanesii' has purple stems with dark-green leaves. 'Illustris', or Imperial Taro, has violet leaf stalks and green leaves with dark-purple coloration between the veins.

Other Name
Dasheen

Bloom Period and Seasonal Color
Foliage is the ornamental feature

Mature Height × Spread
2 to 4 ft. × 2 to 3 ft.

When, Where, and How to Plant
Put potted plants outdoors in late spring when air temperature has warmed to around 70 degrees Fahrenheit. Taro likes full sun or some shade; some of the darker-leafed ones show better in shade. Elevate pots in a water garden so the roots are constantly moist, the stalks above the water. Plants can handle as much as 12 in. of water over their roots, but have less vigor. Two or 3 in. are better. Plant Taro in containers that hold a minimum of 3¹/₂ qt. of heavy soil or are at least 5 in. in diameter. Use slightly acid heavy garden soil containing some organic matter in it rather than soilless potting mixes, which do not anchor the plant securely. A mulch of washed gravel or decorative stones over the soil surface keeps soil settled. Set potted plants in only 1 in. of water at first, lowering them as the plants grow to maintain several inches of water over their edges. Pots should have holes in the bottom.

Growing Tips
Taro does not need regular fertilizing.

Care
During the season trim off yellowed, limp leaf stalks to groom plants. Taro stalks yellow and die when frost hits. Store moist tubers in a cool cellar over winter. Divide overgrown clumps in spring. Taro tissues have a sap that may irritate skin. Watch for aphids, mites, or whiteflies on Taro houseplants. Wash them off or spray with insecticidal soap.

Companion Planting and Design
Taro provides a vertical element, plus foliage contrast, color, and texture simultaneously. It doubles as a houseplant, set in a container of water indoors in plenty of light during the winter.

Did You Know?
In Hawaii and other tropical cultures Taro is an agricultural crop. It is a diet staple much like Potatoes are elsewhere. The starchy tuber is served baked, fried, or boiled. Poi, a classic Hawaiian dish, is made of pounded Taro root. Taro must always be cooked to be edible.

Water Hyacinth
Eichhornia crassipes

When, Where, and How to Plant
Water Hyacinths are not usually available commercially in Pennsylvania until well into June. Put plants into any pond over 6 in. deep when its water temperature is over 70 degrees Fahrenheit. They prefer full sun. They do not do well where water is disturbed by a fountain. If they have been accustomed to indoor or greenhouse conditions over the winter, they will need some afternoon shade when first introduced to the outdoors in spring. Simply drop Water Hyacinths into the water. If they land upside down, they will right themselves.

Growing Tips
Water Hyacinths get their nutrients from the water. They need no special care.

Care
A good way to control Water Hyacinths is to corral them. Fashion a large ring from some tubing or other material that floats on the water, and trap the Water Hyacinths inside it. They multiply by means of stem offshoots in several directions. Remove excess plants by just pulling them out of the water. Sometimes their long roots reach into the soil bottom of natural ponds or into accumulations of muck on the bottom of lined ponds, so pulling them may take a bit more effort. Before October frost pull some out to overwinter indoors. The rest will be killed by frost instantly. Scoop them out, and discard them. In a natural setting, turtles may eat them.

Companion Planting and Design
Water Hyacinths are suitable for water gardens in containers such as tubs and kettles.

Did You Know?
Wherever warm water, sunshine, and nutrients exist together, there will be algae. There are many kinds, some good, some bad, in a water garden. The brown type that coats surfaces of liners, pumps, pots, and submerged plants with a furry layer is not a problem. Like organic matter in soil, it supports beneficial microorganisms to maintain a balanced system and water quality. The bright-green, stringy stuff is a problem. Water Hyacinths help control it by taking up the nitrates that would otherwise nourish this algae.

Water Hyacinths have a dual personality. In the South where they survive winters, they are a major invasive pest that chokes waterways. In Pennsylvania where they are too tender to withstand winter outdoors they are ornamental and useful annual plants in water gardens. Their bizarre feathered roots trailing below the pond surface in thick bunches absorb prodigious amounts of water pollutants and they also shelter fish. A single Water Hyacinth is as effective at controlling algae as six bunches of submerged plants. Above the water's surface they sport crisp, glossy-green, rounded foliage with bulbous stalks that enable them to float. They multiply very quickly. Water Hyacinths bloom toward the end of summer, their flowering prompted by water rich in nutrients and overcrowding. Their flowers vaguely resemble Dutch Hyacinths.

Other Name
Water Orchid

Bloom Period and Seasonal Color
Late summer; blooms in lilac-blue

Mature Height × Spread
Individual plants 10 to 12 in. × 6 to 8 in.

Water Lily
Nymphaea species

Tropical or hardy, Water Lilies are the stars of a water garden. Their classic, round, lily pad foliage—green, bronze, maroon, mottled, or ripple edged—is decorative as it shades the water, sheltering fish and discouraging algae growth. Their wonderful blossoms are from 2 to 12 in. wide, semi-double or double, and bloom at the tips of submerged stalks at, or just above, the water surface. Hardies and daytime tropicals bloom between 9:00 a.m. and 4:00 p.m. Night-blooming tropicals open after sundown and close the following midday. Tropical Water Lily flowers bloom higher above water and are more likely to be fragrant than the hardy types. They also bloom longer into the fall, stopping when water temperatures dip to 50 degrees Fahrenheit. They die with frost.

Other Name
Nymphaea

Bloom Period and Seasonal Color
June to September; blooms in red, shades of pink, yellow, white, or lilac

Mature Height × Spread
6 to 8 in. × 1 to 10 ft.

When, Where, and How to Plant
Plant Water Lily rhizomes in pots in the spring. Sink pots of hardy types into the water anytime. Wait until water temperatures reach 70 degrees Fahrenheit to sink pots of tropical ones in the water garden pond. Water Lilies need at least five or six hours of sun daily. Set containers 6 to 18 in. deep under still water on the pond bottom. Plant rhizomes in shallow containers that hold at least 15 qt. of heavy or clay soil. Lay each rhizome horizontally on the soil, its growing tip tilted upward. Cover the rhizome, but not the tip, with soil. Insert two fertilizer tablets near, but not touching, the rhizome. A gravel mulch will settle soil. Soak the soil, then sink the container.

Growing Tips
Fertilize flowering plants with pellets twice a month.

Care
Routinely pinch off dead flowers and yellowed leaves. Winterize hardies by cutting back their stems and setting them on the floor of the pond if that is below the frost line where you live. Otherwise, wrap hardies or tropicals, containers and all, in damp newspaper, then in plastic bags with air holes, and store in a cool basement. Divide hardies every year or two in spring. Remove them from their pots when new leaf shoots appear. Rinse off soil from their rhizomes, then cut them into 4- to 6-in. pieces with a growing tip. Repot, and sink them into the pond. If you notice aphids on the leaves, dunk the affected leaves in water to wash them off; cut off severely affected leaves.

Companion Planting and Design
Use dwarf varieties in container water gardens. Add a tall, narrow plant for vertical interest and a fine-textured floater such as Fairy Moss or Duckweed for contrast.

Did You Know?
Cut Water Lilies last three or four days. Cut blossoms on their opening day. Clip stems about 1 ft. under the water. Display stemmed blossoms in water in a tall vase, or float them stemless in bowls of water. A drop of melted candle wax between petals will keep blossoms open for evening viewing.

Yellow Flag
Iris pseudacorus

When, Where, and How to Plant
Plant Yellow Flag rhizomes in pots either in spring, summer, or early fall. Fall-planted ones will bloom in the spring; spring-planted ones may not bloom until the following spring. Yellow Flags do fine in full or partial sun. They tolerate from 2 to 10 in. of water over their pots; however, double-flowered types prefer only 4 in. of water. Plant up to three rhizomes in a container 9 in. across. Use heavy soil for good anchorage. Lay each rhizome so its growing tip tilts upward. Allow it to protrude from the 2-in. layer of soil that covers the rest of each rhizome. A layer of washed gravel or small stones on the soil holds it. Wet the container and soil first, then lower onto a shallow support at the edge of the water garden.

Growing Tips
In October put fertilizer pellets in the soil as directed on the product label.

Care
Cut off the faded flowers and leaves to groom plants. Cut back limp foliage after the first frost. To overwinter Yellow Flag, lower pots to the bottom of the pond. Divide crowded rhizomes every three to five years after they bloom, mid-summer through early fall. Discard Yellow Flags with virus-streaked foliage or rhizomes that show signs of rot. Dispose of them carefully so that they do not "escape" into the wild.

Companion Planting and Design
Use Yellow Flag as vertical interest. Grow them with Ferns or spring bulbs that like moist soil such as Camassia.

Did You Know?
Many aquatic plants appropriate for Pennsylvania water gardens grow in the wild. Some are native; others have made themselves at home here. It is tempting to dig up plants in a remote area and bring them home; this is illegal and inadvisable. Wild plants may carry disease pathogens or pests that would endanger the fish and plants in your water garden. Buy plants from reputable sources that raise them for ornamental use.

Although not native to Pennsylvania, Yellow Flag Irises are naturalized here in lakes and farm ponds. These plants combine ribbed, bright-green to gray-green strap-like foliage 1 to 2 in. wide with cheery yellow flowers for a lovely effect. Yellow Flag flowers are typical Iris with three inner petals that stand up, and three outer ones that jut out horizontally. They do not have beards as some Irises do. Flowers are typically 3 to 4 in. across, and there are several on each branched stem. Some have brown or violet veins, and various hybrids are paler or darker yellow, or even double. Early bloomers, they are the first of all Water Irises to bloom in spring when air is still quite chilly. They spread slowly.

Other Name
Yellow Water Iris

Bloom Period and Seasonal Color
June and July; blooms in yellow

Mature Height × Spread
3 to 5 ft. × spread as permitted

Gardening Quick Facts

Eastern PA (Philadelphia)

   Average daily high and low temperatures: 63 high; 45 low
   Average relative humidity: 76 percent morning; 55 percent afternoon
   Annual rainfall: 41 inches

Frost Dates

First expected frost (32° F)	On or about October 20
First hard frost (25° F)	On or about November 10
Last hard frost (25° F)	On or about April 10
Last expected frost (32° F)	On or about April 20

Central PA (Harrisburg)

   Average daily high and low temperatures: 62 high; 44 low
   Average relative humidity: 76 percent morning; 55 percent afternoon
   Average rainfall: 38 inches

Frost Dates

First expected frost (32° F)	On or about October 10
First hard frost (25° F)	On or about October 31
Last hard frost (25° F)	On or about April 20
Last expected frost (32° F)	On or about April 30

Western PA (Pittsburgh)

   Average daily high and low temperatures: 60 high; 41 low
   Average relative humidity: 76 percent morning; 55 percent afternoon
   Annual rainfall: 36 inches

Frost Dates

First expected frost (32° F)	On or about September 30
First hard frost (25° F)	On or about October 20
Last hard frost (25° F)	On or about April 30
Last expected frost (32° F)	On or about May 10

Cold Hardiness Zones (see map on page 19).

Soil:

   pH: Typically acidic
   Type: Clay/loam

Soil test kits are available from the office of your County Extension Agent (see page 217).

County Cooperative Extension Office Phone Numbers

Adams . . . . (717) 334-6271

Allegheny . . . . (412) 473-2540

Armstrong . . . . (724) 548-3447

Beaver . . . . 724) 774-3003

Bedford . . . . (814) 623-4800

Berks . . . . (610) 378-1327

Blair . . . . (814) 693-3265

Bradford . . . . (717) 265-2896

Bucks . . . . (215) 345-3283

Butler . . . . (724) 287-4761

Cambria . . . . (814) 472-7986

Cameron . . . . (814) 486-3350

Carbon . . . . (717) 325-2788

Centre . . . . (814) 355-4897

Chester . . . . (610) 696-3500

Clarion . . . . (814) 226-4956

Clearfield . . . . (814) 765-7878

Clinton . . . . (717) 726-0022

Columbia . . . . (717) 784-6660

Crawford . . . . (814) 333-7460

Cumberland . . . . (717) 240-6500

Dauphin . . . . (717) 921-8803

Delaware . . . . (610) 690-2655

Elk . . . . (814) 776-5331

Erie . . . . (814) 825-0900

Fayette . . . . (724) 438-0111

Forest . . . . (814) 755-3544

Franklin . . . . (717) 236-9226

Fulton . . . . (717) 485-4111

Greene . . . . (724) 627-3745

Huntingdon . . . . (814) 643-1660

Indiana . . . . (724) 465-3880

Jefferson . . . . (814) 849-7361

(814) 849-8297

Juniata . . . . (717) 436-7744

Lackawana . . . . (570) 963-4761

Lancaster . . . . (717) 394-6851

Keeping Plants Healthy

The unspoken fear of homeowners and beginning gardeners—and even many experienced gardeners—is that the plants for which they have taken responsibility may fall victim to pest insects, critters, or diseases and that they will not know how to deal with them. It seems as if there are hundreds of potential threats and dozens of possible treatments. It is hard to know what to do—and confusing, too. This is a pretty negative approach to gardening.

The best approach is a positive one. Be proactive rather than reactive. Do not expect problems to develop; prevent them from the outset. There are three ways to do this.

The first proactive measure is to create a healthy environment for your plants by developing a diverse landscape. By mixing a wide variety of shrubs, trees, ground covers, and flowering plants in your yard, you provide a variety of shelter and food for beneficial insects. By creating a landscape that teems with all kinds of creatures, you are reinforcing the natural defense system that is already in place. Depending on that and working to reinforce it is easier than constantly fighting plant health problems. It is important to understand that most of the bugs in a healthy landscape are either beneficial or benign. That means there are plenty of predators waiting for the pests. Absent horrendous environmental disruptions, the resident beneficials in the soil and air will control population explosions of pest insects and disease-causing fungi, bacteria, and viruses.

The second proactive measure is to protect the environment as best you can from major disruptions that upset the balance of pest and predator. Although you cannot control the weather—droughts and storms happen—you can do a lot about other potential problems. Avoid using broad-spectrum pesticides that kill everything, friend or foe. Do not spill or dump gasoline or other foreign substances on the soil. Prune trees and shrubs, and cut lawns properly to avoid creating breeding places for pests and disease spores. Do not overfertilize, plant too deeply, weed or trim too closely, or compact the soil. Do not allow pets to harm your plants and their soil. Protect your soil by grading properly to control and direct drainage and prevent erosion. Mulch all bare soil.

The third way to be proactive about keeping plants healthy is to keep your plants stress free. Try to meet their cultural requirements, described in the individual plant entries, so that they do not have to constantly struggle to cope with deprivation of nutrition or moisture or something. Truly healthy plants rarely have problems. Their immune systems are up and running. When they experience extreme or severe weather, injury by yard care equipment, crowding, or insufficient light, however, the ensuing stress makes them vulnerable to secondary attack by insects or disease. A pest or disease problem is usually a symptom of some underlying stress. Thus, keeping plants healthy requires two steps. First, treat the symptom (see chart on the next page). Second, the most important step, address the possible cause of the underlying stress, and correct that to make sure the problem does not return. By moving the plant to a more congenial spot, pruning its neighbors, putting up a fence, changing the variety, or doing something similar, you can remove the underlying cause of stress and make your plants happy and thus vigorous.

Pest Control Guidelines

- Maintain a healthy, diverse environment to encourage natural control of pest insects and diseases by resident beneficial insects and birds.
- Purchase pest- and disease-resistant varieties of plants.
- Keep plants happy and as stress free as possible by providing them with the sun, soil, and moisture conditions they prefer.
- Observe plants regularly to catch problems at their earliest stage.
- Identify the problem accurately.
- Treat only the specific plants or lawn area that exhibits the problem.
- Use the least toxic measure first.
- Read product labels carefully, and follow instructions exactly.
- After treating the problem, think about the underlying cause and address that.
- Store and dispose of all pesticides safely.

Troubleshooting Pests and Diseases

Pest Name	Common Target Appearance/Damage	Some Control Methods
Aphids (aka. Plant Lice)	*Trees, shrubs, flowers, water plants.* Soft, pear-shaped, spindly legs. / May be green, yellow, pink, black, or white. / Clusters on stems and foliage of tender new growth cause wilted, curling foliage. Sap plant vigor.	Pinch infested tips and discard. Wash with water spray or use insecticidal soap. Predators: green lacewings, ladybugs.
Bagworms	*Needled evergreens.* Bags of fine twigs dangle from branches. /Worms feed on foliage, then retreat to protective bag.	Pick off reachable bags. Spray *B.t.* on foliage while worms feed. Predators: birds.
Borers	*Shrubs (esp. Roses, Lilac), trees, also bulbs such as Iris.* Small worms burrow into plant stems. Larvae of beetles and moths. Infest bulbs. / Leaves wilt. Holes in woody stems, sawdust nearby. Bulbs turn mealy, dry out.	Prune off affected stems below borer holes. Inoculate the soil with predatory nematodes. Spray *B.t.* on stem surfaces. Dust it on bulbs. Predators: birds.

Troubleshooting Pests and Diseases (continued)

Pest Name	Common Target Appearance/Damage	Some Control Methods
Caterpillars—Parsleyworm, Corn Earworm, et al.	*Trees, shrubs, flowers.* Worm larvae of moths, butterflies. / Chew holes in edges of foliage. May leave only veins.	Handpick. Spray *B.t.* on foliage. Predators: Trichogramma wasps; birds.
Chlorosis	*Acid-loving trees and shrubs such as Holly, Azalea, Mountain Laurel.* Indication of iron deficiency in plant. / Foliage becomes yellowish; green veins stand out.	Acidify soil by sprinkling garden sulfur or iron sulfate over root zone.
Critters: Deer, Chipmunks, Squirrels, Voles, Groundhogs, Raccoons	*Trees, shrubs, annuals, perennials, bulbs (except Daffodils and their relatives), water plants.* Animals feed on foliage, stems, and tender twigs (deer), or roots (rodents). Deer will rub off tender bark of young tree and shrub stems. / Foliage is chewed or simply disappears, leaving bluntly cut stem ends. Plants collapse as roots disappear.	Spread winter mulch after ground freezes to prevent rodent nests near woody plant stems. Use barriers—chicken wire over/under bulbs, electrified tape, chain link or polymesh fencing around individual plants or beds or the entire property.
Fall Webworm; Tent Caterpillar Gypsy Moth Caterpillar	*Trees and shrubs at roadsides and other stressful sites. Oak trees, especially.* Nests resemble webbed tents in twigs. Caterpillars are larvae of moths or butterflies. / Caterpillars feed on tree foliage, chewing large holes, possibly skeletonizing it.	Prune out nests. Poke open very high nests with a stick. Spray foliage with *B.t.* when worms hatch and begin to eat. Predators: parasitic wasps; birds.
Fungal Disease	*Turfgrasses.* Blackish or gray coating on foliage; spots, circles of mold or fungi. / Gray or dark streaks on foliage. Tattered or matted blades. Dead patches.	Mow grass dry. Do not walk on wet or frosty grass. Water early in day. Spray fungicide on healthy grass to prevent spread. Change to a new grass variety if the problem is chronic.

Troubleshooting Pests and Diseases (continued)

Pest Name	Common Target Appearance/Damage	Some Control Methods
Grasshoppers	*Turfgrasses, fruits, vegetables.* Chew foliage.	*B.t.*; insecticidal soap; *Nosema locustae* bacteria. Predators: praying mantis; birds.
Japanese Beetle	*Roses, annuals, perennials, shrubs, and trees.* Metallic green and copper beetle. / Ragged holes in buds and leaves. Will skeletonize foliage.	Handpick. Spray Neem or pyrethrum as directed. Predators: starlings. (See White Grubs.)
Lacebugs	*Broadleaf shrubs such as Azalea, Pieris, Rhododendron stressed by too much sun.* Tiny squarish dots with netted wings. Dark excrement specks under leaves. / Suck juices until leaves are pale and stippled. Leaves dry and bleach out.	Move plant to shadier, understory location. Spray undersides of leaves with insecticidal soap. Repeat several times at 2-week intervals.
Pine Sawfly	*All kinds of Pines.* Small blackish-striped caterpillars (larvae) resemble tree twigs. Vertical posture if startled. / Chew needles and defoliate tree.	Handpick. Spray Neem or pyrethrum as directed. Predators: birds.
Powdery Mildew	*Roses, annuals, perennials, shrubs, trees, bulbs.* Grayish blotching or white coating on foliage. / Lower leaves dry, curl, and drop. Unsightly but not fatal in mature plants.	Improve air circulation. Spray garden (sulfur) fungicide or horticultural oil on healthy and new foliage to prevent infection.
Rots: Root Rots, Crown Rot	*Annuals, perennials, and bulbs.* Soil-dwelling bacteria, fungi, or viruses attack roots. / Tissues blacken and turn mushy with decay.	Avoid overwatering, soggy soil. Dig up and dispose of affected plants and nearby soil. Wash tools afterwards.
Scale	*Trees, shrubs, perennials.* Raised, waxy bumps on leaf undersides and stems. / Insects feed on juices of plant tissues. Foliage looks pale.	Scrape off gently with fingernail. Spray horticultural oil to smother. Predators: green lacewings.

Troubleshooting Pests and Diseases (continued)

Pest Name	Common Target Appearance/Damage	Some Control Methods
Slugs, Snails	*Plants in moist, acidic soil in shade. Hosta. Also some bulbs.* Soft-bodied, 1 to 4 in. long. Leave a trail of mucous as they travel. / Feed at night. Chew large ragged holes in leaves.	Place wood planks or upended flowerpots on the ground to collect slugs hiding during the day. Handpick from under debris. Trap with yeast/beer bait. Sprinkle diatomaceous earth on soil around plants. Predators: birds.
Spider Mites	*Feed on foliage of stressed plants suffering dry conditions. Ivy, shrubs, houseplants.* Resemble tiny spiders. Suck juices from foliage. / Pale stippling on leaves; fine webbing on stems. Leaves curl, turn brown.	Wash with forceful water spray. Treat stubborn mite problems with insecticidal soap or spray horticultural oil to smother. Repeat treatment weekly, 3 times.
Thrips	*Roses (esp. red, white, yellow), Citrus, Dahlias, Foxgloves, Daylily, Iris, Gladioli, Mums, Privet.* Tiny, yellowish brown. Burrow into buds, suck juices. / Flowers distorted, droop. Buds fail to open, dry out.	Clip off infested flowers. Use Merit insecticide. Encourage beneficial insect predators.
Whiteflies	*Occasionally on ornamental plants and plants raised in greenhouses.* Tiny white specks fly off when disturbed. Note black dots of excrement under foliage. / Suck juices from foliage, which turns pale. Not life threatening to most mature, healthy plants.	Spray pests with insecticidal soap. Predators: green lacewing larvae.
White Grubs	*Turfgrass roots.* Japanese beetle larvae. Fat, curled worms with brown heads. Overwinter in soil. / Grass dies, sod lifts easily because roots are destroyed.	Cut grass tall to discourage beetles from laying eggs. Spray predatory nematodes on the lawn. Spread milky spore disease on the lawn. Predators: starlings, skunks, moles.
Wooly Adelgid	*Hemlock.* Round fuzzy white bumps at the base of needles. / Needles on infested branches turn brown and drop.	Spray horticultural oil in late March-April, in late June and again in late September to mid-October.

Endangered and Threatened

Pennsylvania's Disappearing Wildflowers

In the beginning, before the European settlers arrived on the shores of this continent, it was densely covered with plants. The survivors of eons of competition between evolving species and environmental upheavals, these native trees, shrubs, bulbs, vines, flowers, and water plants were therefore highly adapted to conditions in their respective regions. They supported a rich variety of native wildlife. The early settlers delighted in the plants, discovering among them resources for food, shelter, and medicine, as well as raw materials for tools, local industries, and agriculture. In many cases they were exported to Europe.

Typically, the settlers collected the fruits, seeds, foliage, and bark from the abundant populations of native plants growing in the wild. In their gardens they cultivated mostly the plants they brought from their own countries, which, being unaccustomed to the New World, needed more attention. Over the centuries this pattern continued as plants introduced into Pennsylvania from Europe, Asia, and other places in the United States took preference in our landscapes over the humble wildflowers that grew in the "natural" areas. While most of these imports coexist benignly with native plants, some have become particularly aggressive and have escaped from gardens into the wild where they have overwhelmed native plant populations, reducing many to alarmingly small numbers. (See Invasive Plant List.)

Today in Pennsylvania and other states the number of species of native plants growing in the wild is rapidly diminishing. There are all kinds of reasons, including loss of habitat from environmental pollution, housing developments, deer browse, commercial exploitation, and competition from the above-mentioned aggressive plants from other regions and countries encroaching into their habitat. The serious loss of plant diversity has far-reaching implications for wildlife preservation, environmental sustainability, and quality of life for Pennsylvania residents.

How Gardeners Can Help

Why is this something gardeners should know about? Well, there are many ways that gardeners and other concerned citizens can help stem the tide of destruction of native plants. Identifying and protecting existing native plant communities in the wild, rescuing the plants that are in the path of bulldozers, resisting the temptation to collect plants in the wild for their gardens, and refusing to buy wild collected plants from unscrupulous nurseries are some of the ways. Of course, in order to do all this, the first step must be to become familiar with some of the most vulnerable of our Pennsylvania native plants.

You can also help sustain populations of Pennsylvania threatened and endangered plant species by incorporating them into gardens and home landscapes. This is not as difficult as it might seem. A close look at the list reveals that among the numerous obscure plants, there are many familiar ones that are presently available commercially. Notice that American Holly, Crested Iris, Sweetbay Magnolia, and

Plants *of Pennsylvania*

American Lotus—excellent garden plants all—are numbered among the vulnerable plants. Also, there are specialty nurseries and wildflower preservation organizations that raise and sell less familiar garden-worthy natives. (See Information Resources, page 250.) There are numerous wetland plants on this list, Rushes and Sedges, victims of the disappearing wetland areas in Pennsylvania. Why not establish a bog garden or water garden, and try some of these plants? Consider including some of the Ferns and grasses in woodland and meadow areas on your property. Endangered or not, native plants will expand your palette of plants and create an authentic sense of place, of Pennsylvania, on your property.

Threatened Native Plants

Common Name	Scientific Name	Status*
American Beachgrass	*Ammophila breviligulata*	PT
American Beakgrain	*Diarrhena obovata*	PE
American Columbo	*Frasera caroliniensis*	PE
American Gromwell	*Lithospermum latifolium*	PE
American Holly	*Ilex opaca*	PT
American Lotus	*Nelumbo lutea*	PE
Annual Fimbry	*Fimbristylis annua*	PT
Appalachian Blue Violet	*Viola appalachiensis*	PT
Appalachian Gametophyte Fern	*Vittaria appalachiana*	PT
Appalachian Sandwort	*Minuartia glabra*	PT
Arrow-Feathered Three Awned	*Aristida purpurascens*	PT
Asterlike Boltonia	*Boltonia asteroides*	PE
Autumn Bluegrass	*Poa autumnalis*	PE
Autumn Willow	*Salix serissima*	PT
Awned Sedge	*Carex atherodes*	PE
Backward Sedge	*Carex retrorsa*	PE
Balsam Poplar	*Populus balsamifera*	PE
Baltic Rush	*Juncus balticus*	PT
Bayonet Rush	*Juncus militaris*	PE
Beach Peavine	*Lathyrus japonicus*	PT
Beach Plum	*Prunus maritima*	PE
Beach Wormwood	*Artemisia campestris* ssp. *caudata*	PE
Beaked Spike-Rush	*Eleocharis rostellata*	PE
Bebb's Sedge	*Carex bebbii*	PE
Beck's Water-Marigold	*Megalodonta beckii*	PE
Bicknell's Hoary Rockrose	*Helianthemum bicknellii*	PE
Bicknell's Sedge	*Carex bicknellii*	PE
Black-Stemmed Spleenwort	*Asplenium resiliens*	PE

*See page 233.

Threatened Native Plants (continued)

Common Name	Scientific Name	Status*
Blue Monkshood	*Aconitum uncinatum*	PT
Blue-Curls	*Trichostema setaceum*	PE
Blunt Manna-Grass	*Glyceria obtusa*	PE
Blunt-Leaved Pondweed	*Potamogeton obtusifolius*	PE
Blunt-Leaved Spurge	*Euphorbia obtusata*	PE
Bog Aster	*Aster nemoralis*	PE
Bog Sedge Aupercula	*Carex p*	PT
Box Huckleberry	*Gaylussacia brachycera*	PT
Bradley's Spleenwort	*Asplenium bradleyi*	PT
Branching Bur-Reed	*Sparganium androcladum*	PE
Braun's Holly Fern	*Polystichum braunii*	PE
Broad-Leaved Beardgrass	*Gymnopogon ambiguus*	PE
Broad-Leaved Water-Milfoil	*Myriophyllum heterophyllum*	PE
Broad-Leaved Water-Plantain	*Alisma plantago-aquatica* var. *americana*	PE
Broad-Winged Sedge	*Carex alata*	PT
Brook Lobelia	*Lobelia kalmii*	PE
Bull Sedge	*Carex bullata*	PE
Bushy Cinquefoil	*Potentilla paradoxa*	PE
Bushy Naiad	*Najas gracillima*	PT
Bushy St. John's-Wort	*Hypericum densiflorum*	PT
Butterfly-Pea	*Clitoria mariana*	PE
Canada Buffalo-Berry	*Shepherdia canadensis*	PE
Canby's Mountain-Lover	*Paxistima canbyi*	PE
Capillary Beaked-Rush	*Rhynchospora capillacea*	PE
Capitate Spike-Rush	*Eleocharis caribaea*	PE
Carey's Sedge	*Carex careyana*	PE
Carey's Smartweed	*Polygonum careyi*	PE
Carolina Grass-of-Parnassus	*Parnassia glauca*	PE
Carolina Leaf-Flower	*Phyllanthus caroliniensis*	PE
Case's Ladies'-Tresses	*Spiranthes casei*	PE
Cat's-Paw Ragwort	*Senecio antennariifolius*	PE
Cattail Sedge	*Carex typhina*	PE
Chamisso's Miner's-Lettuce	*Montia chamissoi*	PE
Cluster Fescue	*Festuca paradoxa*	PE
Coast Violet	*Viola brittoniana*	PE
Collin's Sedge	*Carex collinsii*	PE
Common Hemicarpa	*Hemicarpha micrantha*	PE

Threatened Native Plants (continued)

Common Name	Scientific Name	Status*
Common Hop-Tree	*Ptelea trifoliata*	PT
Common Shooting-Star	*Dodecatheon meadia*	PE
Cooper's Milk-Vetch	*Astragalus neglectus*	PE
Cranesbill	*Geranium bicknellii*	PE
Crepis Rattlesnake-Root	*Prenanthes crepidinea*	PE
Crested Dwarf Iris	*Iris cristata*	PE
Cross-Leaved Milkwort	*Polygala cruciata*	PE
Cuckooflower	*Cardamine pratensis* var. *palustris*	PE
Curtis' Golden-Rod	*Solidago curtisii*	PE
Curtis's Milkwort	*Polygala curtissii*	PE
Cyperus-Like Sedge	*Carex pseudocyperus*	PE
Downey Willow-Herb	*Epilobium strictum*	PE
Downy Lobelia	*Lobelia puberula*	PE
Dwarf Azalea	*Rhododendron atlanticum*	PE
Dwarf Huckleberry	*Gaylussacia dumosa*	PE
Dwarf Iris	*Iris verna*	PE
Dwarf Mistletoe	*Arceuthobium pusillum*	PT
Dwarf Spiraea	*Spiraea betulifolia*	PT
Eared False-Foxglove	*Tomanthera auriculata*	PE
Eastern Baccharis	*Baccharis halimifolia*	PR
Eastern Blue-Eyed Grass	*Sisyrinchium atlanticum*	PE
Eastern White Water-Crowfoot	*Ranunculus longirostris*	PT
Ebony Sedge	*Carex eburnea*	PE
Elephant's Foot	*Elephantopus carolinianus*	PE
Elk Sedge	*Carex garberi*	PE
Ellisia	*Ellisia nyctelea*	PT
Fall Dropseed Muhly	*Muhlenbergia uniflora*	PE
False Gromwell	*Onosmodium hispidissimum*	PE
False Loosestrife Seedbox	*Lludwigia polycarpa*	PE
Farwell's Water-Milfoil	*Myriophyllum farwellii*	PE
Few Flowered Nutrush	*Scleria pauciflora*	PT
Few-Flowered Sedge	*Carex pauciflora*	PE
Few-Flowered Spike-Rush	*Eleocharis pauciflora* var. *fernaldii*	PE
Few-Seeded Sedge	*Carex oligosperma*	PT
Flat-Leaved Bladderwort	*Utricularia intermedia*	PT
Flat-Stemmed Spike-Rush	*Eleocharis compressa*	PE
Floating-Heart	*Nymphoides cordata*	PT

Threatened Native Plants (continued)

Common Name	Scientific Name	Status*
Fogg's Goosefoot	*Chenopodium foggii*	PE
Forked Rush	*Juncus dichotomus*	PE
Four-Angled Spike-Rush	*Eleocharis quadrangulata*	PE
Foxtail Clubmoss	*Lycopodium alopecuroides*	PE
Fraser's Sedge	*Cymophyllus fraseri*	PE
Fries' Pondweed	*Potamogeton friesii*	PE
Fringed-Leaved Petunia	*Ruellia humilis*	PE
Geyer's Sedge	*Carex geyeri*	PE
Glade Spurge	*Euphorbia purpurea*	PE
Golden-Fruited Sedge	*Carex aurea*	PE
Grape	*Vitis novae-angliae*	PE
Grass-Leaved Goldenrod	*Euthamia tenuifolia*	PT
Grassy Pondweed	*Potamogeton gramineus*	PE
Green-and-Gold	*Chrysogonum virginianum*	PE
Green Sedge	*Carex viridula*	PE
Grooved Yellow Flax	*Linum sulcatum*	PE
Handsome Sedge	*Carex formosa*	PE
Harbinger-of-Spring	*Erigenia bulbosa*	PT
Hard-Stemmed Bullrush	*Scirpus acutus*	PE
Harris' Golden-Rod	*Solidago arguta* var. *harrisii*	PE
Hartford Fern	*Lygodium palmatum*	PR
Heart-Leaved Twayblade	*Listera cordata*	PE
Hemlock-Parsley	*Conioselinum chinense*	PE
Hill's Pondweed	*Potamogeton hillii*	PE
Hispid Gromwell	*Lithospermum caroliniense*	PE
Hoary Willow	*Salix candida*	PT
Holly-Leaved Naiad	*Najas marina*	PE
Hooded Ladies'-Tresses	*Spiranthes romanzoffiana*	PE
Horrible Thistle	*Cirsium horridulum*	PE
Houghton's Flatsedge	*Cyperus houghtonii*	PE
Jacob's-Ladder	*Polemonium vanbruntiae*	PE
Jeweled Shooting-Star	*Dodecatheon amethystinum*	PT
Kate's Mountain Clover	*Trifolium virginicum*	PE
Kidney-Leaved Twayblade	*Listera smallii*	PE
Labrador Marsh Bedstraw	*Galium labradoricum*	PE
Lanceolate Buckthorn	*Rhamnus lanceolata*	PE
Large-Flowered Marshallia	*Marshallia grandiflora*	PE

Threatened Native Plants (continued)

Common Name	Scientific Name	Status*
Large-Leafed Water-Leaf	*Hydrophyllum macrophyllum*	PE
Larger Canadian St. John's-Wort	*Hypericum majus*	PT
Leafy Northern Green Orchid	*Platanthera hyperborea*	PE
Leafy White Orchid	*Platanthera dilatata*	PE
Leopard's-Bane	*Arnica acaulis*	PE
Lesser Bladderwort	*Utricularia minor*	PT
Lesser Panicled Sedge	*Carex diandra*	PT
Limestone Adder's-Tongue	*Ophioglossum engelmannii*	PE
Limestone Petunia	*Ruellia strepens*	PT
Little-Spike Spike-Rush	*Eleocharis parvula*	PE
Long-Fruited Anemone	*Anemone cylindrica*	PE
Long-Leaved Aster	*Aster novi-belgii*	PT
Long-Lobed Arrow-Head	*Sagittaria calycina* var. *spongiosa*	PE
Low Showy Aster	*Aster spectabilis*	PE
Maryland Golden-Aster	*Chrysopsis mariana*	PT
Maryland Hawkweed	*Hieracium traillii*	PE
Maryland Meadow-Beauty	*Rhexia mariana*	PE
Matted Spike-Rush	*Eleocharis intermedia*	PT
Minor Nutrush	*Scleria minor*	PE
Missouri Gooseberry	*Ribes missouriense*	PE
Missouri Rock-Cress	*Arabis missouriensis*	PE
Mitchell's Sedge	*Carex mitchelliana*	PE
Mock Bishop-Weed	*Ptilimnium capillaceum*	PE
Moss Pink Phlox	*Subulata* ssp. *brittonii*	PE
Mountain Alder	*Alnus viridis*	PE
Mountain Bugbane	*Cimicifuga americana*	PT
Mountain Fly Honeysuckle	*Lonicera villosa*	PE
Mountain Pepper-Bush	*Clethra acuminata*	PE
Mountain Phlox	*Phlox ovata*	PE
Mountain Pimpernel	*Taenidia montana*	PE
Mountain Wood Fern	*Dryopteris campyloptera*	PE
Mouse-Ear Chickweed	*Cerastium arvense* var. *villosissimum*	PE
Multiflowered Mud-Plantain	*Heteranthera multiflora*	PE
Naked Bishop's-Cap	*Mitella nuda*	PE
Narrowleaf Bushclover	*Lespedeza angustifolia*	PE
Narrow-Leaved Pondweed	*Potamogeton strictifolius*	PE
Narrow-Leaved White-Topped Aster	*Aster solidagineus*	PE

Threatened Native Plants (continued)

Common Name	Scientific Name	Status*
Nodding Pogonia	*Triphora trianthophora*	PE
Nondo Lovage	*Ligusticum canadense*	PE
Northeastern Bullrush	*Scirpus ancistrochaetus*	PE
Northeastern Sedge	*Carex cryptolepis*	PT
Northern Water-Milfoil	*Myriophyllum exalbescens*	PE
Nuttall's Hedge-Nettle	*Stachys nuttallii*	PE
Oblique Milkvine	*Matelea obliqua*	PE
Oblong-Fruited Serviceberry	*Amelanchier bartramiana*	PE
October Ladies'-Tresses	*Spiranthes ovalis*	PE
Passion-Flower	*Passiflora lutea*	PE
Pink Milkwort	*Polygala incarnata*	PE
Pod-Grass	*Scheuchzeria palustris*	PE
Possum Haw	*Viburnum viburnum nudum*	PE
Prairie Dropseed	*Sporobolus heterolepis*	PE
Prairie Sedge	*Carex prairea*	PT
Prairie Violet	*Viola pedatifida*	PE
Purple Rocket	*Iodanthus pinnatifidus*	PE
Purple Sandgrass	*Triplasis purpurea*	PE
Red Currant	*Ribes triste*	PT
Red-Head Pondweed	*Potamogeton richardsonii*	PT
Reflexed Flatsedge	*Cyperus refractus*	PE
Reticulated Nutrush	*Scleria reticularis*	PE
Retrorse Flatsedge	*Cyperus retrorsus*	PE
Richardson's Rush	*Juncus alpinus*	PT
Robbins' Spike-Rush	*Eleocharis robbinsii*	PT
Rock Clubmoss	*Lycopodium porophilum*	PE
Roseroot Stonecrop	*Sedum rosea*	PE
Rough Cotton-Grass	*Eriophorum tenellum*	PE
Rough Dropseed	*Sporobolus clandestinus*	PE
Round-Leaved Fame-Flower	*Talinum teretifolium*	PT
Rush Aster	*Aster borealis*	PE
Sand Dropseed	*Sporobolus cryptandrus*	PE
Sandplain Wild Flax	*Linum intercursum*	PE
Scarlet Ammannia	*Ammannia coccinea*	PE
Schweinitz's Sedge	*Carex schweinitzii*	PT
Scirpus-Like Rush	*Juncus scirpoides*	PE
Sedge	*Carex tetanica*	PT
Serpentine Aster	*Aster depauperatus*	PT

Threatened Native Plants (continued)

Common Name	Scientific Name	Status*
Shale-Barren Evening-Primrose	*Oenothera argillicola*	PT
Short Hair Sedge	*Carex crinita* var. *brevicrinis*	PE
Short-Fruited Rush	*Juncus brachycarpus*	PE
Showy Lady's-Slipper	*Cypripedium reginae*	PT
Showy Mountain Ash	*Sorbus decora*	PE
Shrubby Cinquefoil	*Potentilla fruticosa*	PE
Shumard's Oak	*Quercus shumardii*	PE
Sida	*Sida hermaphrodita*	PE
Silverweed	*Potentilla anserina*	PT
Slender Blue Iris	*Iris prismatica*	PE
Slender Cotton-Grass	*Eriophorum gracile*	PE
Slender Golden-Rod	*Solidago erecta*	PE
Slender Mountain-Ricegrass	*Oryzopsis pungens*	PE
Slender Panic-Grass	*Panicum xanthophysum*	PE
Slender Rock-Brake	*Cryptogramma stelleri*	PE
Slender Sea-Oats	*Chasmanthium laxum*	PE
Slender Spike-Rush	*Eleocharis elliptica*	PE
Slender Spike-Rush	*Eleocharis tenuis* var. *verrucosa*	PE
Slender Water-Milfoil	*Myriophyllum tenellum*	PT
Small Sea-Side Spurge	*Chamaesyce polygonifolia*	PT
Small Swollen Bladderwort	*Utricularia radiata*	PE
Small Yellow Lady's-Slipper	*Cypripedium parviflorum*	PE
Small-Floating Manna-Grass	*Glyceria borealis*	PE
Small-Flowered False-Foxglove	*Agalinis paupercula*	PE
Small-Headed Rush	*Juncus brachycephalus*	PT
Small-Whorled Pogonia	*Isotria medeoloides*	PE
Smith's Bullrush	*Scirpus smithii*	PE
Smooth Swallow-Wort	*Cynanchum laeve*	PE
Southern Bog Clubmoss	*Lycopodium appressum*	PT
Southern Red Oak	*Quercus falcata*	PE
Southern Sea-Beach Panic-Grass	*Panicum amarum* var. *amarulum*	PE
Southern Twayblade	*Listera australis*	PE
Spotted Bee-Balm	*Monarda punctata*	PE
Spotted Pondweed	*Potamogeton pulcher*	PE
Spreading Globe Flower	*Trollius laxus* ssp. *laxus*	PE
Spring Ladies'-Tresses	*Spiranthes vernalis*	PE
Stagger-Bush	*Lyonia mariana*	PE

Threatened Native Plants (continued)

Common Name	Scientific Name	Status*
Stalked Bullrush	*Scirpus pedicellatus*	PT
Sterile Sedge	*Carex sterilis*	PT
Sticky Golden-Rod	*Solidago spathulata* var. *racemosa*	PE
Swamp Beggar-Ticks	*Bidens bidentoides*	PT
Swamp Smartweed	*Polygonum setaceum* var. *interjectum*	PE
Swamp Fly Honeysuckle	*Lonicera oblongifolia*	PE
Swamp-Pink	*Arethusa bulbosa*	PE
Sweet Bay Magnolia	*Magnolia virginiana*	PT
Sweet Bayberry	*Myrica gale*	PT
Sweet Flag	*Acorus americanus*	PE
Tall Gramma	*Bouteloua curtipendula*	PT
Tall Larkspur	*Delphinium exaltatum*	PE
Taper-Leaved Bugle-Weed	*Lycopus rubellus*	PE
Tawny Ironweed	*Vernonia glauca*	PE
Tennessee Pondweed	*Potamogeton tennesseensis*	PE
Thick-Leaved Meadow-Rue	*Thalictrum coriaceum*	PE
Thin-Leaved Cotton-Grass	*Eriophorum viridicarinatum*	PT
Three-Flowered Melic-Grass	*Nitens melica*	PT
Three-Toothed Cinquefoil	*Potentilla tridentata*	PE
Torrey's Bullrush	*Scirpus torreyi*	PE
Torrey's Mountainmint	*Pycnanthemum torrei*	PE
Torrey's Rush	*Juncus torreyi*	PT
Trailing Tick-Trefoil	*Desmodium humifusum*	PE
Tuckerman's Panic-Grass	*Panicum tuckermanii*	PT
Tufted Buttercup	*Ranunculus fascicularis*	PE
Twig Rush	*Cladium mariscoides*	PE
Twinflower	*Linnaea borealis*	PT
Umbrella Flatsedge	*Cyperus diandrus*	PE
Umbrella Magnolia	*Magnolia tripetala*	PT
Upright Primrose-Willow	*Ludwigia decurrens*	PE
Vanilla Sweet-Grass	*Hierochloe odorata*	PE
Variable Sedge	*Carex polymorpha*	PE
Variegated Horsetail	*Equisetum variegatum*	PE
Vase-Vine Leather-Flower	*Clematis viorna*	PE
Vasey's Pondweed	*Potamogeton vaseyi*	PE
Velvety Panic-Grass	*Panicum scoparium*	PE
Walter's Barnyard-Grass	*Echinochloa walteri*	PE

Threatened Native Plants (continued)

Common Name	Scientific Name	Status*
Water Lobelia	*Lobelia dortmanna*	PT
Water Sedge	*Carex aquatilis*	PT
White Monkshood	*Aconitum reclinatum*	PE
White Twisted-Stalk	*Streptopus amplexifolius*	PE
Whorled Nutrush	*Scleria verticillata*	PE
Whorled Water-Milfoil	*Myriophyllum verticillatum*	PE
Wiegands Sedge	*Carex wiegandii*	PT
Wild Bleeding-Hearts	*Dicentra eximia*	PE
Wild Ipecac	*Euphorbia ipecacuanhae*	PE
Wild-Pea	*Lathyrus ochroleucus*	PT
Willow Oak	*Quercus phellos*	PE
Wrights Spike Rush	*Eleocharis obtusa* var. *peasei*	PE
Yellow Sedge	*Carex flava*	PT

*PE = Endangered   *PT = Threatened

Pennsylvania Endangered—Plant species that are in danger of extinction throughout most of their natural range within this Commonwealth, if critical habitat is not maintained or if the species is greatly exploited by man.

Pennsylvania Threatened—Plant species that may become endangered throughout most or all of their natural range within this Commonwealth, if critical habitat is not maintained to prevent their future decline, or if the species is greatly exploited by man.

List courtesy of the Pennsylvania Natural Diversity Inventory (PNDI)

Invasive Plants *of Pennsylvania*

Pennsylvania gardeners and homeowners need to be aware of the increasing threat to our state's native plants from rampant, aggressive species that move into a region's ecosystem and monopolize its moisture, light, and soil nutrients. They deprive the indigenous plants of these basic necessities. They not only threaten native plant communities, but they degrade the health of the wider environment because they reduce plant diversity and therefore limit the availability of food and shelter to wildlife that depends on many kinds of plants. They upset the healthy balance of populations of beneficial insects and pest insects that keep both the wild and the cultivated areas in our state vigorous and productive.

In many cases these plants are familiar roadside weeds, known to prefer sterile, disturbed soil that other plants will not tolerate. However, the spread of many ornamental plants, deliberately cultivated in home gardens, into natural areas such as parks, woodlands, wetlands, recreational areas, and roadsides has compounded the invasive plant problem. Often these plants are species that have been introduced from other countries—called alien, exotic, or introduced plants—and proliferate freely here because they are free from the disease, pest, and environmental constraints of their native regions. Sometimes invasive plants are native to the area, meaning that they occurred in Pennsylvania before the Europeans settled here. They became aggressive after settlers altered the landscape.

Cultivated plants capable of becoming invasive escape from gardens several ways. Typically, they are prolific seeders, and these seeds are widely distributed by birds or the wind. In other cases, garden plants are spread by careless disposal of their running roots. Plants that spread aggressively in the garden or water garden—they need frequent division, they need controlling in pots—are prime candidates for escape if their roots fall on fertile ground elsewhere. As a gardener, you have a real stake in preserving the environment. Therefore, you are on the front lines in the fight to preserve it. Be aware of the plants on the Invasive Plant List, and control or destroy any offenders on your property. Further, avoid purchasing suspect plants, and monitor any plants in your landscape that tend to be aggressive. Protect communities of native plants nearby, and create some in your yard. Use fertilizer with restraint, as high nitrogen often fuels explosive growth of plants used to a lean diet and promotes their aggressiveness. Talk about the problem with your neighbors, garden club, or plant society. Raise people's consciousness about this insidious problem.

Invasive plants tend to:

- Be nonnative
- Spread rapidly by roots or shoots
- Accept a wide range of growing conditions
- Mature quickly
- Disperse copious seeds that sprout easily
- Exploit disturbed and open ground

The following is a partial list of the plants identified in various regions of Pennsylvania as invasive threats to the environment. It is courtesy of the Pennsylvania Department of Conservation and Natural

Resources (DCNR) in collaboration with the Pennsylvania Landscape and Nursery Association (PNLA) and the Rodale Institute. To learn more, visit PA/DCNR Bureau of Forestry at www.dcnr.state.pas.us/forestry/pndi.

Invasive Plants in Pennsylvania

*An asterisk denotes that the species has cultivars that are not known to be invasive.

Common Name	Scientific Name	Form	Notes
Amur Honeysuckle	*Lonicera maackii*	Shrub	Escaped from landscapes
Autumn Olive	*Elaeagnus umbellata*	Shrub	Escaped from landscapes
Bull Thistle	*Cirsium vulgare*	Flower	Noxious weed statewide
Canada Thistle	*Cirsium arvense*	Flower	Noxious weed statewide
Common Reed	*Phragmites australis*	Grass	Forms colonies in wetlands
Garlic Mustard	*Alliaria petiolata*	Flower	Seeds into woodlands
Giant Hogweed	*Heracleum mantegazzianum*	Flower	Noxious in PA; Sap blisters
Goatsrue	*Galega officinalis*	Flower	Noxious weed in SE region
Japanese Honeysuckle	*Lonicera japonica*	Vine	Fragrant, rampant
Japanese Knotweed	*Polygonum (Fallopia) cuspidatum*	Flower	Spreads by roots, seeds
Japanese Stilt Grass	*Microstegium vimineum*	Grass	Annual; spreads by seed
Jimsonweed	*Datura stramonium*	Flower	Noxious weed statewide
Johnson Grass	*Sorghum halepense*	Grass	PA noxious weed
Kudzu	*Pueraria lobata*	Vine	Inroads into southern PA
Mile-a-Minute Vine	*Polygonum perfoliatum*	Vine	Spreading PA noxious weed
Morrow's Honeysuckle	*Lonicera morrowii*	Shrub	Escaped from landscapes
Multiflora Rose	*Rosa multiflora*	Shrub	PA noxious weed
Musk Thistle	*Carduus nutans*	Flower	Noxious weed statewide
*Norway Maple	*Acer platanoides*	Tree	'Crimson King' is okay
Oriental Bittersweet	*Celastrus orbiculatus*	Vine	Escaped from landscapes
Purple Loosestrife	*Lythrum salicaria, L. virgatum*	Flower	Garden escape; Likes wet.
Shattercane	*Sorghum bicolor* ssp. *drummondii*	Grass	Noxious weed statewide
Standish Honeysuckle	*Lonicera standishii*	Shrub	Escaped from landscapes
Tartarian Honeysuckle	*Lonicera tatarica*	Shrub	Escaped from landscapes
Tree-of-Heaven	*Ailanthus altissima*	Tree	Wind spreads seeds

Invasive Plants to Be Watched

Common Name	Scientific Name	Form	Notes
Beefsteak Plant	*Perilla frutescens*	Flower	Escaped from gardens
Bell's Honeysuckle	*Lonicera morrowii* x *tatarica*	Shrub	Escaped from landscapes
Border Privet	*Ligustrum obtusifolium*	Shrub	Escaped from landscapes
Cheatgrass	*Bromus tectorum*	Grass	Annual, spreads by seed
Common Buckthorn	*Rhamnus catharticus*	Shrub	Becoming a problem
Common Privet	*Ligustrum vulgare*	Shrub	Landscape plant escaped
Dame's Rocket	*Hesperis matronalis*	Flower	Escaped garden plant
Eurasian Water-Milfoil	*Myriophyllum spicatum*	Flower	Aquatic plant chokes lakes
European Barberry	*Berberis vulgaris*	Shrub	Escaped from landscapes
Fiveleaf Akebia	*Akebia quinata*	Vine	Major problem near Phila.
Glossy Buckthorn	*Rhamnus frangula*	Shrub	Becoming a problem
Goutweed	*Aegopodium podagraria*	Flower	Escaped garden plant
*Japanese Barberry	*Berberis thunbergii*	Shrub	'Atropurpurea' is okay
Lesser Celandine	*Ranunculus ficaria*	Flower	Moist soil; via roots or seeds
Porcelain-Berry	*Ampelopsis brevipedunculat*	Vine	Escaped from landscapes
Reed Canary Grass	*Phalaris arundinacea*	Grass	Aggressive in wetlands
Russian Olive	*Elaegnus angustifolia*	Shrub	Escaped from landscapes
Siberian Elm	*Ulmus pumila*	Tree	Escaped from landscapes
Star-of-Bethlehem	*Ornithogalum nutans, umbellatum*	Flower	Escaped garden plant
Wild Parsnip	*Pastinaca sativa*	Flower	Roadside weed; seed spread
Wineberry	*Rubus phoenicolasius*	Shrub	Weedy bramble; seed spread

Invasive Plants in Southeastern Pennsylvania

Common Name	Scientific Name	Form	Notes
*Callery Pear	*Pyrus calleryana*	Tree	Escapes from street planting
Empress Tree	*Paulownia tomentosa*	Tree	Prolific seeds spread trees
*Guelder Rose	*Viburnum opulus* var. *opulus*	Shrub	Escapes from landscapes
*Japanese Spiraea	*Spiraea japonica*	Shrub	Overplanted; escapes
*Maiden Grass	*Miscanthus sinensis*	Grass	Some varieties seed around
Sycamore Maple	*Acer pseudoplatanus*	Tree	Escapes from yards by seed
Water Chestnut	*Trapa natans*	Flower	Likes wetlands; do not plant
*Winged Euonymus	*Euonymus alatus*	Shrub	Escapes to moist forests

Gardens to Visit *in Pennsylvania*

The American College Arboretum
> 270 South Bryn Mawr Avenue
> Bryn Mawr, PA 19010
> (610) 526-1229; (610) 526-1100
> http://www.amercoll.edu

This 35-acre campus was developed as an arboretum when the college purchased the property in 1959. It features fine old trees, plus planted annual, perennial, and vegetable gardens.

Amish Farm and House
> 2395 Route 30 East
> Lancaster, PA 17602
> (717) 394-6185
> www.amishfarmandhouse.com

The everyday farm life of an Amish family and their gardens.

Appleford Manor
> 770 Mount Moro Road
> Villanova, PA 19085
> (610) 525-9430
> www.mainlineevents.com/facilities/appleford.htm

This municipally owned 22-acre property features formal and informal planted areas, including a parterre garden.

Arboretum Villanova
> Villanova University
> 800 Lancaster Avenue
> Villanova, PA 19085
> (610) 519-4426
> www.villanova.edu

The 222-acre campus has 100 tree species plus flowering annuals, perennials, and bulbs.

Awbury Arboretum
> The Francis Cope House
> One Awbury Road
> Philadelphia, PA 19138-1505
> (215) 849-2855
> www.awbury.org

This house with its planted grounds, 55 acres of green, was the summer retreat of Henry Cope, Quaker businessman and philanthropist. It features trails and open lawns reminiscent of an English park.

The Barnes Foundation Arboretum
> 300 North Latches Lane
> Merion, PA 19066
> (610) 667-0290
> www.barnesfoundation.org

This arboretum was established by Albert C. and Laura Barnes in 1922 on the grounds of their home, and art gallery filled with Mr. Barnes's unique collection of Impressionist and Post-Impressionist paintings. The gardens were designed to supplement the art appreciation classes held there.

Botanical Gardens of the Reading Museum
500 Museum Road
Wyomissing, PA 19610
(215) 373-1525
www.readingpublicmuseum.org

Bowman's Hill Wildflower Preserve
Washington Crossing State Park
Route 32
New Hope, PA 18938-0685
(215) 862-2924
www.bhwp.org
A subdivision of Washington Crossing Historic Park, this first wildflower preserve in Pennsylvania is dedicated to educating the public about preserving native plants. Among the 800 species of native plants there are 80 that are endangered to some degree. Birders will enjoy the Sinkler Observation Area for nesting and migrating birds and indoor displays.

Brandywine Conservancy and Brandywine River Museum
Route 1 (near Route 100)
P.O. Box 141
Chadds Ford, PA 19317
(610) 388-2700
www.brandywinemuseum.org
On the grounds of the Brandywine River Museum, which features the art of the Wyeth family, naturalistic wildflower plantings in varied habitats, including parking areas, embody the mission of preserving, protecting, and sharing the natural resources of the Brandywine Valley area.

Chanticleer
786 Church Road
Wayne, PA 19087
(610) 687-4163
http://www.chanticleergarden.org
The former estate of Adolph Rosengarten is now a 30-acre pleasure garden featuring thousands of bulbs, Roses, vegetables, fruit trees, containers, and courtyards.

Chatham College Arboretum
Woodland Road
Pittsburgh, PA 15232
(412) 365-1157
http://chatham.edu/

Cliveden of the National Trust
6401 Germantown Avenue
Philadelphia, PA 19144
(215) 848-1777
This was the summer home of Chief Justice Benjamin Chew (1763–67), and scene of the Battle of Germantown, October 4, 1777. There are a museum and 60 acres of trees and gardens.

Colonial Pennsylvania Plantation
Ridley Creek State Park
Sycamore Mills Road
Media, PA 19063
(215) 566-4800
www.colonialplantation.org
This farm museum re-creates daily 18th-century farm life. Authentically dressed staff provide educational demonstrations of traditional tasks on a farm. It features an enclosed vegetable garden and animal pens as well as the farmhouse and outbuildings.

Conestoga House and Garden
8 West King Street
Lancaster, PA 17603
(717) 291-8793
www.demuth.org/garden.htm
Lovely colonial revival mansion surrounded by beds, borders, patios, and pools full of annuals, perennials, hanging baskets, and water plants.

Coover Arboretum
Route 3
Dillsburg, PA 17019
(717) 766-6681
By appointment only.

Crozer Arboretum
1 Medical Center Boulevard
Upland, PA 19018
(610) 447-2281
The grounds of the former theological seminary, now part of a hospital campus, feature fine trees and other plantings.

Curtis Arboretum
Cedar Crest College
100 College Drive
Allentown, PA 18104-6196
(800) 360-1222

Ebenezer Maxwell Mansion
200 West Tulpehocken Street
Philadelphia, PA 19444
(215) 438-1861
This accurately re-created Victorian garden is composed of more than 150 varieties of period plants—trees, shrubs, herbaceous plants, ferns, and vines.

Erie Zoological Park and Botanical Garden
423 West 38th Street
Erie, PA 16508
(814) 874-4091

Fairmount Park Horticulture Center

North Horticultural Drive and Montgomery Avenue
P.O. Box 21601
Philadelphia, PA 19131
(215) 685-0096
www.shofuso.org

The center anchors the 8,000 acres of Fairmount Park, the largest urban park in North America. The conservatory is the site of the Pennsylvania Horticultural Society's annual Harvest Show and contains a year-round display. It is surrounded by lovely grounds with gardens and display areas.

Fallingwater

Mill Run, PA 15464
(412) 767-9200

Site of the famous house built by Frank Lloyd Wright, the woodland landscape of trails bordered by Rhododendrons and Azaleas complements that architectural wonder.

Five Senses Garden

Route 441
Swatara Township, PA
c/o S. Disend
409 Latshsmere Drive
Harrisburg, PA 17109
(717) 564-0488

Garden and nature site.

Friends Hospital

4641 Roosevelt Boulevard
Philadelphia, PA 19124
(215) 831-4781

The grounds of this hospital feature woodland trails through groves of Azaleas and Rhododendrons, plus interesting plantings among its various buildings.

The Grange Estate

Myrtle Avenue and Warwick Road
Havertown, PA 19083
(610) 446-4958

This country estate of Henry Lewis, a Welsh Quaker, is listed on the National Register of Historic Places. It features sheltered gardens and woodlands overlooking Cobb's Creek.

Hartwood

215 Saxonburg Road
Pittsburgh, PA 15238
(412) 767-9200

The grounds of this historic mansion are planted in gardens.

Haverford College Arboretum

370 Lancaster Avenue (Route 3)
Haverford, PA 19041
(610) 896-1101
www.haverford.edu/arboretum/home.htm

This arboretum is on 216 acres of a tract originally deeded to Welsh Quakers and purchased in 1831 for a college. It features 3 Pennsylvania State Champion trees, a duck pond, an herb garden, and a Japanese Zen garden.

Helbling Farms

212 Little Beaver Road
Enon Valley, PA 16120
(724) 336-3276

The Henry Foundation for Botanical Research

801 Stony Lane (off Henry Lane)
Gladwyne, PA 19035
(610) 525-2037

It was founded by Mary Gibson Henry in 1948 for her collection of plants acquired over 40 years of extensive plant-collecting travels.

The Henry Schmeider Arboretum

Delaware Valley College of Science and Agriculture
Route 202 and New Britain Road
Doylestown, PA 18901
215-489-2283
www.devalcol.edu/arboretum

Named to honor a revered professor, this campus arboretum serves as an outdoor laboratory for Delaware Valley College's horticulture programs. In addition to century-old trees, there are special collection gardens to aid study. The Lois Burpee Herb Garden and others are featured on the self-guided tour.

Hershey Rose Gardens

Hershey Hotel
Hershey, PA 17033
(717) 534-3493

Milton Hershey established this 23-acre garden in 1937. Beginning with 3 acres of Roses, it has expanded over the years to include theme gardens full of annuals, bulbs, grasses, perennials, as well as trees and shrubs in view of the Hershey chocolate factory.

The Highlands Mansion and Gardens

7001 Sheaff Lane
Fort Washington, PA 19034
(215) 646-9355

Originally the estate of Anthony Morris, a Quaker lawyer, it represents a remarkable blend of the taste and technology of its day. Caroline Sinkler bought it in 1917 and installed formal gardens, which won a Gold Medal for Excellence from the Pennsylvania Horticultural Society in 1933.

Hill-Physick-Keith House

    321 South Fourth Street
    Philadelphia, PA 19106
    (215) 925-7866

For 20 years, this was the home of Philip Syng Physick, a famous colonial doctor. It features a small 19th-century walled city garden.

Historic Bartram's Gardens

    Fifty-fourth Street and Lindbergh Boulevard
    Philadelphia, PA 19143
    (215) 729-5281
    http://www.bartramsgarden.org

Home of King George III's Royal Botanist for North America and a National Historic Landmark, this is America's oldest living botanical garden. It is a repository of the plants discovered by Quaker farmer John Bartram and his son in the attempt to document all the native plants in the New World. The interesting house reflects the complex character of its owner, and the grounds contain the oldest Ginkgo tree in the country.

Independence National Historical Park

    Visitors' Center
    Third and Chestnut Streets
    Philadelphia, PA 19106
    (215) 597-8974

The historical district of Philadelphia contains plantings and individual gardens at Franklin Court, Independence Square, and other sites that reflect the fact that Philadelphia was the center of American horticulture. Directions and self-guided tour information are available at the visitors' center.

The Japanese House and Garden

    The Horticulture Center
    North Horticulture Drive at Montgomery Drive
    Philadelphia, PA 19131
    (215) 878-5097

Originally landscaped for the 1876 Centennial Exposition held in Philadelphia, the current garden was designed in 1958 when the tea house was moved from the Museum of Modern Art in New York to Fairmount Park. It was subsequently renovated for the 1976 Bicentennial celebration.

Jenkins Arboretum

    Elizabeth Phillippe Jenkins Foundation
    631 Berwyn-Baptist Road
    Devon, PA 19333
    (215) 647-8870
    www.jenkinsarboretum.org

A preserved remnant of the hardwood forest of Southeastern Pennsylvania, it features the native flora of Eastern North America and specializes in Rhododendrons from all over the world.

John Heinz National Wildlife Refuge and Environmental Center
Lindbergh Boulevard and Eighty-sixth Street
Philadelphia, PA
(215) 365-3118
http://www.heinz.fws.gov/
The refuge and center feature a tidal wetlands habitat and trails for biking.

Landis Valley Museum
2451 Kissel Hill Road
Lancaster, PA 17602
(717) 569-0401
Features German rural life in Pennsylvania. Gardens on the grounds include a beautiful herb garden.

Lee and Virginia Graver Arboretum of Muhlenberg College
Bushkill Township
(610) 759-3132
This arboretum serves the educational mission of the college and is available for research and the enjoyment of the beauty of nature. Make advance arrangements for a visit.

Longwood Gardens
Routes 1 and 52
Kennett Square, PA 19348
(610) 388-1000
http://www.longwoodgardens.org
This former home of Pierre duPont is the premier display garden in the United States, featuring 11,000 types of plants on 1,050 acres of meticulously maintained conservatory displays, formal gardens, and woodlands, augmented by fountain and fireworks displays.

Malcom W. Gross Memorial Rose Garden Portraits
2700 Parkway Boulevard
Allentown, PA 18104

Masonic Homes Arboretum
Elizabethtown, PA 17033
(717) 367-1121
This historic property holds a valuable and interesting collection of trees and shrubs.

Maywood University Arboretum
2300 Adams Avenue
Scranton, PA 18509
(717) 384-6265

Mont Alto Arboretum
Mont Alto Campus of Pennsylvania State University
Mont Alto, PA 17237
(717) 749-3111
Features woody plants.

Morris Arboretum of the University of Pennsylvania
100 Northwestern Avenue
Philadelphia, PA 19118
(215) 247-5777
http://www.upenn.edu/morris
Established in 1932 on the site of the home of siblings John and Lydia Morris, it is today 92 acres of rare woody plants set in a Victorian landscape. It is the official arboretum of the Commonwealth of Pennsylvania.

Mount Assisi Monastery
Loretto, PA 15940
(814) 472-8971

Olmstead Manor and Gardens
Box 8, Route #6
Ludlow, PA 16333
(814) 945-6512

Pennsbury Manor
East of Bordentown Road and north of Exit 29 of Pennsylvania Turnpike
Morristown, PA
(215) 946-0400
http://www.libertynet.org/pensbury
The grounds of this former county home of William Penn have 23 buildings and gardens that represent colonial living of his era. Among them are a formal flower garden, a kitchen garden, a vineyard, and an orchard.

Pennsylvania State University Test Gardens
Bigler Road and East Park Avenue
University Park, PA 16802
(814) 865-2571
Site of extensive trials of hundreds of annuals, vegetables, and Rose varieties.

Philadelphia Zoological Garden
Thirty-fourth Street and Girard Avenue
Philadelphia, PA 19104
(215) 243-1100
www.phillyzoo.org
The oldest zoo in America is also a garden, featuring some fine old trees and naturalistic plantings to complement the animals on display and provide them habitat.

Phipps Conservatory
Shenley Park
Pittsburgh, PA 15213
(412) 622-6914
www.phipps.conservatory.org
The lovely Victorian conservatory, which displays an impressive array of plantings and theme gardens, is surrounded by landscaped gardens and a downtown park.

Phipps Garden Center
1059 Shady Avenue
Pittsburgh, PA 15232
(412) 441-4442

Physick Garden
Eighth and Pine Streets
Philadelphia, PA 19107
(215) 829-3971

This tiny garden of 18th-century medicinal plants was the dream of doctors at nearby Pennsylvania Hospital in 1774. It would provide them a source of botanical compounds for treatment of patients. Only in 1976, as a celebration of the bicentennial, were appropriate plants actually planted at the site.

Reading Rehabilitation Hospital
Morgantown Road
Reading, PA 19607
(610) 777-7615

An official All-America Display Garden, this site for horticultural therapy is also planted with trees, shrubs, perennials, and annuals.

Renzeehausen Park Rose Garden and Arboretum
McKeesport, PA 15131
(412) 672-1050

Rodale Institute
611 Siegfriedale Road
Kutztown, PA 19530
(215) 683-6383
www.rodaleinstitute.org

A demonstration and workshop garden open to self-guided tours May through October. Gardens of ornamental and food crops grown by organic methods are on display.

Rodef Shalom Biblical Botanic Garden
4905 Fifth Avenue
Pittsburgh, PA 15213
(412) 621-6566

Scott Arboretum
Swarthmore College
Route 320 (Chester Road)
Swarthmore, PA 19081
(610) 328-8025
www.scottarboretum.org

Integrated into the 300-acre campus of Swarthmore College, this arboretum showcases trees, shrubs, and perennials recommended for Philadelphia-area gardens. Labeled collections of Hollies, Maples, Lilacs, Rhododendrons, and many others share the grounds with several special gardens and a remarkable outdoor amphitheater where graduation is held annually.

Stonehedge Gardens
RD #3, Box 190
Tamaqua, PA 18252
(570) 386-4276
Six acres of garden. Open to the public.

Sunken Garden of Riverfront Park
Front and Verbecke Streets
Harrisburg, PA 17101
(717) 255-3020
This public garden features lovely landscaping in a wonderful setting.

Taylor Memorial Arboretum
10 Ridley Drive
Wallingford, PA 19086
(610) 876-2649
These 30 acres nestled along Ridley Creek were dedicated to the public for their health, education, and pleasure in 1931 by Chester lawyer and banker Joshua C. Taylor. The arboretum features a Fern grotto at a former quarry site and a waterfall and millrace dating from 1740. The Bald Cypress marsh supports Cattails and other water plants, which are habitat for a variety of wildlife. Trails reveal meadows and collections of Azaleas, Viburnum, and three Pennsylvania Champion trees.

Temple University, Ambler Campus
School of Landscape Architecture/Horticulture
Butler Pike and Meeting House Road
Ambler, PA 19002-3994
(215) 283-1292
http://www.temple.edu/
Around this campus garden 800 species of plants are on view. Among the attractions are special dwarf shrubs, woodlands, and an herb garden, as well as an orchard and formal perennial garden.

Tyler Arboretum
515 Painter Road
Media, PA 19063
(610) 566-5431
www.tylerarboretum.org
Presently encompassing 650 acres, the arboretum is composed of several parcels of land dating from a land grant in 1681, including one owned by the Quaker Painter brothers who planted enormous numbers of shrubs and trees. There are trails through woods and planted collections, and a meadow maze for fun. Two especially unique features are the huge Sequoia and a remnant of serpentine barrens.

Wildflower Reserve
Raccoon Creek State Park
3000 SR 18
Hookstown, PA 15050
(724) 899-3611

Wildwood Arboretum and Botanical Garden

3300 North Cameron Street Road
Harrisburg, PA 17110
(717) 780-2300.
www.hac.edu/COLLEGE/UNIQUE/ANSOR

Two hundred acres showcase wetland, meadow, and woodland habitat. Gardens on the grounds feature use of wild native plants among cultivated garden ones.

The Woodlands

4000 Woodland Avenue
Philadelphia, PA 19104
(215) 386-2181

The 55 acres of this Victorian garden cemetery and remarkable home are a National Historic Landmark.

Wyck House

6026 Germantown Avenue
Philadelphia, PA 19144
(215) 848-1690
www.wyck.org

This was home to generations of the horticulturally inclined Quaker families of Wistars and Hainses. The landscape includes a garden of old Roses and has not been altered since the 1820s.

The Pennsylvania Horticultural

Since 1988 the Pennsylvania Horticultural Society's Gold Medal Plant Award program has honored little-known and underused woody plants of exceptional merit for gardens. They are chosen for their beauty, superior performance, and hardiness in zones 5 through 7 and are, therefore, appropriate for landscapes and gardens throughout Pennsylvania.

Each year a distinguished committee of the Philadelphia area's most knowledgeable horticulturists from local arboreta, public or private gardens, and allied industries evaluate plants that have been nominated for the Gold Medal. They choose from among the candidates several annual award winners. Some of these plants are familiar standbys, others obscure or virtually unknown to the average home-owner. They may be native to Pennsylvania or introduced from elsewhere in this country or other parts of the world.

For additional information, please feel free to contact the Pennsylvania Horticultural Society at 215-988-8800.

Plants are listed here by common name, followed by their botanical name and the date they were awarded the Gold Medal. (An asterisk indicates that the genus is mentioned in this book.)

American Yellowwood (*Cladrastis kentukea*) 1994
Arborvitae* (*Thuja* 'Green Giant') 1998
Birch*:
    River Birch (*Betula nigra* 'Heritage') 1990
Boxwood*:
    Buxus 'Green Velvet' 1995
    Buxus sempervirens 'Vardar Valley' 2002
Buckeye:
    Bottlebrush Buckeye (*Aesculus parviflora*) 1998
    Red Buckeye (*Aesculus pavia*) 1995
Chinese Trumpetcreeper (*Campsis grandiflora* 'Morning Calm') 2002
Clematis*:
    Clematis 'Betty Corning' 1992
Crabapple*:
    Malus 'Adirondack' 1989
    Malus 'Donald Wyman' 1989
    Malus 'Jewelberry' 1989
Daphne*:
    Caucasian Daphne (*Daphne caucasica*) 1990
Dawn Redwood (*Metasequoia glyptostroboides*) 1999
Deutzia:
    Slender Deutzia (*Deutzia gracilis* 'Nikko') 1989
Dogwood*:
    Cornelian Cherry Dogwood (*Cornus mas* 'Golden Glory') 2001

Japanese Dogwood *Cornus kousa* (*C. florida* 'Rutban' Aurora™) 1993
Japanese Dogwood *Cornus kousa* (*C. florida* 'Rutlan' Ruth Ellen™) 1993
Redosier Dogwood (*Cornus sericea* 'Silver and Gold') 1990
Eastern Ninebark (*Physocarpus opulifolius* 'Diablo' Diablo™) 2002
Eastern Redcedar (*Juniperus virginiana* 'Corcorcor' Emerald Sentinel™) 1997
English Ivy* (*Hedera helix* 'Buttercup') 1998
Fothergilla*:
    Dwarf Fothergilla (*Fothergilla gardenii* 'Blue Mist') 1990
Goldenrain Tree* (*Koelreuteria paniculata* 'September') 1997
Hawthorn*:
    Green Hawthorn (*Crataegus viridis* 'Winter King') 1992
Holly*:
    American Holly (*Ilex opaca*) 2002
    Blue Holly (*Ilex meserveae* 'Mesid' Blue Maid™) 1996
    Inkberry (*Ilex glabra* 'Densa') 1994
    Winterberry (*Ilex* 'Harvest Red') 1991
    Winterberry (*Ilex* 'Sparkleberry') 1998

Society's Gold Medal Awards

Winterberry (*Ilex verticillata* 'Scarlett O'Hara') 1996

Winterberry (*Ilex verticillata* 'Winter Red') 1995

Hydrangea*:

Bigleaf Hydrangea (*Hydrangea macrophylla* 'Blue Billow') 1990

Oakleaf Hydrangea (*Hydrangea quercifolia* 'Snow Queen') 1989

Smooth Hydrangea (*Hydrangea arborescens* 'Annabelle') 2001

Japanese Cedar (*Cryptomeria japonica* 'Yoshino') 1993

Japanese Climbing Hydrangea* (*Schizophragma hydrangeoides* 'Moonlight') 1998

Japanese Plum Yew (*Cephalotaxus harringtonia* 'Prostrata') 1994

Japanese Umbrella Pine (*Sciadopitys verticillata*) 1991

Japanese Zelkova* (*Zelkova serrata* 'Green Vase') 1998

Korean Stewartia (*Stewartia pseudocammellia* var. *koreana*) 1990

Lilac*:

Japanese Tree Lilac (*Syringa reticulata* 'Ivory Silk') 1996

Meyer's Lilac (*Syringa meyeri* 'Palibin') 2000

Magnolia*:

Magnolia 'Elizabeth' 1998

Magnolia 'Galaxy' 1992

Magnolia grandiflora 'Edith Bogue' 1992

Star Magnolia (*Magnolia kobus* var. *stellata* 'Centennial') 1997

Mahonia*:

Leatherleaf Mahonia (*Mahonia bealei*) 1998

Maple*:

Japanese Maple (*Acer palmatum* 'Tamukeyama') 1997

Japanese Maple (*Acer palmatum* 'Waterfall') 1999

Paperbark Maple (*Acer griseum*) 1993

Three-flowered Maple (*Acer triflorum*) 1996

Trident Maple (*Acer buergerianum*) 2000

Nordmann Fir (*Abies nordmanniana*) 1992

Oriental Spruce (*Picea orientalis*) 1992

Ornamental Cherry*:

Prunus 'Hally Jolivette' 1994

Prunus 'Okame' 1998

Persian Parrotia (*Parrotia persica*) 2000

Purple Beautyberry* (*Callicarpa dichotoma*) 1989

Red Chokeberry (*Aronia arbutifolium* 'Brilliantissima') 2000

Rose of Sharon* (*Hibiscus syriacus* 'Diana') 1991

Seven-son Flower (*Heptacodium miconioides*) 1995

Silverbell (*Halesia diptera* var. *magniflora*) 1995

Summersweet*:

Clethra alnifolia 'Hummingbird' 1994

Clethra alnifolia 'Ruby Spice' 1998

Viburnum*:

Burkwood Viburnum (*Viburnum* x *burkwoodii* 'Conoy') 1997

Burkwood Viburnum (*Viburnum* x *burkwoodii* 'Mohawk') 1993

Double File Viburnum (*Viburnum plicatum* f. *tomentosum* 'Shasta') 1991

Linden Viburnum (*Viburnum dilatatum* 'Erie') 1993

Smooth With-rod (*Viburnum nudum* 'Winterthur') 1991

Viburnum 'Eskimo' 1992

Virginia Sweetspire* (*Itea virginica* 'Henry's Garnet') 1998

Weigela* (*Weigela florida* 'Alexandra' Wine and Roses) 2000

White Enkianthus (*Enkianthus perulatus* 'J. L. Pennock') 1999

White Oak* (*Quercus alba*) 2000

Witchhazel*:

Chinese Witchhazel (*Hamamelis mollis* 'Pallida') 1989

Hybrid Witchhazel (*Hamamelis intermedia* 'Diane') 1991

List courtesy of Pennsylvania Horticultural Society

Information Resources

All-America Selections

Nona Wolfram-Koivula

1311 Butterfield Road

Suite 310

Downer's Grove, IL 60515

(630) 963-0770

American Rose Society

P.O. Box 30,000

Shreveport, LA 71130-0030

(318) 938-5402

http://www.ars.org

International Society of Arboriculture

Derek Vannice

P.O. Box 3129

Champaign, IL 61826

(217) 355-9411

E-mail: isa@isa-arbor.com

National Audubon Society

700 Broadway

New York, NY 10003

(212) 979-3000

http://www.audubon.org

National Wildlife Federation

Backyard Wildlife Habitat Program

8925 Leesburg Pike

Vienna, VA 22184-0001

(703) 790-4434

http://www.carskaddan@nwf.org

Netherlands Flower Bulb Information Center

Sally Ferguson

30 Midwood Street

Brooklyn, NY 11225

(718) 693-5400

http://www.bulb.com

Pennsylvania Department of Agriculture

2301 North Cameron Street

Harrisburg, PA 17110

(717) 787-4737

Pennsylvania Horticultural Society

100 North Twentieth Street

5th Floor

Philadelphia, PA 19103-1495

(215) 988-8800

http://www.libertynet.org/phs

Turfgrass Producers International

Douglas H. Fender

1855-A Hicks Road

Rolling Meadows, IL 60008

(800) 405-TURF

www.TurfGrassSod.org

Western Pennsylvania Conservancy

209 Fourth Avenue

Pittsburgh, PA 15222

(412) 288-2777

www.paconserve.org

Mail-Order Sources

Bowman's Hill Wildflower Preserve

P.O. Box 685

New Hope, PA

(215) 862-2924

www.bhwp.org

Native plant seeds

Brent and Becky's Bulbs

7463 Heath Trail

Gloucester, VA 23601

(804) 693-3966

Bulbs

Burpee Seed Company

300 Park Avenue

Warminster, PA 18974

(215) 674-9633

http://www.burpee.com

Seeds, flowering plants

Conard-Pyle Co.

372 Rose Hill Road

West Grove, PA 19390

(800) 458-6559

www.starroses.com

Roses, shrubs

Duncraft

102 Fisherville Road

Concord, NH 03303-2086

(800) 593-5656

www.duncraft.com

Bird supplies

Ernst Conservation Seeds

9006 Mercer Pike

Meadville, PA 16335

(814) 425-7276

www.cernst@gremlan.org

Native plants

Ferry-Morse Seeds

P.O. Box 488

Fulton, KY 42041-0488

(800) 283-3400

www.ferry-morse.com

Seeds

Forest Farm

990 Tetherow Road

Williams, OR 97544-9599

(541) 846-7269

http://www.forestfarm.com

Trees, shrubs, perennials

Gardener's Supply Company

128 Intervale Road

Burlington, VT 05401

(802) 863-1700

http://www.gardeners.com

Tools and supplies

Lilypons Water Gardens

7000 Lilypons Road

P.O. Box 10

Buckeystown, MD 21717-0010

(301) 874-5504

Aquatic plants, fish, supplies

Musser Forests

P.O. Box S-91M

Indiana, PA 15701

(412) 465-5685

Park Seed Company

P.O. Box 31

Greenwood, SC 29647

(800) 845-3369

http://www.parkseed.com

Flower and vegetable seeds

Plow and Hearth

560 Main Street

Madison, VA 22727

(800) 627-1712

www.plowhearth.com

Tools and supplies

Seeds of Change

P.O. Box 15700

Santa Fe, NM 87506-5700

Organically grown vegetable and flower seeds

Wayside Gardens

1 Garden Lane

Hodges, SC 29695-0001

(800) 845-1124

http://www.waysidegardens.com

Perennials, shrubs, roses, bulbs

We-Du Nurseries

Route 5, Box 724

Marion, NC 28752-9338

(704) 738-8300

Perennials, wildflowers

Glossary

Acclimate, acclimatize: to foster a plant's ability to adjust to significantly cooler or warmer conditions. Commonly used when discussing moving houseplants or seedlings that spend time indoors and outdoors either out or in. See Hardening off.

Acidic: soil with a pH that measures below 7.0, indicating acid conditions. This type of soil is typical of Pennsylvania. Some degree of acidity is preferred by most plants that grow well here.

Alkaline soil: soil with a pH measuring greater than 7.0. It lacks acidity, often because it has limestone in it. Pennsylvania has no significant areas of naturally alkaline soil.

All-purpose fertilizer: powdered, liquid, or granular fertilizer with a balanced proportion of the three key nutrients—nitrogen (N), potassium (P), and phosphorus (K). It is suitable for maintenance nutrition for most plants.

Amendment: material added to inferior soil to improve its fertility, texture, or both. Organic materials, such as compost, manure, peat moss, and chopped leaves, are commonly used amendments.

Annual: a plant that lives its entire life in one season. It is genetically determined to germinate, grow, flower, set seed, and die the same year.

Anti-transpirants: also called anti-desiccants, these products are designed to reduce the loss of moisture through plant foliage by means of transpiration. They are typically sprays that thinly coat leaf surfaces.

Arborist: a person who cares for trees as a profession. A certified arborist is specially trained and certified to be an expert in planting, pruning, and treating tree problems.

Backfill: to return the loose soil dug from a planting hole after the tree or shrub rootball has been set into it.

Balled and burlapped: describes a tree or shrub grown in the field whose soilball has been wrapped with protective burlap and twine when the plant is dug up to be sold or transplanted.

Bare root: plants that have been packaged without any soil around their roots. (Often young shrubs and trees purchased through the mail arrive with their exposed roots covered with moist peat or sphagnum moss, sawdust, or similar material, and wrapped in plastic.)

Barrier plant: any plant that has intimidating thorns or spines and is sited purposely to block foot traffic or other access to the home or yard.

Beneficial insects: insects or their larvae that prey on pest organisms and their eggs. They may be flying insects (such as ladybugs, parasitic wasps, praying mantids, and soldier bugs) or soil dwellers such as predatory nematodes, spiders, and ants.

Berm: soil mounded up to form an elevated area in the landscape for planting. Also, it is the small ridge of packed soil made after planting trees that rings their root zone, creating a water-holding reservoir.

Biennial: plants that take two years to complete their life cycle. They grow vegetatively the first growing season, winter over, then produce reproductive parts, flower, set seed, and die the second season.

Botanical name: a plant's formal or scientific Latin name. It is binomial, having two parts—the name of the genus and the name of the species. Because it is in a foreign language, it is italicized when written.

Bract: a modified leaf structure on a plant stem near its flower that resembles a petal. Often it is more colorful and visible than the actual flower, such as in Dogwood.

Bud union: see Graft.

Bulbs: a general term for plants that have organs formed from modified stems (bulbs, rhizomes, tubers, corms) for storing starches to provide energy for next season's growth. True bulbs feature a compressed stem and growing point or flower bud packaged in scales or thick, modified leaves as a fully formed miniature plant.

Canopy: the overhead branching area of a tree, usually referring to its extent including foliage.

Chlorosis, iron chlorosis: a nutritional disorder that sometimes occurs in acid-loving plants. Their foliage turns yellow, its veins remaining green, indicating that the plant is deprived of iron. Either the soil is depleted of iron, or more likely, the soil is not acid enough to provide its iron in a form the plant roots are able to take up.

Climber: a plant that grows vertically by means of upright stems attached to supports; a common synonym for *vine*.

Clinger: a vine, such as English Ivy, that attaches itself to walls and other supports by means of sticky rootlets (holdfasts) along the stems. It does not need trellises or arbors for support.

Cold hardiness: the ability of a perennial plant to survive the winter cold in a particular area. Plants that are listed as cold hardy to -10 degrees Fahrenheit do well in the Philadelphia area. In central and western parts of Pennsylvania plants must be cold hardy to -20 degrees or colder to overwinter safely. (See zone map, page 19.)

Composite: a flower that is actually composed of many tiny flowers. Typically, it has flat clusters of tiny, tight florets, sometimes surrounded by wider-petaled florets. Composite flowers are highly attractive to bees and beneficial insects. Examples are Daisies or Sedums.

Compost: organic matter that has undergone progressive decomposition by microbial and macrobial activity until it is reduced to a spongy, fluffy texture. Added to soil of any type, it improves the soil's ability to hold air and water and to drain well.

Conifer: a tree or shrub that produces cones. Conifers usually have needled foliage, which is evergreen, but there are exceptions such as Baldcypress, whose needles are deciduous.

Corm: the swollen energy-storing structure, analogous to a bulb, under the soil at the base of the stem of plants such as Crocus and Gladiolus.

County agent: an employee of the Pennsylvania State University's Agricultural Extension Service. Agents are assigned to each of the sixty-seven counties in the state. As trained horticulturists, they assist farmers and homeowners with information about soil, pest control, and state regulations. Soil test kits are usually available from their offices. (See page 217.)

Crown: the base of a plant at, or just beneath, the surface of the soil where the roots meet the stems. (This term is sometimes used synonymously with *canopy* to mean the upper, branching part of a tree.)

Cultivar: a CULTIvated VARiety. It is a naturally occurring form of a plant that has been identified as special or superior and is purposely selected for propagation and production.

Deadhead: a pruning technique involving clipping or pinching faded flower heads from plants to improve their appearance, abort seed production, and stimulate further flowering.

Deciduous plants: unlike evergreens, these trees, shrubs and vines lose their leaves each fall as they enter dormancy.

Desiccation: drying out of foliage tissues, usually due to drought, harsh winter sun, or wind.

Diversity, biodiversity: the presence of many species of plants and animals in a particular ecosystem. This is desirable to promote environmental health and stability.

Division: the practice of splitting apart perennial plants to create several smaller-rooted segments. It is useful for controlling the plant's size and for acquiring more plants; it is also essential to the health and continued flowering of certain ones.

Dormancy: the period, usually the winter, when perennial plants temporarily cease active growth and rest. Some plants such as spring-blooming bulbs go dormant in the summer to cope with the heat.

Dwarf: forms of plants that are smaller than the normal mature size of their species. This does not necessarily mean that they are tiny.

Escape: the spreading of cultivated plants into natural areas by means of careless handling, transporting of seeds by wind or birds, or running roots or stems.

Established: the point at which a newly planted tree, shrub, or flower begins to produce new growth, either foliage or stems. This is an indication that the roots have recovered from transplant shock and have begun to grow and spread.

Evergreen: describes woody perennial plants that do not lose their foliage annually with the onset of winter. The term refers to needled or broadleaf foliage that persists and continues to function on a plant through one or more winters, aging and dropping unobtrusively in cycles of three or four years or more.

Fast-acting (fertilizers): either liquid fertilizer products or granular ones whose nutrients, especially the nitrogen, dissolve in water. Water-soluble nutrients are easily and quickly absorbed through plant roots or foliage tissues.

Fertilizer: a product intended to supplement the soil's natural supply of essential plant nutrients—nitrogen (N), phosphorus (P), and potassium (K). Complete, or all-purpose, fertilizers contain proportions of these three major nutrients and often trace amounts of others, whereas special purpose or incomplete products feature just one or a few.

Foliar: of or about foliage. This term usually refers to the practice of spraying plant foliage (foliar spray), as in fertilizing or treating with insecticide. Leaf tissues absorb liquid directly for much faster results, and the soil is not affected.

Floret: a tiny flower, usually one of many, forming a cluster that comprises a single blossom such as a Lilac or Spider Flower.

Fungicide: any product or compound that acts to prevent, control, or eradicate plant diseases caused by fungi, such as mildew, rust, or certain leaf spots and rots.

Genus: the main classification of a plant and the first word of its binomial scientific name. Hydrangea and Rhododendron are genus names. (The plural of genus is genera.)

Germinate: to sprout. Germination is a fertile seed's first stage of development.

Glaucous: description of foliage with a waxy coating that gives it a bluish or whitish tinge, such as the coloring on the needles of Blue Spruce.

Grabber: a type of vine that climbs by means of special tendrils that typically develop from their leaf stems for this purpose.

Graft (union): the point on the stem of a woody plant having sturdier roots where a stem from a highly ornamental plant is inserted so that it will join with it. Roses are commonly grafted.

Habitat: the natural environment of a plant. A plant removed from its habitat and brought into cultivation in a residential landscape does best when the new conditions are similar to those of its native habitat to which it is adapted.

Handpick: to eliminate pest insects or slugs and caterpillars by plucking them from plant foliage, usually followed by knocking them into a plastic bag or jar of soapy water to kill them.

Hardening off: the process of gradually acclimating indoor plants—houseplants or seedlings raised under lights—to outdoor weather in the spring.

Hardscape: the permanent, structural, nonplant part of a landscape, such as walls, sheds, pools, patios, arbors, and walkways.

Hardy: refers to the capacity of a plant to withstand temperature variations. Cold-hardy plants have roots that can survive some cold where they grow during the winter; heat-hardy plants can survive the highest summer temperatures where they are cultivated. See zones.

Herbaceous: plants having fleshy or soft stems that die back with frost; the opposite of woody.

Herbicide: any product, compound, or chemical agent that kills plants. Some act on foliage, stem, or root tissues; others (pre-emergent) act on seeds. Broad-spectrum types kill all vegetation indiscriminately. Selective ones limit their effect to broadleaf plants or grasses specifically.

Hybrid: a plant that is the result of intentional or natural cross-pollination between two or more plants of the same species or genus.

Hydrophytic: the capacity to grow in water. Hydrophytic plants have roots that are adapted to an aquatic environment.

Insecticide: any product, compound, or garden aid formulated, designed, or used for the purpose of killing insects. It may either be natural or of laboratory origin.

Invasive: the tendency of a vigorous plant to spread rapidly and inappropriately. Often denotes an aggressive habit that overtakes and destroys less rampant species, especially plants introduced from other regions that engulf native plants.

Leader: synonym for tree trunk, or main stem.

Lime: limestone processed as granules, pellets, or powder used to raise the pH of the soil (reduces its acidity, especially where turfgrass is cultivated). It adds calcium to soils in planted beds. Dolomite limestone also provides magnesium to the soil.

Low-water-demand: describes plants that tolerate dry soil for varying periods of time. Typically, they have succulent, hairy, or silvery-gray foliage and tuberous roots or taproots.

Microclimate: the special climate conditions in small portions of an area that deviate from the prevailing climate. For instance, areas sheltered by masonry walls or hedges are typically warmer than the yard as a whole.

Mulch: a layer of material over bare soil to protect it from erosion and compaction by rain, and to discourage weeds. It may be inorganic (gravel, fabric) or organic (wood chips, bark, pine needles, chopped leaves).

Native plant: a plant that is documented to have existed in a particular region or ecosystem in the U.S. before the arrival of European settlers. Also, a plant that is indigenous to North America.

Naturalize: (*a*) to plant seeds, bulbs, or plants in a random, informal pattern as they would appear in their natural habitat; (*b*) to adapt to and spread throughout adopted habitats (a tendency of some nonnative plants).

Nectar: the sweet fluid produced by glands on flowers that attract pollinators such as hummingbirds and honeybees for whom it is a source of energy.

Node: the ridged scar, swollen joint, or visible ring on a plant stem that indicates a growing point for a leaf or stem.

Organic material, organic matter: any material or debris that is derived from plants. Carbon-based material capable of undergoing decomposition and decay.

Peat moss: organic matter from peat sedges (United States) or sphagnum mosses (Canada) often used to improve soil texture. The acidity of sphagnum peat moss makes it ideal for boosting or maintaining soil acidity while also improving its drainage.

Perennial: a flowering plant that lives over two or more seasons. Many die back with frost, but their roots survive the winter and generate new shoots in the spring.

pH: a measurement of the relative acidity (low pH) or alkalinity (high pH) of soil or water based on a scale of 1 to 14, 7 being neutral. Individual plants require soil to be within a certain range so that the nutrients they need can be available for uptake by their roots. Pennsylvania soils are typically acidic. Little naturally alkaline soil is to be found here.

Photosynthesis: the process whereby plants create sugar, carbohydrates, from carbon dioxide and water using energy from the sun. A way of describing plant metabolism.

Phytotoxic: poisonous to plants. Certain insecticides destroy foliage tissues on some plants. To determine their phytotoxicity, apply them to a small test area on a leaf first.

Pinch: to remove tender stems or leaves by pressing them between thumb and forefinger. This pruning technique encourages branching, compactness, and flowering in plants. It also removes aphids clustered at growing tips.

Pollen: the yellow, powdery grains in the center of a flower. A plant's male sex cells, they are transferred to the female plant parts by means of wind or animal pollinators to fertilize them and create seeds.

Pond liner: a molded fiberglass form or a flexible butyl or poly fabric that creates an artificial pond for the purpose of water gardening.

Rhizome: a swollen energy-storing stem structure, similar to a bulb, that lies horizontally in the soil, with roots emerging from its lower surface and growth shoots from a growing point at or near its tip, as with Bearded Iris.

Rootbound (or potbound): the condition of a plant that has been confined to a container too long, its roots having been forced to wrap around themselves and even swell out of the container. Successful transplanting or repotting requires untangling, cutting through, or trimming away some of the matted roots.

Root flare: the transition area at the base of a tree trunk where the bark tissue begins to differentiate and roots begin to form just prior to entering the soil. This area should not be covered with soil when planting a tree.

Self-seeding: the tendency of some plants to sow their seeds freely around the yard. It creates many seedlings the following season that may or may not be welcome.

Shearing: the pruning technique whereby plant stems and branches are cut uniformly with long-bladed pruning shears (hedge shears) or powered hedge trimmers. It is used in creating and maintaining hedges and topiary.

Slow-acting fertilizer: fertilizer that is water insoluble and therefore releases its nutrients gradually as a function of soil temperature, moisture, and related microbial activity. Typically granular, it may be either organic or synthetic.

Soil test: an analysis of the soil from a property by a laboratory to determine the presence of nutrients and their proportions, the soil type, and pH.

Species: indicated by the second word of a plant's binomial scientific name. Species names often describe a distinguishing feature of the plant or contain the name of the person who discovered it or introduced it into cultivation. Example: *purpurea* = purple. ("Species" is both singular and plural.)

Stolon, stoloniferous: a plant stem that grows horizontally aboveground, rooting at various points and producing young plants at those points. The means by which some turfgrasses and other ground cover plants spread and create a mat of plants.

Sucker: a new growing shoot. Underground plant roots produce suckers to form new stems and spread by means of these suckering roots to form large plantings, or colonies. Some plants produce root suckers or branch suckers as a result of pruning or wounding.

Transpiration: the process whereby plants give off moisture through their foliage as a cooling mechanism.

Tuber: a type of underground storage structure in a plant stem, analogous to a bulb. It generates roots below and stems above ground (example: Dahlia).

Twiner: a vine that grows by means of twisting stems that wrap around available supporting structures.

Understory: the area beneath large shade trees that is roomy enough for smaller trees and various shrubs that prefer dappled sunlight or bright, indirect light.

Variegated: having various colors or color patterns. The term usually refers to plant foliage that is streaked, edged, blotched, or mottled with a contrasting color, often green with yellow, cream, or white.

Water sprouts: weak, suckering branch shoots that grow from tree or shrub limbs. Often indicates the plant is under stress.

White grubs: fat, off-white, wormlike larvae of Japanese beetles. They reside in the soil and feed on plant (especially grass) roots until summer when they emerge as beetles to feed on plant foliage.

Wings: (*a*) the corky tissue that forms edges along the twigs of some woody plants such as Winged Euonymus; (*b*) the flat, dried extensions of tissue on some seeds, such as Maple, that catch the wind and help them disseminate.

Woody plant: perennial plants whose stems do not die back with the arrival of frost. Their bark toughens and thickens each season.

Zones (hardiness zones): geographical designations determined by temperature pattern, each zone representing a 10 degree difference in lowest temperature. Useful in characterizing a plant's ability to withstand summers or winters in specific regions of the country. Numbered from 1 to 10, the lower the number, the colder the winter temperatures.

Bibliography

American Horticultural Society. *A-Z Encyclopedia of Garden Plants*. Ed. Christopher Brickell. New York: Dorling Kindersley, 1997.

Bagust, Harold. *The Gardener's Dictionary of Horticultural Terms*. Strand, London: Cassell Publishers, 1992.

Barash, Cathy Wilkinson. *Edible Flowers from Garden to Palate*. Golden, Colo.: Fulcrum, 1993.

———. *Evening Gardens*. Shelburne, Vt.: Chapters Publishing, 1993.

Baron, Robert, ed. *The Garden and Farm Books of Thomas Jefferson*. Golden, Colo.: Fulcrum, 1987.

Bown, Deni. *Encyclopedia of Herbs and Their Uses*. New York: Dorling Kindersley, 1995.

Cox, Jeff. *Perennial All-Stars*. Emmaus, Pa.: Rodale Press, 1998.

Cresson, Charles O. *Charles Cresson on the American Flower Garden*. New York: Prentice Hall Gardening, 1993.

Cutler, Sandra McLean. *Dwarf and Unusual Conifers Coming of Age*. North Olmsted, Ohio: Barton-Bradley Crossroads Publishing Co., 1997.

Dennis, John V., and Mathew Tekulsky. *How to Attract Hummingbirds and Butterflies*. San Ramon, Calif.: Ortho Books, 1991.

Dirr, Michael A. *Manual of Woody Landscape Plants*. Champaign, Ill.: Stipes Publishing, 1998.

DiSabato-Aust, Tracy. *The Well-Tended Perennial Garden*. Portland, Oreg.: Timber Press, 1998.

Fell, Derek. *The Pennsylvania Gardener*. Philadelphia: Camino Books, 1995.

Greenlee, John. *The Encyclopedia of Ornamental Grasses*. New York: Michael Friedman Publishing Group, 1992.

Hart, Rhonda Massingham. *Deer Proofing Your Yard and Garden*. Pownal, Vt.: Storey Communications, 1997.

Healey, B. J. *A Gardener's Guide to Plant Names*. New York: Charles Scribner's Sons, 1972.

Heriteau, Jacqueline, and Charles B. Thomas. *Water Gardens*. New York: Houghton Mifflin, 1994.

Hightshoe, Gary L. *Native Trees, Shrubs, and Vines for Urban and Rural America*. New York: Van Nostrand Reinhold, 1988.

Klein, William M., Jr. *Gardens of Philadelphia and Delaware Valley*. Philadelphia: Temple University Press, 1995.

Krussmann, Gerd. *Manual of Cultivated Conifers*. Portland, Oreg.: Timber Press, 1985.

Loewer, Peter. *The Annual Garden*. Emmaus, Pa.: Rodale Press, 1988.

McVicar, Jekka. *Herbs for the Home*. New York: Viking Studio Books, 1994.

Ney, Betsey, ed. *Ornamental Grasses*. Kennett Square, Pa.: Longwood Gardens, 1993.

Ottesen, Carole. *The Native Plant Primer*. New York: Harmony Books, 1995.

Pennsylvania Natural Diversity Inventory. Pennsylvania DCNR, Bureau of Forestry.

Roth, Susan A. *The Four-Season Landscape*. Emmaus, Pa.: Rodale Press, 1994.

Seitz, Ruth Hoover. *Philadelphia and Its Countryside*. Harrisburg, Pa.: RB Books, 1994.

Still, Stephen M. *Manual of Herbaceous Ornamental Plants*. 4th ed. Urbana, Ill.: Stipes Publishing Co., 1994.

Stokes, Donald and Lillian. *The Butterfly Book*. Toronto: Little, Brown, 1991.

———. *The Hummingbird Book*. Toronto: Little, Brown, 1989.

Thomas, Charles B. *Water Gardens*. New York: Houghton Mifflin, 1997.

Tice, Patricia M. *Gardening in America 1830-1910*. Rochester, N.Y.: Strong Museum, 1953.

Todd, Pamela. *Forget-Me-Not: A Floral Treasury*. Boston: Bulfinch Press, 1993.

Tomlinson, Timothy R., and Barbara Klaczynska. *Paradise Presented*. Philadelphia: Morris Arboretum of the University of Pennsylvania, 1996.

Welch, Humphrey J. *Manual of Dwarf Conifers*. New York: Theophrastus Publishers/Garland STPM Press, 1979.

Photography Credits

Thomas Eltzroth: pages 21, 22, 23, 24, 26, 27, 28, 29, 30, 32, 33, 34, 36, 37, 40, 42, 43, 47, 49, 50, 53, 54, 55, 56, 58, 60, 63, 64, 66, 67, 68, 69, 72, 74, 77, 82, 84, 85, 86, 87, 88, 89, 90, 91, 93, 94, 96, 97, 98, 99, 100, 102, 103, 105, 108, 109, 11, 112, 113, 114, 115, 117, 118, 125, 128, 135, 136, 137, 138, 140, 141, 146, 150, 151, 152, 155, 156, 157, 159, 163, 166, 167, 168, 177, 186, 187, 188, 189, 190, 191, 192, 193, 194, 200, 203, 204, 209, 212 and the first photo on the back cover

Liz Ball and Rick Ray: pages 8, 10, 13, 14, 17, 20, 31, 35, 38, 39, 41, 44, 48, 51, 52, 61, 65, 70, 73, 75, 79, 80, 81, 83, 92, 95, 101, 106, 110, 116, 119, 122, 123, 124, 126, 129, 130, 139, 142, 143, 144, 147, 148, 154, 158, 160, 161, 162, 165, 171, 174, 175, 180, 181, 182, 184, 195, 196, 202, 206, 207, 208, 210, 214 and the second through the fourth photos on the back cover

Pam Harper: pages 71, 104, 121, 127, 132, 145, 170, 172, 173, 179, 183, 199, 201, 215

Dency Kane: pages 62, 107, 120, 149, 153, 185, 198

Charles Mann: pages 45, 59, 78, 134, 178

Ralph Snodsmith: pages 46, 88, 131, 169

William Adams: pages 76, 211, 213

Michael Dirr: pages 164, 176, 197

Bruce Asakawa: page 133

Lorenzo Gunn: page 25

Robert Lyons: page 57

Plant Index

Meet Liz Ball

Liz Ball is a horticultural writer, photographer, researcher, and teacher whose articles and photographs have appeared in numerous books, magazines, and catalogs. Ball has written for the National Garden Bureau and Burpee's website. Her weekly "Yardening" column has appeared in her local newspaper for more than 12 years.

In addition to this book for Cool Springs Press, Ball has authored or co-authored 10 books on plant care and landscape gardening. These include *The Philadelphia Garden Book: A Gardener's Guide to the Delaware Valley* (Cool Springs Press, 1999), *My Pennsylvania Garden: A Gardener's Journal* (Cool Springs Press, 2000), and *Month-by-Month Gardening in Pennsylvania* (Cool Springs Press, 2000), as well as *Step by Step Yard Care* and *Step by Step Garden Basics* (Better Homes and Gardens, Meredith, 1999).

A long-time gardener herself, Ball specializes in addressing the issues that concern non-gardening homeowners who have lawns and plants to care for, but who have limited time. Ball's career includes teaching courses on gardening at community forums and teaching classes at arboretum programs. Ball has also taught garden writing at Temple University and Longwood Gardens. She speaks frequently to gardening clubs, horticultural societies, civic groups, as well as at nationally recognized events such as the Philadelphia Flower Show.

She is a national director of the Garden Writers Association of America, and also is a member of the Hardy Plant Society Mid-Atlantic Region and the Rock Garden Society. In addition to writing, Ball manages her own stock photography business and licenses images to book and magazine publishers. In fact, many of her photos are in this book for Cool Springs Press.

Ball recently moved to a new home in Springfield, Pennsylvania where she is currently at work establishing plants in a floodplain, designing and planting garden beds, and coping with deer.